CONTENTS

1 Making the most of our leisure time

FOCUS

> "We all need empty hours in our lives or we will have no time to create or dream."
> (Robert Coles, American child psychiatrist)

> "The best intelligence test is what we do with our leisure."
> (Laurence J. Peter, Canadian educator)

> "Free time was the most precious time, when you should be doing what you loved, or at least slowing down enough to remember what made your life worthwhile and happy."
> (Amy Tan, American writer)

A Discuss these questions in class:

1 Which photo represents best your idea of leisure? Explain your choice.
2 Which photo illustrates one of the quotes? Which doesn't? Justify your choices.
3 What is your favourite leisure activity? Explain why.

B Do this with a partner:

1 Write a short sentence about leisure. Start like this: "Leisure for me is …".
2 Collect the sentences on the board and be prepared to explain your sentence.

Leisure time

Leisure time is generally defined as the time that you spend doing what you enjoy when you are not working or studying. There is no doubt that free time or vacation time is indispensable for our well-being, as it allows us to unwind, to relax and to recover from our daily routine and possibly to pursue our real passions. Yet, even today some advocates of the Protestant work ethic see leisure time as an idle waste of time. However, now more than ever, people require a proper work-life balance in which an equilibrium is achieved between the hours spent at one's job and the time spent doing leisure activities. Polls suggest that although Americans work more hours annually than Europeans, their satisfaction with the amount of leisure time they have is paradoxically higher than in any European country: 69% of the Americans were completely or fairly satisfied, compared to 68% of Germans and 57% of Swedes.

How do people generally spend their free time? In our stressful world the majority of people probably subscribe to the statement: "Whenever I have free time, I basically want to do nothing – just lie in my bed and watch movies." While doing nothing can be relaxing, the trend towards sedentary free-time activities is actually becoming a health issue. Too many people are just passive watchers – in the worst case couch potatoes, whose only leisure pursuit is watching TV, as is the case with 88% of the British and 79% of the Germans. Other passive leisure interests include listening to music, reading a book, playing board games and, of course, playing video games.

Others relax best when they pursue hobbies such as photography, singing in a choir or playing a musical instrument. Following your passion to your heart's content is a great way to relax and develop your character and skills.

Another group are the active doers, who pursue activities that encourage a healthy lifestyle, exercising regularly and often taking part in team games. However, the figures are pretty sobering here: the percentage of those keen on playing football or volleyball, cycling, jogging or doing any other sports activity is quite low in most countries.

Do leisure activities reveal what kind of people we are? Are passive activities like watching TV a sign that someone has a limited imagination? But what about reading a novel? And why might participating in a team sport be seen as a sign of character? Taking part in any form of activity can form the basis for social interaction. People meet and talk about the last football match, they exchange views on TV series or discuss movies they have seen.

There is one other category of leisure activity: volunteering. About 40% of people in Britain and Germany do voluntary work at least once a month. Helping others by taking part in charity work makes us feel part of a community, as well as making us feel good about ourselves.

Doing things you enjoy can have a positive effect on your well-being and happiness, as it enhances your satisfaction with life, builds your self-esteem and encourages a positive outlook on life. This includes any free-time activity, even the non-physical ones. It is the fun of indulging in a free-time activity, the social interaction and the work-life balance which count. After all, all work and no play would make us very dull indeed. (555 words)

First of all, make sure you understand the meaning of each of the highlighted words and phrases in the text above. If you are not sure, look them up in your dictionary. Then complete the tasks on the following page.

1 WORD FIELDS

1 Find two terms in the first paragraph used to express the German word "Freizeit".
2 Which collocations with the word "leisure" can you find in the text?
3 Note down two negative expressions used to describe leisure in the text.
4 Note down five positive aspects of leisure in the text.

2 DEFINITIONS

Go to File 1 on p. 176.

Explain to a partner the meaning of:
1 couch potato (l. 18) 2 all work and no play (ll. 39–40)

3 WORD FAMILIES

Use a member of the word family of the word in brackets to fill the gaps.

There is one way to stay ▬ [1] (health) and that is by ▬ [2] (participation) in leisure activities. Any leisure ▬ [3] (pursue) is rewarding, whether it is passive or active, as long as you do it regularly and with ▬ [4] (passionate). The fun factor of leisure activities mustn't be underestimated as it guarantees real ▬ [5] (satisfy). But leisure is not just about fooling around with friends, playing soccer or watching sport on TV. You can derive pleasure from ▬ [6] (voluntary) for a ▬ [7] (charitable) as well as from singing in a choir. No leisure activity can be called a ▬ [8] (wasteful) of time if it gives people a feeling of happiness or facilitates social ▬ [9] (interactive).

4 PHRASES

Complete the sentences, using highlighted words and phrases from the text for the German equivalents in brackets.

1 Participation in leisure activities ▬ *(ist unverzichtbar)* for a healthy life.
2 What my parents don't understand is that video games help me ▬ *(sich entspannen)* after school.
3 Polls reveal that ▬ *(bewegungsarm)* free-time activities are becoming more and more common.
4 Even ▬ *(Brettspiele zu spielen)* fosters social interaction.
5 Pursuing free-time activities ▬ *(nach Herzenslust)* doesn't only make you happy but also healthy.
6 Many kids are ▬ *(scharf auf)* taking part in team sports.
7 Participating in free-time activities is known to ▬ *(Zufriedenheit mit dem eigenen Leben zu erhöhen)*.
8 Helping others or the environment are activities which ▬ *(das eigene Selbstwertgefühl aufbauen)*.
9 ▬ *(Arbeit alleine)* doesn't make you a happy person.

5 TALKING ABOUT LEISURE

1 Make a list of the active and passive leisure activities mentioned in the text.
2 Then add further activities to the list.

SITUATION

Your school has become worried that not all students are taking part in leisure activities. Some students do not enjoy social activities, some prefer the company of their computers, some are on exchange programmes from abroad, while some are from immigrant backgrounds with a different attitude to social activities. So the school wants to inform all students about how to benefit from leisure activities in and around the town. Groups of students have, therefore, been asked to **prepare posters for a gallery walk**, which display their views and ideas on the topic and which are intended to appeal to all types of students.

STEP 1 Brainstorming

Read the headline of the text below and in groups think what successful people might do and how this might be different from your way of spending free time. First collect ideas individually and then compare them with your group members.

STEP 2 Thinking about how others spend their free time

To find out about the ways successful people spend their free time, skim the text below and compare the findings with your brainstorming in Step 1.

HOW SUCCESSFUL PEOPLE SPEND THEIR FREE TIME

Jayson Demers

A How people spend their free time can actually have a big impact on their success in the professional world. Successful people tend to spend their free time in these ways (and more, of course), so read below and find out why:

B Physical exercise is important for both physical and mental health. Exercising a half hour after work or on a weekend can get your blood pumping, get your endorphins flowing, and revitalize your spirit. You'll build muscle, burn calories, and oxygenate your brain – giving you a release after a day of stress. Exercising regularly also helps you remain disciplined, which can be valuable in a demanding work environment, and can reduce the long-term effects of stress. You'll also look better and feel better, which gives you greater confidence.

C Reading is a lifelong skill, and successful people never stop reading new books. Whether it's fiction or nonfiction, books help give you a greater understanding of the world around you. They introduce you to new characters, new environments, new cultures, new philosophies, and new ideas, and might even help you build new skills (if you're reading nonfiction, at least). Similarly, reading

11 **endorphin:** a hormone produced in the brain that reduces the feeling of pain

13 **oxygenate sth:** supply sth with oxygen

regularly helps to build your vocabulary and your semantic comprehension, giving you greater communication skills.

D Education shouldn't stop at college, and shouldn't be restricted to institutions. The most successful people in the world are the ones who make a commitment to never stop learning. They're always incorporating new skills for their résumés and learning new aspects of the world around them. Instructional courses aren't particularly difficult to find, either, especially in the modern era. Many local colleges offer courses for free. And don't underestimate the value of free online courses. If you have a free hour and an Internet connection, you can start learning a new skill.

E Volunteering, no matter where or how you do it, is beneficial for you and your community. Whether you're helping to clean up a highway, working in a soup kitchen, or providing mentorship to a group of young professionals, your time goes a long way toward improving the community around you. Professionals realize the importance of giving back to the community, and feel happier because of it. Volunteering is also a valuable networking experience, introducing you to other people who, one way or another, can help you drive your career forward. […]

F Focusing exclusively on work might seem like a fast track to success. With nothing else distracting you, you can funnel your full effort into your job and do in one week what would take most people two. But this approach has a nasty downside; it stresses you out, sets you up for burnout, and prevents you from

developing skills in any other areas. Finding and pursuing a hobby, on the other hand, helps you relieve stress, put your job in perspective, and build skills that complement ones you use at work. It's a breath of fresh air that keeps you grounded, and if it's a social hobby, also offers networking opportunities.

G I implied it in the last point, but I'll reiterate it more strongly here: your job isn't everything. Focusing too much on your career is self-sabotage, no matter how counterintuitive that might sound. If you want to be successful in life, you have to prioritize your personal relationships – your bond with your friends and family members. No matter how much you want to be successful, you can't neglect your friends and family to do it.

H If you don't spend your free time like this, it doesn't mean you have no chance of being successful. Start incorporating a few of them into your free time routines and you might just be surprised at the results. (620 words)

Source: *the website of inc*, 23 June 2015

32 semantic: connected with the meaning of words and phrases
53 mentorship: *Betreuung*
75 complement sth: *etw ergänzen*
80 reiterate sth: *etw wiederholen*
83 counterintuitive: *kontraintuitiv*
85 prioritize sth: *etw priorisieren*

STEP 3 Collecting and selecting information

A **Successful people might be useful role models for considering how free time could be well spent. Each group collects and structures the information in the text. The grid below can serve as a table for you to copy and use, but you can design your own. Add all the relevant information you can find on activities and positive aspects for each item mentioned in the text. (Leave out paragraphs A and H.)**

ways of spending your free time	physical exercise	reading	education/ lifelong learning	volunteering	pursuing a hobby	spending time with friends and family
activities			…	…		…
positive aspects	…	…	…	…	…	…

B **As there is just enough space on your gallery walk poster for three ways of spending free time, each group has to decide on a list of the three most beneficial ones. After discussing which items should be presented, come up with a ranking list for them.**

STEP 4 Boosting your word power

You have noticed that the text contains language that might be helpful for your poster. Make the language your own by doing the following exercises.

A **Rewrite the following sentences so that their meanings don't change. Use words and phrases from the text to replace the underlined parts. You will find the word/phrase needed in the paragraph given in brackets.**

1 Leisure activities can <u>have a powerful effect on</u> a person's well-being. [A]
Leisure activities … a person.

2 Going to the gym makes you feel alive again after a stressful work day. [B]
Going to the gym ▬ after a stressful work day.
3 Having a training plan at the gym helps people keep to their schedule. [B]
Having a training plan at the gym helps people ▬.
4 Some leisure activities help you to feel much more secure about your abilities. [B]
Some leisure activities ▬.
5 There is no denying that certain free-time activities will help you develop abilities that you did not have. [C]
Certain leisure activities without doubt help you ▬.
6 What you should do is promise yourself to never stop learning. [D]
What you should do is ▬ to never stop learning.
7 A hobby helps you have a sensible and realistic attitude to life. [F]
A hobby helps you ▬.
8 You might find the outcome not what you expected. [H]
You might ▬.

B Now find paraphrases of the underlined expressions from the text in the following sentences. Use your dictionary, as it gives you explanations and words you can use in your paraphrases.

1 Exercising can be valuable in our hectic world. [B]
2 Exercising can reduce the long-term effects of stress. [B]
3 Some people underestimate the value of online courses. [D]
4 People believe that work is a fast track to success. [F]
5 My friend's illness put life in perspective. [F]

Exercising reduces stress.

STEP 5 Preparing the posters

The information in your poster should focus on the positive outcomes of leisure and the best and/or most creative leisure activities in and around your hometown. Your poster should make good use of the information collected from the text.

Find pictures, cartoons and/or graphs on the internet to visualize the information presented. Students of each specific group should be ready to answer questions.

Check the pronunciation of all the words on your poster. There is usually a loudspeaker symbol in online dictionaries, which you can click to hear the word.

STEP 6 Evaluating the posters

Now look at the posters of the other groups. If a question arises, ask the students who made the poster. Then evaluate the posters.

BEFORE YOU READ

How important are digital leisure activities in your free time? Which ones do you use most?

Some people claim that leisure activities such as online gaming are evil and must be banned. Do you agree?

DIGITAL AGE
HAPPINESS, RELAXATION AND LEISURE

Suren Ramasubbu

A Every culture in the world has divided waking hours of a human day into "formal" working hours, and "leisure hours" where they are not formally required to be "productively" engaged. Despite work being considered the most important predictor of happiness [...], research has often shown that leisure is as important for happiness and productivity as work. All work and no play is certainly known to make us dull people.

B Leisure activities of children have always changed over time, but the digital age has probably changed them most in the least amount of time. Traditional forms of leisure activities such as outdoor play, travel, reading, indulging in the arts and socializing have been modified beyond recognition, or at least augmented by newer technology-induced activities. It would be an unfair accusation to say that technology has ruined leisure; it has merely changed (even productively) the way traditional leisure activities have been pursued over the years. For example, while in the past, one had to visit a library to read a variety of books, an entire library can now be carried in a glowing screen; thus, the activity of "reading" has not died, it has merely moved to a different medium. [...] Pursuing

certain hobbies has become easier with the internet; 83 percent of online Americans used the internet to pursue their hobbies in 2007. The digital age has also led to the creation of new hobbies, blogging being a classic example. [...]

C Some other leisure activities have changed for the worse. What used to be outdoor play time for children is increasingly being replaced by sedentary device-based gaming time. However, parents do not seem to be overly concerned, despite media-induced concerns. A report [...] noted that over half of the parents surveyed believed that devices had no impact on children's play time at all. This 51 percent notwithstanding,

07 **predictor:** *Indikator*
19 **augment sth:** *etw erweitern*
20 **induced:** *verursacht (durch)*
46 **notwithstanding:** *trotz*

the survey does point out that most parents seek to establish a balance between the world of devices and apps, and traditional play. While most parents do recognize the educational potential of electronic devices, they are equally concerned that too much technology could foster laziness and unhealthy solitary experiences, or lead to "over-connectedness".

D A serious adverse outcome of the intrusion of technology into a child's outdoor play time is deterioration of health. [...] A study showed that an increasing number of children can no longer hold their own weight when hanging from wall bars, a technique that children learned in the past from climbing trees and hanging from branches.

E But there are contradictory reports as well. According to a study presented to the American College of Sports Medicine, exergaming can raise children's activity levels to meet guidelines for moderate-intensity activity level. There are conflicting reports on the effect of gaming on psychiatric health as well. A research paper in *Pediatrics* shows that children and young adults who overdo TV and video games are nearly twice as likely to suffer from a variety of attention-span disorders. [...] Another unsavory effect of technology on leisure is that it has blurred the boundary between work and play. Technology has removed the barrier between home and place of work (or school) and the former is no longer only a place of simple leisure. It has transformed into a place to study, work, exercise, listen to music, watch movies and even socialize. Communication technology such as email and smartphones exacerbates impatience and anxiety in that one is on call 24/7 and leisure is not simply leisure anymore.

F Despite general unrest about the adverse effects of technology on leisure and play time, the idea of mixing play and technology is not new. Toys have always been tools of play for children, and digital developments of the 21st century have merely brought electronics into these tools. Electronic toys and digital games have become a child's first hands-on introduction to the world, giving children an opportunity to learn about technology as well as with technology. It is logical to believe that parental guidance is absolutely necessary in the use of electronic gadgets/devices/screens by children for leisure activities. It is thus up to the parents to analyze the benefits and risks of technology-driven leisure of their own and their children's lives and limit tech time accordingly. (702 words)

Source: *The Huffington Post*, 16 September 2015

68 **exergaming:** video games that are also a form of exercise
73 ***Pediatrics:*** journal concerned with the study of children
77 **unsavory:** *unangenehm*
78 **blur sth:** *etw verwischen*

1 SHORT-ANSWER QUESTIONS / SENTENCE COMPLETION

→ Skills, p. 200

Answer the questions or complete the sentences with information from the text. [Paragraphs A–C]

1 Which phrase does the author use to describe *that something has totally changed*? It has ___.
2 What does "it" (l. 29) refer to?
3 While in the past children spent most of their free time in the open air, the trend nowadays is towards ___.

4 While parents see a positive role for electronic devices, they are also concerned that technology encourages negative developments. What benefit and which negative developments do they see?

positive effect	negative developments
___	___
	___
	___

2 GAPPED SUMMARY

→ Skills, p. 202

Fill in the gaps with words from the corresponding sections of the text. Use only one word for each gap. Give the number of the line in which you found the word/expression. [Paragraphs D–F]

Using technology in one's free time has positive and negative effects. One of the negative aspects is that the ___[1] of some children suffers if they use too much technology in their free time. For example, watching too much TV or playing too many computer games can lead to ___[2] ___[3]; another negative ___[4] is the fact that sometimes youngsters find it hard to distinguish between ___[5] and ___[6].
In the end it is the ___[7] who have to weigh up the pros and cons of technology as used by their children in their free time. After all, ___[8] gives their children the possibility to learn an enormous amount. It should, however, be clear that ___[9] by the parent is necessary when the children are using their various devices.

3 WORKING WITH WORDS

A With the help of a dictionary, use one of the words from the box on the right to complete the sentence sets.

age ▪ effect ▪ game ▪ medium ▪ on

1 Why don't we **have a** ___ **of** table tennis?
I think we **are back in the** ___ again, don't you think so?
Let's stick to the rules and **play the** ___.

2 You should worry about a possible **long-term** ___.
I guess the antibiotics will soon **take** ___.
Children are warned about the dangers of the internet, but often **to no** ___.

3 The game went ___ **and** ___ for hours so that I got totally bored and left.
I do some exercises ___ **and off**.
___ **average**, British children play online games for more than an hour a day.

4 He started playing online-games **at an early** ___.
The boys pretty much **acted their** ___.
If you don't exercise, you will ___ much faster.

5 He is of ___ **height**, he is neither a giant like John nor short like Bill.
Video clips are an excellent ___ to get your message across.
I hate sport but going for a walk is **a happy** ___, as I exercise a bit but don't get tired.

B **The expressions printed in bold in 3A above are commonly used phrases, collocations or idioms. List them and find their German equivalents. Copy the table.**

English phrases	German equivalents
to have a game of	___

C **Find phrases from the text to complete the sentences. You will find the word/phrase needed in the paragraph given in brackets.**

1 Children still play games but the games they play have ___. [B]
2 If I want to read a book but I don't want to buy it, I just ___ and borrow it. [B]
3 People tend to glorify the past and to think badly of the present, which is why many people are of the opinion that leisure activities have changed ___. [C]
4 Playing soccer, running around in the garden or biking, kids just love that kind of ___. [D]
5 There are ___ in some papers on today's leisure activities. While some say the situation is deplorable, others say exactly the opposite. [E]

4 WORD FAMILIES

Copy and complete the table. The words given are all in the text.

Noun	Verb	Adjective
variety	___	___
activity	___	___
creation	___	___
___	___	contradictory
communication	___	___
___	analyse (BE)/analyze (AE)	___

Go to File 2 on p. 176.

5 EXCHANGING INFORMATION

You are hanging out with your friend Lukas, who has brought along Jonny, an exchange student from Britain, but Jonny doesn't understand any German at all. As Lukas's English isn't great, he asks you to help him out.

EXAMPLE: Lukas will von Jonny wissen, ob er glaubt, dass Geld den Fußball ruiniert.
Do you think that money ruins soccer?

1 Lukas möchte Jonny sagen, dass Fußball seine liebste Freizeitaktivität ist.
2 Lukas will von Jonny wissen, wer seiner Meinung nach das Champions-League-Endspiel gewinnen wird.
3 Lukas möchte Jonny sagen, dass das Fußballspiel gestern Abend ziemlich langweilig war.
4 Lukas will von Jonny wissen, welche Freizeitbeschäftigungen in Großbritannien beliebt sind?
5 Lukas möchte Jonny sagen, dass es in der Stadt eine große Auswahl an Sportmöglichkeiten gibt.

1 LISTENING

→ Skills, p. 196

You are going to hear Patti Neighmond, a reporter for National Public Radio, discussing a study by psychologist Matthew Zawadzki on how leisure activities affect our health.

A Look at the word list first, as it will help you to understand the report. Match the English words (1–8) with their German equivalent (a–h).

1 to kick back	5 to back sth up	a eindeutig, unzweideutig	e ruhend
2 stationary	6 antidote	b bekräftigen, belegen	f Nähen
3 sewing	7 unequivocal	c grübeln	g Gegenmittel
4 to ruminate	8 to add up	d sich summieren	h abschalten, relaxen

03

B Listen and decide which option is the most suitable.

1 According to the report, doing stationary leisure activities to reduce stress is ▬
- a as good as doing exercise.
- b not at all beneficial.
- c much better than watching TV.

2 Even watching TV can be helpful if you find the programme you watch ▬
- a monotonous.
- b educational.
- c interesting.

3 Leisure activities are good as they allow us ▬
- a to feel a positive emotion.
- b not to think too much about things.
- c to play and move as much as we want.

4 Which aspect was not taken into consideration in the study done by Matthew Zawadzki?
- a gender b ethnic origin c health status

5 The study data were collected using ▬
- a questionnaires.
- b electrodes.
- c electronic tags.

6 If was found that ▬ lower(s) the heart rate.
- a any leisure activity
- b no leisure activity can
- c only one leisure activity

7 As far as health goes, leisure activities have ▬
- a only a short-term effect.
- b an effect in the long run.
- c an effect just for a day.

2 GROUP DISCUSSION

→ Skills, p. 210

You and some friends of yours are going to Britain on an exchange trip for six weeks. As your time and budget are limited, you think you can do only one activity during your stay, but there might be time for a second. Discuss the proposals and make a ranking list of the three activities according to how interesting you find them.
The activities can be found in File 1 on p. 188.

Presentation phase

Each of you presents one of the activities in a one-minute speech. Explain why you think it is the best for your group.

Interaction phase

Exchange arguments, try to convince your friends that your activity is the best or at least should be the second on the list. Be willing to compromise.

3 MATERIAL-BASED ESSAY

→ Skills, pp. 206, 208

Inactive free time is a problem both for the individual and for society. Comment on this statement, using the cartoon and statistics as help. Write 300 words.

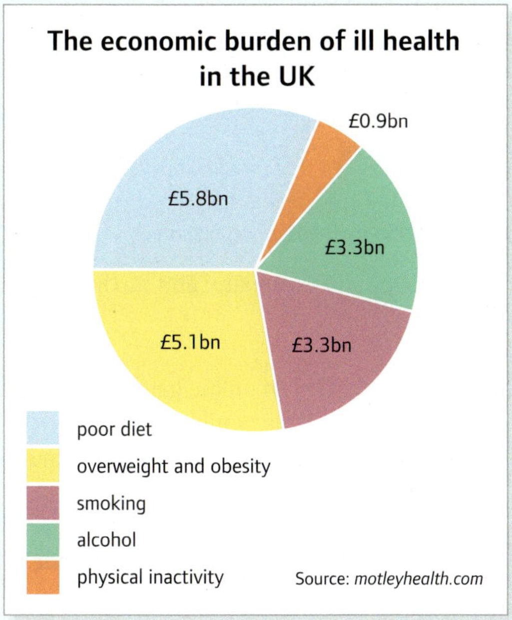

"My mom wants us to stop watching cartoons and go outside. Let's take my laptop outside and watch cartoons on it."

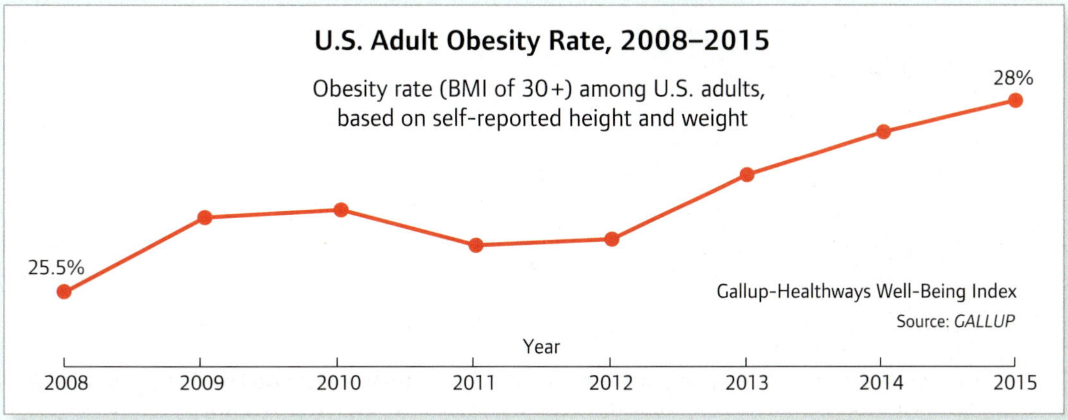

4 ARGUMENTATIVE WRITING

→ Skills, pp. 206, 208

1 **Go to File 3 on p. 176.**

"Watching TV is the most popular leisure activity in Britain. I find that very depressing."

(Jeremy Paxman, journalist and author)

Comment on Paxman's view.

2 **Leisure time makes people happy and there can't be enough of it. Do you agree?**

SIMPLE PRESENT – PRESENT PROGRESSIVE

→ Grammar summary, p. 216

1 SPOT THE MISTAKES

Spot the mistakes and correct them. Explain why they are wrong.

1 ~~In the photo a boy digs a hole in the garden.~~
2 ~~Is the pie tasting good?~~
3 ~~John always go to work by bus.~~
4 ~~Hi, Jill. What do you do at the moment?~~
5 ~~Joe is having a house in Bristol.~~

2 **Complete the sentences using the *simple present* or the *present progressive*.**

1 My new girlfriend is from California. She ___ (work) for an IT company and ___ (live) in Los Angeles.
2 Look, Sally ___ (leave) her parents' house to go to work.
3 Brian usually ___ (study) hard, but at the moment he ___ (play) an online game.
4 I ___ (be) sure he ___ (enjoy) his holiday in the USA, otherwise we would have heard from him.
5 Mary and her mother ___ (live) in Cornwall, but this week they ___ (stay) in London with her sister.
6 They often ___ (play) soccer, but right now they ___ (work) on a physics project.

3 **Read the following cartoon description and decide which is correct: the *simple present* or the *present progressive*.**

The cartoon shows / is showing [1] a couple in the wilderness. The location is / is being [2] a river valley, framed left and right by a forest with a mountain range in the background. A man blows / is blowing [3] up a mattress. He sits / is sitting [4] among lots of other inflated items. He looks / is looking [5] determined. The various items show / are showing [6] that he has already spent some time blowing things up. His wife sits / is sitting [7] behind him and she looks / is looking [8] at him. Judging by her expression, she appears / is appearing [9] to be really annoyed. Maybe she was expecting a more romantic holiday. In my opinion, the message of the cartoon is that many people just don't want / aren't wanting [10] to do without the comforts they are used to.

WATCH OUT! mustn't – needn't

Read the example sentence and then complete each sentence with *mustn't* or *needn't*.

You ~~mustn't~~ donate a lot of money – even a small amount can make an effective contribution.
→ *You needn't donate …* (= *nicht brauchen*; mustn't = *nicht dürfen*)

1 You ___ play sport every single day – every other day is more than enough.
2 You ___ play sport if you have an injury.
3 Doctors are always telling me that I ___ eat fatty foods, but I never listen to them.
4 If you are feeling stressed out, you ___ take work home from the office.
5 I just read on the website that we ___ pay for the hotel now. We can do so when we arrive.

2 From school to work

FOCUS

A Look at the photos and do these tasks:

1. What does "school" mean to you? Close your books and write down the first five things connected to "school" that come to mind.
2. Collect your ideas on the board. Which ideas are mentioned the most often?
3. Which ideas on the list are positive aspects of school? Which of them are negative aspects?

B Discuss these questions in class:

1. What makes a school good?
2. Apart from the subjects on your timetable, what other things do you learn at school?
3. How does your time at school prepare you for the career that you want?

Education and training

Education is compulsory for children in all developed countries and most developing countries, although not all young people have equal access to good schools, colleges or universities. Traditionally, school education is divided into primary education (from about 5 or 6 to 10 or 11 years old), secondary education (from about 11 to 18 years old). Some young people then choose to go on to tertiary or further education at a university or technical college.

Vocational schools that train students for particular types of career are widespread in Germany. These schools usually prepare students for working life with work placements in local companies as part of the course. In the dual system of training, apprentices attend vocational schools in blocks of several weeks as part of their apprenticeship.

All schools have a curriculum which states which subjects students must learn. At secondary level, most schools have a mixture of compulsory subjects which all students have to do, and a range of elective subjects which students can choose from, depending on their interests or their plans for the future. Schools require students to follow a timetable of lessons. As the students get older, the timetable becomes increasingly flexible, with more elective subjects and with free periods which students can use to do homework tasks and independent study. In homeschooling, which is popular in the USA, parents educate their own children at home.

Assessment is an important part of education, to check that students are progressing as they should. This may take the form of written or oral exams or assessed coursework. In either case, the results play an important role in determining a student's success and whether he or she is suitable for the next level of education, e.g. a place at university.

The aim of education is not only to give young people subject knowledge and help them to pass exams, but also to help them to gain skills that will be useful after they leave school: study skills that they can use to learn anything during their lives; work skills that will help them in their careers; life skills which will help them whatever they do in the future; and perhaps most important of all, social skills that will help them interact with others.

Many young people hope for admission to a university after they graduate from school at 18. A university degree is a necessary qualification for many professions and the competition for places is high. The process of applying for university can be very stressful for young people, particularly as they are often revising for final exams at the same time. Applications usually consist of a CV (*AE*: résumé) and a cover letter or personal statement, explaining why the applicant is suitable for the course on offer. Many students try to make their applications stand out from the others by doing volunteer work or getting work experience in the summer vacation of their last years at school.

Like society itself, every school has different social groups among the students. Some students thrive on the social interaction in the classroom and during break; others feel under pressure to "fit in" and in some extreme cases may become the victims of bullying. However, many people look back on their school days as "the happiest time of their life", before childhood comes to an end and the serious business of work and a career begins. (560 words)

First of all, make sure you understand the meaning of each of the highlighted words and phrases in the text above. If you are not sure, look them up in your dictionary. Then complete the tasks on the following page.

1 WORD FIELDS

A Make a list of words and phrases from the text related to the given categories.

a	types/levels of education	*compulsory,* ___
b	curriculum and exams	*subjects,* ___
c	applications for further education / a job	*a place at university,* ___

B Add any other words/phrases that you know to your list.

2 WORD FAMILIES

A Copy the table below and add the missing words. Use your dictionary if necessary.

verb	noun (person)	noun (abstract)
___	applicant	___
assess	___	___
___	___	education

verb	noun (person)	noun (abstract)
___	___ / examinee	___
___	___	study
___	trainer / ___	___

B Complete the paragraph with the English equivalent of the German word in brackets. They are all in the table in 2A.

___ [1] *(Klausuren)* are one of the downsides of school life. Many people say that the purpose of ___ [2] *(Bildung)* is to teach young people how to ___ [3] *(studieren)* rather than to undergo constant ___ [4] *(Beurteilungen)* of how much subject knowledge they have learned. Unfortunately, good grades still play an important role when pupils ___ [5] *(sich bewerben)* for places at universities or on ___ [6] *(Ausbildung)* courses. ___ [7] *(Studierende)* often work as volunteers to make themselves stand out from the other ___ [8] *(Bewerber/innen)* for the best jobs. However, universities and employers know how to ___ [9] *(bewerten)* these perfect ___ [10] *(Bewerbungen)*.

3 COMPOUND NOUNS

A Match words from box A and box B to make compound nouns. They are all in the text.

A cover ▪ homework ▪ life ▪ subject ▪ university ▪ volunteer ▪ work ▪ work

B degree ▪ experience ▪ knowledge ▪ letter ▪ placement ▪ skills ▪ task ▪ work

B Complete the paragraph with a suitable compound noun from 3A.

One of the important ___ [1] that all teenagers should learn is how to write a proper ___ [2] for an application to university or for a job. While the ___ [3] that your teacher gives you are important to help you learn, it is the exam results on your CV that will give an employer a good idea of how much ___ [4] you have acquired. But exam results alone don't say much about whether you are a good candidate for the job or whether you will be able to complete a ___ [5]. That's why it's important to have some ___ [6] on your CV: this might come in the form of a ___ [7] in a company during the holidays or your vocational training, or in the form of ___ [8] with a charity.

SITUATION

Your city theatre is organizing a youth drama festival on the topic of tolerance. The festival is being run under the motto "If they're OK, we're OK" and will feature performances by amateur drama groups on any aspect of tolerance. Your English class decides to **create a 5-minute sketch** that you can perform at the festival.

STEP 1 Brainstorming ideas

While you are thinking about what your sketch could be about, your teacher shows you the following quote: *"The highest result of education is tolerance" (Helen Keller)*. You decide to think about how tolerant you are at school towards people who "don't fit in". Answer these questions for yourself and discuss your answers in class.

1 Who do you socialize with …
- **a** on the way to/from school?
- **b** in class?
- **c** during breaks/lunchtime?
- **d** during extra-curricular activities?

2 Is it always the same group of people, or does it change? Why/Why not?

STEP 2 Identifying social groups

You decide to base your sketch on the interaction of social groups at a school. While you are researching some ideas, you come across the extract on p. 25 from a young adult novel, which describes cliques at a US high school.

A Work in groups of four, divided into two pairs.

Pair A: Read the text and find the names of the cliques that Greg, the narrator, mentions. Make short notes on how he describes each group's potential to dominate the social life at school.

cliques	description in text
affluent kids	*rich;*
non-affluent kids	*equal numbers as rich kids*

Pair B: Read the text and make notes on the narrator, Greg.

Greg	notes
what he thinks about high school	
how he describes the social situation	
what he does to survive	

ME AND EARL AND THE DYING GIRL

JESSE ANDREWS

A So in order to understand everything that happened, you have to start from the premise that high school sucks. Do you accept that premise? Of course you do. It is a universally acknowledged truth that high school sucks. In fact, high school is where we are first introduced to the basic existential question of life: How is it possible to exist in a place that sucks so bad?

B Most of the time middle school sucks even worse, but middle school is so pathetic that I can't even bring myself to write about it, so let's just focus on high school.

C All right. Allow me to introduce myself: Greg S. Gaines, seventeen. During the period described in this book, I was a senior at Benson High School in lovely inner-city Pittsburgh, Pennsylvania. And before we do anything else, it is necessary for us to examine Benson and the specific ways in which it sucks.

D So, Benson is on the border of Squirrel Hill, an affluent neighborhood, and Homewood, a non-affluent neighborhood, and it draws about equal numbers of students from both. On television, it's usually the rich kids who assert control at a high school; however, most of Squirrel Hill's genuinely rich kids go to the local private school, Shadyside Academy. The ones that remain are too few to impose any kind of order. [...]

E So the rich kids aren't the alpha group of the school. The next most likely demographic would be the church kids: They're plentiful, and they are definitely interested in school domination. However, that strength – the will to dominate – is also their greatest weakness, because they spend so much time trying to convince you to hang out with them, and the way they try to do that is by inviting you over to their church. "We've got cookies and board games," they say, or that sort of thing. "We just got a Wii set up!" Something about it always seems a little off. Eventually, you realize: These same exact sentences are also said by child predators.

F So the church kids can never be the alpha group, either. Their tactics are just too creepy. At many schools, the jocks would be a good bet to ascend to the throne, but at Benson, they're pretty much all black, and many of the white kids are afraid of them. Who else is there to lead the masses? The smart kids? Please. They have no interest in politics. They're hoping simply to attract as little attention as possible until high school is over. Then they can escape to some college where no one will mock them for knowing how an adverb works. The theater kids? My God, it would be a bloody massacre. They would be found beaten to death with their own dog-eared *The Wiz* songbooks. The stoners? Too lacking in initiative. [...] The band kids? It would be like with the theater kids, except somehow even sadder. The gothy dorks? Impossible even as a thought experiment.

G So at the top of the Benson social hierarchy, there is a vacuum. The result: chaos. →

21 **demographic:** a group of people who are in some way similar
27 **child predator:** *Kinderschänder/in*
29 **jock:** a boy who plays a lot of sport
34 **dog-eared:** *abgewetzt*
35 **stoner:** *Kiffer*
35 **lacking:** not having enough of sth
36 **gothy dork:** eccentric person who dresses in goth fashion

[...] So there are a bunch of groups, all jockeying for control, and consequently all of them want to murder each other. And so the problem is that if you're part of a group, everyone outside of that group wants to murder you.

H But here's the thing. There's a solution to that problem: Get access to every group.

I know. I know. This sounds insane. But it's exactly what I did. I didn't join any group outright, you understand. But I got access to all of them. The smart kids, the rich kids, the jocks, the stoners. The band kids, the theater kids, the church kids, the gothy dorks. I could walk into any group of kids, and not one of them would bat an eye. Everyone used to look at me and think, "Greg! He's one of us." Or maybe something more like: "That guy's on our side." Or at the very least: "Greg is a guy who I am not going to flick ketchup at." This was a brutally difficult thing to accomplish. (684 words)

Source: Jesse Andrews, *Me and Earl and the Dying Girl, 2012*

38 **jockey for sth:** *um etw ringen*
42 **outright:** *voll und ganz*
45 **not bat an eye:** *nicht mit der Wimper zucken*

B When you have finished, share your notes from Step 2A with the other pair in your group, and talk about these questions:

- What do you think of Greg? Would you like to have him as one of your friends?
- Do you think he is serious when he describes the situation at his high school? Why/Why not?
- What do you think of his strategy for surviving high school? Do you think it will work?

STEP 3 Boosting your word power

The text contains some useful phrases for describing the interaction of social groups. Rewrite the following sentences so that their meanings are the same. Use words and phrases from the text to replace the parts in brackets. You may have to adapt them to fit.

EXAMPLE: There weren't enough rich kids for them to *assert control* (make other people recognize their authority) at our high school. [Paragraph D]

1 At some high schools the rich kids are the ▬ (kids with the most influence). [Paragraph E]
2 The way the church kids try to convince you to ▬ (spend a lot of time) with them is just too creepy. [Paragraph E]
3 Many of the smart kids at our school ▬ (really worry about) what the jocks and the stoners might do to them. [Paragraph F]
4 The smart kids want to ▬ (stay in the background as much as they can) until they can go to college. [Paragraph F]
5 Some groups ▬ (make fun of) the smart kids because they are so clever. [Paragraph F]
6 There is no ▬ (system of groups organized into levels of importance) at Benson, so there is chaos. [Paragraph G]
7 There are just lots of different groups, all ▬ (fighting to be in charge). [Paragraph G]
8 Greg's plan is to ▬ (be allowed to socialize with) all the groups of kids at his high school. [Paragraph H]
9 When the kids at high school see Greg, they all think, "He's ▬ (a member of our group)." [Paragraph H]

STEP 4 Thinking about your cliques

A **The text describes cliques at an American school. Work in your groups of four: Pair A are students from the American school in the text, while Pair B are students from your German school. Each side explains the different types of students in their school; the "Americans" use information from the text, the "Germans" from their own experience. Exchange views and discuss whether the differences between cliques in both countries are culturally based.**

B **Now start preparing ideas for your sketch by talking about the cliques at Greg's high school. (Your notes from Step 2 and the phrases from Step 3 will help you.) You can use your imagination and you don't have to be completely serious.**

- What do they look like? What do they wear?
- What are they interested in? What do they talk about?
- What don't they like? What are they afraid of?
- How do they behave/act in school?

C **Now choose three (or four) of the cliques to include in your sketch.**

STEP 5 Deciding on a situation

A **In your group of four, choose an everyday school situation for your sketch. It should be one that could present a problem for someone who "doesn't fit in" or who is an "outsider", for example …**

- finding somewhere to sit in the school canteen.
- finding a seat in class on the first day of the school year.
- finding a seat on the coach at the start of a school trip.

B **Brainstorm what the problems might be and what could go wrong for the "outsider".**

STEP 6 Writing the sketch

Now write your sketch, using your situation from Step 5 and the cliques you chose in Step 4. Imagine the problem(s) that Greg (or any other "outsider") is faced with and decide …

- how the cliques behave towards Greg/the outsider.
- how Greg/the outsider reacts to them.

You can give your sketch a "happy" or a "sad" ending.

STEP 7 Performing the sketch

A **Practise your sketch and act it out in front of the class. (You may need to "borrow" actors from other groups to make sure you have enough members in your cliques.)**

B **Vote on which sketch should enter the youth drama competition "If they're OK, we're OK".**

BEFORE YOU READ

What are you planning to do when you finish school? How hard do you think it will be to find the job or get on the further education course you really want? What can you do to make your application more successful?

By: Tracy McVeigh and Joanna Mason — June 28, 2015

SUMMER'S HERE, BUT STUDENTS HAVE TO TOP UP CVS AND NOT THEIR TANS

A

Who doesn't envy a school student with the slothful days of summer ahead? Carefree, work-free and with only an enviable social calendar to worry about – the last responsibility-free gasp of childhood. But if that's the picture that school holidays conjure up in older minds, then increasing numbers of stressed-out teenagers would like to put the record straight.

As schools break up [...], more 16- and 17-year-olds than ever before are concentrating on curating their curricula vitae rather than chilling out.

B

"I don't think, 'tops, the exams are over, it's time to chill'. The pressure is still on," said Daniel Hall, 17. "Big time. It's like, what are you doing to get a job? What are you doing to get work experience? Write a letter here, write to these people. Then a mate will have got something because their dad works in a big company and you feel you're being left behind. You get a bit scared and it's like you're under pressure to try harder.

"We've got to start working on our Ucas personal statements now, and you have to have something to say to back up your application. My mum works as a hospital cleaner, so not much doing there. You get told if you haven't got things to put on your CV, you won't get the place at university, and if you don't get into university, forget about a job."

Hall, from near Epsom in Surrey, says he has sent out 13 CVs to local companies and had one reply – a rejection. "I was too young," he said glumly.

C

Sixth-formers have until the end of the year to make a personal statement for Ucas, the Universities and Colleges Admissions Service. The Ucas chief executive, Mary Curnock Cook, has urged people to be more realistic with their summers and to use them to enhance their suitability for courses they want to do. [...]

D

Rob Evans, head of admissions at the University of Sussex, said: "The personal statement can be critical. We look at all personal statements when reviewing applications, but how much it is used does vary between courses, and even between applicants. [...]

"They can be especially important for applicants whose academic results are more borderline. If, for example, someone has slightly lower results than our offer level, the admissions tutor will look very carefully at the personal statement and it can make the difference between an offer and a rejection. [...]

"What is important is not just to tell us in the application that you have done work experience, but to reflect upon what you have gained from that experience and demonstrate what you have learned from it. [...]

E

At Warwick University the advice for teenagers is to "take it easy". "Cramming a load of extra activities or work experience in is just piling on extra stress. We read all the personal statements and the teachers' statements, but we want to know who you are as a person," said a spokesman.

01 **slothful:** *faul*
04 **gasp:** *Atemzug*
20 **UCAS:** British organization that deals with applications to study at universities and colleges
30 **sixth-former:** *(in GB) Oberstufenschüler/in*
54 **cram sth in:** *mit etw vollstopfen*

F

That is music to the ears of Emily Mason. Aged 16, she has just finished 22 exams for her GCSEs and starts her A-levels at Queen Mary's College in Basingstoke in September.

She dreamed of having a few weeks off to "watch Netflix", but she feels that she should be out looking for a job. "I've applied for basically every part-time job I can find and looking for jobs is taking up a lot of time. It's really difficult because the government scrapped work experience [for year 10s] and you need experience to get a job, but there's no way of getting that experience. Also I'm not old enough to drive, so I have to find a job I can get to and the buses here are pretty bad.

"I feel like I should get stuff and do experience so that I can get a job and go to a good university, but there aren't really that many opportunities out there in Basingstoke. The application is definitely in my mind, but I don't really know what I want to do. But it's obviously something really important that I can't just forget about. It's daunting."

G

Hannah Dearden teaches media and communication to sixth-formers at Northampton College. "I feel quite sorry for them. It's really difficult. They're told they need to build up work experience from the age of 16, but then many places won't take them until they are 18. There's a lot of pressure on them, and for some it's easier than others if they have the right parents and the right connections, which of course isn't really fair." For those with connections and those without, the school summer holidays just ain't what they used to be. (776 words)

Source: *The Guardian*, 28 June 2015

60 GCSEs: (in UK) exams taken at the age of 16
61 A-levels: (in UK) exams taken at the age of 18
68 scrap sth: *etw streichen*

1 MULTIPLE MATCHING

→ Skills, p. 200

Match the statements (a–i) with the corresponding speakers (1–6) in the text. Two of the statements don't match. For one speaker there are two statements.

1 Daniel Hall
2 Mary Curnock Cook
3 Rob Evans
4 University of Warwick spokesman
5 Emily Mason
6 Hannah Dearden

a Applicants should show how they have benefitted from their work experience.
b It's not extra summer jobs or doing lots of extra-curricular activities that will get you into university.
c It's really difficult to find a job or to write a good application if you don't know what you want to do.
d Not everybody has the same opportunities to find suitable work experience, and a lot of places won't take 16 or 17-year-olds.
e Personal statements can sometimes turn an unsuccessful application into a successful one.
f The best way to get work experience is to offer to work as a volunteer.
g Universities don't accept any applicants who haven't done any work experience in the summer.
h You feel a lot of pressure if your friends have a summer job and you don't.
i You should use the vacation in a sensible way to improve your chances of being accepted for a university course.

2 MEDIATION ENGLISH–GERMAN

→ Skills, p. 198

Beantworten Sie die folgenden Fragen auf Deutsch.

1 Worauf bezieht sich der von vielen Teenagern geäußerten Wunsch, „to put the record straight“ (l. 7)?
2 Was sagt „concentrating on curating their curricula vitae“ (ll. 9–10) über die Pläne der SchülerInnen für die Sommerferien aus?
3 In welchem Fall könnten *personal statements* eine entscheidende Rolle bei der Bewerbung um einen Studienplatz spielen?
4 Was gefällt Emily Mason so an den Ratschlägen der Warwick University?
5 Was schränkt die 16-jährige Emily Mason bei der Suche nach einem Job stark ein?
6 Welchen Vorteil genießen Teenager mit „the right parents and the right connections“ (ll. 86–87)?

3 WORKING WITH WORDS

A The words on the left are all from the text. Match them to their meanings on the right.

1 envy sb sth	a frightening in a way which makes you feel less confident
2 conjure sth up	b improve the quality, value or status of sth
3 rejection	c make sth appear as a picture in your mind
4 glum	d refusal to accept sb for a job, position, etc.
5 urge sb to do sth	e sad, quiet and unhappy
6 enhance sth	f strongly advise sb to do sth
7 reflect upon sth	g think carefully and deeply about sth
8 daunting	h wish you had the same qualities, possessions, etc. as sb else

B Use the words (1–8) from 3A to complete these sentences. You may have to make some changes.

1 For many students, getting the right work experience to create the perfect CV is a ▬ task.
2 He looked at the pile of rejections ▬ and wondered if he would ever be offered a place at university.
3 His mother strongly ▬ him to do some volunteer work to create a good impression on his CV.
4 I don't ▬ him the job of writing all those university applications.
5 She spent the summer ▬ her CV with a whole string of volunteer projects with homeless people.
6 Long summer holidays ▬ a picture of lazy students doing nothing all day long.
7 We like students to ▬ their work experience in their personal statements and give us an idea of what they have learned from it.

8 When he opened the letter from the university, he saw that it was only another ▬.

C Use the English equivalents of the German words in brackets to complete the email on p. 31. They are all in the text.

Hi Stella,
You asked me about applying for university. Here's what you need to do:
First of all, you should make a list of all the schools you've been to, the exams you've taken and your ▬ 1 (*Prüfungsergebnisse*), even if they are not as good as you might like. You'll need these as the basis of your ▬ 2 (*Lebenslauf*). The second part of your ▬ 3 (*Bewerbung*) is a ▬ 4 (*Motivationsschreiben*), in which you tell the university why you are suitable for the ▬ 5 (*Studiengang*) you are applying for, what sort of ▬ 6 (*Praktikum*) you have and what you have learned from it. There are lots of ▬ 7 (*Bewerber/innen*) all trying to get a ▬ 8 (*Studienplatz*) and if you can show the university the type of person you are, this might make the difference between an ▬ 9 (*Angebot*) of a place and a ▬ 10 (*Absage*). I hope this helps. Good luck!
Lisa

D ⊙ **Go to File 4 on p. 177.**
Complete this paragraph with the correct prepositions. All the prepositions can be found in the text with the verbs or nouns they are used with.

Even when their GCSE exams are over at the age of 16, many British students still feel that the pressure is ▬ 1 because they have to look ▬ 2 work experience or other activities to put ▬ 3 their CVs. Students who want to go ▬ 4 university often worry ▬ 5 their applications and work hard ▬ 6 their personal statements because they know that the universities look ▬ 7 them very carefully. Even those students who concentrate ▬ 8 polishing their CVs still feel ▬ 9 pressure as a good application can make the difference ▬ 10 getting ▬ 11 a good university or just getting a place ▬ 12 a university they might not really want to go to.

4 GROUP DISCUSSION

→ Skills, p. 210

Next year you and your friends will take your final exams and apply for places at university. You are discussing what you should do together in the summer before your final year.

Presentation phase

Choose one of the plans for the summer listed below and in one minute say why you favour it.

- Find work experience in a local company to add to your CV.
- Do voluntary work for a charity or local organization to help society (e.g. Red Cross, fire brigade).
- Take extra tuition in a school subject to improve your chances of good exam grades.
- Travel around Europe to broaden your horizons.
- Stay at home, meet your friends and enjoy the summer while you can.

Interaction phase

Discuss all the suggestions above and try to reach an agreement on which one(s) is/are most suitable. Be prepared to compromise if your suggestion isn't accepted.

5 ARGUMENTATIVE WRITING

→ Skills, pp. 206, 208

Do you agree with the saying that "Your school days are the happiest days of your life"? Write about 200 words.

1 LISTENING

→ Skills, p. 196

05

Michel Martin of National Public Radio in the USA is talking to author and educator Alvin Hall about how teenagers can get a good summer job.

Go to File 5 on p. 177.

A Listen to the first part of the interview and complete these sentences:

1 A generation ago, ▬ of teenagers in the USA worked during the summer vacation.
2 Nowadays, that number has fallen by ▬.
3 One reason for the drop in the number of teenagers with summer jobs is the increased competition from ▬.
4 Alvin Hall gives teenagers two pieces of advice: first of all, they should go around and ▬; secondly, they need to ▬.
5 Teenagers are unlikely to get internships in well-known companies because these mostly go to ▬.

06

B Listen to the second part of the interview and answer these questions.

1 What two qualities make young people attractive to small businesses as candidates for summer jobs?
2 What do employers no longer do if you drop off a résumé to get a summer job?
3 Why do many employers not give summer jobs to black and Latino teenagers?
4 What should black and Latino teenagers do in order to get good summer jobs?
5 Which three-word phrase sums up Alvin Hall's tips on how to get a good vacation job?

2 VIEWING

→ Skills, p. 196

At a job interview, it is not only important what you say, but also how you act. You are going to watch a video with tips about interview body language.

03

A First of all, watch the video clips. Which of the tips below are illustrated in the extracts?

Interview body language: Dos and Don'ts

1 Greet the interviewer with a firm handshake.
2 Be relaxed but not too relaxed.
3 Don't form barriers with your body.
4 Keep your hands away from your face.
5 Stay focussed on the interviewer.
6 Don't fidget with your hands and feet.
7 Don't fiddle or pick at your clothes.
8 Maintain normal eye contact with the interviewer.
9 Sit facing the interviewer.
10 Use sensible hand gestures.

04

B Now watch the whole video and make sure you understand all the tips above.

C **Work with a partner. Chose one tip from the list in 2A and demonstrate for the class (without talking) some incorrect and then some correct body language. The others have to guess which tip you have chosen.**

D **Mediation: A friend of yours is going for a job interview with a German company next week. Explain the body language tips to him/her in German.**

3 MATERIAL-BASED ESSAY

→ Skills, pp. 206, 208

A **Look closely at the cartoon on the right. What is the boy worried about? Do you share his worries?**

B **You have to write an essay on the topic below. Use the cartoon to help you write the introduction to the essay.**

If you need help writing the introduction, turn to File 6 on p. 178.

"If you haven't got things to put on your CV, you won't get the place at university, and if you don't get into university, forget about a job." (Daniel Hall)

Comment on this statement. Write about 300 words.

4 WRITING A PERSONAL STATEMENT

Choose one of the following job adverts and write a personal statement, saying why you are interested in the job and what makes you suitable for the position.

Student Summer Job – Waiting Staff
Beach Café, Watergate Bay, Cornwall

Pay:	Starting at £7.20 per hour
Sector:	Catering/Hospitality/Leisure
Category:	Part-time/Holiday
Type of work:	Waiter/Waitress

Job Description
We are currently recruiting waiting staff to work at the Beach Café, located on Watergate Bay, the premier surfing beach in Cornwall.
The ideal candidate:
- Previous experience not absolutely necessary
- Must be 16 years of age or older
- Must have a "can-do" and positive working attitude
- Ability to work under pressure
- Must have the confidence and ability to deal with a wide range of people
- Must be happy to walk/stand during the entire shift
- On-site accommodation available (caravan)

Summer Camp USA
Work in the USA at one of 500 summer camps

TYPES OF ROLES:
Work as a camp counsellor. This involves living and working with the campers. Your day will involve caring for and supervising the children at meal times, in the bunk and at night-time. You also lead a specific activity area of camp which can include a whole host of activities on the waterfront from sailing to swim teaching, kayaking and much more.

WHAT'S INCLUDED?
Return transatlantic flights
Between \$800–\$1500 pay
Up to 90 days' medical insurance
Visa assistance and sponsorship

REQUIREMENTS:
Age 18 by June 1st
Fluent English speaker
Available for 9 weeks and able to depart prior to June 19th
Active interest in working with children

SIMPLE PAST / PAST TENSE – PRESENT PERFECT

→ Grammar summary, p. 217

1 SPOT THE MISTAKES

Spot the mistakes and correct them. Explain why they are wrong.

1 ~~Rob has sent out twelve applications last week.~~
2 ~~He is receiving only one reply since January.~~
3 ~~Lisa has been to an interview in London two days ago.~~
4 ~~Jenna didn't go to an interview for several weeks now.~~
5 ~~Nicola has been working for a charity since three months.~~

2 Decide whether the *past tense* or the *present perfect* is most suitable in each case.

James went / has been [1] to an interview yesterday. He didn't attend / hasn't attended [2] any interviews since he started / has started [3] writing applications two months ago, so that was / has been [4] the first. He left / has left university [5] in June and he then decided / has decided [6] to travel for a few months before starting to apply for a job. He flew / has flown [7] to Thailand in September and travelled / has been travelling [8] in South-East Asia. He came / has come [9] home at Christmas and was working / has been working [10] hard since then at getting his CV up to date. Altogether he wrote / has written [11] 250 applications in the last two months, but until now he only received / has only received [12] 35 replies, most of them rejections.

3 Complete the paragraph with the *past tense* or the *present perfect*.

Melissa ___ [1] (sit) her final exams at vocational college six weeks ago. Since then she ___ [2] (get) her results back – all As and Bs – and she ___ [3] (go) on holiday to Portugal. She ___ [4] (have) an interview at a design college last week and yesterday she ___ [5] (hear) that she had been accepted on the fashion course. She ___ [6] (phone) her mum and dad straight away and in the last 24 hours she ___ [7] (write) literally hundreds of messages to all her friends and ___ [8] (invite) them to a big party at her house.

WATCH OUT! Wie übersetzt man das deutsche „machen"?

Complete the sentences with the English equivalents of the German phrases in brackets.

Luisa had to ~~make~~ a short break while she was ~~making~~ her final exam.
→ *Luisa had to take a short break while she was doing / sitting / taking her final exam.*

1 Don't forget to ___ (*deine Hausaufgaben machen*) when you get home from school.
2 I won't get a good grade for English because I always ___ (*viele Fehler machen*) in the oral exam.
3 When are you going to ___ (*deine Fahrprüfung machen*)?
4 Robert is a trainee electrician. At the moment, he ___ (*macht seine Ausbildung*) at a company in Munich.
5 First of all, I'm going to ___ (*Abitur machen*) then I'm going to ___ (*Urlaub machen*) for six weeks!
6 We always ___ (*gute Erfahrungen machen*) with trainees from vocational schools.
7 What does Harry ___ (*beruflich machen*)? – Oh, he's a doctor.
8 Sally isn't interested in going out at the weekends. All she wants to do is ___ (*Karriere machen*).

3 Keeping healthy

FOCUS

- Take it in turns to throw a dice and move your counter.
- When you land on a square, read the situation aloud to the other players. They discuss how healthy or unhealthy your lifestyle is.
- The other players decide if you should move two squares forward (very healthy), one square forward (healthy), one square backwards (unhealthy) or two squares backwards (very unhealthy).
- Move your counter according to the other players' decision. (If they can't decide, you can stay where you are.) The first one to "Finish" is the winner.

START

1. You decide to give up chocolate and sweets for Lent.

2. Your boy/girlfriend takes you to his/her favourite – vegan – restaurant; you can't say no.

3. You eat a hamburger and chips and have two alcoholic drinks on a night out on the town.

4. Your moped has broken down, so now you have to cycle to school until it has been repaired.

5. Your boy/girlfriend leaves you. You drown your sorrows with two tubs of chocolate chip ice cream.

6. You train twice a week with a local football team and afterwards you all go to a pizza place to relax.

7. You have an important test and want to stay up all night to revise. Three cans of an energy drink help you to keep awake.

8. You go snowboarding with friends. You're out on the slopes all day and enjoy the après ski parties at night.

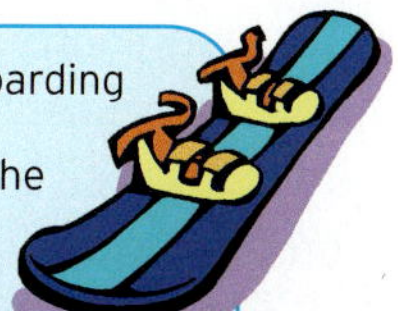

9. You go jogging with your new boy-/girlfriend every morning before school, but there's no time for breakfast.

10. Your friends decide to watch a model casting show. In desperation you drink 1 litre of cola and eat 2 bags of crisps.

11. Summer's coming and you need to lose weight. You cut back on meals and just eat a few snacks.

12. Your mum has become a vegetarian so now there are vegetarian meals 3 times a week at home.

13. You've given up smoking at last, but you've become addicted to juicy fruit chewing gum.

14. Your dad has put a cycling machine in the basement. Sometimes you use it when no one else is at home.

FINISH

3 WORDS IN CONTEXT A

Healthy eating

For a fit and healthy body we need a balanced diet and regular exercise. How much we should eat depends on how active we are: the amount of calories we consume should correspond to the amount of energy we use. If we eat or drink too much, we put on weight or become obese. If we eat and drink too little, we lose weight. Men usually need around 2,500 and women around 2,000 calories per day. We also need to drink about 1.6 to 2 litres of fluid every day to stop dehydration.

Experts recommend that teenagers get 60 minutes or more of moderate to vigorous physical activity per day. Physical exercise produces endorphins, substances that can help us to relax, sleep better and feel happier. The right amount of exercise can also boost our energy levels and improve our mood. People who exercise regularly burn more calories (= energy), which helps them to lose weight and reduce the risk of heart disease, type-2 diabetes and strokes.

Starchy foods (= carbohydrates), which make up a large part of most diets, include potatoes, cereals, pasta, rice and bread. Wholegrain varieties contain more fibre and make us feel full. Some people think starchy foods are fattening, but gram for gram the carbohydrates they contain provide fewer than half the calories of fat.

Nutritionists recommend that we eat at least five portions of different types of fruits and vegetables a day. A glass of unsweetened fruit juice counts as one portion, as do vegetables cooked into dishes or a fresh salad.

For many people in developed countries, meat is the main source of protein, but we do not need it more than once or twice a week, and we should eat lean meats and cut off visible fat for healthy nutrition. Fish is also a good source of protein and contains many vitamins and minerals. Two portions of fish a week are recommended, including at least one portion of oily fish, such as salmon, trout, fresh tuna or sardines. These contain omega-3 fats which may help to prevent heart disease.

The type of fat in our diet is just as important as the amount of fat we eat. There are two main types of fat: saturated and unsaturated fats. Too much saturated fat can increase the level of cholesterol in the blood, which increases the risk of heart disease. Saturated fat is found in many foods, such as hard cheese, cakes, biscuits, sausages, cream, butter and pies. Foods that contain unsaturated fats include vegetable oils, oily fish and avocados.

Sugary fizzy drinks, alcoholic drinks, sugary breakfast cereals, cakes, biscuits and pastries all contain added sugars, they are often high in calories and, if eaten too often, can contribute to weight gain. They can also cause tooth decay, especially if eaten between meals. Reducing our intake of sugar is vital for good health and preventing diabetes and obesity.

Many people consume too much salt, even if they don't add salt to their meals. About three quarters of the salt we eat is already in processed food such as breakfast cereals, soups, breads and sauces. Eating too much salt can raise our blood pressure: high blood pressure increases the risk of heart disease or strokes.

(536 words)

First of all, make sure you understand the meaning of each of the highlighted words and phrases in the text above. If you are not sure, look them up in your dictionary. Then complete the tasks on the following page.

1 WORD FIELDS

A Make a list of words and phrases from the text related to the given categories.

a	medical conditions	*put on weight, become obese,* ___
b	forms of nutrition	*calories,* ___
c	healthy types of food	*fruit and vegetables,* ___
d	unhealthy types of food	*starchy foods,* ___
e	fitness and health	*balanced diet,* ___

B Add any other "health and fitness" words or phrases that you know to your list.

2 WORD FAMILIES

Find the correct adjectives from the text to complete these sentences.

1 Experts say that the key to fitness and a healthy body is a ___ (balance) diet and a regular amount of ___ (physics) exercise.
2 Too much ___ (starch) food is a major cause of obesity, but there are many ___ (health) varieties of carbohydrates such as wholegrain wheat.
3 ___ (oil) fish is a good source of protein, but too many ___ (saturate) fats, such as those in cheese and butter, increase the risk of heart disease.
4 ___ (sugar) drinks and ___ (alcohol) drinks are usually high in calories and can contribute to weight gain.
5 There are large amounts of ___ (add) sugar and salt in many ___ (process) foods such as breakfast cereals and packet soups.

3 COLLOCATIONS

A Look through the text and find more collocations with the words below.

1 *prevent* / ___ tooth decay
2 *consume* / ___ / ___ calories
3 *lower* / ___ blood pressure
4 *gain* / ___ / ___ weight
5 *increase* / ___ the risk of heart disease
6 *cause* / ___ obesity

burn ▪ cause ▪ lose ▪ prevent ▪ provide ▪ put on ▪ raise ▪ reduce

B Complete the following paragraph with the most suitable verb from 3A.

For a healthy lifestyle, we need a certain amount of physical activity to make sure that we ___ [1] as many calories as we ___ [2] as food. Too many calories and too little exercise will cause us to ___ [3] weight; too few calories, however, and we are in danger of ___ [4] weight, which can also be unhealthy if it is taken too far. Everyone knows that fizzy drinks and sweets ___ [5] tooth decay, but nutritionists warn that added sugar in processed food can also ___ [6] the risk of heart disease. Too much salt in processed food can also ___ [7] our blood pressure. They say that it is important to ___ [8] our intake of sugar to ___ [9] diabetes and obesity.

SITUATION

Your school is doing a project week on the theme of health and fitness. In your English class you decide to take a closer look at one particular aspect: the vending machines in your school and the snacks and soft drinks they sell. During the project week, you will hold a **class discussion** on what to do with **the vending machines** and then you will put your chosen solution into practice.

STEP 1 Brainstorming ideas

You start thinking about vending machines and quickly realize that most of the snacks and drinks that they sell contain added sugar, which can cause obesity, diabetes and tooth decay.

Brainstorm some ways in which you could persuade your fellow students to buy fewer unhealthy snacks from vending machines. Collect your ideas on the board.

STEP 2 Reading about a possible solution

While researching the topic of unhealthy snacks and soft drinks, you come across the article on p. 39 about warning labels.

A Work in groups of three. Read the heading and introduction together and quickly discuss these two questions:

- Should sugary drinks carry warning labels?
- Do warning labels really change people's minds?

B Partner A: Read the introduction to the text and lines 1–27 and collect arguments for warning labels on sugary drinks.

Partner B: Read the text from line 28 to the end and collect arguments for warning labels on cigarettes.

Partner C: Read the text from line 28 to the end and collect arguments against warning labels.

A	arguments for warning labels on sugary drinks	*parents will buy fewer sugary drinks for children;* ...
B	arguments for warning labels on cigarettes	*warnings ... have saved 8 million lives (ll. 41–42);* ...
C	arguments against warning labels	*labels ... fade into the background (ll. 47–50);* ...

C Each partner completes one sentence below to sum up the information in the text.

Partner A: There should be warning labels on sugary drinks because they might help ...
Partner B: Warning labels on cigarette packets are necessary because ...
Partner C: Some people say warning labels don't have any effect any more because ...

D Share your notes with your partners. Did the text answer the questions in Step 2A?

By LUCY SCHOUTEN • January 14, 2016

Should sugary drinks carry warning labels?

A new study claims to show that parents will buy fewer sugary soft drinks for their children if a warning label advises against it, but the dire warning labels on cigarettes seem to have lost their touch. Do warning labels really change minds?

Some Americans could see one more warning label during trips to the grocery store.

Legislators in California and New York are considering requiring warning labels on high-sugar drinks as a weapon against childhood obesity, and a study claims the labels would dissuade parents from giving them to their children [...].

The study used an online survey to show 2,381 parents a series of beverages and used labels featured in California's proposed law: "Drinking beverages with added sugar(s) contributes to obesity, diabetes and tooth decay."

When the parents saw sodas and sugary juices with the label, only 40 percent of parents said they would give their child the sugary drink, compared with 53 percent who saw the calorie-count label used currently or 60 percent of parents who saw the drinks with no labels.

"[Health warning labels] provide an extra layer of information that people can understand," said David Hammond, lead researcher and professor in the school of public health at the University of Waterloo in Ontario [...].

This study, published Thursday in the *Journal of Pediatrics*, joins a body of research with demonstrated ambivalence on the subject of warning labels. A useful comparison can be found in cigarettes, first

packaged with warning labels in 1965. The dire pronouncements about smoking ought to make any potential smoker think twice, but do they?

The US surgeon general says, "yes". In the 50th anniversary report on smoking and health in 2014, Acting Surgeon Gen. Boris Lushniak claimed warnings on individual cigarette packs had saved 8 million lives. Yet at an estimated 500,000 deaths per year, smoking is still considered the leading cause of preventable death in the United States [...].

The stern warning labels are on every package, but for many smokers they fade into the background, research indicates.

"Unfortunately, since the current requirements for warning labels were established in 1984, their effect on smokers has →

14 soda: *Limonade*
29 pediatrics: *Kinderheilkunde*
31 ambivalence: *Zwiespältigkeit*
35 pronouncement: formal public statement
38 surgeon general: (in USA) head of the public health service
47 stern: *ernst, hart*
53 current: happening now

drastically weakened, and the current labels are now virtually meaningless," according to a report by Campaign for Tobacco-Free Kids, an advocacy group in Washington, D.C. "Moreover, smokers have become habitualized to the style of labels, to the point that the labels go unnoticed altogether."

Recognizing this, some anti-tobacco advocates supported the US Family Smoking Prevention and Tobacco Control Act of 2009, which would have required graphic pictures to accompany the warning labels on cigarette packs. Research in 2007 by the Center for Disease Control suggested that warning labels with frightening images of children in danger and black lungs might dissuade potential smokers, at least at first.

Even in that study, however, researchers looked at results from Canada, which already used the colorful pictures to describe what they see as the harms of smoking, and wondered whether the graphic warning labels would have lost their shock value over time.

For similar reasons, the ubiquitousness of warning labels may reduce their effectiveness in the case of sugar. Warning labels now appear on everything from music to grocery bags and printer cartridges. (531 words)

Source: *Christian Science Monitor*, 14 January 2016

60 advocacy group: *Lobbygruppe*

80 ubiquitousness [juːˈbɪkwɪtəsnəs]: *Allgegenwärtigkeit*

STEP 3 Boosting your word power

In the text there are phrases that you could use in a discussion about warning labels.

Go to File 7 on p. 178.

A Find the phrases in the text that match the following explanations. They are in the same order as in the text.

1 signs on a product that tell the buyer in explicit terms how dangerous it is
2 persuade sb not to do sth
3 soft drinks with a lot of extra sugar
4 make sb who wants to start smoking have second thoughts
5 get used to sth
6 shocking or disturbing images

B Find at least five expressions in the text that express the idea that warning labels no longer have the same effect on smokers.

C Some compound adjectives could be useful in your discussion. Using the words in the box and a dictionary, find phrases that mean the same as the following:

anti- ▪ -free ▪ high- ▪ low- ▪ multi- ▪ non- ▪ pro-

1 beverages with a lot of added sugar — *high-sugar drinks*
2 a diet with a small amount of calories
3 a restaurant where you're not allowed to smoke
4 a business worth many millions of dollars
5 a drink that doesn't contain any sugar
6 a snack bar with a lot of protein
7 people who support measures to restrict smoking

STEP 4 Discussing a solution

A **In class, discuss ways to persuade your fellow students not to buy unhealthy snacks and drinks from the vending machines. Consider the options from the list below, or add your own ideas from Step 1. Use your notes from Step 2 and the phrases in Step 3 to help you. Make sure you have checked the pronunciation of important thematic vocabulary.**

- Provide an informative warning sign to stick on or next to the vending machines, stating how much sugar, salt and fat is contained in each product.
- Hang up a poster with a graphic warning next to the vending machines, showing the negative health effects of consuming too much salt, sugar or fat.
- Create a video showing the negative health effects of consuming too much salt, sugar or fat (google "public health videos", for example).
- Raise the price of the items sold in the vending machines to make them less attractive.
- Ban the vending machines from the school building completely.

Use these phrases and the "Language for discussion" on the back cover flap.

You can't buy ... in ... unless ...

We have to pay ... because ...

I think you should be able to ... whatever you want.

I don't agree with you. I think we ought to ...

You're not allowed to ... in Germany if ...

B **At the end of the discussion, come to a decision on the best course of action.**

STEP 5 Putting the solution into practice

A **Work again in your group of three. Now put the decision from the class discussion into practice and create whatever you have decided on: a warning sign, a label, etc. If you have decided to ban the vending machines completely, write a flyer explaining the decision.**

B **In your groups, present your "result" to the class.**

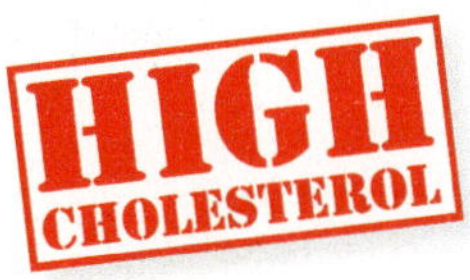

3 THE PALEO DIET C

BEFORE YOU READ

Imagine you are on a diet that doesn't permit anything made from grain (wheat, maize, etc.), sugar or dairy products – and all forms of processed food. Make a quick list of all the things that you couldn't eat. Which of them would you miss most?

THE PALEO DIET:
can it really be good for you?

A Most reformed serial dieters can remember a defining moment that got them off the starvation treadmill. Mine came in 2008. I was meeting an old friend, the nutritionist Charlotte Watts, for brunch. She walked in and something – everything – had changed. Her skin was clear and glowing, her eyes were bright. Her body looked stronger and leaner.

"You look amazing," I said.

"I've gone paleo," she replied.

B Over the three months since I'd last seen her Charlotte had been "eating the way our ancestors did": she'd given up sugar, processed foods, grains and legumes, focusing instead on meat, fish, vegetables and fruit. As a health writer, I pooh-poohed the idea (All that meat? There's a global food crisis! And what healthy diet says give up lentils?) and continued to jump on and off whichever new [diet] I happened to be writing about. […]

Then, in 2011, Charlotte and I wrote a book together and in the interests of research I tried her approach. Six weeks in, I had lost 4lb and felt unbelievable. I was back at the gym after years of desperate tiredness, had lost my afternoon crisp cravings, was sleeping better and thinking more clearly.

C Although the idea of eating "what we're programmed to" has been around since the 1960s, it was only in 2001, when the high priest of paleo, Loren Cordain, published *The Paleo Diet*, that it began to grow in popularity in America. By 2013 it had become the most Googled diet on the internet. […]

D Cordain's thesis is simple. A professor in the department of health and exercise science at Colorado State University, he argues that certain foods entered our diets only about 10,000 years ago with the agricultural revolution, when we began cultivating grains in larger amounts, and that isn't long enough for us to adapt to eating them.

Instead, he believes we should stick to what the cavemen ate – meat, vegetables, fruits, seeds and nuts – and avoid grains, along with anything that prehistoric man wouldn't have recognised, such as dairy, pulses, sugar and, of course, processed food. […]

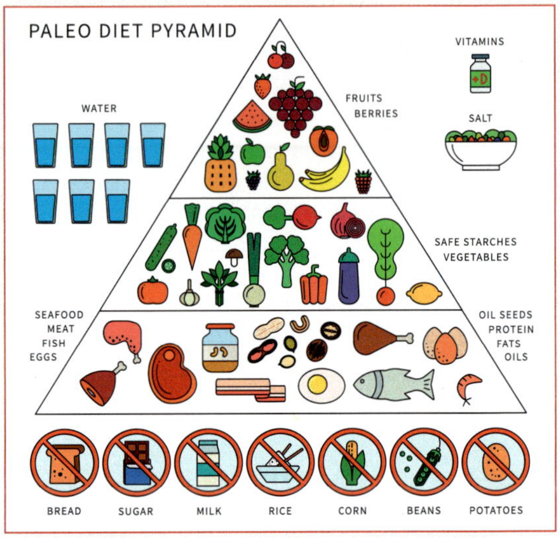

E Whatever you call it – primal, caveman or paleo – no diet is quite so divisive. John Briffa, a doctor, nutritionist and ardent supporter of primal eating, points to evidence from fossilised remains that show "our ancestors pre-agriculture were robust physically, tall, strong and lean". Remarkably, a study of the hunter-gatherer people of the Trobriand Islands in Papua New Guinea found an absence of heart disease or diabetes, while a three-week trial of the paleo diet at Karolinska Institute in Sweden recorded an average weight loss of 2.3kg and a drop in blood pressure among participants.

01 **serial dieter:** sb who goes from one diet to the next
12 **legume:** *Hülsenfrucht*
14 **pooh-pooh sth:** say that sth is not true or not worth thinking about
20 **lb = pound:** 0.453kg
40 **pulse:** *trockene Hülsenfrucht*
43 **divisive:** *polarisierend*
44 **ardent:** *leidenschaftlich*

But large-scale studies are non-existent – the Swedish one involved 14 people – and, in light of their absence, many nutritionists remain vehemently opposed to the paleo diet. [...]

F "The paleo diet trend is a dangerous fad," says Lucy Jones, a spokeswoman for the British Dietetic Association (BDA). "There isn't any proof that it improves health, and its demand that you exclude food groups essential to health such as dairy, grains and legumes could leave people seriously deficient in essential vitamins and calcium [...]." (One thing dietitians do agree on is sugar, which is increasingly blamed for poor health, with the Action on Sugar campaign comparing it to smoking and alcohol in harmfulness.) Besides, asks Jones, what was the life expectancy for hunter-gatherers? About 20? Indeed, only a minority of our paleo ancestors would have made it to their forties, and many children would have died before they reached the age of 15. [...]

G Jones's concerns do make sense to me, but, after three years, paleo eating is the one diet that has made me forget about dieting. It's given me, at 44, huge reserves of energy, and I no longer feel hungry. [...] And yet I find a truly paleo diet a struggle [...]. At restaurants friends have called me a pain in the a—, because I'm always asking whether things contain dairy and opting out of potatoes or rice. It becomes boring and repetitive, and so I have made my own concessions to the hardcore rules laid out in Cordain's covenant – as do most people who eat primally long-term. [...]

H "I would always recommend people be flexible," says Sarah Bowles-Flannery, [a naturopath and nutritionist]. "If you love porridge and want to have a lentil curry a few times a week, that's fine. Most of the benefits come from cutting out sugar and processed foods and not eating grains all the time."

Now I eat red meat only once a fortnight [...]. I'll rarely have more than 100g to 150g of meat or fish (a portion the size of an iPhone) and avoid processed or charred meats altogether [...]. "That's the big mistake everyone makes on paleo diets," says Bowles-Flannery. "They go mad on meat but their diet should be three-quarters vegetables and fruit, the rest lean protein and healthy fats such as nuts, avocados and seeds." (818 words)

Source: Anna Magee, *The Daily Telegraph*, 29 January 2014

57 **fad:** *Modeerscheinung*
62 **deficient:** not having enough of sth that is very important
79 **hardcore:** *extrem*
80 **covenant:** *Bündnis*
90 **charred:** *angebrannt*

1 SHORT-ANSWER QUESTIONS

→ Skills, p. 200

Go to File 8 on p. 179.

Answer the following questions by providing information from the text (Paragraphs A–C).

1 Which phrase describes the author's feeling that dieting is a never-ending form of torture?
2 Which expression is a synonym for: "I've started eating the way our ancestors did"?
3 Why was the author sceptical of the paleo diet at first? (*2 aspects*)
4 What visible benefit of the paleo diet did the author experience?
5 Which piece of information demonstrates the growing interest in the paleo diet?

2 MULTIPLE CHOICE

→ Skills, p. 204

Choose the most suitable option in each case.

1 According to the theory of the paleo diet, we should adopt a diet that resembles the nutrition prior to the agricultural revolution because ...
  - **a** modern humans eat too much and don't get enough exercise.
  - **b** our bodies can process meat and fish better than fruit and vegetables.
  - **c** processed foods are fattening and contain too much salt.
  - **d** our bodies are not able to properly process grains and dairy products.

2 Which idea is not expressed in paragraph E?
   a The paleo diet is very controversial among doctors and nutritionists.
   b Prehistoric men and women were shorter on average than we are today.
   c The paleo diet can provide certain health benefits for modern people.
   d There is not enough scientific evidence to evaluate the paleo diet.

3 Lucy Jones says that the paleo diet is dangerous because …
   a there is no evidence that it provides health benefits.
   b foods such as milk and wheat products are necessary for a balanced diet.
   c sugar is just as harmful as smoking and alcohol.
   d it is not suitable for adults who are in their 40s and over.

4 Which sentence best summarizes the author's current attitude to the paleo diet?
   a She finds it hard to follow because it is boring and repetitive.
   b She is amazed that she no longer feels hungry while dieting.
   c She doesn't mind not eating potatoes and rice in restaurants.
   d She feels fitter and stronger, although she doesn't follow all the rules.

5 According to Sarah Bowles-Flannery, which mistake do lots of people on the paleo diet make?
   a They don't eat processed foods but still eat some grains.
   b They don't add enough lentils and porridge to their diet.
   c They eat too much meat and not enough vegetables and fruit.
   d They eat too much processed or overcooked meat.

3 WORKING WITH WORDS

A The words in the box are all taken from the text. Match them with the definitions (1–8).

approach ▪ concession ▪ cultivate sth ▪ essential ▪ life expectancy ▪ participant ▪ repetitive ▪ vehement

1 saying or doing the same thing many times so that it becomes boring
2 a way of dealing with or doing sth
3 showing very strong feelings, especially anger
4 prepare and use sth, e.g. land, for growing sth, e.g. plants or crops
5 a person who is taking part in an activity or event
6 absolutely necessary for sth, e.g. for life
7 the number of years that people are likely to live on average
8 sth that you allow or do, or allow sb to have, in order to make a situation less difficult

B Use words from 3A to complete this paragraph about the paleo diet. You may have to change the form of some of the words.

The ___ 1 of the paleo diet is to only eat what cavemen ate before humans started ___ 2 grain about 10,000 years ago. ___ 3 critics of the diet say that cavemen only had a short ___ 4 and that the diet excludes some ___ 5 items, such as grain and pulses. ___ 6 in a study on the diet in Sweden quickly noticed several health benefits, such as lower blood pressure. However, even some of the most ardent followers of the diet say that it is ___ 7 and they sometimes have to make ___ 8 to the strict rules.

C Choose a verb from box A and prepositions from box B to replace the underlined phrases in the sentences below. The answers are all in the text. You may need to adjust the forms.

A cut ▪ focus ▪ forget ▪ give ▪ go mad ▪ jump ▪ opt ▪ stick

B about ▪ on (2×) ▪ on and off ▪ out ▪ out of ▪ to ▪ up

1 Is there a healthy diet anywhere that says you should ___ stop eating lentils?
2 The idea behind the paleo diet is to ___ concentrate on eating meat, fish, vegetables and fruit instead of grains, dairy products and sugar.
3 Anna has ___ started and stopped every new dieting fad since she became single.
4 Cordain thinks humans should ___ only eat foods that cavemen would have recognized.
5 According to the author, the paleo diet is the only one that has allowed her to ___ stop thinking of dieting all the time.
6 In restaurants, she often ___ chooses not to have potatoes or rice as side dishes.
7 The main benefits of the paleo diet come from ___ excluding sugar and processed foods from your diet.
8 The biggest problem is that people tend to ___ eat far too much meat instead of more fruit and vegetables.

D The photo shows a general recommendation of how much of each type of food we should include in a healthy, balanced diet. With a partner, decide on a healthy set of meals for a day. Try to agree on foods that are healthy and that both of you like. The verb phrases from 2C and the speech bubbles below will help you.

I'd prefer to have ... instead.

I think we should have ... for breakfast.

I think we ought to have ... . It contains much more ... and is good for ...

I can't stand ... . Why don't we have (some) ... instead?

When you have finished, present your ideas to the class.

4 GIVING A PRESENTATION

→ Skills, p. 212

Choose one of these diets, or a diet that you know about. Research the diet on the internet and prepare a 3-minute presentation. Make sure you use websites that give a balanced view of the diet.

Diets

Atkins diet	low-carb diet
Breatharian diet	Mediterranean diet
fruitarian diet	paleo diet
gluten-free diet	vegan diet
juice fasting	vegetarian diet

Topics

- origins of the diet
- what the diet consists of
- claimed benefits of the diet
- famous ardent supporters of the diet
- possible negative effects of the diet

1 LISTENING

→ Skills, p. 196

08

You are going to listen to a report about a primary school in Scotland that has started an unusual scheme to help their pupils stay fit and concentrate on their work.

A Listen to the first part of the report and say if these sentences are true or false.

1 The children at St. Ninian's primary school in Stirling run one mile at the same time every day.
2 Lots of nursery and primary schools across Britain have started similar schemes.
3 One in five children are overweight when they start primary school in Britain.
4 Thirteen schools in Stirling have already started or are about to start the daily mile.
5 The children really enjoy their daily run around the playing field.
6 The daily mile takes place every school day unless it is raining heavily or is icy.

09

B Listen to the second part of the interview and match the speakers to the statements. Two speakers match more than one statement. There is one more statement than you need.

a "Children should have at least one hour of physical exercise every day."
b "I saw the kids at St. Ninian's and now we're going to build our own running track."
c "The daily mile helps parents to teach their children good habits for their health and fitness."
d "The pupils seem happier and fitter, but there are no scientific facts to support this yet."
e "This scheme is not only good for kids, but also for their parents and teachers."
f "We sent St. Ninian's an email asking them how they get the kids out on the track every day."
g "We want to offer our pupils more than just the compulsory two hours of PE per week."
h "We want to see the scheme in action and then we hope to introduce it to our local schools."

1 Dr Colin Moran, Stirling University
2 Kevin Clelland, teacher, Leeds
3 spokesperson for Active Cheshire
4 Tanni Grey-Thompson, chair of ukactive
5 Scottish government spokesperson

2 ARGUMENTATIVE WRITING

→ Skills, pp. 206, 208

Choose one of the following topics and write at least 200 words.

1 **Go to File 9 on p. 179.**
"Sugary drinks are just as dangerous to health as cigarettes. They should have warning labels and higher taxes as well." Do you agree with this statement?
2 "You are what you eat." Comment on this statement.

3 RESEARCH PROJECT

Look back at the ideas you collected for Part B, Step 1. How many ways are there in which people can be persuaded not to buy products that are unhealthy?

A **Work in groups of four. Research two items each from the list of products below. Find out if they are freely available in the UK, the USA and Germany, or whether there are any kind of sales restrictions, taxes or warning labels. Make a note of the websites you took your information from in case someone questions your findings.**
Copy the table below and write the items under the headings. Some items may appear under more than one heading.

alcopops ▪ beer & wine ▪ cigarettes ▪ energy drinks ▪ hard drugs ▪ soft drugs ▪ spirits ▪ sugary drinks

	warning signs	(age) restrictions	higher taxes	forbidden
United Kingdom	*cigarettes,* ...	*cigarettes,* ...	*cigarettes,* ...	...
United States	...	...	...	...
Germany	...	...	...	...

B **Compare your table with another group. Have you found the same results? Do you agree with the way the items are restricted by governments? Should they be more, or less, freely available. Explain your reasons.**

4 GROUP DISCUSSION

→ Skills, p. 210

As part of your school's project week on health and fitness, you have been asked to discuss general ways in which schools could be made healthier places.

Presentation phase

Choose one of the suggestions listed below and in one minute say why you favour it.

- ban all students from coming to school by car or moped; students should use public transport, bikes or go on foot
- introduce a compulsory sports lesson every day; always to be done at different times on the timetable, not just in the afternoon
- remove all snack vending machines from the school premises
- introduce a school canteen selling healthy meals, vegetarian meals and a salad buffet
- introduce "health and nutrition" as a compulsory school subject for all students
- ...

Interaction phase

Discuss all the suggestions above and discuss the merits of each one and how it could be implemented. Try to reach an agreement on which one(s) is/are most suitable. Be prepared to compromise if your suggestion is not accepted.

MODAL AUXILIARY VERBS

→ Grammar summary, p. 220

1 SPOT THE MISTAKES
Spot the mistakes and correct them. Explain why they are wrong.

1 ~~You mustn't go on a diet. Your weight is just right. I wish I had your figure.~~
2 ~~I will must go to the doctor's tomorrow. I'm feeling tired and I don't have any energy.~~
3 ~~You couldn't eat bread and lentils if you want to do the paleo diet properly.~~
4 ~~You can reduce your risk of heart disease if you ate less sugar and salt.~~
5 ~~With this diet we'd like to can help you lose weight.~~
6 ~~You needn't forget to do physical exercise if you want a healthy body.~~

2 **Complete the dialogue between an American high-school principal and a student with the English equivalent of the German verb in brackets.**

Principal: We ___ 1 (*müssen*) get rid of the new vending machine. Too many students are buying candy and sodas. It ___ 2 (*nicht können*) stay on the campus any longer.
Student: (*können*) ___ 3 we keep it until the summer vacation? We ___ 4 (*nicht müssen*) get rid of it straight away.
Principal: No. We ___ 5 (*sollen*) get the company to take it back right away. Students ___ 6 (*nicht sollen*) be able to buy all these high-sugar snacks at school.
Student: But we ___ 7 (*nicht dürfen*) smoke at school or drink alcohol anywhere. There's nothing that we ___ 8 (*dürfen*) do! You closed down the cafeteria as well last year.
Principal: We ___ 9 (*mussten*) close down the cafeteria, because the food was too unhealthy and we ___ 10 (*nicht können*) find a better company to run the cafeteria.
Student: It's not fair. We ___ 11 (*nicht dürfen*) vote on the question …
Principal: When you're older, you ___ 12 (*können*) do whatever you want. But while you're at high school, you ___ 13 (*müssen*) do what the high-school board says.
Student: Why ___ 14 (*nicht können*) adults just leave us kids alone!
Principal: You ___ 15 (*nicht müssen*) be angry with me. We ___ 16 (*müssen*) think of what's best for our students. Now you ___ 17 (*sollen*) get back to your class …

WATCH OUT! want
Read the example sentences and then translate the sentences into English.

Some people ~~want that diets~~ help them lose weight.
→ *Some people want diets to help them lose weight.*
Other people ~~not want~~ to eat foods that make them feel unhealthy.
→ *Other people don't want to eat foods that make them feel unhealthy.*

1 Die meisten Leute wünschen sich ein langes und gesundes Leben.
2 Meine Freunde wollen nur Junk Food essen und keinen Sport treiben.
3 Du kannst alles essen, was du willst.
4 Ich möchte nicht, dass du diese Paleo-Diät machst.
5 Warum wollen Experten, dass wir weniger Fleisch essen?
6 Garry möchte nicht, dass seine Freundin eine Diät macht.

4 The world of sport

FOCUS

1

2

3

4

5

6

7

8

Together in class do the following tasks:

10

1 Listen and match the five sounds to the photos above. Explain your choices, using the speech bubble and words from the box.

> That sounds like someone hitting a ... / people watching a ... match. I think it must be ...

bounce (sth) ▪ catch sth ▪ dive (into/from sth) ▪ hit sth ▪ jump (over sth) ▪ run ▪ skate ▪ ski ▪ swim ▪ throw sth

2 Write a "sports" word list, matching places and equipment to each sport. Start with the sports in the photos and add any other sports that you know. In the box you will find useful vocabulary.

places: course ▪ court ▪ diamond ▪ pitch ▪ pool ▪ ring ▪ rink ▪ track

equipment: bat ▪ boots ▪ club ▪ costume ▪ gloves ▪ goggles ▪ gumshield (*BE*) / mouthguard (*AE*) ▪ helmet ▪ puck ▪ racket ▪ shin pads ▪ shirt ▪ shoes ▪ shorts ▪ stick ▪ tee ▪ trunks

sport	place	equipment
athletics	*track*	*(running) shoes,*
baseball		

3 What do you like or love about sports? What do you dislike or really hate about sports?

4 WORDS IN CONTEXT A

11

06

The business of sport

"Sport" can be any activity that we do for pleasure and that needs physical effort or skill: sport includes many different types of activities, from jogging to karate, gymnastics to swimming, volleyball to ice hockey. Most sportsmen and women are amateurs: people who do whatever form of sport they do for the love of the sport and out of a desire to keep fit and healthy.

Sports can be divided into individual sports, such as tennis, and team sports, such as football. There are also winter sports, such as skiing or biathlon, ball games, such as handball or basketball, indoor and outdoor sports, such as darts and orienteering. Some sports, such as motor racing, cycling or sailing, need expensive equipment; other sports, such as dancing or judo, can be done without.

Sports such as archery are niche sports that don't have many active participants and don't attract a large following or a television audience. The most obvious example of a spectator sport is football. There are millions of amateur players, men and women, in non-professional leagues all over the world, and the professional football leagues have a global fan base. Many top football clubs regularly play in front of crowds of over 50,000, and supporters happily pay more money to support their favourite team by buying fan merchandise, such as football shirts or scarves. Football clubs have done a lot in recent years to combat the problem of hooliganism and make their stadiums more family-friendly.

The huge popularity of some sports, such as tennis, golf and American football, has turned them into highly attractive partners for sponsors and advertisers, and professional sport has become a multi-billion dollar industry. Top clubs such as Barcelona, Bayern Munich and Manchester United are well-run businesses and some of them are even quoted on the stock exchange. They have lucrative sponsorship deals with multinational corporations to display their logos on their shirts or in their stadiums. Sportswear is also a huge industry, with brands such as Adidas, Nike and Reebok paying sports stars millions of dollars a year to endorse their products.

The number of professional sportsmen and women who make a living from sport is small compared to the millions of amateurs. However, there are a few top stars who can market their success and image and become brand names in their own right. The financial rewards are enormous and so it is no surprise that the temptation to cheat, for some individuals, is considerable, too. The most common form of cheating in sport is doping, and there have been a number of doping scandals in recent years, particularly in athletics and cycling, which require great reserves of strength and endurance from the athletes. Match-fixing has also been uncovered in some sports, where betting syndicates have bribed a player or a team to lose matches.

These scandals have damaged the image of some sports, but major sporting events, such as the football World Cup or the Olympic Games, make an enormous profit from sponsorship and selling the TV rights worldwide. However, the prestige of hosting an event is also priceless and, unfortunately, a number of officials in international sports federations have been accused of corruption for their role in awarding events to particular countries.

Despite the scandals, sport still continues to flourish at the grass-roots level and provides hours of enjoyment and excitement for active participants and spectators. (562 words)

First of all, make sure you understand the meaning of each of the highlighted words and phrases in the text above. If you are not sure, look them up in your dictionary. Then complete the tasks on the following page.

1 WORD FIELDS

A Find all the different sports mentioned in the text and write them in the correct list.

a	you **play**	*volleyball,* ___
b	you **go**	*jogging,* ___
c	you **do**	*karate,* ___

B Add any other sports that you know to your lists.

C Draw a mind map for "types of sport" and add the sports to the different categories.

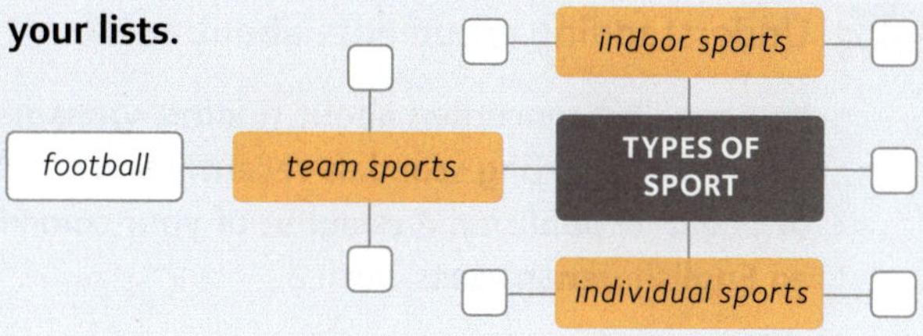

2 WORD FAMILIES

Complete the text with a member of the word family of the word in brackets. The words you need are all in the text. Use your dictionary if necessary.

Most amateur ___ [1] (participate) in sporting events simply take part because they love their sport and want to keep fit. However, in the world of some ___ [2] (profession) sports, finding ___ [3] (sponsor) deals is almost as important as winning games. ___ [4] (advertise) are keen to have famous sports stars ___ [5] (endorsement) their brands and wear their logos. Where large sums of money are involved, there is a great ___ [6] (tempt) to bend the rules and ___ [7] (cheat) has become a problem in certain sports. One way of doing this is by ___ [8] (dope); another is by fixing the results of matches to make sure that betting syndicates get the right result. Moreover, there is often a suspicion of ___ [9] (corrupt) when major sporting events, such as the World Cup or the Olympic Games, are awarded to cities or countries. In the long term, it's not just the other competing athletes who are being cheated but also the ___ [10] (spectate) who come to watch them.

3 PHRASES

Find highlighted phrases in the text that can replace the words in brackets. You may have to make some changes.

1 Darts has been transformed from a ___ (sport with only a few players) to one that ___ (is popular with lots of supporters) because of the increase in television coverage.
2 The last World Cup final had one of the biggest ___ (people who watch an event from the comfort of their own homes) for a sporting event ever.
3 The club was only able to invest in new players because they had ___ (an extremely valuable advertising agreement) with an airline from one of the Gulf states.
4 Compared to the top stars, many tennis players who are low down the ranking struggle to ___ (earn enough money). Most of these players don't have contracts to ___ (advertise the sports-wear) of companies such as Adidas and Nike.
5 ___ (Arranging to lose a game) has become a big problem in some non-professional leagues now that ___ (groups of illegal gamblers) are able to gamble money on the result of their games.
6 There have been lots of scandals with ___ (office-holders) in some large ___ (sporting organizations), but sport ___ (among amateur players) is still very much alive and kicking.

SITUATION

Your school is organizing a sports tournament for teams of young players from several EU countries. You are part of the organizing committee and you need to find sponsors to help fund the event. At the end of this section, you will **write a proposal** to send to firms with international connections, asking them to **sponsor the tournament**.

STEP 1 Understanding arguments about sport

You are a bit concerned about finding sponsors for your tournament as there have been a number of sporting scandals recently and sport, professional sport in particular, has had a lot of negative publicity. A member of your committee finds the following letters to the editor in an English newspaper.

A **Work in groups of three. Read the letter below and talk about the point the writer is making. Summarize his arguments in one sentence.**

http://www.independent.co.uk

Letter to the editor of the *Independent*, 19 January 2016

YET ANOTHER SPORT CORRUPTION SCANDAL

Now it's the turn of tennis, and I can't say I'm surprised. The money's too tempting, the egos too inflated.

If I were king for a day, I would ban all professional sport. It's the source of massive corruption. Millions are spent on short-lived vanity projects by governments looking to boost misplaced national pride or the personal status of foul dictators. With their narcissistic behaviour and obscene spending habits, sports superstars are the worst role models for young people and impressionable adults.

"Professional sport"? The phrase itself is a contradiction in terms. (97 words)

Patrick Cosgrove
Chapel Lawn, Shropshire

COMMENTS

02 **inflated:** higher than is acceptable or reasonable

07 **obscene:** (here) so large that most people find it unacceptable or offensive

09 **impressionable:** easily influenced

B **Now each partner reads one of the replies A–C on the opposite page and makes notes on the writer's opinion of sport and sports stars.**

http://www.independent.co.uk

A Patrick Cosgrove (Letters, 19 January) cannot go unchallenged. It is a human trait to want to be the best at things we are good at, whether they be sport, art, music, research, or writing. People don't initially strive for excellence because of the money, but because they love the thing they do.

The logical follow-on from Mr Cosgrove's argument that professional sport (i.e. people getting paid to do the thing they are good at) shouldn't be allowed is that all "pointless", non survival-related activities should be done only for love, not money. So out would go the arts, because some of these practitioners also get paid enormous, unjustifiable amounts.

Sport is a valid human endeavour and the vast majority of people who do it and enjoy it are not corrupt or motivated primarily by the money. There are ways to deal with criminal activity and inflated salaries without condemning the whole shebang. (152 words)

Rosy Leigh
London W3

B Patrick Cosgrove is right: "professional sport" is an oxymoron. The cause of the trouble is simple: the involvement of big money. There is one major exception to this unhappy situation and that is the game of hockey (called field hockey in North America).

Since the advent of AstroTurf pitches in the mid-1970s hockey has become a faster and more exciting and skilful game, and thus more popular. It is played equally by both men and women and, being a non-contact sport, can be played from the age of six to 60. At the 2012 London Olympics hockey was the third most watched sport, and globally it is the third most popular team sport after football and cricket, with some three million players in 100 countries over five continents.

Hockey, however, has remained defiantly amateur. No money equals no corruption. As far as Britain is concerned, the sport has dropped off the radar and, generally speaking, is neither reported in the national newspapers nor shown on television. Long may this innocence continue! (171 words)

David Ashton
Shipbourne, Kent

C Football has a zero tolerance towards cheating and corruption … boxing has a zero tolerance … athletics has a zero tolerance … horse racing has a zero tolerance … cricket has a zero tolerance … rugby … snooker … tennis … And yet, day after day, we discover that all of them are mired in cheating and corruption, up to the highest levels.

I wouldn't even trust the World Conker Championship any more, even though it, too, doubtless has a zero tolerance towards … , etc.

But you can bet on conkers; and so far every sport in the world has proven that if you can place a bet on it, then it cannot be trusted to be honest.

And sport is used as an impetus to invigorate, and supposedly teach some sort of honest, moral ethic to our youth? (130 words)

Alistair Ordeman
Northolt, Middlesex

Letters to the editor: 20 January 2016

A
07 **unjustifiable:** *nicht zu rechtfertigen*
10 **the whole shebang:** (slang) *das Ganze drumherum*

B
01 **oxymoron:** *Widerspruch in sich*
10 **drop off the radar:** (slang) disappear from media coverage

C
03 **be mired in sth:** be completely covered in sth

C **Report back to your partners the opinion(s) of the writers. Who agrees with Patrick Cosgrove; who disagrees with him? What points do they make?**

STEP 2 Collecting ideas for your proposal

Use your notes from Step 1 to complete the table and write phrases from the letters under the headings:

positive qualities of sport	negative qualities of professional sport
Sport is … *a valid human endeavour*	The problem with professional sport is … *massive corruption*
Sportsmen and women (are) …	Professional sports stars (are) …

STEP 3 Boosting your word power

The letters also contain some useful expressions that you could use in your proposal. Find the highlighted words or phrases in the letters that match these German expressions.

1 Angehörige einer Berufsgruppe
2 Anschub/Impuls
3 ein Widerspruch in sich
4 etw/jdn verurteilen
5 jdm/etw neue Energie geben
6 menschliche Eigenschaft
7 menschliches Streben
8 nach etw streben
9 Prestigeprojekt
10 selbstverliebtes Verhalten

STEP 4 Listening to interviews with sportspeople

12

Before you start your planning, listen to some interviews with professional sports stars to find out what they have learned from sport. You can use some of these ideas when you write your sponsorship proposal.

Match the aspects the sports stars mention (1–10) to their photos below. There are four more aspects than you need.

Marcie, a football player

Jamal, a sprinter

Sunil, a cricketer

1 listening to the coach
2 respecting your opponents
3 taking your chances
4 playing as part of a team
5 not letting the fans down
6 learning from your mistakes
7 pushing yourself to the limit
8 winning or losing graciously
9 pursuing your ambition
10 representing your country well

STEP 5 Planning your sports competition

Work in your groups of three. As mentioned at the beginning, you are the organizing committee for the invitation tournament to be held at your school. Eight teams will take part: a team from your school and seven other teams from schools in your partner town(s) in the EU.

A **First of all, decide which type of sport you want to hold the tournament in.**

B **Discuss what you will need to provide for a) the participating teams from the different schools, and b) the spectators. Think about these points:**

accommodation ▪ advertising ▪ cups and medals ▪ food and drink ▪ parking ▪ printed programmes ▪ showers, changing rooms and lockers ▪ sponsorship ▪ training facilities ▪ transport ▪ website

We'll need a snack bar / a restaurant / ... if lots of spectators come to watch.

If we find a sponsor, we can pay for ...

If we invite other teams, we'll have to provide more showers / changing rooms / ...

C **Present your ideas to the class.**

STEP 6 Writing the proposal

You decide to write a letter to Ms Mary O'Kane, the European Marketing Manager of Renidas PLC, a British sportswear company that has a factory in your area. You want to ask Renidas to sponsor your competition. In your letter, you should ...

- describe the competition (time, place, participants, etc.).
- outline the benefits of sport for young people.
- explain how Renidas PLC can help and what they will receive in return.

Write about 200 words.

Useful phrases

Dear Ms O'Kane
We are writing to you to request that ...
The tournament will consist of ...
As you know, sport and sporting events ...
We would like to ask you to ... because ... . In return, we can offer ...
We look forward to ... and hope for a positive reply.
Yours sincerely

IF-SENTENCES

→ Grammar summary, p. 224

1 **SPOT THE MISTAKES**

Spot the mistakes and correct them. Explain why they are wrong.

1 ~~When we had a sponsor for our handball competition, we could invite teams from our partner towns.~~
2 ~~If Sammy had done more sport in his free time, he had put on less weight.~~
3 ~~The athletes had not have started doping if their coaches had told them about the dangers.~~
4 ~~Lou-Ann Tierney wouldn't have lost her gold medal if she wouldn't have been caught doping.~~

2 **Which statements are correct, a, b, c or d?**

1 "Athletes would stop doping if people stopped watching their races."
The speaker thinks people are a) likely / b) unlikely to stop watching races.
2 "Jimmi Floyd will lose his sponsors if he is banned from athletics for two years."
The speaker thinks a ban is a) likely / b) unlikely.
3 "If Jimmi hadn't taken steroids, he would have lost the race."
Jimmi a) has / b) hasn't taken steroids. Jimmi c) lost / d) didn't lose the race.

3 **Complete these *if*-sentences with the correct form of the verb in brackets.**

1 Experts say that if there ___ (be) more doping tests, athletes wouldn't take illicit substances.
2 If Terry takes EPO, he ___ (improve) his medal chances at the next world championships.
3 Steffi Müller probably wouldn't have won the gold medal if she ___ (not take) anabolic steroids.
4 Jimmi Floyd will be banned for life if the members of the commission ___ (find) him guilty.
5 If Wada had been set up earlier, we ___ (not have) such a problem with doping now.
6 Would you take steroids if you ___ (have) a chance of winning a gold medal?
7 I wouldn't have run in that race if I ___ (know) that the other competitors were doping.
8 If FIFA knew a top football star was taking drugs, what ___ (they / do) with him?
9 ___ (people – watch) the games on TV if they think some athletes are cheating?

WATCH OUT! much – many, (a) little – (a) few, a lot of

Read the sample sentences and complete the gaps with the correct word.

~~Much~~ sports federations are trying to rid their sports of drugs cheats.
→ *Many sports federations are trying to rid their sports of drugs cheats.*
Mass spectometry can detect even a ~~little~~ milligrams of illegal substances in blood samples.
→ *Mass spectometry can detect even a few milligrams of illegal substances in blood samples.*

1 Only ___ sports cheats are put off doping by the threat of a lifetime ban.
2 ___ people think that top sports stars earn far too much money.
3 Jimmi Floyd has ___ chance of returning to athletics. There is just too ___ evidence against him.
4 Players lower down on the ranking list don't have ___ money to pay for hotels and trainers.
5 We only have ___ time before the match starts. Let's take a taxi to the stadium.
6 There are ___ professional tennis players but only ___ of them have lucrative sponsorship deals.

5 Travelling when young

FOCUS

A Discuss these questions in class:

1 What do you like about travelling?
2 What kind of travelling do you personally prefer?

B Do this task with a partner:

More and more niche markets are opening up that cater for particular tastes and needs. With your partner look at the different ways of spending a holiday below. Pick three examples each and with the phrases in the speech bubbles try to explain:

- what this particular kind of tourism is about.
- where you would have to travel to find this particular niche market tourism.

I think ... tourism attracts people who enjoy ...

If you like ... tourism, you should travel to ..., because

LGBT: lesbian, gay, bisexual, trangender

14

07

Tourism: a pleasure and an industry

The *Encyclopedia Britannica* defines tourism as "the act and process of spending time away from home in pursuit of recreation, relaxation and pleasure, while making use of the commercial provision of services". Tourism, a word coined at the end of the 18th century, has always existed. Romans flocked to the coast to escape the heat of the city, while in the Middle Ages pilgrims went on journeys to holy places. The advent of modern transportation in the 19th century allowed for more comfort and speed for the traveller, while at the same time making holidays affordable. The 20th century saw an enormous increase in international tourism due to cheaper air travel. Package tours to the Mediterranean that included flights and hotels became popular.

Nowadays, modern tourism has become a well-organized business catering to every kind of customer. From high-end to low-budget trips and all-inclusive holidays, from Antarctica to Zambia, anything is available. While the traditional two-week standard beach holiday remains popular, many people take advantage of weekend city trips and mini-breaks, which have become popular thanks to the rise of low-cost carriers. Another trend is the emergence of niche markets focussing on certain aspects of travelling, for example adventure tourism, culinary tourism, medical tourism, stag-party tourism or ghetto tourism. Travellers can now construct their own itinerary through online platforms.

Tourism currently supports more than 284 million jobs worldwide and generates 9.8% of world-wide gross domestic product (GDP), making it the fourth largest global export sector after fuels, chemicals and automobile products. Tourism has grown dramatically since the 1950s from 25 million international arrivals to over one billion in 2012. 2012 was also the year when the Chinese overtook the Germans on money spent on travelling. A wide variety of services benefit from tourism: airlines, cruise ship companies, car rental companies, taxis, private and commercial accommodations, amusement parks, casinos, theatres, souvenir retailers, online platforms, restaurants, etc. For one third of all developing countries tourism is the main source of income, making it a means to reduce poverty and an engine for economic growth. Increasing tourist numbers does, however, also have a downside. Creating a tourist infrastructure with all kinds of services can lead to the overuse of natural resources and the destruction of valuable ecosystems, and may have a negative impact on animal habitats and result in the loss of local culture. The money spent by tourists does not necessarily benefit the local community, but often goes to foreign investors and tour operators.

In order to help minimize tourism's potentially negative impact, many countries are trying to promote responsible and sustainable tourism across the globe. One of the most important parts of sustainable tourism is ecotourism, which can be defined as responsible travel that protects the environment and respects and sustains the lifestyle of the locals. Many people, however, see ecotourism as an oxymoron, since any flight produces more CO_2 emissions than can ever be compensated for on an eco-friendly holiday. True eco-travellers stay in the close vicinity of their home, and if they travel, then they don't fly, but go by bus, train, bicycle or on foot.

But no matter what kind of tourist you are, everyone should be a responsible traveller and keep the damage done to the environment to a minimum. (535 words)

First of all, make sure you understand the meaning of each of the highlighted words and phrases in the text above. If you are not sure, look them up in your dictionary. Then complete the tasks on the following page.

1 WORD FIELDS

A **Make a list of all the words and phrases from the text according to the given categories. The first two are already filled in.**

type of tourism/travel	means of transport
■ *package tours*	■ *flight*
▬	▬

B **Copy the table below and fill it in with aspects mentioned in the text.**

positive aspects of tourism	negative aspects of tourism
▬	▬

2 SENTENCE FORMATION

Use these verbs and phrases to create sentences.

1. to escape sth
2. to cater to sth
3. to take advantage of sth
4. to benefit from sth
5. to respect sth

the cold weather ▪ eco-friendly holidays ▪ the guests' wishes ▪ the local culture ▪ low-cost carriers

3 VISUALIZATION

Use highlighted words from the text to complete the visualization of the information. Then work with a partner to add more aspects of sustainable tourism.

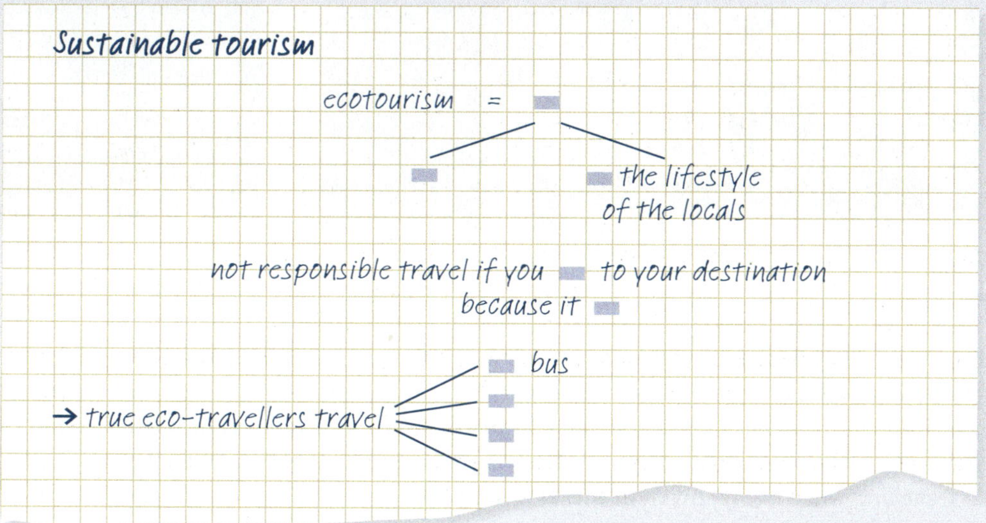

SITUATION

You and some classmates are on an exchange programme in Australia. At your Australian school you are often confronted with your Australian classmates' indecision about what to do after finishing school. Many are interested in the fact that you have travelled across the world to Australia and will travel around the country after the programme is over. So your teachers organize a workshop for you and your classmates, in which you create a **presentation entitled "Reasons for travelling when young"** for the **Open School Day** followed by a **question-and-answer session** with the Australian audience.

STEP 1 Brainstorming

Get into groups of five people (Group 1) and do some brainstorming with the help of the questions and pictures below. You can talk to all the members in your group or form subgroups.

1 Do you know people who have spent some time or even a whole year abroad?
2 Can you think of advantages and/or disadvantages of travelling when young?

1

2

3

4

5

6

7

8

9

STEP 2 Preparing your part of the presentation

Now give every member of your group a number between 1 and 5 and go to a new group consisting of all the 1s, 2s, 3s, etc. (Group 2). Exchange the results of your brainstorming from Step 1. As you have an overview of all the opinions in your class now, each group reads <u>one</u> of the five reasons (the group of 1s reads paragraph 1, the 2s read paragraph 2, etc.) for travelling when young given in the following text.

FIVE REASONS FOR TRAVELLING WHEN YOUNG

When you are young, you have spent most of your life at school and at home, and you've been preparing yourself for your future career. At a certain age you have reached the point where you have to take decisions for yourself and discover the sort of person you are. Travelling is one of the best ways of moving ahead. Here are our top five reasons why you should spend time abroad while you are young.

1. Travelling

Until now you've probably spent your life in the safety of your family with friends whom you've known for ages. Even if your childhood and adolescence were not idyllic, nevertheless decisions were probably being made on your behalf. Being far away from home and staying in a place where everything is different and the people don't speak your language can be quite scary. But by being in an unfamiliar setting with no one to rely on except yourself, you are quickly put in the position of having to learn to make your own decisions and stand on your own two feet. Being far from home will allow you to end up trying out new things that you had never even imagined you'd do. After all, life only starts once you've left your comfort zone. And however much you value family face time, there's always Skype to keep in contact.

2. Travelling

You've learned a lot at school and you've learned a lot at home. You may be popular and fun. Or you may be reserved and shy. But as soon as you arrive in a foreign country, you will be meeting other travellers and locals, all of whom you'll have to interact with in order to profit from your time abroad. Whatever you do – whether you have to find your way around or decide what to buy and eat – you'll be gaining new experiences. Once you figure out that you can connect with people despite differences, you'll learn more about yourself. Once you feel you have liberated yourself from your daily routine, you'll do things you never thought you were capable of. You'll gain self-confidence, you'll become smarter and more interesting, and exude maturity. Whether you like your travels or not, you will still come back with more worldly knowledge than you had before.

3. Travelling

The first thing you need to do before travelling is to plan a budget. This requires organization and research. Through websites and forums you can find out how much your trip may set you back. Then you have to decide how you are going to access money abroad: How much cash should you take? Which credit cards can you use and where? You will master the art of budgeting when you travel. And when you're young you can be frugal and budget-conscious, and learn how to haggle at markets. You'll learn the value of money. You'll have to discover how to get around, which are the hot spots you want to visit, how to get the all-important simcard for your phone. And what happens if the worst happens and you get robbed? How do you replace your passport, your credit card? Who can you turn to for help? Before you leave, you will probably have found out the answers to these questions. If you do end up in trouble, you will find out how effective your survival strategies are. Don't underestimate how valuable these skills will be in your future life.

4. Travelling

When you travel you get exposed to different cultures. Your tolerance will grow as you experience different lifestyles, different religions or simply anything foreign to you. Until now you've just presumed that the way you and your society do things is the best way. But you'll learn how to see things from a different perspective. Every culture is different, and so is every individual in it. You will probably start to see how certain aspects of each culture could enrich your own life. There's no perfect society – try and understand why people do things differently. Even if there are elements you dislike, you must learn to respect other cultures and customs, as you are, after all, the guest. Cultural sensitivity is essential in a globalized world. And don't just dip into a culture – get immersed in it.

→

5. Travelling

It's always a good idea to spend some time in one particular country, even if you speak little to none of the language, as you will certainly pick up some of it. Or you may choose a country where you can deepen your knowledge of the language. In today's globalized world, the more you can offer, the better your future prospects. Become fluent in another language and you will have opened up a whole new world of people to connect with. Even having a grasp of another language gives you insight into other ways of expressing yourself. From a networking perspective, you will meet a whole host of people with different skills and experiences, all of whom will further your knowledge in one way or another. Any experience abroad gives a person a competitive edge. And who knows if any of them turn out to be valuable connections who might come in handy in the future?

(871 words)

A **With your Group 2 identify four important phrases from the box on the right and use them to write one sentence explaining your group's reason for travelling.**

B **The headline to each of the five reasons (except for the initial word "travelling") has been left out of the text. Work out what it might have been. Then use your headline as the title of your part of the presentation. Each part should have a similar layout (cf. grey box on the right).**

C **Together choose one of the photos on p. 66 that you think suits your part of the presentation best and include it in your presentation. You may also use a photo from another source. Be prepared to explain your choice of photo.**

keywords and phrases

- become fluent in
- comfort zone
- competitive edge
- cultural sensitivity
- discover how to get around
- enrich your own life
- experience different lifestyles
- find your way around
- future prospects
- gain self-confidence
- haggle at markets
- interact with sb.
- learn more about yourself
- master the art of budgeting
- see things from a different perspective
- stand on your own two feet
- survival strategies
- try out new things
- unfamiliar setting
- valuable connection

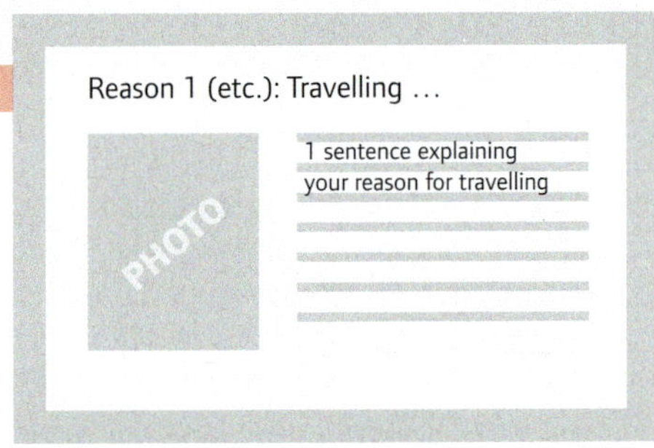

STEP 3 Completing your presentation

Now go back to your original Group 1, taking your presentation materials with you. Explain your presentation materials to the others. Make sure they understand your headline, your reason for travelling and the photo you selected.

STEP 4 Boosting your word power

Together with your Group 1 prepare for the question-and-answer session after the presentation by brushing up your language skills. Each of you now reads the whole text for the first time. Rewrite the following sentences using words and phrases from the text, but in such a way that their meaning remains the same. You may have to adapt them to fit.

1 Many people in southern countries, in Spain for example, think that seeing one's family regularly is very important. [Paragraph 1]
2 While travelling you can make friends although they might come from different backgrounds and have different viewpoints. [Paragraph 2]
3 Even if you do not like the idea of travelling, you will return more self-confident. [Paragraph 2]
4 And don't think that networking is not important. [Paragraph 3]
5 In order to understand another culture really well, it is best to live in it on an intense day-to-day basis. [Paragraph 4]
6 Travelling may be difficult if you do not know the language well or not at all. [Paragraph 5]
7 Knowing people all over the world might be very useful later in your life. [Paragraph 5]

STEP 5 Preparing for the Q&A session with the audience

With a partner prepare for critical questions from parents or students who may still have doubts about the wisdom of young people travelling by themselves. Partner A: Use the critical statements in the box below, and add your own doubts. Partner B: Try to refute the criticism, using information from the text and your own arguments. Change roles every now and then. Correct each other's pronunciation and intonation if necessary.

It is much safer for youngsters to relax at home with their own friends.
How will they find their way around in a foreign country?
They don't even speak the country's language!
There will be no one to comfort my son/daughter if they feel lonely or homesick.
Why should they have to respect other countries' customs? They're just visiting the country.
It's a waste of time – the sooner young people go to university or find a job, the better.
Young people have enough friends on- and offline – they don't need to make even more friends.

Useful phrases for a discussion

It seems to me (that) ...
Do you see what I mean?
If you ask me, ...
I don't entirely agree with you.
So do you mean (that) ...?
Oh, I don't agree.
So is the general idea that ...?
In fact, I think (that) ...

STEP 6 Giving your presentation

It's Open Day now. Give your presentation to the class (either individually or in your Group 1) and answer critical questions from the audience (i.e. your other classmates).

BEFORE YOU READ

What does sustainable tourism mean to you? Would you be willing not to visit exotic countries in order to contribute less to global warming?

The paradox of sustainable tourism

A A tourist flying economy class from Britain to Kenya and back generates around a tonne of carbon emissions, according to the International Civil Aviation Organisation. No matter how many times he reuses his towels or sits on a composting toilet when he is there, he could never hope to offset the burning of all that jet fuel. Does that mean the very notion of "sustainable tourism" is an oxymoron?

B The phrase has three possible meanings. The first is ecological. Given the contribution that transport, especially by air, makes to global warming, on this definition it is almost guaranteed to fall short. The only truly sustainable holiday would be camping in the back garden eating berries, says Harald Zeiss of the Institute for Sustainable Tourism at Harz University in Germany. The second is social. Ideally, when cultures meet and gain in mutual understanding the long-term benefits will be intangible, but real. The final one is economic. Tourists who step off the beaten track have a chance to help lift the poor out of poverty and encourage them to preserve their environments for financial gain. The question is how much weight to give to each.

C According to the World Tourism Organisation (UNWTO), a UN agency, 1.1 billion international trips were made in 2014, a 4.4% increase on the year before. As popular destinations become overcrowded, more people seek places that remain comparatively unspoilt. But pristine wildernesses don't stay pristine for long once they are on the holiday trail. The paradox of sustainable tourism is that it can be "both a destroyer of nature and an agent for its conservation", notes Andrew Holden of Bedfordshire University in Britain.

D Keeping resorts small, and perhaps even temporary, can help resolve that paradox in favour of conservation. Maurice Phillips and Geri Mitchell opened Sandele, an eco-resort, in Gambia in 2008. Locals are too often persuaded to sell their land to developers for less than it is worth, says Mr Phillips, and villages can vanish once the hotels go up. Instead, he leased the land for Sandele from villagers, and employs them in the resort. When the lease runs out in 20 years' time the property will revert to locals, who should by then have the skills to manage

07 **offset sth:** *etw ausgleichen*
21 **mutual:** *gegenseitig*
22 **intangible:** *nicht genau zu bestimmen*
35 **pristine:** *unberührt*
52 **revert to sb:** *an jdn wieder zurückgehen*

it. The pair also run courses for locals, including on how to make "rocket stoves" that require very little wood for fuel, thereby reducing deforestation.

E Those on larger-scale eco-tourism packages may be doing good in other ways. Concentrating large numbers of visitors in a single location increases their local impact – which can be for the better. If a resort buys local food, says Mr Zeiss, or invests in renewable-energy generation that can be used by those who live nearby, then the surrounding area can receive a boost.

F But hotels must seek ways to mitigate their negative effects. Though signs suggesting that guests can help "save the planet" by reusing their towels overstate the case, water-guzzling is one of the biggest evils of mass tourism. An analysis by Thomas Cook, a large holiday firm, suggests that on average each tourist around the world accounts for around 350 litres of water per day by showering, using the swimming pool and the like – which rises to 6,000 litres when indirect use such as food production is added. In Greece, for example, each tourist directly uses around three-fifths more water than a local. Being more frugal with water can boost firms' profits. TUI, another big travel company, says it saved €2.2m ($2.5m) in 2014 by cutting energy and water use at 43 of its hotels.

G But often it is the guests themselves who kick against energy-saving initiatives. To stop patrons leaving lights and air conditioning on when they are out, many hotels have keycards that control the electrics in rooms. Yet some report that guests override the system by inserting a business card into the control slot before heading out, rather than wait to recharge portable devices or put up with a stuffy room for a few minutes on their return.

H Overall, the benefits of sustainable tourism outweigh the harms, thinks Dirk Glaesser of the UNWTO. Mr Zeiss argues that the most unnecessary flights are taken not by tourists but by businessfolk who fly abroad for a toe-touch meeting that could easily have been replaced by a video-call, and then fly home the same day. Perhaps. But it is unclear how many such trips actually occur. Executives already have an incentive to avoid unnecessary business travel – it is less fun than the frivolous sort. (735 words)

Source: *The Economist*, 27 August 2015

Eco-tourism: going against the crowd?

71 **guzzling:** *verschwendend, fressend*

1 MEDIATION ENGLISH-GERMAN

→ Skills, p. 198

Beantworten Sie die folgenden Fragen auf Deutsch mit Information aus den Absätzen A und B.

1 Anhand welchen Beispiels erläutert der Autor die Frage, ob nachhaltiger Tourismus ein Widerspruch in sich ist?
2 Ergänzen Sie die Begriffe in der ersten Spalte und konkretisieren Sie diese in der zweiten Spalte.

(Teil)aspekte des Begriffs nachhaltiger Tourismus:	Konkretisierung der Aspekte:
▪ ___ Aspekt	nachhaltiger Tourismus schließt ___ aus, da ___
▪ sozialer Aspekt	nachhaltiger Tourismus ermöglicht ___
▪ ___ Aspekt	nachhaltiger Tourismus fördert ___ und ___

2 GAPPED SUMMARY

→ Skills, p. 202

Fill the gaps in the summary with appropriate words or expressions (one word per gap) from paragraphs C–F of the text. Do not make any changes or adjustments to the text. Provide the number of the line in which you have found the word or expression.

As soon as popular tourist destinations become ___[1], travellers try to find areas which are still ___[2]. This is a vicious circle, which also applies to sustainable tourism. People go off the beaten track, but then this soon becomes *the* beaten track. On the one hand, tourism can be a destructive force, on the other, it can actually contribute to the ___[3] of a place.
Sandele is an ___[4] which will be given back to the local population after two decades when the ___[5] expires. This gives them enough time to learn the ___[6] necessary for running a holiday business.
Bigger holiday businesses than Sandele can also raise their ___ ___[7] by providing their customers with food and energy produced in the area.
Hotels everywhere now invite their customers to act in a way that is environmentally friendly, for example by reducing water consumption – tourists in an eco-sensitive area on average ___ ___[8] 350 l of water per day. This not only helps the environment but can also ___[9] the companies' revenues due to the savings made only on this particular resource.

3 SHORT-ANSWER QUESTIONS

→ Skills, p. 200

Answer the questions with information from paragraphs G–H of the text. Use words from the text.

1 Which phrase is used to explain that in many cases it is the guests themselves who stop energy-saving devices on purpose?
They ___
2 Which example shows that tourists are not the only people who contribute to the destruction of the environment?

4 WORKING WITH WORDS

With a partner sum up the article's most important facts by each of you giving a one-minute speech, concentrating on the aspects listed below. Make sure you understand the words and phrases and that you use all of them in your speech. Copy all the words your partner has to use and, while listening to his or her speech, tick all the words and phrases he or she used correctly. You may need two rounds before all the words have been used.

Partner A

Talk about …
the paradox of sustainable tourism, possible criticism of sustainable tourism and ways to solve the paradox. [Paragraphs A–E]

- to reuse
- oxymoron
- global warming
- to gain in mutual understanding
- intangible
- off the beaten track
- pristine
- temporary
- to vanish
- to lease
- to run a course
- deforestation
- to receive a boost

Partner B

Talk about …
the contribution of various hotels to safeguarding the environment, the problems they face and the real culprits (according to the UNWTO). [Paragraphs F–H]

- to mitigate
- water-guzzling
- mass tourism
- to account for
- more than a local
- to be frugal with
- energy-saving initiative
- patron
- rather than wait
- to recharge portable devices
- benefits
- toe-touch meeting
- incentive

5 ARGUMENTATIVE WRITING

→ Skills, pp. 206, 208

Choose one of the following topics and write at least 200 words.

1. "If everybody travelled more, the world would see more understanding and tolerance between countries and fewer wars." What do you think about this statement?
2. **Go to File 13 on p. 181.**
   Student exchange programmes of six months should be mandatory for every young person. Discuss.

6 PANEL DISCUSSION

Imagine an eco-tourist resort is being planned in an ecologically sensitive area in the Amazon region. Have a panel discussion to find out the pros and cons of the project, using information from this unit and your own research. Focus on the ideas of different interest groups: the entrepreneurs who want to build it, eco-activists who are worried about the effect on the eco-systems, and locals who need work but worry about the impact on their culture and lifestyle.

1 VIEWING

→ Skills, p. 196

The Poverty-Environment Initiative (PEI) is a global programme which helps poor countries develop sustainable projects in order to help the local population benefit from tourism in an environmentally friendly and also socially sustainable way.

08

A Watch the first five minutes of the film without sound and do the following tasks as partner work. Partner A answers one section, Partner B the other section.

Partner A	Partner B
→ What makes this country appealing?	→ What do you not like about this country?
→ List the following words in the order in which they appear in the video. *sewage – tourist shop – deforestation – chemicals*	→ List the following words in the order in which they appear in the video. *lake – fishing net – air balloon – clear water*
→ How does the lady explain sustainability? (Use the subtitles.) ■	→ What is special about the hotel? (Use the subtitles.) ■ ■
→ Which country do you think is presented in this video?	→ Which country do you think is presented in this video?

B Exchange your answers with your partner.

C Now watch the whole video with sound and together try to find out more about:

- how the businesses of Daw Yin Myo Su are all eco-friendly – find at least four examples.
- how contract farming works in the case of the vineyard.

D The film ends with the following statement: "Quality investments … are a reminder that running a profitable business does not mean having to sacrifice … ecosystems, cultural heritage or vulnerable groups". Do you regard this as a feasible way of planning tourism projects?

2 GROUP DISCUSSION

→ Skills, p. 210

Presentation phase

You are planning a ten-day holiday with three or four friends. Each of you has found an interesting holiday offer and presents the suggestion in one minute.
You can find the holiday offers in File 2 on p. 189.

Interaction phase

Weigh up the pros and cons of each destination and try to find a destination everybody can agree on at the end of your discussion.

3 MATERIAL-BASED ESSAY

→ Skills, pp. 206, 208

Ecotourism is just window dressing when it comes to saving the environment. Discuss.

Write about 300 words. Use the information from the material provided below to support your argumentation.

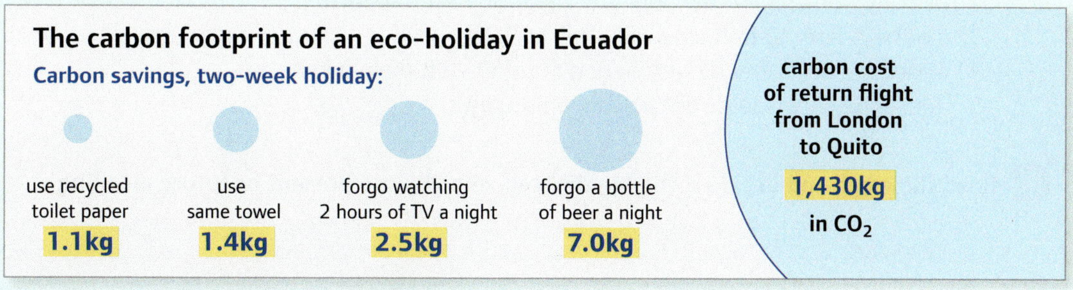

BUENA VISTA LODGE

Ecofriendly, sustainable and yet adventurous!

- Buena Vista Lodge does not use air conditioning. It cools the rooms by using a combination of fans and large well-ventilated rooms.
- Buena Vista Lodge's cabins are made from fast-growing bamboo which is produced by the local community.
- Buena Vista Lodge only returns filtered and cleaned waste water to the environment.
- Buena Vista Lodge composts all waste material which is used as fertilizer.
- Buena Vista Lodge serves meals with locally grown ingredients.
- Buena Vista Lodge provides many jobs for the local community.
- Buena Vista Lodge asks its guests to reuse towels and bed linen.
- How to get to Buena Vista Lodge: we will pick you up at Quito Airport, from there you will take a 30-minute flight to Pico, from there a river canoe will take you on a very romantic 2-hour river journey to Malarez, after a short walk through the jungle a hand-paddled canoe will bring you across the river to the lodge.

Umweltfreundliche Fernreisen gibt es nicht. Man kann zwar den Aufenthalt vor Ort möglichst umweltfreundlich gestalten, aber die An- und Abreise kann man nicht vermeiden. Wer zum Beispiel von Europa aus nach Bangkok reist, überzieht durch den Flug das Jahresbudget einer Person an CO_2 Emissionen bereits mehr als das Doppelte.

Eine gute Möglichkeit die produzierten Schadstoffe auszugleichen sind Spenden an Klimaschutzprojekte in Entwicklungsländern. So kann z. B. der durch den Hin- und Rückflug nach Bangkok verursachte Schaden durch einen Aufpreis von 150 EUR kompensiert werden.

Auch bei konventionellen Pauschalreisen kann man durch etwas Umdenken die eigene Umweltbilanz verbessern. Muss es denn der Jetski sein? Oder ist auch das ruhigere Stand-up Paddling erholsam? Muss die Klimaanlage im Zimmer den ganzen Tag laufen, obwohl niemand im Zimmer ist? Kann man nicht auch die Aussicht vom selbst erklommenen Berg genießen ohne den (sicherlich teureren) Rundflug?

FUTURE FORMS

→ Grammar summary, p. 219

1 SPOT THE MISTAKES

Spot the mistakes and correct them. Explain why they are wrong or improbable.

1 ~~Look at the clouds. It will rain in a minute.~~
2 ~~We buy Viv a pint at the pub after the tour – she's so nice.~~
3 ~~The next ferry to Koh Lipe will leave at 9.25.~~
4 ~~I pack the bags after dinner, so don't bother with them now.~~
5 ~~Tom and Len will leave for Taveuni on Friday.~~

2 Read the email and decide if the highlighted verbs have a present or future meaning.

How are you? I'm [1] fine. Actually, I'm sure that you won't believe [2] me when I tell you that I'm currently waiting [3] in the departure lounge at Ulan-Bator airport, fresh from a Yurt trip in the steppes. I'm heading [4] back home to Bristol in an hour (my plane lands [5] at 6 a.m.) so you'll find [6] me back at my desk the day after tomorrow! I find [7] that somewhat hard to believe at the moment. Anyway, I'll be [8] back in mobile phone reach again within a few hours. I also wanted to tell you that Karen is coming [9] on Monday. You know, my pen friend from Munich. She's going to do [10] some research at the uni here for a couple of months. When she gets [11] here, I thought we could get together for a ladies' night.

3 Look at the various ways of expressing future meaning in the email. Which ones can you find?

4 Read this dialogue and say which tense is correct – and why.

Judith: I'm really fed up with this winter. I'm starved of sun. I think I'll have / 'm going to have [1] a nervous breakdown. Let's go to Portugal for Christmas!

Simon: Hold on, dear! Have you forgotten that your cousin comes / is coming [2] in two weeks?

Judith: OK, but we could go after that, couldn't we? She will leave / is leaving [3] on the 22nd. I call / 'll call [4] the travel agent now.

Simon: I think we'll probably get / 're probably going to get [5] cheaper last-minute offers on the internet … I don't believe it! The computer has crashed again! I hope the hotline is going to be able / will be able [6] to help me. Sometimes I hate this thing!

Judith: Oh, no! That will take / is going to take [7] hours! I'll get / 'm getting [8] my laptop from the office.

WATCH OUT! Problem words (1)

Choose the correct word or phrase so that each sentence makes sense.

1 For two days / Two days ago I was really annoyed because I had lost my passport.
2 The latest / last surveys show that some places are being damaged by mass tourism.
3 The travel brochures / prospects always make the hotels sound perfect.
4 Some handys / mobile phones don't work when you are abroad.
5 They were discussing / discussing about where to go on holiday next year.
6 Hannah said she could possibly / eventually go on holiday if she finished her project on time.
7 Ruth was nervous when the plane started / took off.

6 Saving the planet

FOCUS

A Look at the photos and do the following tasks with a partner:

1 Describe what you can see in the photos.
2 What underlying problem do the photos have in common?

B Get together with another couple and do the following:

1 Exchange your results from your partner work.
2 Discuss the most urgent steps that are needed to solve the problem.
3 Think of ways in which you personally can become part of the solution.

15

09

Energy and the environment

Human actions have a serious impact on the environment. Probably the most important green issue of the day is energy. The way we use energy causes harm to the environment. We produce most of our energy through power stations, which emit toxic gases that cause acid rain. Fossil fuels (oil, coal and gas), which represent 80% of the world's total energy consumption, contribute to air, soil, river and sea pollution. Today many countries use fracking to recover gas and oil from rock, a technique which is controversial because of environmental concerns. Road transport is the main source of toxic gas emissions, which also result in pollution and global warming. In many cities in developing countries there is an unhealthy layer of smog, while many rivers throughout the world have become contaminated by industrial waste and fertilizers. Greenhouse gases such as carbon dioxide and methane trap heat from the sun in the earth's atmosphere so that the temperature rises around the earth, creating the greenhouse effect.

Due to the detrimental effect of having to provide energy for an ever-expanding global population, we need to ensure that we use energy in a sustainable way. Great hope rests on the development of non-polluting, renewable energy sources, such as solar and wind energy and biofuels. Encouraging consumers to be more economical with their daily energy consumption is also an important factor in the success of an energy management plan. According to statistics, one person in the USA consumes 30 times more energy than one person in India.

Another cause of global warming is the deforestation of tropical rainforests for wood, pulp and farmland. Forests extract carbon dioxide from the atmosphere and store it in trees. Deforestation releases carbon, as well as reducing the amount of carbon dioxide capture on the planet. According to research, climate change could lead to the extinction of more than a million species on Earth and seriously affect the biodiversity of the rainforests, which are the world's most diverse ecosystems. Another result of global warming is that glaciers and the polar ice caps are melting, which is causing a rise in sea levels and an increase in the intensity of storms.

We also have to deal with the problem of waste. The increase in the amount of waste is a reflection of modern consumer lifestyle, and developed countries are producing more and more waste, e.g. 900kg a year per inhabitant in the USA. Germany has been successful in its fight against growing landfill sites by introducing a sophisticated waste disposal system, the Green Dot system. A major part of the success of this programme is the proper sorting of domestic waste such as returnable bottles or glass jars, paper, cardboard and plastic materials. By having to pay for plastic bags, consumers are encouraged to use reusable shopping bags instead. Biological waste makes up almost 50% of the total waste produced in Germany. The rest of the household rubbish is usually incinerated. Hazardous waste, for instance batteries or paint, has to be disposed of in the proper manner.

Educating people to use less energy and to recycle are the best ways to address the environmental problems we face. If humanity does not act, irreparable damage will be done to the planet.

(534 words)

First of all, make sure you understand the meaning of each of the highlighted words and phrases in the text above. If you are not sure, look them up in your dictionary. Then complete the tasks on the following page.

1 DEFINITIONS

Find the highlighted words and phrases in the text that match these definitions.

1 a place where rubbish is buried
2 make a substance or place dirty or impure by adding a dangerous substance
3 materials that are no longer needed and are thrown away
4 burn sth until it is completely destroyed
5 involving the use of energy in a way that does not affect the environment negatively
6 the existence of a large number of different kinds of animals and plants which make a balanced environment
7 poisonous
8 a type of energy derived from plant and animal material

Go to File 14 on p. 181.

2 COLLOCATIONS

Find collocations in the text that correspond to these German expressions.

EXAMPLE: *eine Auswirkung haben auf* → *to have an impact on*

1 Schaden anrichten
2 Gase ausstoßen
3 Energiekonsum
4 ein Abfallentsorgungs-System einführen
5 Hausmüll trennen
6 zur Luftverschmutzung beitragen

3 A SHORT ARTICLE

Write a short article on the preservation and protection of our environment for a blog for a website for young Europeans and their views on the environment. Use ten words from tasks 1 (definitions) and 2 (collocations).

4 WORD FAMILIES

A Copy the table below and add the missing words.

noun (abstract)	noun (person)	verb	adjective
▬	▬	produce	▬
▬	▬	represent	▬
consumption	▬	▬	▬
▬	▬	contribute	▬
pollution	▬	▬	▬
development	▬	▬	▬
waste	▬	▬	▬

B Make five sentences with words from the table, but leave a gap for the words. Ask a partner to complete the sentences with the appropriate words.

SITUATION

Feldheim is Germany's first energy self-sufficient community, and visitors from around the world come to learn about its experiment with renewable energy. You are an intern at Feldheim's "New Energy Forum Foundation" and your job is to **produce an audio guide** in English informing international visitors about the project that has made Feldheim a model renewable-energy village.

STEP 1 Reading about Feldheim's energy self-sufficiency

When preparing the audio guide, you come across the following article by Edvard Glücksman, an environmental specialist, explaining how the village has become energy self-sufficient.

A Work with a partner. Read the text and take notes. Partner A collects information on the wind and solar farms in Feldheim, Partner B on the biogas plant and the woodchip furnace.

wind and solar farms	biogas plant and woodchip furnace

The energy self-sufficient village of Feldheim

On the spectrum of climate-friendly projects, Feldheim represents a microcosm showcase of a zero-emissions future: it is Germany's first energy self-sufficient community, a pioneering working example of economically beneficial renewable use.

The Feldheim project dates back to 1995, when a local entrepreneur paid for the first wind turbines to be installed on nearby fields. Next, the village bought its own electricity grid, severing ties with the regional grid and the major national provider that operates it. Finally, the village forged links both with a local energy firm, which agreed to install a fleet of wind turbines in return for the right to sell excess power back to the market, and with a regional agricultural cooperative, which provided over 350 hectares of land to grow corn required for biogas.

Feldheim derives its electricity and heating from three main sources. Firstly, from a 43-turbine wind farm one mile east of the village, which provides power to 7,000 homes. Simultaneously, at the eastern edge of the village there is a biogas plant (500 kW) operated by the local agricultural cooperative which provides power to over 200 homes from an input of manure and corn. Electricity from the biogas plant is sold on the public market, but the heat produced during power generation

01 represent a microcosm showcase of sth: *etw im Kleinen vorführen*
05 sever ties with sth: *sich von etw trennen*
06 forge links: *Kontakte herstellen*

is fed into a separately-installed heating grid, which heats the village's private homes, commercial enterprises, and livestock enclosures. Finally, on particularly cold days, additional heating is supplied by a woodchip furnace, which uses wood collected locally and in a sustainable manner (by using branches only). It is located opposite the biogas plant.

woodchip furnace and wind turbines

This three-pronged approach provides Feldheim an existence that is less dependent on fossil fuels, something its inhabitants are very proud of. However, perhaps more importantly from a global perspective, and certainly what has raised most eyebrows in Germany and internationally, is that the project clearly demonstrates that renewable energy investments can have tangible long-term economic benefits.

Feldheim consumes under 1% of the electricity produced annually by its wind turbines, selling the remainder to the market. Local electricity bills are around half of the national average. The village's biogas plant saves the inhabitants of Feldheim over 160,000 litres of heating oil each year. The whole project is set to break even on the initial investment of €1.75 million for the construction of the plant within a decade.

biogas plant

Having understood the economic potential of renewables, Feldheim took yet another pioneering step when, in 2008, it constructed a solar farm comprising 284 panels. The installation produces enough to cover the annual power requirements of around 600 four-person households. The construction of the panels has also created 20 local jobs and rejuvenated the 45-hectare area of Selterhof, a former Soviet telecommunications centre north-east of Feldheim, which was dismantled and restored to its natural state as a result of the project.

Understandably, the small population of Feldheim is optimistic about the nation's renewable energy future and their enthusiasm seems to be catching on. Every single resident of Feldheim is employed, mostly working at one of the sites of the renewables.

solar panels

Yet Feldheim remains just a small piece in the wider context of Germany's energy transition, by which the country hopes to generate 80% of its power through renewable sources by 2050. (529 words)

From: Edvard Glücksman, *Blogs of the European Geosciences Union*, 4 December 2013

19 **woodchip furnace:** *Hackschnitzelheizung*

22 **three-pronged approach:** *dreigleisiger Ansatz*

29 **tangible:** *konkret, spürbar*

B **With your partner, make notes from the text on the importance of Feldheim's pioneer work for the whole of Germany.**

STEP 2 Boosting your word power

The text contains some useful words and phrases for writing your audio guide script.

A **Find idiomatic English expressions in the text for the German phrases below.**

1 energieautarke Gemeinde
2 ein bahnbrechendes funktionierendes Beispiel
3 auf nachhaltige Weise
4 weniger von fossilen Brennstoffen abhängig sein
5 den Rest weiterverkaufen
6 die Energiewende
7 etw in seinen Urzustand zurück versetzen
8 ein kleines Teil in einem großen Puzzle

B **Complete the following text with phrases from Step 2A. Take care with the verb constructions and tenses.**

Feldheim is Germany's first ___ [1]. It produces energy ___ [2] showing that there is no need to continue using nuclear energy or fossil fuel plants. It is also a ___ [3] that demonstrates how a disused military area can be ___ [4]. In fact, we have a model example of how a town can use renewable energy so that it is ___ [5] such as oil, coal and gas. If renewable energy is generated efficiently, more electricity can be produced than required and these communities can ___ [6] the market. Though Feldheim may only be ___ [7] of a zero-emissions future, it is an example of how Germany intends to carry out its ___ [8].

STEP 3 Preparing and writing your audio guide script

A **Form groups of four. Each group selects one renewable source of energy in Feldheim: the wind farm, the biogas plant, the woodchip furnace and the solar panels.**

Start preparing your part of the audio guide script using the information from Step 1, the phrases from Step 2 and the "Audio script writing guide" below.

Audio script writing guide

General guidelines:
- Gather information on the topic (from the text and your own research).
- Write down your audio text.

Script elements:
- an introduction to the topic
- a body in which you develop the idea
- an ending in which you also thank the listeners

Advice:
- Write clearly, use plain English and short sentences. A sentence should not take more than one breath to say.
- Add an anecdote to get the attention of the audience.
- Write like you talk, which means write for the ear, not for the eye. Read your script out loud at the end.

Words and phrases:

Introduction:	Hello, welcome to …
Main body:	Let's have a look at … Here/Over there/Opposite you can see …
Listing items:	next, furthermore, in addition
Comparing and contrasting:	on the one hand …, on the other hand …, however, although
Showing results and consequences:	as a result, for this reason
Summarizing:	in conclusion, in other words
Conclusion:	Thanks for listening. We hope that this audio guide was informative.

B **Form a new group in which there is at least one member of the other groups to exchange information.**

Decide on the order of the visit to the four elements that make up Feldheim's alternative energy sources and write a group version of the complete tour. Do not forget to add an introduction and a conclusion.

STEP 4 Reading out the audio guide tour

Practise reading your group version of the audio guide out loud. Make sure you know how to pronounce all the words. Practise your intonation and speed of delivery.

STEP 5 Recording the audio guide

Decide which of the audio guides best serves the purpose of presenting Feldheim as an energy self-sufficient village. Record this guide using a recording software. Upload it to your mobile phone or computer.

BEFORE YOU READ

Would you be willing to lower your living standards to help improve the environment? Give reasons for your answer.

By: Oliver Milman — 19 January 2015

LIFE ON EARTH AT RISK

A

Humans are "eating away at our own life support systems" at a rate unseen in the past 10,000 years by degrading land and freshwater systems, emitting greenhouse gases and releasing vast amounts of agricultural chemicals into the environment, new research has found.

Two major new studies by an international team of researchers have pinpointed the key factors that ensure a livable planet for humans, with stark results.

Of nine worldwide processes that underpin life on Earth, four have exceeded "safe" levels – human-driven climate change, loss of biosphere integrity, land system change and the high level of phosphorus and nitrogen flowing into the oceans due to fertiliser use.

Researchers spent five years identifying these core components of a planet suitable for human life, using the long-term average state of each measure to provide a baseline for the analysis.

They found that the changes of the last 60 years are unprecedented in the previous 10,000 years, a period in which the world has had a relatively stable climate and human civilisation has advanced significantly.

Carbon dioxide levels, at 395.5 parts per million, are at historic highs, while loss of biosphere integrity is resulting in species becoming extinct at a rate more than 100 times faster than the previous norm.

Since 1950 urban populations have increased seven-fold, primary energy use has soared by a factor of five, while the amount of fertiliser used is now eight times higher. The amount of nitrogen entering the oceans has quadrupled.

B

All of these changes are shifting Earth into a "new state" that is becoming less hospitable to human life, researchers said.

"These indicators have shot up since 1950 and there are no signs they are slowing down," said Prof Will Steffen of the Australian National University and the Stockholm Resilience Centre. Steffen is the lead author on both of the studies.

"When economic systems went into overdrive, there was a massive increase in resource use and pollution. It used to be confined to local and regional areas but we're now seeing this occurring on a global scale. These changes are down to human activity, not natural variability."

Earth's nine life-support systems

1. Acid oceans: More carbon dioxide in the atmosphere means more is absorbed by the oceans, creating carbonic acid.
2. Ozone depletion: With most of the culprit chemicals now banned, the worst of the danger has passed.
3. Fresh water: A quarter of the world's river systems no longer reach the ocean for at least part of the year, which is drying out the landscape.
4. Biodiversity: Individual species may not matter much on their own, but collectively they form ecosystems that provide a range of vital "ecosystem services".
5. Nitrogen and phosphorus cycles: We produce around 121 million tonnes of nitrogen a year, far more than nature can cope with.
6. Land use: Half the world's tropical rainforests are gone, and large areas of grasslands once open to wildlife are now fenced in for livestock.
7. Climate change: Greenhouse gasses are raising the Earth's temperature.
8. Aerosol loading: We have more than doubled the global concentration of aerosols such as soot since pre-industrial times.
9. Chemical pollution: There are thousands of human-made chemical compounds in use around the world which harm humans and wildlife.

09 **stark:** *schonunglos, nüchtern*
13 **integrity:** *Unversehrtheit*

Steffen said direct human influence upon the land was contributing to a loss in pollination and a disruption in the provision of nutrients and fresh water.

"We are clearing land, we are degrading land, we introduce feral animals and take the top predators out, we change the marine ecosystem by overfishing – it's a death by a thousand cuts," he said. "That direct impact upon the land is the most important factor right now, even more than climate change."

C

There are large variations in conditions around the world, according to the research. For example, land clearing is now concentrated in tropical areas, such as Indonesia and the Amazon, with the practice reversed in parts of Europe. But the overall picture is one of deterioration at a rapid rate.

"It's fairly safe to say that we haven't seen conditions in the past similar to ones we see today and there is strong evidence that there [are] tipping points we don't want to cross," Steffen said.

"If the Earth is going to move to a warmer state, 5–6 °C warmer, with no ice caps, it will do so and that won't be good for large mammals like us. People say the world is robust and that's true, there will be life on Earth, but the Earth won't be robust for us.

"Some people say we can adapt due to technology, but that's a belief system, it's not based on fact. There is no convincing evidence that a large mammal, with a core body temperature of 37 °C, will be able to evolve that quickly. Insects can, but humans can't and that's a problem."

D

Steffen said the research showed the economic system was "fundamentally flawed" as it ignored critically important life support systems.

"It's clear the economic system is driving us towards an unsustainable future and people of my daughter's generation will find it increasingly hard to survive," he said. "History has shown that civilisations have risen, stuck to their core values and then collapsed because they didn't change. That's where we are today." (856 words)

From: *The Guardian*, 19 January 2015

50 pollination: *Bestäubung*
54 feral animals: *wildlebende Tiere*

1 MULTIPLE CHOICE

→ Skills, p. 204

Choose the most suitable option in each case. [Paragraph A]

1 "Eating away at our own life support systems" means that …
- **a** we consume so much that soon we'll not have enough to eat.
- **b** our life support systems are being destroyed by excessive food production.
- **c** we are destroying the things that keep us alive.
- **d** we need to stop the destruction of our environment.

2 Which of the following processes that underpin life on Earth has not exceeded safe levels?
   a pollution of oceans by chemical farming
   b ozone depletion in the atmosphere
   c climate change caused by humans
   d destruction of diversified ecosystems

3 The international team of researchers found out that …
   a human civilization has progressed significantly in the last 60 years due to climate change.
   b the climate has been relatively stable in recent years compared to the previous 10,000 years.
   c the planet has undergone more change in the last 60 years than in the 10,000 years beforehand.
   d human civilization has led to a stable climate.

4 What is the reason given for the fast rate of extinction of so many species?
   a More and more of our biosphere is disappearing.
   b Carbon dioxide levels are exceptionally high.
   c Chemical substances used in farming are polluting soil and water.
   d Cities are spreading into the countryside.

2 GAPPED SUMMARY

→ Skills, p. 202

Fill in the gaps with words from the corresponding sections of the text. [Paragraphs B and C]

The Earth is undoubtedly not as ___ [1] as it used to be, as life on earth has got more difficult for many species. ___ [2] hinting at this development have been around for many decades, according to the main ___ [3] of two studies. As economic activity accelerated, ___ [4] use increased significantly. Whereas beforehand the overuse of raw materials and increased pollution had been ___ [5] to particular areas, now it is happening everywhere. Humans have been ___ [6] massively to the degradation of the land and sea, and their ___ [7] on the environment is the most serious threat to the planet at the moment. While some activities like forest clearance are ___ [8] in certain areas, it is clear that ___ [9] is taking place throughout the world and human beings will be unable to ___ [10] to the new conditions.

3 MEDIATION ENGLISH–GERMAN

→ Skills, p. 198

Beantworten Sie folgende Fragen auf Deutsch. Beziehen Sie sich auf Absätze C und D.

1 Wann sieht Prof. Steffen einen Punkt erreicht, der dem Menschen wirklich Probleme bereiten wird?
2 Wer oder was auf der Erde wäre „robust“ genug, einen weiteren Klimawandel zu überleben?
3 Was sieht Prof. Steffen als eine trügerische Hoffnung der Menschheit an?
4 Prof. Steffen zieht eine Lehre aus der Geschichte. Was braucht seiner Meinung nach eine Zivilisation fürs Überleben?

4 WORKING WITH WORDS

A The words on the left are all from the text. Match them to their meanings on the right.

1	degrade sth	a	rise quickly
2	pinpoint sth	b	make sth become worse
3	exceed sth	c	never having happened or existed in the past
4	unprecedented	d	be able to show/give the exact reason for sth
5	extinct	e	be greater than a particular number or amount of sth
6	soar	f	facts that make you believe that sth is true
7	fertilizer	g	(of a plant or an animal) no longer in existence
8	predator	h	a substance added to soil to make plants grow more successfully
9	evidence	i	an animal that kills and eats other animals

B Use eight of the words from 4A to complete this article on "Spaceship Earth" in a magazine.

Spaceship Earth

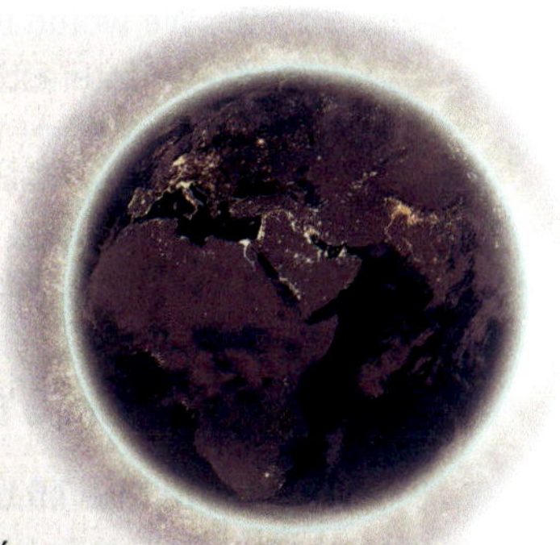

Earth is like a spaceship, in that it has limited resources and a crew that has to work together towards the greater good. Yet the ___[1] indicates that the spaceship team is devouring the spaceship's resources without thinking of its future. Humans, unlike insects, cannot evolve and adapt rapidly to changing surroundings. As we continue to consume ravenously, like ___[2] intent on satisfying our selfish needs, so more life forms on the spaceship become ___[3]. As the trend towards urbanization continues at an ___[4] rate and as the need for more resources ___[5], some of the spaceship's scientists are trying to ___[6] the exact time when the team will no longer be able to survive on the spaceship. Once the environment on the spaceship is ___[7] to such an extent that life is no longer sustainable, what will the team do? Some suggest moving to another spaceship like Mars, but the problem of getting there and establishing settlements ___[8] our present scientific capabilities.

5 GROUP DISCUSSION

→ Skills, p. 210

The earthquake and tsunami in Japan that damaged the Fukushima nuclear power plant triggered a heated energy debate in Germany and other European countries. Imagine you are members of the Youth Commission for European Energy discussing energy concepts for the future which could replace nuclear power and coal in the long run.

The energy concepts can be found in File 3 on p. 190.

Presentation phase

Present your energy solution and say why you think it should be an important component of a new European energy concept.

Interaction phase

As a group, discuss the suggestions and try to reach an agreement as to which three would be the most effective for a future European energy concept.

GRAMMAR CHECK

THE PASSIVE

→ Grammar summary, p. 223

1 **SPOT THE MISTAKES**
Spot the mistakes and correct them. Explain why they are wrong.

1 ~~At the moment a lot of houses are being insulating to reduce energy costs and pollution.~~
2 ~~Will global warming reduce by these measures?~~
3 ~~We act because our environment has endangered for a long time.~~

2 **Use the correct passive form of the verbs in *italics*.**

Organic material ___ [1] (*feed*) into the biogas plant. Manure can ___ [2] (*also – put*) into the plant. In the fermenter the substrate ___ [3] (completely – *decompose*) by microorganisms. Biogas ___ [4] (*produce*) as the final product of the fermentation process. Once the substrate ___ [5] (*ferment*), it ___ [6] (*transport*) to the storage tank. The residue can ___ [7] (*utilize*) as high-quality fertilizer. The biogas ___ [8] (normally – *store*) in the roof of the tank. From there it has to ___ [9] (*burn*) to generate electricity and heat. The electric power ___ [10] (then – directly – *transfer*) into the power grid.

3 **Decide which form is the most suitable in each case.**

1 The government ___ (has often been criticized/has often criticized) for not doing enough to encourage builders to use energy-saving measures in their houses.
2 Critics argue that renewable energy should ___ (promote/be promoted) ___ (from/by) the government to ensure energy-efficient housing.
3 In 2002 a law ___ (was passed/passed) in Germany aimed at ___ (improving/being improved) the energy-efficiency of houses.
4 As a consequence, more high-efficient heating and cooling systems ___ (have installed/have been installed) in new housing.
5 Experts say a huge contribution towards protecting our environment can ___ (achieve/be achieved by) proper wall insulation of the houses.
6 It is a fact that heat ___ (absorbs and stores/is absorbed and stored) during winter if solid material ___ (provides/is provided by) sufficient thermal mass.
7 From now on the question of how to reduce your individual footprint can easily ___ (answer/be answered).

WATCH OUT! as, like, than
Choose the correct options to translate the German "wie" or "als".

Consumers are using more renewable energy ~~as~~ in the past.
→ *Consumers are using more renewable energy <u>than</u> in the past.*

1 Martin used to work as/like an engineer in a nuclear power station in England. (*als*)
2 However, he wanted to leave the Earth as/like it was. (*wie*)
3 So he used his experience as/like an engineer to work for the renewable energy sector. (*als*)
4 More renewable energy is being produced as/than in previous years, but he thinks that is still not enough. (*als*)
5 His aim is to encourage an energy transition as/like the one in Germany, where the use of renewable energy is higher as/than it has ever been. (*wie; als*)

7 Information in a digital age

FOCUS

Social media board game: How to play:

- Get together in groups of three or four.
- Throw a dice.
- Move your counter.
- Talk for one minute about the subject on the square.

SITUATION

Young people often understand social media better than older people. For this reason your class has been invited to a **panel discussion** at an international technology and education fair being held in Munich. The topic is "Should teenagers be allowed uncontrolled access to social media?". You have to think of arguments that you can use and then participate in the panel discussion.

STEP 1 Brainstorming

Work in two groups and list five good and five bad aspects of social media.

good aspects of social media	bad aspects of social media
▒	▒

STEP 2 Preparing ideas

The text "How Social Media Has Changed Us" presents the positive and negative sides of social media. Read it and find arguments in favour and against social media. Group 1 finds the arguments in favour of social media as presented in the text and Group 2 the arguments against social media. Compare them to the lists you made in your brainstorming and add any new ideas to the table.

How Social Media Has Changed Us

A It's hard to believe that, only a decade ago, social media was little more than a budding trend. Back in 2005, Facebook was still in its early stages of its spread across the world. Twitter appeared around that time, but a lot of us saw it as a pointless toy. Fast forward to 2014, and social media has become a key part of the modern lifestyle. Yesterday, a friend commented that her elementary age kids were stunned to know that phones were only used for conversations a few years ago. They were dumbfounded to hear that we didn't even carry phones with us 15–20 years ago. This tells me that everything has officially and permanently changed. There is a generation of kids coming up who can't even conceive of a world without smartphones and social networking.

B Let's look at ways that social media improves our life experience, and also a few ways that it uncovers a few of the more unsightly parts of humanity.

C Given all the consolidation of media companies in the United States, it is pretty easy to question whether the news we get from the major media is the full story or not. After all, it's not a rare occasion to hear more about the latest celebrity death than a political uprising in Turkey or elsewhere in the world. One of the things that attracted me personally to Twitter was the immediate access to other sources of information. Back when the government raided Osama Bin Laden's fortress in Pakistan, there was a neighbour live tweeting his observations of the whole situation through the night.

D Social media is also very helpful for expanding our sources of content as a whole. With so much being blogged and written, the volume of content has grown exponentially. Now, there is no shortage of viewpoints and sources from which we can draw our own conclusions. It's less important to have a news team interpret it on our behalf.

E I remember the days of phones with old style dials. We didn't even have answering machines back then. If you called someone and they didn't answer the phone, you had to call back and try to catch them in real time. It was

10 **consolidation:** *Fusion, Zusammenlegung*

sometimes hard to catch up with people, so you had to handwrite and send a letter to communicate if you were both leading busy lives. Today, if you can't catch someone on the phone, you can leave a voicemail or send a text. Or even better, tweet, Facebook message, or touch base by some other means. You can see what others are doing within seconds of them doing it, assuming they share it on a social network of some sort.

F Similar to the phone situation it was extremely difficult to access a globally reaching platform where one could share their opinions or findings back a mere 25 years ago. I recall in the early 1990s when it was a huge deal to send in a letter to the editor of a local newspaper, and have them actually decide to include the letter in the paper. Today, all we have to do is login to our platform of choice. We can rant, rave, share images, and generally mix and mingle to our heart's content. For those of us who can write, it takes only a couple of minutes to create a new blog and start putting our thoughts into words. And those thoughts could grow legs of their own once the social sphere grabs hold of them. It is far easier to do something remarkable and noticeable, and have it reach people across the planet, than it has been at any time in our history. We now have truly globalized voices.

G It would be short-sighted to only highlight the good from social media. Here are some of the things that make me want to close the browser window. I know, it's been mocked and made fun of ad nauseam – the selfie. Whether it's a shirtless guy flexing in front of a mirror or people with bad judgment taking selfies in front of natural disasters, we're stuck with them. I get why so many selfies make their way out onto the social networks. Phones come with high res cameras now. You don't even need anyone present to take a picture from the top of Mount "Amazing-est View in the World." But really, it's not hard to ask some friendly passer-by to take a picture if you really want one. Everyone can see right through your brag about the cool places you're visiting or the awesome people you are hanging out with.

H When it comes to politics, religion, or any other very personal area of life, discussion becomes contentious almost immediately. If you have a different belief system from someone else, you are both more likely to fight to defend it rather than cave in to the other's argument. These are very delicate topics, and all too easily the conversation can devolve into personal attacks and negative judgments of each other's characters. Social media is meant to be social, not a boxing rink.

I Anonymity has been a key piece of the internet since its early days. It's amazing to see how people behave when their true identity is masked. Now we have everything from outright trolls to habitual pranksters. If you want to say something and are afraid to have anyone know you said it, perhaps you should buck up and use common sense before putting it out there. Being offensive anonymously is not only cowardly, it shows a lack of character.

J In recent years, we've seen a ton of hashtag activists across social media. It has become a trend to take a selfie while holding a sign with a political or social message on it, and a new hashtag, of course. Or take a video in the case of the Ice Bucket Challenge. The idea is to get likes and shares for the picture or video, or challenge others to take part, with the aim of having a message spread. While that's fine in concept, hashtag activism is all talk. If an issue is important enough to take action, why not take real action? Facebook is crawling with people ready to go to social media war with anyone on a topic they care about, but what else are they doing to fix the problem? Venting on social media doesn't fix a thing; it just stirs the pot.

K I love social media. As with any communication medium, it comes with its ups and downs, pros and cons. Overall, I truly believe it makes the world a better place in many ways. (1109 words)

From: Tommy Landry, the website of business2community, 5 September 2014

45 **high res camera:** *hochauflösende Kamera* 52 **devolve:** *übergehen* 56 **buck up:** *sich zusammenreißen*

STEP 3 Following an argument

Stay in the two groups and analyse the structure of each argument. Find …

- the topical sentence
- supporting reason 1
- the example/or: supporting reason 2

Group 1 works on the arguments in favour of social media and Group 2 on the ones against social media again. Afterwards, each group presents their results to the class.

EXAMPLE for paragraph F:

Topical sentence	we have a global voice due to social media
Supporting reason 1	use a platform which might give us a global readership or: share your views and findings; no longer dependent on a newspaper to print your letter to the editor
Example	write a blog

STEP 4 Finding further arguments

Stay in the two groups and find further arguments in favour of (Group 1) or against (Group 2) social media which you can use in the discussion in addition to the ones from above. Think about items such as:

- staying in touch with people
- privacy
- impact on political development/movements
- learning/education
- bullying

Report to the class.

STEP 5 Making a ranking list

In the discussion, which will be held at the end, each group is allowed four arguments only. Group 1 discusses the arguments in favour of social media and comes up with a ranking list of the four most convincing ones to be used in the discussion. Group 2 works on the arguments against social media.

STEP 6 Boosting your word power

The text contains language that might be useful in the discussion. Work on the following exercises.

A ⊙ **Go to File 17 on p. 183.**
Replace the underlined parts with idiomatic phrases from the text.

1 Social media at the turn of the century was <u>just starting out</u>.
Social media at the turn of the century was ▬

2 Social media allows you to spread as many rumours as you want.
You can spread rumours ▬ on social media.
3 You can take selfies with your smartphone again and again until you get sick of it.
You can take selfies with your smartphone ▬.
4 Why did you do that? Have you no ability to think about things reasonably?
Why did you do that? Have you no ▬?
5 Why don't you tell me everything that has happened?
Why don't you tell me ▬?

B Find the English equivalents of the following German expressions in the text which describe social media and its activities negatively.

1 ein sinnloses Spielzeug [Paragraph A]
2 sprachlos/verdutzt sein [Paragraph A]
3 jdn wüst beschimpfen/schimpfen wie ein Rohrspatz [Paragraph F]
4 Prahlerei, Angeberei [Paragraph G]
5 beleidigend sein [Paragraph I]
6 Charakterlosigkeit [Paragraph I]
7 nur Geschwätz [Paragraph J]
8 seinen Ärger an jdn/etw auslassen [Paragraph J]

C Complete the sentences by using collocations and idioms based around the words in the box to replace the German phrases in brackets. Your dictionary will help you find the collocations/idioms under the listed words.

news ▪ source ▪ voice ▪ volume

1 The unexpected turn of events became ▬ (*Aufmacher auf Seite 1*).
2 I heard about the attack ▬ (*in den Nachrichten*).
3 Due to the media everyone now ▬ (*ein Sprachrohr haben*).
4 She's the only ▬ (*Stimme der Vernunft*) in Parliament – the rest are clowns.
5 The ▬ (*bloße Menge*) of data is overwhelming.
6 Your silence ▬ (*spricht Bände*).
7 Journalists need information from a ▬ (*verlässliche Quelle*).
8 What was your ▬ (*Nachrichtenquelle*)?

STEP 7 Holding a discussion

"Should teenagers be allowed uncontrolled access to social media?"

In groups of four (two members supporting the statement, two members opposing the statement) discuss the question. Exchange sound arguments and try to convince the opposite group of your view. The other students listen and assess the discussion.

BEFORE YOU READ

Do you or does anyone in your family read any newspapers? Which ones, and why and how (print, app or online)? Which sources of information do you prefer to get your news from, and why?

ARE MILLENNIALS REALLY MORE INFORMED?

This article was written by teen reporters from The Mash, *a bi-weekly publication distributed to Chicago high schools.*

A Our generation, sometimes referred to as Millennials, has entered unknown territory when it comes to methods of collecting information. Nowadays, social media has allowed the spread of information at a rate that has never been seen before.

B But speedy methods of communication don't necessarily guarantee that said information is actually being consumed. Some argue that this generation's increased access to information results in teens being more informed than any group before them. But others insist that while young people are exposed to more information, they fail to accurately learn from it. So which side is correct?

C The perception that Millennials are less informed is backed by recent research. In 2012, a Pew Research survey reported that members of the Silent and Boomer generations spent almost twice the amount of time following the news as Millennials. But polls like this fail to take social media into account as a news source; earlier this year, the Media Insight Project released research that found 88 percent of Millennials use Facebook as a source for their news.

D So does social media keep Millennials as informed as newspapers kept other generations informed? Well, it does allow people to become more informed if they choose to use it that way. "We are a generation that is completely aware of everything going on," Jones junior Audrey James said. An example of this is the rise of the Black Lives Matter movement, which owes a lot of its success to social media. The 2014 events in Ferguson, Mo caught the attention of millions even as law enforcement worked to keep journalists at bay – people could get a glimpse of what was going on through social media. And when people become aware of a major

Police in Ferguson arrest protesters following the killing of Michael Brown.

19 **Silent generation:** generation born from the late 1920s to the early 1940s
19 **Boomer generation:** generation born from the late 1940s to the early 1960s
32 **Jones:** school in Chicago
32 **junior:** student in second-to-last year of high school
36 **Ferguson, Mo.:** the shooting of an African-American, Michael Brown, by a white police officer in Ferguson, Missouri

news event, they also have the capability to learn more about it. "I believe it's a lot easier to find the information because there are a lot more resources at our fingertips," Glenbard East journalism teacher Jeffrey Kargol said. "People can pretty much go online and get informed about something, while other generations couldn't do that. So, does this generation have the capability to be more informed? Absolutely."

E While many agree that the widespread use of technology is key in keeping the Millennial generation informed of current affairs, many think young people don't take advantage of that technology. "I don't believe we are informed as much as we should be," Glenbard East sophomore Kelly Tautkus said. "Our generation is all about texting, video games, how many likes we have got on social media. It's sad that more teens will know what the Kardashians are doing and have no idea what's going on in Syria or what the European immigration crisis is about."

F Jones junior David Flores believes that being informed is a matter of choice. While teens have the capability to be more informed than previous generations, many of them don't take steps to do so. "People just seek what interests them," Flores said. "For example, there can be a Twitter post that says, 'CPS goes on strike,' and that's as informed as people want to be. They won't search as to the exact reasoning for the strike and why it's happening."

G Unlike sitting down and watching the evening news, Twitter and Facebook provide users with the ability to pick and choose what information they see and investigate more closely. While this is a powerful tool, it requires responsible use to actually serve its purpose. "We subconsciously filter out what we don't want to be informed on," Whitney Young senior Avelardo Rivera said. "Such as people with a news app can choose what sort of news they want to see. People filter the information they are fed."

H So are teens actually less informed than past generations? Not necessarily, according to Paul Booth, an associate professor for media and cinema studies at DePaul University. "It's only in the past hundred years or so that children and teenagers have had free time to become engaged with the world around them," Booth explained. "For many years, people went to school and then went to work, and the idea that you might have free time to spend on media- or technology-related issues would be laughable! So, the rise of leisure time goes hand-in-hand with technological growth."

I Of course, to be informed doesn't mean one has to know everything. Decades ago, all the news of the day had to fit into a newspaper, but now there's significantly more information available. "Today we have access to almost all the news around the world, so it's literally not possible to know everything," Booth said. "Teenagers know more today than they did in the past, but it's just a drop in the bucket compared to all the news that's out there. No one can know all that!"

J Even if older generations aren't fond of social media, it's hard to deny that the way we consume news is changing. Many newspapers are beginning to move their business online. As the generation who grew up on the internet, teens already have a head start to understanding the information that can be gained online. "Adults have always looked with fear at new technology and what it's doing to young people – from the invention of writing to the invention of Snapchat, there have always been people bemoaning changes in culture," Booth said. (886 words)

From: Darcy Palder and Syeda Sameeha, *The Mash*, teen edition of *The Chicago Tribune*, 16 December 2015

44 **Glenbard East:** school in Chicago
57 **sophomore:** student in second year at high school
70 **CPS:** Chicago Public Schools
81 **Whitney Young:** school in Chicago
81 **senior:** student in final year of high school

7 FURTHER ACTIVITIES D

1 VIEWING

→ Skills, p. 196

11

A First, listen to the presenter of the news story talking about print journalists going digital. Complete the sentences below.

1 The presenter says that just ___ is not enough to attract online readers.
2 The presenter calls the important newspapers the big ___ .
3 The report focuses on how ___ and ___ are coming together.

B Now listen to three people working in America's top newsrooms.

A	Jim Joseph
B	Gabriel Dance
C	Meghan Ventura

Decide which journalist made which statements. All the journalists made more than one statement.

1 Readers of all age groups like the interactive elements of online newspapers.
2 Even traditional journalists see that they can reach more readers through interaction.
3 Previously, stories were written but there was little reaction from the readership.
4 Interactive elements like games help to attract the interest of readers in the content itself.
5 The articles on the website of *The New York Times* are not always its most popular attractions.
6 It is the mutual exchange between reader and writer which the writer finds exciting.

2 ARGUMENTATIVE WRITING

→ Skills, pp. 206, 208

1 **Go to File 19 on p. 183.**

"What is interesting is the power and the impact of social media. So we must try to use social media in a good way."
(Malala Yousafzai, Nobel Peace Prize laureate)

Comment on her view in at least 200 words.

2 **In the text on p. 99 Kelly Tautkus says: "Our generation is all about texting, video games, how many likes we have got on social media. It's sad that more teens will know what the Kardashians are doing and have no idea what's going on in Syria or what the European immigration crisis is about."**
Give possible reasons for this attitude, and say whether you agree with this statement. Write about 200 words.

3 MATERIAL-BASED ESSAY

→ Skills, pp. 206, 208

"Social media has turned from a blessing into a curse for many."

Comment on this view with reference to the material offered here. Write at least 300 words.

"Kids are going to post photos and personal information. At least they should be aware of the risks. At least they should use the privacy tools built into the sites to keep people they don't know from accessing their information and their data. And at least moms and dads should learn about what they are doing."

(Ernie Allen, President & CEO, National Center for Missing & Exploited Children)

4 GROUP DISCUSSION

→ Skills, p. 210

Your family (parents and two kids) has decided to do something about your excessive media consumption. Therefore, your parents have pinned a list to the refrigerator door with proposals of how to cut down on media for the period of one month, and they want you to add a proposal, too. All the proposals should be discussed in the next family meeting where you should reach an agreement on what you all can do without for a month.

Presentation phase

First, put forward one of the proposals in the list below, which you must present in one minute to the family council.

- No TV
- No smartphone at all
- No PC games or online games
- No Facebook or other social media
- Two hours per week for watching TV, using the smartphone, Facebook or playing games; free decision when to take it and when to split it into smaller units
- No media at all: no newspaper, radio, TV
- No pay-TV (Sky, Netflix, etc.)

Interaction phase

Exchange arguments on the different proposals listed. Weigh up the pros and cons of each. Be ready to compromise. Come to an agreement on which proposal you will accept as the detox measure.

GERUND / INFINITIVE

→ Grammar summary, p. 225

1 **SPOT THE MISTAKES**

Spot the mistakes and correct them. Explain why they are wrong.

1 ~~He would like surfing the internet every day if he had enough time.~~
2 ~~He refuses listening to his friend's advice to stop to download songs illegally.~~
3 ~~He enjoys to meet his friends online.~~
4 ~~He cannot imagine to do without his computer.~~
5 ~~He's looking forward to buy the new computer game.~~
6 ~~He doesn't mind to sit at the computer playing games most of his spare time.~~

2 **Complete this report on the dangers of the internet by using the gerund or the infinitive form of the verb in brackets.**

Most young people enjoy ___ [1] (surf) the internet nowadays. But people who are too negligent about security and personal information risk ___ [2] (become) the victims of internet crime. Many people do not mind ___ [3] (give) their personal data in social networks when they are asked to do so, and many do this without ___ [4] (realize) the dangers involved. This information can be used ___ [5] (commit) crimes such as internet fraud and identity theft. Many employers now also decide ___ [6] (check) the internet ___ [7] (get) information on job applicants before offering them a job. Many young people simply refuse ___ [8] (listen) to experts who urge them ___ [9] (be) on the alert when using the internet.

3 **Complete the sentences by using the gerund or the infinitive form of the verb in brackets.**

1 The minister thanked the journalists for ___ (come) to the press conference and said that he had enjoyed ___ (talk) with them.
2 However, one reporter couldn't resist ___ (ask) him one final question.
3 The reporter asked the minister ___ (explain) why the taxpayers' money had been wasted on the failed tunnel project.
4 The minister didn't give any details, but promised ___ (inform) him as soon as he had any further information.
5 The reporter considered ___ (drop) the matter, but then he decided ___ (follow) it up with another question.
6 After that, the minister refused ___ (answer) any more questions and left the meeting.

WATCH OUT! Problem words (2)

Choose the correct word to complete the sentences.

1 George spent the whole night looking / watching films on his computer.
2 He could hardly stand up / get up the next morning.
3 He knew he would disgrace / blame himself if he arrived at work looking so tired.
4 He had to borrow / lend his flatmate's bike so that he could get to work on time.
5 In the end, he was lucky / happy that his chef / boss wasn't there when he arrived just a little bit late.
6 During his lunch break / pause he sat outside on a bench / bank and wondered how he would get together enough money to pay next month's rent / pension.

8 Multiculturalism in a diverse world

FOCUS

A Listen to the song "Coming to America" and decide if the following statements about the immigrants are true or false. Explain your answers by quoting from the song.

18

1 The immigrants …

- **a** come from a neighbouring country.
- **b** are dreaming of a better life.
- **c** are penned in during their voyage.
- **d** bring a lot of possessions with them.
- **e** are probably fleeing from oppression.
- **f** want to retain their cultural identity on arrival.

2 With a partner decide which of the following adjectives could be used to describe how the singer feels towards the immigrants. Explain your choice.

angry ▪ compassionate ▪ enthusiastic ▪ hopeful ▪ indifferent

B Look at the photos and talk about these questions with your partner.

1 What associations do you have when you see the Statue of Liberty?
2 What do the photos say about migration?
3 Have you ever thought of emigrating? Which country would you choose, and why?
4 Do you think you would face problems trying to settle in a different culture? Explain.

19

12

Immigration and integration

Migration is a worldwide phenomenon. Poverty and a desire for better economic opportunities and living conditions are the driving force behind economic migration. In times of an economic boom countries recruit foreign workers, e.g. when Germany hired "guest workers" in the 1950s. In the USA immigrants gave rise to the concept of the melting pot, where all ethnic identities were merged to form one – the American. Environmental catastrophes, religious persecution, political oppression, war and civil war are events that can bring about mass migration, where people leave a place in droves in search of liberty and safety. After World War II Europe had to cope with millions of displaced people, while today refugees are fleeing the unrest of the Middle East.

Millions of people worldwide risk their lives illegally crossing borders because of circumstances beyond their control. Many illegal immigrants become the victims of human traffickers who exploit their desperate situation. The dangerous passage to a new home often results in death, and the asylum seekers often face discrimination, racism, xenophobia and resentment, even in wealthy host countries.

Anti-immigration groups claim that migrants are a drain on society, that they claim too many benefits and take jobs away from locals, but there is evidence that these fears are not justified. Migrants actually pay more taxes than they take in benefits. Often well-educated in their countries of origin, migrants tend to be young and healthy, which is an advantage for countries suffering from demographic problems like an ageing population, in which a shrinking workforce has to support a growing number of pensioners. Migrants often bring needed professional skills, but often their qualifications are not recognized and their skills go to waste and they end up doing menial jobs locals don't want to do.

With the arrival of many migrants in Europe, right-wing movements and racial tensions are on the rise, with attacks on refugee shelters increasing. Governments have introduced quotas to curb the influx of immigrants, while newly introduced citizenship tests put the onus on foreigners to successfully integrate into their adopted country.

Migrants establish the open pluralistic multicultural environment and the ethnic diversity which is an asset for a country. These qualities are often sought out by multinational companies when searching for workers. Migration broadens our horizons, enriches our culture, creates an atmosphere of tolerance and becomes part of a local identity.

However, many migrants feel torn between two cultures and feel they don't really belong to either. Alienation and uncertainty about their identity are often the result. (412 words)

First of all, make sure you understand the meaning of each of the highlighted words and phrases in the text above. If you are not sure, look them up in your dictionary. Then complete the tasks on the following page.

1 WORD FIELDS

Make a list of words and phrases from the text related to the given categories.

a	different groups who come to a country	*immigrants,* ▬
b	negative responses to immigration	*a drain on resources,* ▬
c	positive aspects of immigration	*pay more taxes,* ▬
d	problems faced by immigrants	*discrimination,* ▬

2 PARAPHRASES

Replace the phrases in the brackets with a phrase from the text.

1 Ruthless traffickers who ▬ (take advantage of the deplorable and hopeless circumstances) that some refugees find themselves in should be punished.

2 Many erroneously believe that migrants are ▬ (a burden on all the people living in a country).

3 Some countries try desperately to ▬ (cut down the numbers of non-citizens coming into the country).

4 Many immigrants ▬ (are confronted with intolerance, racism and prejudice).

5 Syrians are fleeing from the IS jihadists ▬ (in large numbers).

6 There is evidence that immigrants are ▬ (a valuable and useful benefit) for the host country.

3 PHRASES

Complete the sentences with highlighted phrases from the text for the German equivalents in brackets.

1 The American ▬ (*Bild des Schmelztiegels*) seems now a little outdated.

2 It is the duty of the ▬ (*Gastland*) to ensure the safety of refugees once they cross its borders.

3 ▬ (*Staatsbürgerschaftstests*) will be introduced for immigrants to encourage them to integrate.

4 Large international companies appreciate ▬ (*ethnische Vielfalt*) in a city.

5 Many immigrants and their offspring are ▬ (*zwischen beiden Kulturen hin- und hergerissen*).

6 Despair is the ▬ (*treibende Kraft*) behind mass migration.

7 Many ▬ (*Flüchtlingsunterkünfte*) have been built in Germany over the last year to house the newcomers.

8 A multicultural environment usually helps ▬ (*den Horizont erweitern*) of the local residents.

9 Right-wing movements try to stir up negative feelings towards immigrants among local citizens. But most realize that ▬ (*diese Ängste sind unberechtigt*).

10 Many Christians and Yazidis have fled their homes in the Middle East due to ▬ (*religiöse Verfolgung*).

DON'T SIT ON THE FENCE: YOU'RE EITHER FOR US OR AGAINST US.

At the bottom in small print it said, *Published and printed by*, with Dad's name and our address. The flyer had been printed before the bomb, so naturally there was no mention. November the twelfth was a week from today. I had no idea what a non-violent direct action was, or that Dad was actually campaigning against the asylum seekers. If Asra's people were aware of his involvement it would explain how the men on guard knew his name, and why they'd slammed the gates in my face. (268 words)

STEP 3 Thinking of a title

Is there a general topic or problem common to all the stories which could be used in the title of your article? Discuss this in your group.

STEP 4 Examining the characters

Each group draws a mind map for each of the characters in the three stories. Visualize in your mind map the relationships of the characters. Then add information about the characters that helps us to understand them and which helps you to write the article. Pin the mind maps of all the groups to three different walls of the classroom. Each group evaluates the mind maps of the other groups.

STEP 5 Understanding intercultural conflicts

In order to try and understand the different cultural conflicts in the three texts, separate into three groups, and prepare the following discussions.

A **Group 1:** Prepare a discussion between Mrs Iqbal and the headteacher of Magid's school, in which both sides explain why Magid should or should not attend the Harvest Festival.

B **Group 2:** Prepare a discussion between the protagonist and a young British person about changes in attitudes to race since the events in the text.

C **Group 3:** Prepare a discussion between people from the village and the refugees, in which the villagers explain their anxieties and the refugees explain why they have come to England.

STEP 6 Boosting your word power

The text extracts contain vocabulary that can help you write your article. Work with the vocabulary to make it your own.

TEXT A

A Complete the sentences with phrases from the text.

1 Magid writes down his message ▬ (*aufgeregt*).
2 Both Magid and his mother ▬ (*gestanden den schmerzhaften Vorfall ein*).
3 Mrs Iqbal ▬ (*war den Tränen nahe*) because of her son's ▬ (*Brüskierung*).
4 Trying not to reveal her shock, Mrs Iqbal offers ▬ (*ein warmherziges Lächeln*).

B Find phrases in the text which show that Magid is embarrassed.

TEXT B

C The author uses phrases that you want to put into more standard English. Match the phrases (1–7) from the text with a more common English version (a-g).

1 in his best suit
2 I pinch myself so my eyes do not close
3 in a pause between his breaths
4 I thought him to be talking sense
5 all hell would break loose
6 God slipping from me like a freshly launched ship
7 nearly knock him into an early meeting with the Almighty

a I am so bored that I will fall asleep
b believed that what the man was saying was reasonable
c when he stops talking for a moment
d is totally disillusioned
e get so angry with the man that I want to hurt him
f it would cause a riot
g well dressed

TEXT C

D Rewrite the sentences by replacing the underlined parts with phrases from the text. They follow the order of the text.

1 More than half the people believe that immigrants are a benefit.
The … believes that immigrants are a benefit.
2 There are, of course, foreigners who have made it to Germany without showing their real papers.
There are, of course, … in Germany.
3 Our protest is not going to use either weapons or force.
Our protest is strictly … .
4 The police, of course, do know that he took part.
The police, of course, are … .

E Which expression in the text …

EXAMPLE: indicates there is nobody but Ruby in the house?
→ *Ruby is home alone.*

1 associates the asylum home with something unpleasant?
2 shows that Ruby's dad can be pretty annoying?
3 explains why information about the action won't be given beforehand?
4 shows that the guards closed the gates with violence before Ruby could enter?

STEP 7 Writing the article

In your groups write your article. Your article should focus on the problems faced by immigrants and asylum seekers, especially the emotional and social aspects of dealing with a new culture. Use the information and vocabulary from the extracts as far as possible. Add a proposal for a solution. Write about 200 words.

BEFORE YOU READ

Which do you think is the largest ethnic group in the USA? Why do you think they are?
You have probably heard about the USA being a melting pot. What does this metaphor mean?

AMERICA'S LARGEST ETHNIC GROUP HAS ASSIMILATED SO WELL THAT PEOPLE BARELY NOTICE IT

A On a snow-covered bluff overlooking the Sheboygan river stands the Waelderhaus, a faithful reproduction of an Austrian chalet. It was built by the Kohler family of Wisconsin in the 1920s as a tribute to the homeland of their father, John Michael Kohler, who had immigrated to America in 1854 at the age of ten. John Michael moved to Sheboygan, married the daughter of another German immigrant, who owned the local foundry, and took over his father-in-law's business A . Today Kohler is the biggest maker of loos and baths in America. Herbert Kohler, the boss (and grandson of the founder), has done so well selling tubs that he has been able to pursue his other passion – golf – on a grand scale. The Kohler Company owns Whistling Straits, the course that will host the Ryder Cup in 2020.

B B . In 2013, according to the Census bureau, 46m Americans claimed German ancestry: more than the number who traced their roots to Ireland (33m) or England (25m). In whole swathes of the northern United States, German-Americans outnumber any other group. Some 41% of the people in Wisconsin are of Teutonic stock.

C Yet despite their numbers, they are barely visible. Everyone knows that Michael Dukakis is Greek-American, the Kennedy clan hail from Ireland and Mario Cuomo was an Italian-American. C . Companies founded by German-Americans tend to play

down their roots, too: think of Pfizer, Boeing, Steinway, Levi Strauss or Heinz. Buried somewhere on their websites may be a brief note that "Steinway & Sons was founded in 1853 by German immigrant Henry Engelhard Steinway in a Manhattan loft on Varick Street". D .

D German immigrants have flavoured American culture like cinnamon in an *Apfelkuchen*. They imported Christmas trees and Easter bunnies and gave America a taste for pretzels, hot dogs, bratwursts and sauerkraut. E . Germans in Wisconsin launched America's first kindergarten and set up *Turnvereine*, or gymnastics clubs, in Milwaukee,

01 **bluff:** *Klippe* 10 **foundry:** *Gießerei* 24 **swathe:** *Landstrich*

Cincinnati and other cities. After a failed revolution in Germany in 1848, disillusioned revolutionaries decamped to America and spread progressive ideas. "Germanism, socialism and beer makes Milwaukee different," says John Gurda, a historian. F , of whom two, Emil Seidel and Frank Zeidler, were of German stock.

E As in so many other countries where Germans have settled, they have dominated the brewing trade. Beer barons such as Jacob Best, Joseph Schlitz, Frederick Pabst and Frederick Miller made Milwaukee the kind of city that more or less had to call its baseball team the Brewers. "Germans were not part of the colonial aristocracy," says Rüdiger Lentz, director of the Aspen Institute Germany. Many Italian and Polish immigrants were middle-class, and they quickly became politically active. German immigrants tended to be poor farmers, which is why they headed for the vast fertile spaces of the Midwest. "The Italians stormed the city halls; the Germans stormed the beer halls," went the saying.

F During the first world war, parts of America grew hysterically anti-German. Some Germans were spat at in the street. The teaching of their language was banned in schools. Sauerkraut was renamed "liberty cabbage". German books were burned, dachshunds kicked and German-Americans forced to buy war bonds to prove their patriotism. When New Ulm, a predominantly German town in Minnesota, refused to let its young men join the draft, the National Guard was sent in. After the war, German-Americans hunkered down. Many stopped speaking German and anglicised their names.

G The second world war saw less anti-German hysteria, although some 10,000 German-Americans were interned as enemy aliens. President Franklin Roosevelt conspicuously appointed military commanders with names like Eisenhower and Nimitz to fight the Axis powers. But the Holocaust gave German-Americans yet another reason to hide their origins.

H Today German-Americans are quietly successful. Their median household income, at $61,500, is 18% above the national norm. They are more likely to have college degrees than other Americans, and less likely to be unemployed. A whopping 97% of them speak only English at home. They have assimilated and prospered without any political help specially tailored for their ethnic group. "The Greeks and the Irish have a far stronger support network and lobby groups than we do," says Peter Wittig, Germany's ambassador in America. There was no German-American congressional caucus until 2010, though there were caucuses for potatoes, bicycles and Albanian affairs. The German caucus has quickly grown to about 100 members, who lobby for trade and investment as well as the preservation of their common cultural heritage.

I Five years ago a small German-American Heritage Museum opened in Washington, DC. "Germany has never been as popular as it is today," says Petra Schürmann, the museum's director. German fests and Oktoberfests have sprung up all over the country, and they are not only about brats and beer, but also about tracing genealogy and displaying traditional dress and craftsmanship. Stuff made by Germans sells. And Americans travel to Germany in droves: the young to hip Berlin and older folks to pretty Heidelberg.

J On February 9th Angela Merkel, Germany's chancellor, will meet Barack Obama in the White House. They will discuss the war in Ukraine, transatlantic trade, the wobbling euro zone and the upcoming G7 summit in Bavaria. Unlike Indian-Americans, who went wild when their new prime minister visited America, German-Americans will barely notice. (983 words)

From: *The Economist*, 7 February 2015

51 decamp: *aufbrechen* **84 hunker down:** *sich klein machen* **89 conspicuous:** *auffallend* **99 whopping:** *enorm*

8

1 MULTIPLE MATCHING

→ Skills, p. 200

Go to File 20 on p. 184.
Copy the table and match sentences (1–8) with gaps (A–F). Two sentences do not fit.

Gap	A	B	C	D	E	F
Sentence						

1 They built big Lutheran churches wherever they went
2 He transformed it from a maker of ploughshares into a plumbing business
3 Milwaukee is the only big American city that had Socialist mayors for several decades
4 German-Americans are America's largest single ethnic group (if you divide Hispanics into Mexican-Americans, Cuban-Americans, etc.)
5 German-Americans will some day even exceed Hispanics in the USA
6 But firms that play up their Germanic history – as Kohler does, in a short film shown at the Waelderhaus – are rare
7 Milwaukee never saw a Socialist mayor, though
8 Fewer notice that John Boehner, the Speaker of the House of Representatives, and Rand Paul, a senator from Kentucky with presidential ambitions, are of German origin

2 MULTIPLE CHOICE

→ Skills, p. 204

Choose the most suitable answer according to the information given in the text. [Paragraphs E–J]

1 The name Brewers for the Milwaukee baseball team refers to …
a the first German owner of the team.
b a German aristocrat in the city.
c the city's major German-controlled businesses.
d the fact that Germans drank beer when working in the fields.

2 With the saying "The Italians stormed the city halls; the Germans stormed the beer halls," the author means that …
a Italians get easily upset and violent.
b Italians had political ambitions.
c Germans were poor drunkards.
d Germans were skilled craftsmen.

3 During the First World War Germans in America …
a were feared. **b** kept their language. **c** volunteered. **d** faced hostility.

4 What is not mentioned in Paragraph F about Germans in the years after the First World War?
a They changed their names from Müller to Miller.
b They kept a low profile.
c They became more anti-American.
d They switched from speaking just German to just English.

5 Which information is mentioned in paragraph G? Many Germans …
a were kept in camps.
b denied the Holocaust.
c were removed from the army.
d openly showed their German ancestry.

6 Which information is not mentioned in paragraph H? Germans on average …
a are pretty well-off.
b use English as their main language.
c are well-educated.
d want to return to Germany.

7 In paragraph H the writer uses examples of caucuses in order to make the point that …
  - **a** bizarre traditions are popular in America.
  - **b** the Germans have never really organized as an ethnic group.
  - **c** Germans are good at spotting a business opportunity.
  - **d** German-Americans want to integrate into American life.

8 According to paragraph I, Germany …
  - **a** is a cliché for Americans associated with beer and brats.
  - **b** has become a favourite destination with young and old.
  - **c** is a faint memory to most German-Americans.
  - **d** tries but fails to sell its goods to Americans.

9 The text describes German-Americans as …
  - **a** beer-loving immigrants.
  - **b** the scapegoats of anti-German feelings.
  - **c** the perfect example of integration.
  - **d** a caricature of integration.

3 WORKING WITH WORDS

A Complete each gap with an appropriate form of the word in brackets.

Many famous Americans are of German ___ [1] (originate), a fact that has not been ___ [2] (noticeable) by a lot of Americans. Levi-Strauss, John Boehner and Henry Steinway all share a common ___ [3] (inherit): their German ___ [4] (ancestor). German immigrants to the USA came from all over Germany. Originally they did not have political ___ [5] (ambitious), as they were mostly poor farmers. But their influence on America is obvious wherever you are. They became successful ___ [6] (brew), they brought pretzels, the Dachshund and bratwurst to the New World. They ___ [7] (prosperity) without a political lobby. At Oktoberfests all over the USA you can see people wearing traditional dress, eating German specialities and selling typically German pieces of arts and crafts, all of which contribute to the ___ [8] (preserve) of German culture in the USA.

B Go to File 21 on p. 184.

Take 3–4 words from the word bank below to write a sentence about the German-Americans in the USA. Share your sentences with your neighbour. Then collect all the sentences on the board.

origin	play down	successful/ly
culture	become	ethnic/ally
heritage	support	active/ly
group	build	cultural/ly
help	settle	integrate
immigrant	assimilate	common/ly

EXAMPLE *origins – play down – become – successful*

The German origins of many people were played down in order for those people to become successful in business.

SIMPLE PAST / PAST TENSE – PAST PERFECT

→ Grammar summary, pp. 217, 218

1 SPOT THE MISTAKES

Spot the mistakes and correct them. Explain why they are wrong.

1. ~~The president knew about the crisis for a long time when he was sworn into office.~~
2. ~~The police came into the room and arrested the man. He came to the USA illegally.~~
3. ~~He had been so happy to reach Germany, because he almost died during the journey.~~
4. ~~When his wife had come home, her husband had gone out, but he left a note on the table.~~

2 Complete the gaps with the correct verb form.

Javier Hernandez ___ [1] (be) born to Mexican immigrants in the USA. His parents ___ [2] (leave) Mexico years before. After they ___ [3] (come) to the "promised land", they soon ___ [4] (realize) how difficult it was to settle in this new and strange country. By the time the young boy ___ [5] (be) four years old, he ___ [6] (learn) to speak English fluently and even to read the local newspaper. At school he ___ [7] (take) an interest in languages and by the end of school he ___ [8] (outdo) his US-born peers completely. At the age of 16 his parents ___ [9] (decide) to move back to Mexico. When they ___ [10] (arrive) at their former hometown, most of the inhabitants there ___ [11] (move) somewhere else. Javier ___ [12] (convince) his parents to return to the USA again. After he ___ [13] (finally – achieve) full legal status in the USA, he ___ [14] (enrol) at a university in Boston. By the time he ___ [15] (be) 25, Javier ___ [16] (find) a well-paid job and ___ [17] (buy) a nice house for his family. If more illegal immigrants ___ [18] (have) a fairer chance in former years, the USA would have had less trouble with the immigration problem.

3 Translate the following sentences.

1. Nachdem die Familie aus ihrem Heimatland geflohen war, hofften sie auf ein besseres Leben in ihrem neuen Gastland.
2. Als wir das letzte Mal in den USA waren, erfuhren wir, dass das Einwanderungsgesetz vom Senat abgelehnt worden war.
3. Als der Junge nach Arizona kam, konnte er kein Wort Englisch sprechen.
4. Die Gruppe der Mexikaner wartete schon über 2 Stunden, als die Schleuser kamen.

WATCH OUT! Problem words (3)

Choose the correct word so that each sentence makes sense.

1. Immigration policy proves to be too sensible / sensitive an issue for many voters.
2. The cost of monitoring the Mexican-American border has actually / currently turned out be much higher than many politicians expected.
3. During / While the presidency, there was no overhaul of the immigration policy.
4. The new measures are the most sensible / sensitive so far with regards to the integration of illegal immigrants.
5. The Prime Minister is actually / currently on holiday and is unable to comment on the situation.
6. During / While many US states have opted for stricter immigration laws, the president has decided to campaign for an open-door policy.
7. The actual / current immigration figures published by the Home Office are misleading.

9 Living one's life

FOCUS

In our day and age, young adults like yourselves have lots of options in life. Both young men and women can freely do any of the following:

1 choose their friends
2 make use of various post-16 education options
3 select their sexual partners
4 decide whether they want to be married or not
5 determine if they want to have children or not
6 use all kinds of public spaces freely (transport, bars and pubs, sports venues, etc.)
7 decide how to dress
8 decorate their bodies in a variety of ways (including piercings, tattoos)
9 decide whether to eat and use animal products or not
10 choose what music to listen to and what films to watch, etc.

THINK:
A **Which of these freedoms do you fully enjoy, and where may there be some restrictions?**

PAIR:
B **Exchange your answers with a partner.**

Also, think of parts of the world where young adults do not enjoy one or more of these freedoms, and discuss the reasons why. The text on the following page ("Personal choices") may help you to tell each other what you think and know. Make a note of the words/ expressions you want to use.

SHARE:
C **Share your thoughts with the whole class. The following phrases may help you:**

We thought about young people in ... . We believe that they ...

We agreed/disagreed that ...

We were talking about point ...

The reason is / The reasons are ...

SITUATION

You're taking part in an international exchange programme for students sponsored by the German and the US governments. The project you're currently involved in requires you to conduct a series of interviews with young Americans living in rural areas. So you need to find someone to interview and prepare a number of possible **interview questions**.

STEP 1 Picturing the scene

A **Looking for someone who might be interesting to talk to, you've come across a young woman called Amie Shea who, in 2015, uploaded an article about her father onto the internet. You find the title appealing and so you start reading, and a picture of Amie's hometown and her dad appears in your mind.**

My Dancing Dad

Growing up, I always knew my dad was different, but it took me many years to figure out exactly how he was different from all the other dads. I grew up in a small town of about 3,000 people, in Northern Montana. With Glacier National Park 50 miles to the east our town slogan 'Where the Rockies meet the Plains' reflected our literal geographic location. It's the heart of oil, farming, and ranching country. The winters are long, cold, and dark. The summers are short, intense, and dry. People are tough, the men very rugged. It was not uncommon for dads to pick up their children from school or sports practice in oil-stained rig clothes or well-worn cowboy boots. ... →

06 **rugged:** rau

B **Which of the photos come(s) close to the idea you have of the dad when reading the text. Be prepared to explain your choice.**

3

4

1

2

8

9

5

6

7

C Now read the rest of the article and select the photo or photos that you think best fit(s) Amie's description of her dad. Be prepared to explain your choice.

In a town so small that everyone knew each other I feared people knowing that my dad was different. My dad loved music and the arts. His closet wasn't full of [...] Wrangler. His closet was full of boot-cut polyester pants straight from the '70s that spanned the full spectrum of the rainbow. My dad wasn't the classic rock or die-hard country fan like many of the other dads in town. My dad rocked the classics. And by classics I mean Mozart, Bach, Gershwin, and Brahms. By 'rocked' I mean listened peacefully to on a Sunday afternoon. Because my dad kept to himself more and didn't frequent the local bars or town gatherings, we all pretty much flew under the radar. [...]

In the fall of 1997, the year my dad was to turn 50, he decided to take dance lessons. In what I think was his attempt to prove he was still footloose and fancy free in his middle age, my father signed up for tap class at the only dance studio in town. My younger sister and I had been taking dance classes there for years and had worked our way into the most advanced classes our teacher had to offer. Michael Flatley, the Irish stepdancer, and his chorus of ladies were huge that year, touring the world and blowing up commercial slots on television with advertisements for *Riverdance* and the much anticipated follow up *Lord of the Dance.* I was excited that our studio was going to do our own version of *Riverdance* because it felt like something larger than my small town – or even the entire state. *Riverdance* was something performed on iconic stages in populous cities far away from our small town in Northern Montana. [...]

I'd love to recall happy memories of the three of us, dad, my sister, and me, practicing our *Riverdance* steps and bonding over our shared love of music and dance. Instead, I remember dreading dance class each week and worrying about what the kids at school would say when they saw my dad onstage in his black v-neck sequin shirt. I was certain I would die of embarrassment come our annual spring recital in May. As a teenager, all you want to do is fit in. And my tap dancing, harmonizing dad made me feel very different. The truth was, I desperately wanted my dad to be like the other dads. I wanted him to drink beer, chew tobacco, drive a big truck, work on the rigs, and listen to anything but NPR and classical music. Instead, my dad made his own wine and soap, drove a two-door Toyota from the '80s, sewed his own buttons back onto his shirts when they fell off, and struggled to understand my love for MTV and pop music.

In 8th grade, it was utterly embarrassing that my dad's midlife crisis was to become *Lord of the Dance* when it seemed like all the other dads were having affairs with younger women or buying flashy new cars. "Why can't he just buy a candy red convertible or run off with a 20-something blonde?" I often found myself wondering. Did he really have to be so different? Why did I have to be born into this!? Woe was me.

Years later, when my dad did finally come out to me, I was a junior in college at San Diego State University. It was September and my Grandma, his mom, was in the hospital waiting to have open-heart surgery. I was hundreds of miles away from everything when Dad called to update me. I thought the purpose of our phone call was Grandma, but my stomach flipped as he stumbled over some words about me maybe knowing something about him ... but he wasn't really sure. I remember wanting him to spit it all out – to simply say the words, "I AM GAY," and be done with it. But it wasn't that easy, for either of us. →

10 **span:** *umfassen*
30 **recital:** *Aufführung*
33 **NPR:** National Public Radio
40 **Woe was me:** *Wehe mir*

[...] I wish my dad had been able to be himself sooner. I think back to the tense years full of resentment and anger and I wish we could somehow go back and do them over. I wish there was a way to replace some of the yelling and tears with more conversations and laughs. I'm sure tap class would be much different now that I no longer resent having a 'different' dad. It helps that my dad's sexuality isn't the hefty secret it once used to be. However, life doesn't give 'do-overs,' so I'm thankful my dad is still here and that we have the relationship we do today. At 66, my dad's dancing abilities have become somewhat of a tradition at family gatherings and weddings now. [...] When I think back to the year my dad took tap classes, it makes me smile. We were and always have been slightly different. But, today, as an adult, I'm finally able to celebrate my dad for all the ways that he doesn't fit the mold. (954 words)

From: the website of Give a Damn Campaign, 18 June 2016

52 hefty: *groß*
57 not fit the mold (BE: mould): *unangepasst sein*

STEP 2 Identifying important moments

A You are interested in the development of Amie's feelings towards her dad. Find the phrases she uses to describe her feelings and put them into a chronological list. Make sure you understand what Amie's words mean.

- *I **feared** people knowing that my Dad was different*
-
-

B Find the passages in the text where Amie tells us about the following important moments in her life, and make a note of the language she uses to describe these moments:

1. when she feels as if she is entering another, more exciting world
2. when her family starts to become conspicuous
3. when her dad reveals that he is homosexual

STEP 3 Boosting your word power

You've noticed that the text contains language that might be useful for the task at hand. Work with this language to make it your own. Your solutions from Step 2 will enable you to do the following exercises.

A **Find the English equivalents of the following German expressions.**

German	English
sich outen	
… und fertig / … und Schluss, aus!	
versuchen nicht aufzufallen	
für sich alleine bleiben / sich von anderen fernhalten	
kultig / mit Kultstatus	
sich zu Tode schämen	
frei und ungebunden	

B **Go to File 22 on p. 184.**
Rewrite the following sentences using words or expressions from Step 2 instead of the underlined ones. The meaning of the sentences must remain the same, but you may have to adapt the sentence structure!

1 I <u>am really anxious about</u> telling my parents that I've damaged their car.
2 I'm trying <u>very hard</u> to convince my mother not to be my friend on Facebook.
3 I'm horrified by my friend's comments about women. They are <u>absolutely</u> ridiculous.
4 When former lovers talk about the end of their relationship, more often than not they <u>feel bitter and angry</u>.
5 I would <u>feel extreme</u> embarrassment if someone saw that photo of me.

STEP 4 Preparing for the interview

A **Together with a partner, formulate a series of interview questions. Try to make use of the words and expressions you've worked on in this unit so far, and make sure you know how to formulate questions. The box below serves as a reminder.**

Past	When exactly **did** you **realize** that …?
	Did you **experience** any antagonism due to …?
	Were you **raised** by …?
Present	**Does** your dad still **live** …?
	How **do** you **feel** about …?

B **Exhibit your questions around the classroom and take a communal vote on the 15 most interesting questions. Make sure they are written in good English.**

BEFORE YOU READ

Who are your role models: are they members of your family or community or are they public figures? In what ways do they qualify as role models? Do you think media celebrities can serve as role models?

CELEBRITY, YOUTH CULTURE AND THE QUESTION OF ROLE MODELS

Kirsty Fairclough-Isaacs

A The 2015 MTV Video Music Awards event was notable – not for the recognition of award recipients, but for the public spat between host Miley Cyrus and hip-hop artist Nicki Minaj. Whether real or staged, the hurling of insults and aggressive behaviour dominated mainstream press coverage of the ceremony surely much to the delight of MTV.

B Both Minaj and Cyrus are known for courting controversy and have been criticised for being "bad" role models for young people, particularly girls and young women. But what if the mainstream media considered that young people actually use incidents such as this and celebrity culture in a wider sense in a whole host of complex ways to negotiate their identities?

C A well-publicised survey of UK parents with children under ten years old voted both Cyrus and Minaj as the worst role models for their daughters. [...] The dislike of Minaj and Cyrus appears to be centred on their penchant for dressing provocatively and being outspoken about their sexuality. In predictable contrast, the Duchess of Cambridge was considered the most positive influence on young girls. The worst male offenders were musicians and performers Kanye West, Justin Bieber and former One Direction band member Zayn Malik.

Nicki Minaj

03 spat: *Zoff*
11 court controversy: (hier) *gerne Skandale provozieren*

Obsessed with celebrity

D Discourse in this vein is not a new phenomenon. Musicians and performers have long been considered to influence young people in negative ways. In the 21st century, the impact of celebrity culture on society, especially on young people, has come under scrutiny. Are today's youth obsessed with celebrity? Is this detrimental to society? Can celebrities ever have a positive influence on young people? Does celebrity culture really matter? These are complex questions to which there are few, if any, concrete answers. However, what is routinely ignored in mainstream media is young people's sense of agency.

E Much of the research and commentary surrounding such questions is centred on how celebrity culture may impact upon health and well-being in terms of eating disorders or mental health issues. The rise and dominance of social media sites such as Instagram and their links to the glorification of "super-skinny" celebrities have been cited as influences in the rise of eating disorders in young people. The British Psychological Society recently said experts warned that youngsters are finding it increasingly difficult to cope with images permeating from a celebrity culture in which thin bodies are celebrated, larger ones are ridiculed and children are sexualised.

Sense of identity

F It is logical to suggest that continual exposure to celebrity culture impacts in negative ways on some young people's senses of identity. This may well affect health and well-being, but how this happens and to what degree is incredibly complex. We must also consider the ways in which the media choose to present rather narrow ideas about how celebrities – particularly female ones – should behave. [...] Those whose behaviour falls outside of these narrow ideas are often condemned as being wayward, controversial and difficult. [...]

G The Celeb Youth project in the United Kingdom is an excellent example of much needed academic research into the field of celebrity and identity. It focused on the influence of celebrities in the construction of young people's aspirations. What is omitted from the media conversation about celebrities as role models is that many young people are more than capable of making informed, intelligent choices about which celebrities they follow and are becoming increasingly aware of the ways in which the media positions celebrities against each other in terms of race and class. Young people may connect with those that they feel best represent them as well as those that do not. Indeed, it is also fair to suggest that many young people have no interest in celebrity culture at all.

H It is the active and complex use of celebrity culture by young people to negotiate the world around them that is often lost in favour of sweeping generalisations about negative impacts. Perhaps rather than eliminating celebrity culture from the classroom, it could be used productively and constructively to allow young people to make sense of the world they are growing up in.

(679 words)

From: the website of The Conversation, 15 September 2015

34 **discourse:** (hier) *Gerede*
41 **detrimental:** *schädlich*
48 **sense of agency:** (hier) *Handlungskompetenz, Kontrolle*
62 **permeate:** *sich verbreiten, in die Gesellschaft eindringen*

1 MULTIPLE CHOICE

→ Skills, p. 204

Choose the most suitable option in each case.

1 At the 2015 MTV Awards …
  a the winners for once really deserved their awards.
  b the excellence of the ceremony was reported all over the media.
  c Miley Cyrus and Nicki Minaj were among the winners.
  d a public row on stage was exploited by the media.

2 Kanye West, Justin Bieber and Zayn Malik are mentioned as examples of …
  a criminal celebrities.
  b mainstream media darlings.
  c role models parents worry about.
  d singers slowly losing their celebrity status.

3 The writer thinks that mainstream research into the impact of celebrity culture on young people …
  a is an exciting new field of research.
  b asks too many difficult questions.
  c has not come up with any findings yet.
  d has focused too much on health issues.

4 According to experts, young people have problems with …
  a the large number of different social media sites.
  b the fact that celebrity culture is everywhere.
  c the one-dimensional media image of beauty.
  d the handling of child abuse in the media world.

5 Which of the following is not a view held by the writer?
  Young people …
  a are often misrepresented as helpless victims of celebrity culture.
  b need the right celebrities as role models to develop as persons.
  c are clever enough to tell a good from a bad celebrity role model.
  d should be exposed to discussions on celebrity culture at school.

2 SHORT-ANSWER QUESTIONS / SENTENCE COMPLETION

→ Skills, p. 200

Answer the following questions by providing the required information from the respective paragraphs.

1 Who do parents prefer to Miley Cyrus as a role model for their girls? [Paragraph C]
2 What, according to the writer, needs to be looked at more closely by those who research into the impact of celebrity culture on young people? [Paragraph F]

3 Which phrase tells us that the media tend to <u>dismiss</u> female celebrities <u>as disagreeable</u> if they don't act as expected? [Paragraph F]

4 The writer thinks it is important to find out what's going on in young people's minds when they admire someone and follow their example. She praises the ▬ for concentrating on this question. [Paragraph G]

5 Which phrase tells us that the writer criticizes the media for playing one celebrity off against another? [Paragraph G]

3 WORKING WITH WORDS

A **Go to File 23 on p. 185.**

Find the words/expressions in the text that match the following definitions. They follow the order of the text.

a	people who are presented with a prize for outstanding work	▬
b	shout abusive words	▬
c	what the papers report	▬
d	be carefully and closely examined	▬
e	ambitions	▬
f	left out	▬

B **Find German translations for these words/expressions.**

C **In the text you'll find the English equivalents of the following German expressions. Complete and match them.**

1 sich kein Blatt vor den Mund nehmen
2 auf ganz unterschiedliche Art und Weise
3 sehr zur Freude von
4 in Bezug auf
5 eine Vorliebe für
6 im weiteren Sinn
7 zugunsten

a ▬ ▬ *the delight of*
b *a penchant* ▬
c *be* ▬ *about*
d *in* ▬ *of*
e *in* ▬ ▬ ▬ *of ways*
f ▬ ▬ ▬ *sense*
g ▬ *terms* ▬

4 WRITING

Do <u>one</u> of the following writing tasks.
Make use of as many of the expressions from task 3 as possible.

1 Write about a celebrity of your choice who has been involved in some scandal(s) recently.

2 Write about somebody you would never recommend as a role model to your younger siblings.

3 Write about a recent society event that was received with a lot of media attention.

ADJECTIVES / ADVERBS

→ Grammar summary, p. 226

1 SPOT THE MISTAKES

Spot the mistakes and correct them. Explain why they are wrong.

1 ~~Same-sex marriage is viewed critical by many people in Muslim countries.~~
2 ~~The way some minor celebrities behave is total embarrassing.~~
3 ~~Women with careers often have significant fewer children.~~
4 ~~Hugely tattoos are popular these days, which many grandparents find shocking.~~
5 ~~You need to take the dress code in our bank serious if you want to work here!~~
6 ~~I wouldn't say I belong to any particularly youth culture.~~

2 Complete the sentences with adjectives or adverbs.

In the summer when everyone dresses in T-shirts, short dresses and shorts, we are ___ [1] (inevitable) faced with the fact that tattoos are everywhere: ___ [2] (reliable) work colleagues who know ___ [3] (exact) how best to present spreadsheets at a meeting, youngsters who ___ [4] (kind) give up their seats on the bus, ___ [5] (earnest) people who refuse to eat meat for ___ [6] (ethical) reasons but who ___ [7] (rare) make a fuss when you do. All of a sudden, their arms and legs display dragons, roses and, for the ___ [8] (especial) clever, quotes in foreign languages. Whereas in the past, tattoos were ___ [9] (large) associated with sailors and criminals, with time the tattoo has become an ___ [10] (acceptable) form of expression, so that today just about every celebrity sports one.

3 Translate these sentences into English.

1 Unsere Gesellschaft hat unglaublich langsam auf die rasch steigende Zahl fremdenfeindlicher Angriffe auf die Flüchtlinge reagiert, die vor kurzem bei uns angekommen sind.
2 Viele Flüchtlinge sind sich absolut sicher, dass sie hier ein besseres Leben führen werden, wenn sie hart arbeiten.
3 Oft sind sie furchtbar stressigen Befragungen und den unerwarteten Feindseligkeiten der einheimischen Bevölkerung ausgesetzt.
4 Die meisten Experten sind der Meinung, dass nur drastische Maßnahmen das Problem der Fremdenfeindlichkeit wirklich lösen können.
5 Sie raten den jungen Leuten in Deutschland, sich intensiv in der Lokalpolitik zu engagieren und so dafür zu sorgen, dass die richtigen politischen Entscheidungen getroffen werden.

WATCH OUT! Position of adverbs

Put the words in the correct order to make sentences. You may have to change the verb.

at the seaside / last summer / eat / the children / lots of ice cream
→ *The children ate lots of ice cream at the seaside last summer.*

1 look at / at the moment / Mary / some photos
2 happy / money / people / rarely / make
3 in London / find / last year / Nick / happiness
4 some people / in their lives / find / never / happiness
5 matter / all over the world / really / friends / to people
6 to London / he / never / be

10 In conflict with the law

FOCUS

A Match the crimes to the words in the box.

arson ▪ burglary ▪ fraud ▪ graffiti-spraying ▪ manslaughter ▪ murder ▪ rape ▪ robbery ▪ shoplifting ▪ vandalism

1 A woman kills her husband with poison; he has been physically abusing her for years. murder
2 Two teenagers threaten a pensioner and force her to give them her handbag. burglary
3 A group of drunken hooligans destroy the seats in a railway carriage; they are on their way to a football match. vandalism
4 A young man forces a teenage girl to have sex with him in his car; they are on the way home from a party where they have just met. rape
5 Two thieves break into the home of a billionaire; they steal works of art worth £5 million. robbery
6 A group of neo-nazis sets fire to an empty hotel that is being turned into a home for asylum seekers; nobody is injured. arson
7 Environmental activists cover the wall of a new bank building with colourful pictures of trees and flowers; the building stands on the site of an old park. graffiti-spraying
8 A British man meets a woman online who lives in Eastern Europe. She asks him to send her some money so that she can travel to the UK to meet him. "She" doesn't really exist. fraud
9 A twelve-year-old girl steals some lipstick from a supermarket; her parents are unemployed. shoplifting
10 A man speeds through a red light to get his wife, who is in labour, to hospital; he hits and kills a child crossing the street. manslaughter

B Rank the crimes in order, from the most to the least serious. Explain your ideas to the class.

In my opinion, ... is the most/least serious crime, because ...

I think vandalism / destroying a railway carriage is more/less serious than fraud/graffiti-spraying.

I disagree. I think ... is less / far more serious than ...

Crime and juvenile delinquency

When it is time to sentence convicted criminals, judges are always faced with the task of finding a punishment that fits the crime on the one hand, yet treats offenders in a fair and humane way on the other hand.

Repeat offenders and violent criminals can expect mandatory prison sentences, sometimes without the possibility of parole, particularly in cases of burglary, robbery, assault, sex-related crimes such as rape or drug-related offences such as drug trafficking and dealing. In the case of serious crimes, a judge may have to decide if the person accused of the crime should remain in custody or if they can be released on bail before they go on trial in a court of law. More lenient punishments may come in the form of suspended prison sentences, fines or community service for first-time offenders who become involved in petty crimes such as graffiti-spraying or vandalism. Rehabilitation centres, which prepare convicts for the time after they are released from prison, can help to re-integrate ex-convicts back into society and prevent them from reoffending.

Law enforcement agencies – police, prosecutors, courts, prisons – consume enormous sums of money yet are not very effective as a crime deterrent. A more cost-effective use of resources would be to prevent crime from happening in the first place. Some of the many reasons why people commit a crime are broken families, poor education or long-term unemployment. Although these factors are more common among disadvantaged social groups, wealthier members of society may also feel the temptation to commit "white-collar" crime such as bribery or tax evasion, for the simple reason of greed. Some people even consider committing a crime a game, or a way to overcome boredom.

Whatever crime prevention measures governments take, they need to focus on juvenile delinquency, as young offenders under the age of 18 may become the big-time criminals of the future. In many families both parents often work long hours away from home simply to make ends meet. As a result, many kids spend the afternoons after school without parental supervision. Lacking the maturity needed to make sensible decisions, they may be willing to take a risk to get their kicks. Peer pressure from other kids living in similar circumstances may also push them into breaking the law. Truancy or binge-drinking may be the first steps to shoplifting, hooliganism, gang violence or drug abuse. Such activities may, of course, also be influenced by the graphic images commonly projected by the media on TV shows, in the movies, in computer games or in cyberspace. Some juvenile delinquents may not be able to differentiate between fiction and reality and may see certain forms of anti-social behaviour as acceptable.

Some of the measures that have been adopted to get a grip on the problem include placing first-time offenders on probation or forcing them to take part in some form of "alternative" punishment. This may include various forms of community work that put something back into the community. Offenders can also be made to experience the consequences of their actions first-hand by being confronted with the victims of crime and their individual ordeals. An alternative way to deal with drug offenders is to offer them reduced sentences if they agree to attend drug rehabilitation programmes or counselling sessions. Such offenders may also be eligible for early parole from prison. (554 words)

First of all, make sure you understand the meaning of each of the highlighted words and phrases in the text above. If you are not sure, look them up in your dictionary. Then complete the tasks on the following page.

1 WORD FIELDS

A Make a list of words and phrases from the text related to the given categories.

a	types of crime/delinquency	*burglary,*
b	types of offender	*convicted criminals,*
c	types of punishment / alternative sentences	*prison sentence,*
d	possible causes of crime	*broken families,*

B Match the crimes you listed in 1A with the following categories:

a	crimes against people	
b	crimes against property	*burglary,*
c	both a and b	
d	neither a nor b	

C Add any other offences from the Focus page (p. 133) or that you can think of.

2 COLLOCATIONS

A Match words from box A to words from box B to make crime collocations.

A anti-social ▪ community ▪ convicted ▪ drug-related ▪ first-time ▪ juvenile ▪ parental ▪ peer ▪ rehabilitation ▪ white-collar

B behaviour ▪ crimes ▪ criminal ▪ delinquency ▪ offences ▪ offender ▪ pressure ▪ programme ▪ service ▪ supervision

B Go to File 24 on p. 185.
Complete the sentences with the most suitable collocation from 2A.

1 The ___ was taken from court and driven to prison to start his sentence.
2 Because she was a ___, Rachel was given a suspended sentence for possessing drugs.
3 The number of offenders under the age of 18 has risen sharply, so the new government has made tackling ___ its top priority.
4 Binge-drinking, vandalism, hooliganism and graffiti-spraying are all examples of ___.
5 The young offender became involved in petty crime because there was no proper ___ at home after school and too much ___ from the group of friends that he hung around with.
6 One alternative to a prison sentence or probation is some form of ___, where offenders work for the benefit of society.
7 Dealing, trafficking and other ___ are on the increase in many developed countries.
8 ___, such as tax evasion, bribery and fraud, are often considered less serious than violent crime, although the victims often suffer huge losses.
9 Drugs offenders are often sent on a ___ to try to get them to break their drug addiction.

10 THE DANGERS OF DRUG SMUGGLING B

SITUATION

Your school is doing a project week on drugs and drug abuse. As part of the project, your English class decides to look at the problem of drug smuggling, particularly of young people who return from holidays abroad carrying drugs. At the end of the project, you will **produce an information leaflet** warning young tourists about the dangers of drug trafficking.

STEP 1 Thinking about how innocent people get tricked

A Discuss these questions:

- Do you always know what is in your bag when you travel through an airport?
- Why do you think someone would carry something onto a plane for somebody they don't know well? Would you do so? Why/Why not?

B To find some background information for your leaflet, you click on several news articles about people who have been caught smuggling drugs while on holiday. One particular story, "I was tricked into smuggling drugs" (see text below), catches your attention. Before you read the article, skim the first three paragraphs quickly and discuss with a partner the following question:

- What basic mistake did Jessica make?

STEP 2 Looking for useful tips

You think Jessica's story might contain some useful tips for your information leaflet, so you decide to read it more closely.

A Work in groups of three and each make notes under one of the following headings:

"warning signs" Jessica didn't see	*Rose's "brother" would pay for holiday, …*
people affected by her actions (and how)	*uncle (because …), …*
stages of the legal process	*"routine" security check at airport, …*

I was tricked into smuggling drugs

*The names in this article have been changed.

Jessica, 23, was arrested and imprisoned after she was tricked into smuggling two kilograms of cocaine back from holiday.*

Looking back at it, I can't believe I was so naive. But at the time I didn't know anything about drug trafficking. I'm sure people who listen to my story will see the warning signs I missed and think "how could she be so stupid?" I definitely know a lot about drug smuggling now.

I was 21 and studying broadcast journalism at university when I got a call from my friend Rose* asking me if I wanted to go on holiday. I couldn't afford it and she told me her brother would pay. We were more good-time friends than best buddies. Rose kept on at me about the holiday and I eventually agreed to go to St Lucia with her for a week, and pay her brother back in instalments.

08 **St Lucia:** island state in the Caribbean 09 **in instalments:** *in Raten*

Rose said she knew a lot of people out there and was on her mobile the moment we landed. When we arrived at our hotel there was already a man waiting to greet us. He asked us if we were OK and then gave Rose quite a bit of spending money. I didn't think much of it, assuming he was a family friend. [...] On our last drunken night of the holiday, Rose told me she had ordered some duty-free alcohol to bring back home with us. She said friends from England had paid her to bring back the cheap booze and asked if I could carry some so she wasn't over the duty-free limit. I didn't question it. Why would I? It never occurred to me that Rose would smuggle drugs. She had never taken drugs before.

Excess baggage

At St Lucia airport, Rose handed me a duty-free receipt so I could pick up the alcohol. Once we got through customs, we were each given two large bottles of rum in blacked out bottles. I jokingly asked her: "It's not drugs is it?" and she laughed. "Come on. You know I don't do drugs," she said.
We flew home without consequence, landed in England, and picked up our baggage. But as we were strolling through 'nothing to declare', a security lady approached us. She asked to check our bags and I agreed, thinking it was a routine check. She found our rum, shook the bottles, and then asked Rose and I to talk to security staff in separate rooms.
At this point I still thought everything was a big misunderstanding and wasn't at all worried. That was until security staff told me our rum bottles were filled with class A illegal drugs. I was totally confused.
[...] And then I was arrested [and] driven to a police cell and left there for the weekend, shivering in the summer dress I had flown home in.

Behind bars

[...] I was allowed to make one phone call, and let my uncle know what had happened. I didn't want to worry my parents unnecessarily – I honestly still believed it was all a big misunderstanding that would be sorted out quickly. Everything hit home as soon as I got into the court room. My father was sitting in the public gallery, crying.
That was the moment I realised it could be really serious. I honestly thought I was going to get bail – if only I could explain my point of view, they would let me go. So when the magistrates said the charges were too serious for bail and that Rose and I had to remain in custody, I cried. We were driven to a women's prison where all my clothes and possessions were taken. I was put in a shared cell with an open toilet. [...] I thought I would never see my friends, boyfriend, or my family ever again.

Awaiting the trial

I spent three long weeks in prison until my uncle cleared out his bank account bailing me out. Then there was an agonising year-long wait until my crown court trial. Rose and I were facing charges of trafficking five kilograms of crack cocaine between us. If a jury found me guilty, my lawyer told me I would be looking at ten to fifteen years jail time. The sheer enormity of that didn't register. I had to go back to university and try to get on with normal life knowing I could soon be spending a decade behind bars. During this time, I cut off all contact with Rose and began to realise she might not be as innocent as she claimed. But my lawyer told me that if she was convicted, I would then have a higher chance of being found guilty – so at the same time I wanted her to be OK. →

23 **without consequence:** (here) without any problems
24 **stroll:** walk casually
31 **class A illegal drugs:** drugs that are considered to be the most dangerous
38 **hit home:** *plötzlich klar werden*
46 **agonising:** extremely worrying
46 **crown court:** court in the UK which deals with serious criminal cases, with a judge and jury
47 **crack cocaine:** highly addictive form of cocaine
47 **look at sth:** (here) be threatened with sth (e.g. a prison sentence)

The trial finally began, and it was then that the cracks in Rose's story began to show. Under interrogation she kept changing her mind about what happened and told the court she didn't have an older brother. I was shocked – I thought he was the one who paid for the holiday. It was terrifying when it was my turn to give evidence. I was scared I would slip up on a lawyer's question and come across as guilty. The jury then couldn't reach a verdict that day, so I had to go home and wait for morning. I didn't sleep a wink that night. I instead spent my time saying goodbye to everybody and hugging my dog. I felt sure the jury would find me guilty.

Justice?

Rose and I were to get our verdict together. Her name was read out first … (933 words)

From: *the website of themix*, 29 September 2015

55 slip up: *einen Fehler machen*

B Share your notes with the other members of your group.

STEP 3 Thinking about a suitable punishment

The story ends before you find out what happened to Rose and Jessica, but you have your own ideas. Discuss these questions in your group.

1 Think about the two young women, Jessica and Rose. How would you describe their characters? Why do you think they acted the way they did?
2 Speculate about what happened to each of the two women in court. Were they found guilty or not guilty? What punishment would you hand out to them? Explain your reasons.
3 Your teacher has the end of the article. Read what happens and compare it with your ideas. Do you agree with the outcome?
4 Add a fourth category to your notes in Step 2 based on the last part of the story.

the effects on Jessica	*upset in magistrates' court,*

STEP 4 Boosting your word power

Jessica's story contains useful words and phrases that you could use in your leaflet.

A Which "legal" words and phrases match these definitions? They are all in the text (ll. 35–59).

1 an official who acts as a judge in the lowest courts of law
2 an official claim made by the police that somebody has committed a crime
3 a room for one or more prisoners in a prison or police station
4 a formal examination of evidence in court by a judge and often a jury, to decide if somebody accused of a crime is guilty or not
5 a person who is qualified to advise people about the law and to represent them in court
6 the information that is used in court to try to prove something
7 a group of members of the public who listen to the facts of a case in a court and decide whether or not somebody is guilty of a crime
8 a decision that is made by a jury in court, stating if somebody is considered guilty of a crime or not

B Complete this paragraph with the correct form of the verbs from the box. Seven of them are in the text (ll. 35–59).

face ▪ find ▪ get ▪ give ▪ reach ▪ release ▪ remain ▪ spend ▪ stand ▪ walk

At first, Jessica thought that she would ___[1] bail when she appeared at the magistrates' court. However, the magistrate said the charges against her were too serious to ___[2] her on bail and she had to ___[3] in custody. The magistrate told her that she was ___[4] charges of smuggling class A drugs into the UK and she would have to ___[5] trial at a crown court. At this point, she started to worry that she might have to ___[6] ten years behind bars. She was also afraid that if the jury ___[7] Rose guilty of smuggling, she would be convicted too. However, Rose's story fell apart when she started to ___[8] evidence at the trial. Even so, it took the jury more than a day to ___[9] a verdict. After the jury announced their verdict the next day, Jessica was told she could ___[10] free from court.

Write a short paragraph explaining what happened to Jessica, from the moment she was given the bottles of rum to the time she left the court. (Don't forget that you can use the passive to describe things that happened to somebody.)

Jessica was given two blacked out bottles of rum at St Lucia airport. At Heathrow she was asked …

STEP 5 Brainstorming tips

In your information leaflet you want to give tips on how to avoid the mistakes that Jessica made. Look again at the "warning signs" in your notes from Step 2 and think of four or five tips on how to avoid them.

Never … !

Don't (ever) … !

Always (make sure that) … !

STEP 6 Preparing the information leaflet

A Work in your groups. Use the information you have collected in Steps 2 and 3, the phrases from Step 4 and your tips from Step 5 to write an information leaflet, warning young travellers of the dangers and consequences of drug smuggling. In your leaflet, you should:

- Give tips to avoid being tricked into smuggling.
- Explain the legal consequences of drug smuggling.
- Warn of the effects legal proceedings can have on your life.
- Point out the effect the situation can have on your family and friends.

B Present your leaflet to the class.

BEFORE YOU READ

Collect reasons on the board why people commit crimes or criminal acts? Which factors do you think are most important? Are there different reasons for young people?

THE 16-YEAR-OLDS
who have committed 86 crimes each

A A delinquent minority will commit an average of 86 crimes each by the age of 16, with less than 4 per cent responsible for nearly half of all youth crime. A lack of a sense of morality – rather than the opportunity to commit crime or social background – was found to be the most important factor in teenagers breaking the law. The 16 per cent who admitted having the weakest moral sense and self-control were responsible for 60 per cent of all the recorded crimes.

B Cambridge researchers studied 700 teenagers over five years in Peterborough, chosen […] for its average size, crime level and social make-up. From the age of 12 to 16 youngsters were asked about their attitudes to lawlessness and asked what criminal things they had done. Their answers were cross-checked with police records. Crime occurred when teenagers with little sense of right and wrong were in areas where people were unlikely to intervene – primarily city centres or run-down housing estates.

C The findings could have profound implications for policing and youth crime policy. Last year the number of under-18s in custody in England and Wales averaged more than 2,000, and youth offending remains a source of political controversy. Nationally, the latest crime figures show that under-17s are responsible for 23 per cent of police recorded crime – more than a million crimes.

D The study suggests that most of those crimes will be committed by a tiny minority of young people. A typical example of this lawless group is Nathaniel Moffett, a 16-year-old from Bristol who was jailed for five years last February after committing a string of armed robberies. In a single court case Moffett admitted five robberies, three attempted robberies and three charges of possessing a bladed article. He led an older accomplice in a series of attacks on women and children last year, including threatening a 14-year-old with a rusty blade to get his mobile phone and 21p in change. He was caught after punching a pregnant woman in the stomach to steal her wallet while her five-year-old daughter looked on. He wrote on his Facebook page: "I'm nothing but a bully that can't hit a man cus I no I will get banged [beaten] so I have to hit girls."

18 social make-up: the different groups in society
62 cus: (slang) because
62 no: (slang) know

E The research also offers some insights into last year's riots, notably on the question why some young people went on a lawless rampage while others did not. Teenagers who avoided crime did so not because they feared the consequences or lacked the chance, but because they saw it as wrong. The research, the most comprehensive study of youth crime in Europe, found that a third of teenagers did nothing wrong at all over five years.

F Professor Per-Olof Wikstrom, who led the Cambridge study, said: "Many young people are 'crime averse' and simply don't perceive crime as a possible course of action ... The idea that opportunity makes the thief – that young people will inevitably commit crime in certain environments – runs counter to our findings." He added that policy-makers should put an emphasis on teaching young people moral boundaries. "We need to focus on developing policies that affect children and young people's moral education and cognitive nurturing – which aids the development of greater self-control."

G Camila Batmanghelidjh, the founder of Kids Company, [...] said: "Society is lecturing children and young people about how well behaved they should be but it's not behaving in a way that warrants respect. It's a given that it's a good thing to teach right from wrong, but really where children observe it the most is in experience: it's 'have you looked after me?' and 'do you do what you preach?'"
One 14-year-old boy who attends a Kids Company youth club in London said: "I got caught stealing and was given a second chance. That's when I realised it was wrong. Nobody told me I shouldn't do it and my mum still doesn't know I did it."

H Graham Beech, the director of the crime reduction charity Nacro, said: "In my view the key to preventing crime by the small number of young people who are most likely to get entrenched in crime is to get in early, instil positive attitudes and teach them how to solve their everyday problems in a better way."

(752 words)

From: Emily Dugan, *The Independent*, 24 June 2012

85 **cognitive:** connected with mental processes of understanding
86 **nurturing:** *Erziehung*
92 **warrant sth:** deserve sth
92 **it's a given that ...:** everybody knows that ...
107 **entrenched in sth:** *in etw verstrickt*
107 **instil sth:** *(jdm) etw anerziehen*

1 MULTIPLE MATCHING

→ Skills, p. 200

Match the following aspects (1–10) to the paragraphs (A–H) in the text. There are two more aspects than you need.

1 a description of the methods of the Cambridge study
2 a typical career of one of the minority of criminal youths
3 many juveniles think that crime is morally wrong
4 international reactions to the study's findings
5 reasons why teenagers did not take part in urban unrest
6 some recent statistics on juveniles in prison
7 the fundamental findings of the Cambridge study
8 the importance of role models in society
9 the political controversy caused by the study
10 three suggestions to prevent juvenile crime

2 GAPPED SUMMARY

→ Skills, p. 202

Fill in the gaps with words from the corresponding sections of the text. Use only one word for each gap. Give the number of the line in which you found the word/expression. [Paragraphs A–C]

A huge number of juvenile crimes, i.e. those carried out by underage teenagers, are committed by a tiny ___[1] ___[2] that is responsible for almost 50% of recorded crimes. According to a recent survey, these criminal teenagers are characterized by a complete absence of ___[3]. Those teenagers who commit crimes do so because they have too little ___[4], rather than because they have the opportunity or come from a deprived social background. The study compared teenagers' ___[5] to delinquency and found that most crimes took place in ___[6] residential areas or in city centres. The report may have ___[7] ___[8] for the way law-enforcement agencies deal with young offenders in future. The high number of youths under the age of 18 ___[9] ___[10] and the latest official crime figures mean that youth crime is still a topic of ___[11] ___[12].

3 SHORT-ANSWER QUESTIONS / SENTENCE COMPLETION

→ Skills, p. 200

Answer the following questions and complete the following sentences with information from paragraphs D–H of the text.

1 Nathaniel Moffett was charged with a number of ___ at his court case, because he had tried to steal money or other items from different people without success.
2 Those teenagers who didn't go ___ in the riots of the previous year obviously saw crime as something that is wrong.
3 In paragraph F young people who have a strong sense of morality are described as ___.
4 The common belief that young people faced with an opportunity are likely to commit crimes ___ the findings of the report.
5 According to Professor Wikstrom, we need to improve teenagers' ___ to help them make the right decisions in future.
6 What does Graham Beech want to encourage in children and young adults in order to prevent them from becoming criminals?

4 WORKING WITH WORDS

A Rewrite the following sentences so that their meaning remains the same. Use words and phrases from the text to replace the parts of the sentence in brackets. You may have to adapt them to fit.

1 A tiny minority of teenagers who have ___ (absolutely no idea of what is right or wrong) is responsible for the majority of juvenile crime. [Paragraph A]
2 Other factors leading to youth offending are the social background of the offenders and the ___ (chance to break the law). [Paragraph A]
3 This report presents the ___ (results) of a recent study on juvenile crime. [Paragraph C]
4 Two 16-year-olds ___ (said that they were responsible for) carrying out the robberies in Lake Street. [Paragraph D]
5 The burglar was caught when the police arrived, but his ___ (person who helps a criminal) managed to escape. [Paragraph D]

6 The rioters turned back at the bridge because they ___ (were worried about what might happen) if they attacked the police station. [Paragraph E]

7 The majority of young people never come into contact with the law because they don't see crime as a possible ___ (thing to do). [Paragraph F)

8 The best way to prevent juvenile delinquency is to give young people lessons about ___ (the difference between right and wrong). [Paragraph F]

9 Behaving responsibly and sensibly unfortunately does not always ___ (make people admire and look up to you). [Paragraph G]

B **Go to File 25 on p. 185.**

Complete these sentences with the correct prepositions. Use your dictionary if necessary.

The majority ___[1] young people have a positive attitude ___[2] obeying the law, although there are a few juveniles who have no sense ___[3] morality. In one recent example ___[4] delinquency, two youths admitted ___[5] the police that they were responsible ___[6] vandalizing a bus stop. The police charged them ___[7] vandalism, but a charge ___[8] possessing drugs was dropped because ___[9] a lack ___[10] evidence. ___[11] another incident, the police questioned a well-known drug addict ___[12] a robbery ___[13] which a masked man threatened an old lady ___[14] a baseball bat. The addict recently went ___[15] trial ___[16] the attack and he was jailed ___[17] 18 months. The judge also ordered him to take part ___[18] a rehabilitation programme. One way to get a grip ___[19] the problem ___[20] juvenile delinquency is to put more emphasis ___[21] teaching young people ___[22] moral boundaries. We could deal ___[23] the problem more effectively ___[24] focussing ___[25] education and giving people a second chance. ___[26] this way, offenders could learn to see crime ___[27] being wrong.

5 TALKING

Work in pairs. Discuss the following questions together, then share your results with the class.

- Are there any excuses, or mitigating reasons, for young people becoming involved in crime? What might they be? Give examples.
- Does our society do enough to provide positive role models for young people? Who might they be? Give examples.
- What sort of negative role models does society provide? What can we do to reduce their influence?

1 RESEARCH PROJECT

You could add some extra information to your leaflet in Part B by finding out the penalties for drug smuggling in different countries, and the effects of drug-taking and addiction on health. Work in two groups.

Group A: Each person chooses one of the countries from the list and researches the penalties for drug trafficking and possession of different classes of drugs.

Australia ▪ Britain ▪ Egypt ▪ Germany ▪ India ▪ Indonesia ▪ Iran ▪ Malaysia ▪ Mexico ▪ Morocco ▪ the Netherlands ▪ Portugal ▪ Saudi Arabia ▪ Singapore ▪ Sweden ▪ the United Arab Emirates ▪ the USA

Collect your information in a table and share it with the group.

Group B: Each person chooses one of the drugs from the list and researches the negative health consequences of drug-taking or addiction for each drug.

cocaine ▪ ecstasy ▪ heroin ▪ LSD ▪ marijuana ▪ methamphetamines

Collect your information in a table and share it with the group.

2 VIEWING

→ Skills, p. 196

You are going to watch a series of video clips showing a case involving a juvenile offender in a British Youth Court.

16–20

A Watch the first clip, then discuss the following question:
What should be the main aim of sentencing young offenders?
a punishment **b** rehabilitation **c** compensation (i.e. paying for damage caused)

B Watch the second clip, then discuss the following question:
Should Robert's previous convictions influence his sentence?

C Watch the third clip, then discuss the following question:
Should Robert's family situation be considered when he is sentenced?

D Watch the fourth clip, then discuss which of the following sentences Robert should get:
- compensation and reparation: compensating the victim (e.g. £75 for mobile phone and money), and making amends to either the victim or the community at large (24 hours community service)
- a fine (£50 financial penalty + £75 compensation order for the mobile phone and money)
- a youth rehabilitation order: curfew (7 p.m. to 7 a.m.) for 3 months + weekly supervision meetings with a Youth Offending Team for 12 months + required school attendance
- a detention and training order: 4 months (half in custody including education and vocational training + half monitored in the community

E Watch the final clip, then say whether you agree with the judge's sentence. Explain your answers.

3 GROUP DISCUSSION

→ Skills, p. 210

You are now the panel of magistrates in a magistrates' court who have to decide the sentence for Rachel S.

Rachel S., 18, has been caught shoplifting a dress and a pair of jeans worth £270 from a boutique. She wanted to sell the clothes to get money to buy drugs. Rachel has become addicted to heroin since she left school and couldn't find a job. Her mother works as a cleaner in a local factory, her step-father is unemployed and an alcoholic. Rachel usually lives with her boyfriend, a convicted dealer and petty criminal, but she often spends nights sleeping rough when they fight or have rows. Rachel has been caught shoplifting twice before and was let off with a caution. She has also been caught in possession of small amounts of heroin.

Preparation phase

Choose one of these suggested sentences and briefly say why you favour it.

- a prison sentence (you decide how long)
- a suspended prison sentence with a community service order
- a suspended prison sentence with probation
- a suspended prison sentence with a compulsory rehabilitation programme
- a fine and compensation (you decide how much) for the boutique owner
- a warning

Interaction phase

Discuss all the suggestions above and try to reach an agreement on which one(s) is/are most suitable. Be prepared to compromise if your suggestion is not chosen.

4 MATERIAL-BASED ESSAY

→ Skills, pp. 206, 208

Comment on this statement, using ideas from the cartoons below, the video and your discussion.

"It is much more important to rehabilitate young offenders than to punish them."

BEFORE YOU READ

Are you "on call" for your friends 24 hours a day? Do you switch off your smartphone at any time during the day? (When? Why?) How would you feel about being "on call" if your friends were your work colleagues?

By: Gaby Hinsliff January 1, 2013

THE MERGE: HOW OUR WORK-LIFE BALANCE IS CHANGING

Technology is making it easier to juggle work and home – and it's blurring the gap between our public and private lives.

A

How she explained the background drone of the hairdryers is anyone's guess, but the woman next to me at the hairdresser the other week was clearly not there to be pampered. Phone jammed to her ear, laptop open on her knee, she was blithely conducting a conference call while wearing highlighter foils.

B

Welcome to the world of the work-life merge, the term coined by Facebook executive Emily White to describe a life in which work and free time are no longer neatly compartmentalised but seamlessly jumbled up together. It's a world in which it's no big deal to take two hours out of the working day for something personal, but also routine to spend the same time answering emails on a Sunday: where even executives can leave at 5.30pm to have tea with the children [...] but be back on the laptop by 9pm.

C

It's different from the old idea of seeking a balance, which tends to treat work and life as two conflicting opposites – one all hard grind, the other all pleasure – because practitioners of the "merge" tend to be driven people who love their jobs. They want to customise the conventional corporate day to suit them. As Katie Bickerstaffe, the British CEO of Dixons, recently put it: "I love what I do, but I also love my family. I don't think there's any reason you can't do both. You just have to make sure you marshal your resources and yourself." Which for Bickerstaffe means a four-day week, taking Fridays out with her young daughters – but they're long days, often involving overnight trips, and she's in constant contact with the office even on Fridays.

D

The advantages for working parents of this kind of merged lifestyle are obvious, of course: but what's new is that, with the government extending the right to request flexible working patterns to everyone from 2014, it's likely to spread. And what really makes the merge timely is that it taps into two important trends in British working life. The first is a tough new economic reality, which means those torn between work and home life often can't afford to reduce their hours: so the emphasis is on reinventing the time we have. And the second trend is the seamless blurring of private and public life, made possible by technology.

E

Home broadband and Wi-Fi on the move have already liberated us physically from our desks, but the real game-changer is the platforms we use, because that's what has finally dissolved the boundaries between work and play. When I first started on Fleet Street, back in 1996, sitting down at a keyboard simply spelled work: there was nothing much else to do online. Email had yet to catch on, Google was still a twinkle in student eyes and social media didn't exist. Now, work messages jostle with private ones in every inbox, professional contacts become indistinguishable from friends on Facebook, and every work-related search brings up endless other

01 **drone:** *Summen*
05 **blithely:** *unbekümmert*
06 **highlighter foils:** *Folien, die verwendet werden um Strähnchen in die Haare zu färben*
10 **compartmentalise sth:** divide sth into separate sections, so that one thing does not affect the other
19 **grind:** tiring, boring activity
24 **Dixons:** consumer electronics retailer
49 **Fleet Street:** street in London, originally the site of many national newspapers

clickbait. Is surfing Twitter work if you're ostensibly checking for breaking news – or play, given you inevitably become sucked into conversation?

F

The downside of this permanently "switched-on" life, of course, is that there's nowhere to hide. Everyone's permanently checking in, which means the working day has become both longer and more fast-moving: the decision cycle is massively speeded up, as nothing has to wait until people get back to the office tomorrow. Snap judgments in the middle of the night, critical conversations taken on the hoof, are the new norm. […]

G

Merged life can be frantic, messy, and short on sleep: one businesswoman I interviewed recently told me she often knocks off for the school run, but pays for it by getting up at 5am to work before the children are up. But she enjoys the feeling of being able to switch back and forth between school-gate mum and professional across the course of a working day: it's not just about reconciling different demands on her time, but bringing together both facets of her identity, although the mental gear-change required each time isn't easy. […]

H

And while this multitasking lifestyle has been pioneered by working women, the merge may be surprisingly well-suited to many working fathers, too. Surveys suggest working from home, a classic way of blending professional and domestic life, appeals

particularly strongly to men: even David Cameron has described how living over the Downing Street shop makes family life in some ways easier as prime minister than it was in opposition, since he can nip up to see the children during the day. Merged living isn't a panacea, of course. It's not easy for anyone whose job requires fixed physical presence, from binman to brain surgeon. And mingling work and play can be downright miserable for anyone who hates their job, and lives for the moment they can leave it all behind. But at least the occasional chaos of the merge feels more achievable than the smug triumphalism of "having it all" – and far less retrograde than throwing in the towel. Better merged than submerged, perhaps, drowned beneath the weight of guilt and impossible expectations.

(832 words)

From: *The Guardian*, 1 January 2013

67 **snap:** *spontan*
68 **on the hoof:** while doing sth else at the same time
97 **smug:** *selbstgefällig*
98 **triumphalism:** *Triumphiergehabe*
98 **retrograde:** *rückschrittlich*

1 MULTIPLE CHOICE

→ Skills, p. 204

Choose the most suitable option in each case.

1 "The work-life merge" (l. 7) describes a life in which …
- **a** time spent at work and at home are equally balanced.
- **b** executives spend time answering emails on Sundays.
- **c** jobs and personal life can be completely mixed up.
- **d** executives can take time off work to look after their children.

1 LISTENING

→ Skills, p. 196

You are going to listen to part of a radio interview comparing gender equality for professional women in the USA and some emerging economies.

languish: *verkümmern, dahindümpeln*
stall out: stop moving forward
hunch: feeling, suspicion
flash in the pan: sudden, but short-lived, success
leapfrog sb: jump over sb
fatigue: tiredeness
flat-lined: at a low level, not increasing
lose heart: become depressed
cite sth (as a reason): give sth (as a reason)
disengage from sth: move away from sth

Go to File 27 on p. 187.

23

A Listen to the first part of the interview and answer these questions.

1. What are the BRIC countries?
2. What happened to the two branches of Standard Chartered bank in India that were set up for and staffed entirely by women?
3. How many CEOs of top companies in the USA are women?
4. How many CEOs of top companies in Brazil are women?
5. In which of the countries mentioned do women seem to be the most ambitious?
6. In which of the countries mentioned do women seem to be the least ambitious?

24

B Copy the table below and read the questions. Listen to the second part of the interview and complete the notes.

		USA	BRIC countries
a	How much is the economy growing?	▪ *flat-line / nothing*	▪ ___ *% per year*
b	What are the employment opportunities?	▪ ___ *unemployment*	▪ ___ *job opportunities*
c	How do professional women feel about their career chances?	▪ ___	▪ ___ *by the opportunities*
d	What are the options for childcare / maternal leave?	▪ *inadequate options*	▪ *extended* ___ ▪ ___ *domestic help*
e	How does this affect women's career chances?	▪ *average* ___ *year break* ▪ *lose* ___ *% of earning power*	▪ ___

2 RESEARCH PROJECT

Look at the list of emerging technologies mentioned in the text on p. 150 (ll. 36–40). Research one of them and prepare a 3-minute presentation for the class.

Think about these questions:

- What is the technological breakthrough?
- How does it combine with other technologies?
- What possible effects will it have on jobs and the world of work?

3 MATERIAL-BASED ESSAY

→ Skills, pp. 206, 208

"Flexible working hours are the only answer to a better work-life balance."

Write a comment on this statement, using ideas and information from the graph and text below, and giving your own opinion.

Today (June 30, 2014), the UK law has changed, meaning that any employee will have the right to ask their employer to change their working patterns, regardless of why they may need to. [...] Studies show that this is what the public want – and it isn't just mums who want flexibility. Nearly half of British men want to work flexible hours so that they can put their family first, according to a recent survey by Jobsite, and 75 per cent of all 25–34-year-olds would like to request flexible working if they were given the opportunity to do so.
But it isn't just about childcare – the Government has said it hopes the move towards flexible working will remove the "cultural assumption" that flexible working only applies to parents or carers, and make workplaces "fit for the 21st century". From: *The Daily Telegraph*, 30 June 2014

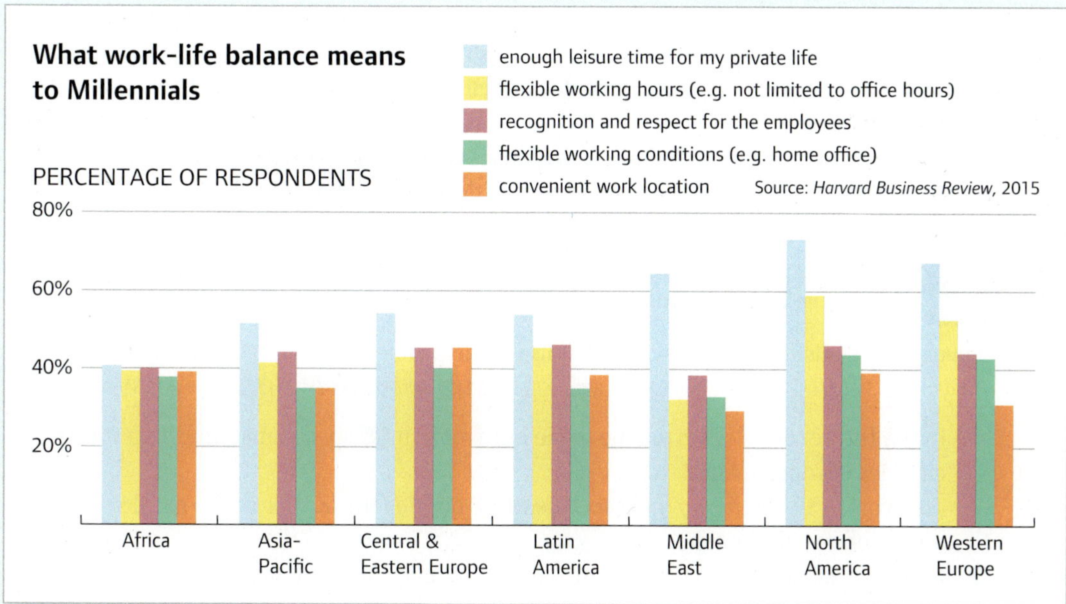

4 ARGUMENTATIVE WRITING

→ Skills, pp. 206, 208

"Robots and computers are soon going to take over all aspects of our working life. Humans will be made redundant."

Do you agree with this statement?

REPORTED SPEECH

→ Grammar summary, p. 221

1 **SPOT THE MISTAKES**

Spot the mistakes and correct them. Explain why they are wrong.

1 ~~I asked Jake's secretary if he left to pick up his kids an hour ago.~~
2 ~~She told that he will be back in the office later this evening.~~
3 ~~When I saw Jake, he said that he was only out of the office for two hours.~~
4 ~~I asked him if he thinks he has to be on call 24 hours a day.~~
5 ~~He replied that the working practices in many companies have changed in recent years.~~

2 **Put the following statements into reported speech.**

1 The Fourth Industrial Revolution will cause many jobs to be lost. *The author stated that* ▬
2 The changes have been gathering pace over the last two decades. *She added that* ▬
3 Steam-driven machines were used to mechanize production in factories in 18th-century Britain. *She pointed out that* ▬
4 The use of electricity at the start of the 20th century turned many factories into production lines. *She explained that* ▬
5 People who can afford to access the digital world have gained the most from the Fourth Industrial Revolution. *She claimed* ▬
6 Low-wage jobs will become rarer in developed economies. *She argued that* ▬
7 I am convinced that talent will be the most important factor in production. *She said that* ▬
8 Will it ever be possible to reduce social tensions? *The author wondered* ▬
9 Why are middle-class incomes stagnating or decreasing? *She wanted to know* ▬

WATCH OUT! Problem words (4)

Choose the correct highlighted word or phrase to complete each sentence.

Levels of dissatisfaction may well rise/raise if the problem of inequality is not solved.
→ *Levels of dissatisfaction may well rise if the problem of inequality is not solved.*

1 In the future, our clothes will be made out from/in/of special materials that create electricity from sunlight.
2 The woman sitting next / next to / nearly / besides the author at the hairdresser's was on the phone all the time.
3 In the actual/actually/current/currently economic situation, many parents can't afford to work less.
4 Rachel and Simone are looking after / looking for / searching after a company where they can share a job.
5 The Fourth Industrial Revolution is expected to cause displacement of jobs in the next day / in the next time / in the next future / in the near future.
6 The managers had to check/control/proof/prove the work that the robots had done.
7 The factory workers stood/stayed/kept/further working until they had finished all the orders.
8 The last/least/latest/newest surveys seems to confirm the theory of a new Industrial Revolution.

12 Our technological future

FOCUS

B

A

C

D

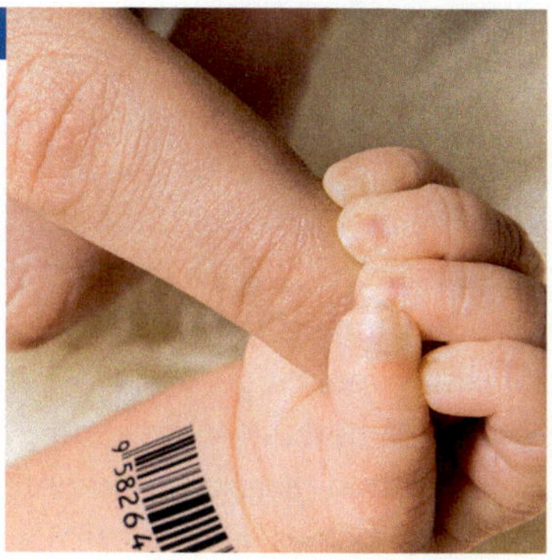

E

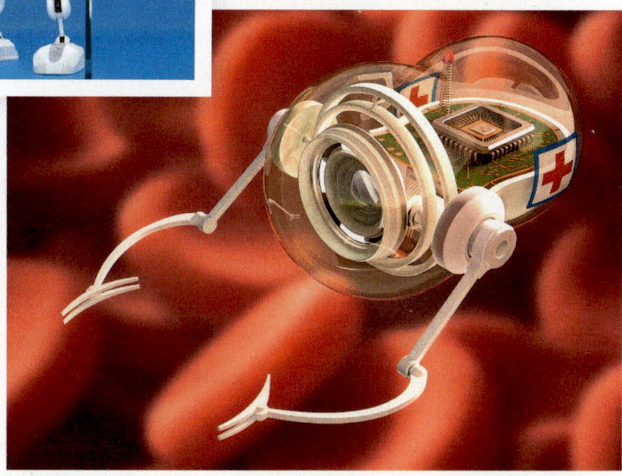

Look at the photos and do the following tasks with a partner:

1 What do the pictures on this page show?
2 Which of these technologies will have the biggest impact on your own lives in the future?
3 Together write a catchy or creative slogan as a caption for each picture, e.g. for Photo A *"A smart house is a happy house"*.

The impact of technological progress

Humanity has seen great leaps in digital technology in recent years. Innovations such as smartphones, cloud computing or multi-touch tablets have transformed the way we work and live. There is no end in sight to the possibilities that might be offered by scientific breakthroughs. Those people who are optimistic about the future point out that new technologies have the potential to change our lives for the better, to improve the way we do business and to enhance the global economy. According to them, we will benefit from technology's rapid growth and could soon be living in a world that looks like a science-fiction film. Whether this turns out to be true or not, one can say for sure that some technology trends will shape our future. For instance, because of greater flexibility and intelligence advanced robotics will be able to take on tasks which used to be considered too delicate or expensive to automate. Modern energy-storage devices are expected to make electric vehicles cost-competitive and may help people in remote areas of developing countries who lack access to electricity.

Yet, one could argue that technological progress is a double-edged sword. Despite the benefits of state-of-the-art technology, our society is also confronted with some immediate problems. Disruptive innovations like the Internet of Things or self-driving cars will make our lives more convenient, but in the developed countries one can already notice an overdependence on technology, which may encourage laziness, reduce social skills or result in health problems. Thanks to environmental technology an increasing number of communities want to become carbon neutral. Yet, it is the products and waste of technological progress that have brought about global ecological problems in the first place. Scientific achievements will help extend the human lifespan. It is predicted that within a few decades we will have nanobots in our blood stream that will keep us healthy and may even increase human intelligence by interacting with our biological neurons. Nevertheless, a greater life expectancy will make it even more difficult to come to grips with the consequences of the world's population explosion. Technological advances may indeed pose a threat to civilization itself. For instance, the development of new nuclear weapons or autonomous military robots could start another arms race between the world's superpowers. Therefore, maybe the biggest challenge for modern society will be to find ways to contain the destructive power of technology.

Another much-debated topic is genetic engineering. One source of controversy is genetic testing, which determines if families can pass on genetically transmitted diseases. Whereas the creation of children with specific genetic material might lead to the elimination of certain diseases, there are ethical concerns about the possibility of producing tailor-made designer babies with particular desirable features. The creation of genetically modified crops like GM maize or potatoes has allowed farmers to improve their yield, reduce their use of pesticides and enhance the quality of crops so that in developing countries vitamin-enriched rice and bananas are now grown. Unfortunately, little is known about the long-term effects of such transgenic plants, and in Europe GM foods are still regarded with suspicion. (514 words)

First of all, make sure you understand the meaning of each of the highlighted words and phrases in the text above. If you are not sure, look them up in your dictionary. Then complete the tasks on the following page.

1 PARAPHRASES

Rewrite the sentences, replacing the underlined parts of the sentences with a synonymous expression from the highlighted phrases. Sometimes you may have to slightly adapt the word order.

1 Technological advances have the potential to improve people's personal circumstances.
2 Will machines eventually do all our jobs?
3 Unfortunately, genetic testing is something which has not only positive consequences but also negative ones.
4 3D printing can be considered a technology which will revolutionize many branches of industry, as it has enabled a new market in large-size and reasonably priced printing to emerge.
5 As the amount of data stored in clouds is growing, it is increasingly difficult to handle data privacy risks.

2 COMPOUND ADJECTIVES

Compound adjectives are adjectives that are made up of two or more words. They are used to make texts more formal by condensing information, e.g. *hard-hitting* documentary, *well-known* author.

A Find at least five examples of compound adjectives in the text.

B Rewrite these sentences by forming other compound adjectives.

EXAMPLE: There are many countries in which English is spoken.
There are many English-speaking countries.

1 There will be many gadgets that can save us time.
2 It is interesting to examine the world of video games which has been changing rapidly.
3 Maize which is resistant to insects is grown in many European countries.

3 WORD FAMILIES

A Copy the chart below and add the missing words. Some of the words you need are in the text. Use your dictionary if necessary.

noun (abstract)	verb	adjective
		accessible
		beneficial
	compete	
destruction		
	disrupt	
		innovative
	threaten	

B Make sentences with five words from the chart but leave a gap for the word. Swap pages with a partner. Can he or she find the missing words?

BEFORE YOU READ

With a partner, think about what the term "smart city" means. Write a short definition. What benefits may smart cities bring about for their residents? Can you think of problems that might arise?

By: Max Opray — March 15, 2016

ADELAIDE TO BECOME AUSTRALIA'S FIRST SMART CITY BUT COULD LOSE OUT ON PRIVACY

A

Stepping into the elevator at the school for computer sciences hub at Adelaide University, Prof Ali Babar shakes his head in exasperation. As the doors close, the head of the Australian centre for smart cities mentions the woman recently found dead in China 30 days after technicians attempting to fix a glitch cut power to the lift she was in and left her stranded inside. "That's the kind of thing that wouldn't happen in a smart city," he says.

B

Babar has just finished another day coordinating with a coalition of government, business and academia about his mission to turn Adelaide into a trial site for such innovations that could one day be rolled out across the rest of Australia and around the world. The goal is to identify ways in which emerging digital technologies can improve how a city functions, whether traffic congestion, reducing carbon emissions or – as in the case of the elevator in Xi'an – personal safety.

C

"Adelaide is small enough to use as a laboratory but large enough to undertake ambitious initiatives," he says. "A proof of concept can be developed and tested here." Central to the idea of a smart city is the Internet of Things – everyday objects that feature online connectivity, such as elevators that actively communicate data to technicians about malfunctions and the number of passengers on board. Other prospective technologies being looked at in the realm of safety include biometric readers that allow paramedics to obtain the medical records of an incapacitated patient via a fingerprint scan, or video recognition techniques capable of identifying suspects of a crime even if they are wearing a mask. […]

Adelaide: a city between past and future

02 **hub:** *Zentrum* 07 **glitch:** *Störung* 12 **academia:** *akademische Welt*

D

Most recently […], Babar secured a memorandum of understanding with tech giants NEC Australia. "We will try to brainstorm suitable projects for Adelaide by partnering with [NEC Australia], sharing findings and making those findings available to the general public," he says. "That in turn will stimulate further collaboration with industry partners and government." NEC Australia's South Australian state manager, Milan Djuricic, says NEC was involved in a similar initiative in Britain as part of the Bristol Is Open project […].

He says Adelaide was attractive for NEC because it offered a solid foundation of infrastructure to build upon, a receptive political environment, and particular challenges that Bristol did not present. "We can take things further in Adelaide in relation to energy management and water management, given South Australia is the driest state in the driest country," he says. "NEC has leading global technologies in relation to water leakage detection which help identify failures before they fail. "That means investment can be made in the right areas to prevent water leakage."

E

NEC also has plenty to offer when it comes to public safety, with the company's biometric identification technologies already being used on the smartphones of South Australian and Northern Territory police to enable immediate identification of members of the public. The company says its biometrics – combined with access control and video monitoring systems – will ensure smart cities are able to rapidly respond to safety incidents when required.

F

Djuricic would like to allay privacy concerns that have arisen over these emerging technologies: "At the end of the day, smart city research is not about private data." Civil Liberties Australia's vice president, Tim Vines, sees it differently. "These smart technologies hold a lot of promise in terms of making better cities and using resources more efficiently," he says. "But they also bring challenges, especially in privacy, and there has to be a public discussion about data being gathered by private companies, city councils and police. "If we can anonymously identify someone, what limitations will be placed?"

G

Vines says even ostensibly benign smart technology advances presented challenges, citing the Australian Centre for Smart Cities' interest in technology that encourages people to dispose of rubbish in the correct type of bin as something that could lead to rubbish detection within smart bins. He asks: "If technology could detect the type of rubbish, what if someone tried to dispose of an illicit substance, would it set off an alarm or message the police?"

H

David Lindsay, vice chair of the Australian Privacy foundation, says he is very concerned about the potential for widespread surveillance offered up by the Internet of Things. "As with any new technologies and applications, we believe that adequate and appropriate privacy protection should be built into the design of the technologies," he says. […]

Babar concedes that smart city technologies present "severe privacy concerns" and society would need to come up with a mechanism to address them […]. "For example we will be looking at who owns the data from the user's point of view, and enabling users to manage their own privacy," he says. "Perhaps at certain times they are willing to share their data, but at other times of day they don't want to and they need to be able to control that." He points out that passive data collection is hardly a new development, pointing to his smartphone. "This phone has a number of sensors collecting data as it is, so all we're looking at is how this sort of data should be used." (851 words)

From: *The Guardian*, 15 March 2016

36 **NEC:** a multinational company that provides information technology services

69 **allay concerns:** *Bedenken zerstreuen*

1 SHORT-ANSWER QUESTIONS / SENTENCE COMPLETION

→ Skills, p. 200

Answer the following questions by providing information from the text. [Paragraphs A and B]

1 Find an expression which shows that a person is upset and annoyed with something.
2 The expression ___ means that Adelaide should become a playing field to test the impact of technological novelties.

2 MULTIPLE CHOICE

→ Skills, p. 204

Choose the most suitable option.

1 Smart technologies could be used to increase people's safety. Yet, which of the following aspects is not explicitly mentioned in paragraphs A–C? Technologies might be used …
- **a** to avoid incidents like the one in China.
- **b** to provide the necessary emergency care.
- **c** to deter prospective criminals.
- **d** to help solve a crime.

2 Among other reasons, why was NEC Australia interested in Adelaide's initiative?
- **a** NEC was involved in a project in Bristol that was a huge success.
- **b** In Adelaide, politicians are open to such projects.
- **c** It will give NEC a chance to improve Australia's infrastructure.
- **d** The initiative will bring more water to Adelaide's population.

3 Which idea is not mentioned in paragraph E? NEC could contribute to Adelaide's public safety by supplying …
- **a** technologies for the recognition of individual identities.
- **b** training programmes for the police.
- **c** technologies to permit or deny entry to a public building.
- **d** video surveillance systems.

3 MULTIPLE MATCHING

→ Skills, p. 200

Match the statements (1–6) on p. 167 with the four people in paragraphs F–H. There are two statements that do not match.

person	statement
Milan Djuricic	
Tim Vines	
David Lindsay	
Ali Babar	

1 Smart technologies themselves must provide the necessary means to protect the data.
2 We have to find similar security measures to those built into smartphones.
3 It should be in the hands of the individual to decide when to share his or her data.
4 We are interested in developing smart technologies and not in getting people's data.
5 Waste sorting is a task which smart technologies will not be able to manage effectively.
6 While new technology offers opportunities, one has to be careful about keeping data private.

4 WORKING WITH WORDS

A Find idiomatic English expressions in the headline/text for the German phrases below.

1 beim Datenschutz ins Hintertreffen geraten [Headline]
2 künftige Technologien [Paragraph C]
3 an die Krankenakte herankommen [Paragraph C]
4 auf Sicherheitsvorfälle reagieren [Paragraph E]
5 sehr vielversprechend sein [Paragraph F]
6 großflächige Überwachung [Paragraph H]
7 [ihre] Privatsphäre selbst verwalten [Paragraph H]
8 [ihre] Daten freigeben [Paragraph H]
9 passive Datenerfassung [Paragraph H]

B Write an example sentence for five of the expressions in 4A, clearly showing their meaning. The sentences should consist of a main and a subordinate clause (*Haupt- und Nebensatz*). The following prompts may help you.

- smart technologies
- Internet of Things
- Adelaide
- citizens
- biometric technologies

people judge their computing devices on the availability of capabilities and features, rather than processing speed, it may not feel like much of a slowdown to consumers.

G For companies, the end of Moore's law will be disguised by the shift to cloud computing. Already, firms are upgrading PCs less often, and have stopped operating their own e-mail servers. This model depends, however, on fast and reliable connectivity. That will strengthen demand for improvements to broadband infrastructure: those with poor connectivity will be less able to benefit as improvements in computing increasingly happen inside cloud providers' data centres. [...]

H For more than 50 years, the seemingly inexorable shrinking of transistors made computers steadily cheaper and more capable. As Moore's law fades, progress will be less metronomic. But computers and other devices will continue to become more powerful – just in different and more varied ways. (845 words)

From: *The Economist*, 12 March 2016

132 **metronomic:** mechanically regular

1 MULTIPLE CHOICE

→ Skills, p. 204

Choose the most suitable option.

1 Which of the following facts is mentioned in paragraph A?
- **a** If cars had improved at the same rate as computers, the fastest car would now be able to drive at the speed of light.
- **b** If skyscrapers had improved at the same rate as computers, now the tallest building would reach to the Moon.
- **c** Moore anticipated an exponential growth of transistors, and thus the doubling of the performance of processors, every two years.
- **d** Nowadays 400,000 times as many tiny transistors as in 1971 can be packed into a single microchip.

2 According to the text (paragraph B), which of the following is correct?
- **a** Moore's law has resulted in billions of people having smartphones.
- **b** Because smartphones have become so powerful, there are fewer computers now than in the 1980s.
- **c** Using supercomputers to simulate nuclear explosions makes real nuclear testing seem slow.
- **d** After five decades of rapid improvement, advances in computing will slow down.

3 What does the example of the ancient game of Go show?
- **a** As improvements in hardware slow down, people will develop better software.
- **b** If computers learn to think like humans, they will be able to teach us any board game.
- **c** Due to better hardware, computers can now outplay the world's strongest Go players.
- **d** The development of better software has shown that the game of Go is not as difficult as it was thought to be.

2 GAPPED SUMMARY

→ Skills, p. 202

Fill in the gaps with words from the corresponding sections of the text. Use only one word per gap. The words do not necessarily appear in the same order as in the text. Write down in which line of the text you found the word. [Paragraphs D–G]

Whereas in the past computers' performance gains relied on the ___ [1] of their processors, nowadays PCs can become more ___ [2] with the same hardware. Today computing muscle is less important, as the devices can ___ ___ [3] the immense resources of the so-called "cloud". The rate of future technological progress will be less ___ [4] owing to the fact that performance gains will be achieved at a much more irregular rate. This will lead in turn to firms initiating a ___ [5] towards cloud solutions. Yet, in order to do so it will be essential for them to have fast and dependable ___ [6]. People sitting in front of their devices at home will not notice the future slowdown of technological innovation since they attach greater importance to the ___ [7] of certain tools and features.

3 WORKING WITH WORDS

A Find the English equivalents of the following German expressions in the text.

paragraph A	paragraphs B–C	paragraphs D–E	paragraphs F–H
starten	das Ende [...] ist in Sicht	sich stützen auf	verschleiert
Faustregel	Tempo	dazu beitragen	zuverlässig
Leistung verstärken	Leistungsgewinne	verfolgen	unaufhaltsam
Fortschritt			

B Which word from 3A completes each group of collocations? (Use the infinitive form of verbs.)

1	to believe in ___	steady ___	the rate of ___	to monitor the ___ of sb/sth
2	Let's not ___ this argument.	___ a career	___ a thief	___ a plan
3	___ a rocket	___ an appeal	___ an attack	___ a campaign
4	from ___ sources	to be a ___ customer	a ___ friend	an un___ software
5	to pick up ___	the fast ___ of life	___ maker	at a breakneck ___

1 LISTENING

→ Skills, p. 196

26

You are going to hear a panel discussion on the controversial use of killer robots in battle.

lethal: *tödlich*
reservation: *Vorbehalt*
first and foremost: *vor allem*
casualty: *Opfer*
accountability: *Verantwortung*
malfunction: *Ausfall, Fehlfunktion*
undermine: *untergraben*

A Listening for gist

Listen to the programme. Before you focus on the details, do the following tasks.

1 Which expert is clearly against the use of killer robots in combat zones?
2 How can the different speakers' participation in the discussion be described? Attribute one description to each expert. One description does not match.

	speaker		description
1	Tessa	A	calm and confident
2	Sean	B	overexcited and insulting
3	Jane	C	emotional and forceful
		D	light-hearted and lively

B Listening for details

Now listen again and do the tasks below. They follow the order of the programme.

1 **Sentence Completion:** Complete the sentence below with information from the text.

The aim of the meeting in Geneva was to make progress on deciding how killer robots ___ .

2 **Multiple Choice:** Which of the following ideas appear in the statements made by the different speakers? The list of items follows the order of the programme but three aspects do not come up at all.

A	There should be a ban on the use of artificial intelligence to manage weapons.
B	Elements of science fiction may now become reality.
C	Autonomous robots can also fulfil peaceful tasks.
D	From a scientist's point of view, no ethical standards are needed.
E	Robots can accept far more risks than humans would.
F	Killer robots have got the potential to decrease the number of people being killed in wars.
G	Even in the future, it will always be a human person who makes the decision and not a robot or weapon.
H	Being killed by a robot that cannot appreciate the value of human life would be a violation of human dignity.

2 ARGUMENTATIVE WRITING

→ Skills, pp. 206, 208

Discuss whether future technological developments will improve or worsen our lives. Write about 200 words.

3 MATERIAL-BASED ESSAY

Genetically modified babies: Is there a line that we as a society should not cross? What is your opinion? Use some of the information from the material below and write about 300 words.

Verletzung der Menschenwürde? Wessen? Des genetisch veränderten Embryos? – Nein. Es ist nicht zu sehen, wie ausgerechnet die Menschenwürde gebieten sollte, einen Embryo schwer geschädigt zur Welt kommen zu lassen, nämlich mit seinem kranken „natürlichen" Genom, statt mit einem medizinisch korrigierten, das gesund ist.

(From: *the website of Deutscher Ethikrat*, 2016)

4 GROUP DISCUSSION

→ Skills, p. 210

Your class has decided to take part in a science and technology fair for young people. You want to focus on potential dangers and downsides of modern science and technology.

Presentation phase

You are one of the 4 or 5 members of a group whose task it is to choose the best cartoon for a poster which will be hung up in the hall to attract visitors to your stand. Each of you presents their suggestion in one minute. For possible cartoons go to File 4 on p. 191.

Interaction phase

Then you weigh up the pros and cons of each example and try to find a cartoon everybody can agree on at the end of your discussion.

5 GIVING A PRESENTATION

→ Skills, p. 212

Work in a group of 3–4 students. Choose an innovation you are really interested in. If you are not sure, you can choose one from below.

- modern energy-storage devices
- self-driving cars
- lethal autonomous robots
- pharma crops
- nanobots
- 3D printing

Do research on the internet and prepare a short speech on what the innovation is about and what benefits it may have and what problems might arise. Every member of the group should talk for 2–3 minutes, highlighting a different aspect.

12 GRAMMAR CHECK E

MIXED GRAMMAR

→ Grammar summary, p. 216

Complete the email by filling in the correct form of the words in brackets. Sometimes you may need to add more words, e.g. prepositions.

Dear Kelly,

I ___ [1] (read) an article in a science magazine the other day. It ___ [2] (write) by a well-known futurologist and was about technological trends to watch out for in the next few decades. The article, although mostly ___ [3] (deal) with emerging technologies, ___ [4] (turn – be) quite interesting reading. After I ___ [5] (look) some of the technical terms, I ___ [6] (write) down the key statements of the text. In general, the article was quite optimistic about the future. At least it gave a ___ [7] (positive) outlook than the article which I ___ [8] (read) the night before. And you know what I think about people who are always pessimistic!

In the article, it ___ [9] (mention) that 3D printing ___ [10] (current – become) much more mainstream. Many people who ___ [11] (recent – undergo) dental treatment may not be aware of the fact that inside their mouths they have some of the first 3D products. Moreover, the article says that 3D printing as a manufacturing technique ___ [12] (already – trust) enough to ___ [13] (use) in aircraft engineering and that it ___ [14] (soon – have) an impact on an even larger number of branches of industry.

Yet the text also deals with the ethical dimension of technological progress. Several years ago the writer ___ [15] (point out) that we ___ [16] (all – confront) with the controversial issue of genome editing in human embryos. This is ___ [17] (hard) surprising as, for instance, in 2016 British scientists ___ [18] (give) permission to alter DNA of embryos, while scientists in China ___ [19] (reveal) that they ___ [20] (try out) a new technique to edit the genomes of human embryos, called CRISPR. By ___ [21] (allow) doctors ___ [22] (put) just the right cancer-hunting genes into a patient's immune system, this ___ [23] (high – sophisticated) technology could one day help people ___ [24] (suffer) from cancer. By and large, it promises ___ [25] (make) it soon possible to edit genetic information ___ [26] (quick) and ___ [27] (precise) and therefore help ___ [28] (develop) therapies for any disease. But in a few decades it may also ___ [29] (use) to make designer babies.

My impression is that if technology ___ [30] (continue) at this pace, our world ___ [31] (bare – be) recognizable in a few years. But in 2125, who ___ [32] (remember) the technological innovations of the first decades of the 21st century? By then all of them ___ [33] (probably – become – outdate).

___ [34] (spend) a whole afternoon ___ [35] (reflect) the article, I ___ [36] (strong – recommend) that you take a closer look at it as well. I really enjoyed ___ [37] (read) it and I ___ [38] (look forward to) the next issue of the magazine.

But that's enough of the future for today! See you next Tuesday!

Yours,
Alex

APPENDIX

Files for differentiation

FILE 1 Unit 1, Part A, Task 2 → Page 9

Decide which paraphrase really explains the expression best.

1 A couch potato is a person who …
  - **a** avoids physical exercise but does some exercises when sitting in a chair or on a couch.
  - **b** enjoys spending his or her free time sitting on a sofa watching a series or sport on TV but occasionally he or she does other things.
  - **c** is lazy and mostly spends his or her free time on a couch and avoids physical exercise.

2 All work and no play means …
  - **a** you have no free time left because you are busy all the time.
  - **b** you are really busy but you don't want to spend your free time playing games.
  - **c** there is a good balance between your free time and the time you spend at work.

FILE 2 Unit 1, Part C, Task 4 → Page 17

Find the idiomatic expression based on the following three words in the table. Use your dictionary.

a the idiomatic expression using the word "variety" which means that new and exciting experiences make life more interesting
b the idiomatic expression using the noun of "contradictory" which means a statement containing two ideas that contradict each other's meaning
c the idiomatic expression using the noun of "analyse" that means what is most important after everything has been considered

FILE 3 Unit 1, Part D, Task 4, Essay 1 → Page 19

Before you write the essay, make sure you understand the following:

a What aspects you have to focus on.
b Whether you have to give only reasons for one side, or if you have to present arguments in favour and against.

(For a detailed discussion of the types of essays you will be asked to write, see Skills, p. 206.)

On p. 19 you find the comment topic:

> "Watching TV is the most popular leisure activity in Britain. I find that very depressing."
> (Jeremy Paxman)
>
> **Comment on Paxman's view.**

Before you write, make sure you know what to do by answering the following true/false questions. Correct the false statements.

1 Your comment should focus on reasons why British people are depressing. T/F?
2 Your aim is to find arguments about why watching TV is the most popular leisure activity in Britain. T/F?
3 Your comment should only include arguments as to why it is depressing that the most popular leisure activity in Britain is watching TV. T/F?

4 You can argue against Jeremy Paxman's view, showing that TV is actually quite good for the viewer. T/F?

5 You have to argue against Paxman's belief that watching TV is the most popular leisure activity in Britain. Doing research is your first step. T/F?

FILE 4 Unit 2, Part C, Task 3D → Page 31

Complete this paragraph with the correct preposition from the box. The highlighted phrases are all in the text on p. 28.

about ▪ at ▪ between ▪ for ▪ into ▪ on ▪ to ▪ under

Even when their GCSE exams are over at the age of 16, many British students still feel that the pressure is ___ [1] because they have to look ___ [2] work experience or other activities to put ___ [3] their CVs. Students who want to go ___ [4] university often worry ___ [5] their applications and work hard ___ [6] their personal statements because they know that the universities look ___ [7] them very carefully. Even those students who concentrate ___ [8] polishing their CVs still feel ___ [9] pressure as a good application can make the difference ___ [10] getting ___ [11] a good university or just getting a place ___ [12] a university they might not really want to go to.

FILE 5 Unit 2, Part D, Task 1 → Page 32

05

A Listen to the first part of the interview and choose the correct alternative to complete these sentences:

1 A generation ago, half / two-thirds / three-quarters of teenagers in the USA worked during the summer vacation.

2 Nowadays, that number has fallen by 14% / 40% / 44%.

3 One reason for the drop in the number of teenagers with summer jobs is the increased competition from adults / illegal immigrants / unemployed people.

4 Alvin Hall gives teenagers two pieces of advice: first of all, they should go around and drop off applications / look for job adverts secondly, they need to visit the job centre / network / ring up shop owners.

5 Teenagers are unlikely to get internships in well-known companies because these mostly go to college students / people with job experience.

06

B Listen to the second part of the interview and choose the correct answer to these questions.

1 What two qualities make young people attractive to small businesses as candidates for summer jobs?
   a ambition and energy   b ambition and curiosity   c energy and curiosity

2 What do employers no longer do if you drop off a résumé to get a summer job?
   a ask for references   b call you back   c read the résumé

3 Why, according to Alvin Hall, do many employers not give summer jobs to black and Latino teenagers?
   - **a** they are uncomfortable with them
   - **b** the teenagers don't have good references
   - **c** the jobs are only for white kids

4 What should black and Latino teenagers do in order to get good summer jobs?
   - **a** do volunteer work
   - **b** network with people from different ethnic backgrounds
   - **c** polish their résumés

5 Which three-word phrase sums up Alvin Hall's tips on how to get a good vacation job?
   a "Don't be pushy." **b** "Make yourself known." **c** "Write a résumé."

FILE 6 Unit 2, Part D, Task 3

→ Page 33

Here is some help on how to write an introduction to your essay. Use the structure and phrases below, and write 80 words for the introduction (cf. Skills, p. 208).

Topic sentence:	*Young people nowadays feel under pressure* ...
Reason:	*They think that they won't get* ... *if* ...
Example:	*As the cartoon shows, even children* ...
Statement of opinion:	*In my opinion, they are right/wrong to be worried and* ...

FILE 7 Unit 3, Part B, Step 3

→ Page 40

A Match the phrases from the text (a–h) to the following explanations (1–6). There are two more phrases than you need

1 signs on a product that tell the buyer in explicit terms how dangerous it is
2 persuade sb not to do sth
3 soft drinks with a lot of extra sugar
4 make sb who wants to start smoking have second thoughts
5 get used to sth
6 shocking or disturbing images

a become habitualized to sth
b beverages with added sugar
c dire warning labels
d dissuade sb from doing sth
e fade into the background
f graphic pictures
g leading cause of preventable death
h make a potential smoker think twice

B Find at least five expressions in the text that express the idea that warning labels no longer have the same effect on smokers.

EXAMPLE: "warning labels on cigarettes seem to have lost their touch" (introduction)

Look for the following keywords in lines 47–63:

fade ▪ weakened ▪ meaningless ▪ habitualized ▪ unnoticed

There are two more phrases in lines 74–84.

FILE 8 Unit 3, Part C, Task 1

→ Page 43

Answer the following questions by providing the required information from paragraphs A–C of the text. Choose from the phrases a–h. There are two more options than you need.

1 Which phrase describes the author's feeling that dieting is a never-ending form of torture?
2 Which expression is a synonym for: "I've started eating the way our ancestors did"?
3 Why was the author sceptical of the paleo diet at first? (*2 aspects*)
4 What visible benefit of the paleo diet did the author experience?
5 Which piece of information demonstrates the growing interest in the paleo diet?

a there's a global food crisis
b I've gone paleo.
c lost 4 lbs weight
d most googled diet on the internet (by 2013)
e she'd given up sugar, processed foods, grains and legumes
f the starvation treadmill
g a healthy diet must contain lentils
h they wrote a book together in 2011

FILE 9 Unit 3, Part D, Task 2, Essay 1

→ Page 46

A Decide whether the following arguments are for or against warning labels and higher taxes on sugary drinks.

- added sugar in drinks causes obesity, diabetes and tooth decay
- despite warning labels, cigarettes are still the leading cause of preventable death
- health-care costs are rising rapidly because of childhood obesity
- parents will buy few sugary drinks for children if they have warning labels
- people don't pay any attention to warning labels
- people will buy sugary drinks even if they are a bit more expensive
- there are already too many warning labels on all sorts of products
- warning labels on cigarette packs have saved 8 million lives

B Use some of the arguments above to write your essay.

FILE 10 Unit 4, Part C, Task 4A

→ Page 59

Which words in the box match the definitions below. The words are all from paragraphs 1–3 of the text.

addictive ▪ aggression ▪ bulk ▪ enhance sth ▪ fatigue ▪ inject sth ▪ restriction ▪ side-effects

1 to improve the good quality, value or status of sth
2 a rule or law that limits what you can do
3 feelings of anger and hatred that may result in threatening or violent behaviour
4 negative reactions that a drug may cause
5 a feeling of being extremely tired, usually because of hard work or exercise

6 tending to make people unable to stop using sth, i.e. a drug
7 weight and size, e.g. of muscles
8 to put a drug or other substance into your body using a syringe

FILE 11 Unit 4, Part D, Task 1B

→ Page 60

Listen again and choose the correct two answers.

1 Why were there so many working-class people in Lancashire in the 19th century? Because it was an important centre of the ___ industry.
a mining **b** ship-building **c** steel and iron **d** textile

2 Why did football matches take place on Saturday afternoons?
a People had to go shopping on Saturday mornings.
b Saturday afternoon was a half-day free of work.
c People had to go to church on Sunday.
d The working day was too long from Monday to Friday.

3 What two things did William Sudell do to improve his team? He ___.
a found players from other areas
b introduced new tactics
c gave his players time off work
d gave players jobs in his mill

4 Why did people start supporting their local football team? Because ___.
a the mill owners told them to
b they identified with the local team
c they were proud when they won
d there was no other form of recreation

5 Which examples show that football had become big business by 1905?
a Training methods had become more professional.
b The teams didn't have any local players any more.
c By 1900 all the clubs in the Football League were limited companies.
d Alf Common was the first player to be sold for £1000 in 1905.

FILE 12 Unit 4, Part D, Task 4, Essay 2

→ Page 61

A Put the following points under the correct headings:

a	arguments in favour of zero tolerance:	___ ___ ___
b	arguments against zero tolerance:	___ ___ ___
c	ideas to sum up:	___ ___

- athletes who dope are cheating supporters and spectators
- bans should be long enough to deter others, but give cheats a second chance
- cheating is unfair to fellow athletes

- everybody deserves a second chance in life
- people found guilty of deliberate doping should be banned
- some athletes have unusual blood test results without doping
- some illegal substances can be taken by mistake
- winning prize money or sponsorship by cheating is a form of fraud

B **Now write the essay, using at least two of the arguments in favour of and two arguments against zero tolerance for anyone caught cheating or doping in sport. Use some examples from the text on pp. 56–57 to support your arguments.**

FILE 13 Unit 5, Part C, Task 5, Essay 2

→ Page 73

In order to find arguments for your essay, you consulted the website of a German company promoting student exchange programmes. Take the content of the website as a source for the essay you are about to write on mandatory student exchange programmes. Note that only the positive aspects are mentioned in the website and that you will have to think of the negative aspects yourself.

SPRACHKENNTNISSE

Du wirst deine Fremdsprachenkenntnisse vertiefen und das ganz nebenbei durch das natürliche Verwenden der Sprache beim Hören, Lesen, Sprechen und Schreiben. Du wirst sogar in der Fremdsprache träumen!

ENTWICKLUNG DER PERSÖNLICHKEIT

Du wirst neue und häufig herausfordernde Situationen meistern müssen. Dabei lernst du mehr über dich selbst, deine Schwächen und vor allem deine Stärken. Du wirst an Selbstvertrauen und Selbstständigkeit gewinnen.

INTERKULTURELLE KOMPETENZ

Du wirst eine in unserer Welt lebenswichtige Kompetenz erwerben: interkulturelle Kompetenz. Diese hilft dir, Dinge aus einer anderen Perspektive zu sehen: Wie handeln, denken, fühlen andere Kulturkreise? Durch das Eintauchen in das landestypische Leben wirst du mehr und mehr alternatives Verhalten akzeptieren und den Umgang damit lernen. Dabei lernst du auch, die eigene Kultur zu reflektieren und vielleicht auch zu relativieren.

KONTAKTE KNÜPFEN FÜR DIE ZUKUNFT

Du wirst mit vielen Menschen mit unterschiedlichen Fähigkeiten und Erfahrungen Kontakte knüpfen. Einige dieser Kontakte kannst du vielleicht für ein Auslandsstudium, für eine Arbeitsstelle oder ein Praktikum nutzen. Zudem schätzen viele Arbeitnehmer junge Mitarbeiter, die bereits Zeit im Ausland verbracht haben.

FILE 14 Unit 6, Part A, Task 1

→ Page 79

Work with a partner and explain to each other the differences between the words below. Use a dictionary if necessary.

fossil fuels ↔ renewable energy
biodiversity ↔ deforestation
biological waste ↔ hazardous waste

FILE 15 Unit 6, Part D, Task 1B → Page 88

Listen to the report again and fill the gaps in the flow chart with the help of the words in the box.

back-up ▪ biogas ▪ experience ▪ grid ▪ height ▪ lease ▪ solar ▪ stages ▪ turbine ▪ two and a half ▪ woodchip ▪ 2.5

<table>
<tr><th colspan="4">Feldheim: Making power gives us power</th></tr>
<tr>
<td>___[1] furnace
as a ___[2] in winter</td>
<td>Own ___[3] farm</td>
<td>___[4] plant
power is fed into national ___[5]</td>
<td>wind ___[6]
starts at wind speed of ___[7] metres in a ___[8] of 100 metres</td>
</tr>
<tr><td colspan="4">Why do villagers welcome the turbines?
• built in different ___[9]
• people receive a land ___[10]

Why do visitors come?
• They learn from Feldheim's ___[11]</td></tr>
</table>

Feldheim wants to get the idea ___[12] around the world so that many villages like this will be built.

FILE 16 Unit 6, Part D, Task 3, Essay 2 → Page 89

In order to get ideas for your essay, look at the short German text below and list ideas that you can use in your essay. Make sure you list the ideas in English; use a dictionary and/or the Words in context text (p. 78) to be certain of the correct terms in English.

Der Klimawandel ist zu einer der größten globalen Herausforderungen geworden. Er ist längst kein Zukunftsszenario mehr, sondern heute schon Realität. Wir spüren bereits weltweit die Folgen des Klimawandels. Gletscher schmelzen in alarmierender Geschwindigkeit. Schwere Stürme oder Überschwemmungen verwüsten ganze Landstriche. Große Trockenheit wechselt sich mit sintflutartigen Niederschlägen ab. Aufgrund der zunehmenden Erwärmung werden sich solche extremen Wetterereignisse immer häufiger zeigen. Durch die Ausbreitung der Wüsten, zunehmende Stürme und Hochwasser und durch den ansteigenden Meeresspiegel werden immer mehr Menschen in Zukunft ihre Heimat verlieren.
Nur durch die konsequente Einsparung von Klimagasen wie Kohlendioxid oder Methan kann der Klimawandel abgemildert werden. Jeder kann einen Beitrag zum Klimaschutz leisten, indem er weniger Energie verbraucht.

FILE 17 Unit 7, Part B, STEP 6A

→ Page 96

Form the idiomatic phrases you need to do the exercise by combining a word from box A with a word from box B. Use your dictionary to help you. Then use these phrases to complete the exercise on p. 96.

Box A		
ad	early	heart's
common	full	

Box B		
content	sense	story
nauseam	stages	

FILE 18 Unit 7, Part C, Task 5

→ Page 101

You're here because you want more vocabulary work, so find idiomatic expressions or collocations with the nouns in the box to complete the following German phrases/expressions.

choice ▪ head ▪ matter ▪ purpose ▪ use

1 The newspaper investigation intends to get to ▬ *(der Kern der Sache)*.
2 *(Ganz egal was passiert)* ▬, we won't reveal our sources.
3 She didn't become a freelance journalist ▬ *(freiwillig/aus freiem Willen)*. The newspaper she worked for fired all its journalists.
4 In her new job, she will be able to ▬ her language skills ▬ *(gut verwenden)*.
5 Her old contacts are ▬ *(nutzlos)* to her any more.
6 Was it an accident or did he reveal the newspaper's sources ▬ *(absichtlich)*?
7 His success ▬ *(ist ihm zu Kopfe gestiegen)* – he's become unbearable.
8 I tried to understand what he was saying about the technological improvements, but most of it ▬ *(ging über meinen Verstand)*.

FILE 19 Unit 7, Part D, Task 2, Essay 1

→ Page 102

A student of your class has lent you some notes on the topic "What is interesting is the power and the impact of social media. So we must try to use social media in a good way." Unfortunately some ideas are in German, while others are incomplete and all of them are jumbled up. Put the ideas/notes into the right order so they make complete arguments and find English equivalents for the German parts.

1 Soziale Medien sind nützlich, um Leute über gefährliche Situationen zu informieren, sie zu warnen oder Entwarnung zu geben.
2 We have to be aware of this negative impact of social media and prevent it.
3 A person – cyberbullied – often not able to defend him/herself adequately → depression/ desperation → there are cases of youngsters – commit suicide
4 Take, for example, the attack in Munich where the police got information via social media and informed people about the danger.
5 Social media help to spread the news of events and incidents taking place immediately.
6 Anonym gepostete Gerüchte, Lügen oder Hassmails verbreiten sich oft rasend schnell.
7 Soziale Medien haben die Macht, Personen zu zerstören.

FILE 20 Unit 8, Part C, Task 1

→ Page 114

Here is some help to find the sentences that fit the gap. Always look at the context first, then parts of the sentence like pronouns or structural words that will indicate a connection between the contents around the gap and the sentence that fits.

gap	context	look for:
A	mention of a business making toilets, baths, tubs	a business which has to do with these items
B	census bureau says that there are 46 million German-Americans	something that might connect with the number and the ethnic group.
C	examples of well-known Americans and their ethnic background	famous people who may have German ancestry or firms founded by German-Americans
D	many companies hardly mention their German origin, they play it down as a rule	something that connects to German-Americans not displaying their heritage
E	lists the contributions of the German-Americans to American culture	an example of German-American contribution to American life
F	Milwaukee and why it is different; two people are mentioned	example of a career that Germans were prominent in

FILE 21 Unit 8, Part C, Task 3B

→ Page 115

Use the elements to make sentences. The elements are in the correct order. Use the correct tense, plurals, adjectives or adverbs and add prepositions or pronouns.

1 In 19th-century – America – some – immigrant – integrate – and – work – hard – become – successful.
2 Local – group – active – help – immigrant – settle – host – country.
3 Cultural – heritage – can – become – part – culture – host – country.
4 Many – immigrant – play down – ethnic – origin – in order to – integrate.

FILE 22 Unit 9, Part B, STEP 3B

→ Page 125

Rewrite the following sentences using one of the words or expressions from STEP 2 in the box below instead of the underlined ones. The meaning of the sentences must remain the same, but you may have to adapt the sentence structure or the words.

be full of resentment ▪ desperately ▪ die of ▪ dread ▪ utterly

1 I am really anxious about telling my parents that I've damaged their car.
2 I'm trying very hard to convince my mother not to be my friend on Facebook.
3 I'm horrified by my friend's comments about women. They are absolutely ridiculous.
4 When former lovers talk about the end of their relationship, more often than not they feel bitter and angry.
5 I would feel extreme embarrassment if someone saw that photo of me.

FILE 23 Unit 9, Part C, Task 3A → Page 129

Match the following definitions to the words and expressions in the box. They are all from the text.

aspirations ▪ award recipients ▪ come under scrutiny ▪ hurl insults ▪ omitted ▪ press coverage

a	people who are presented with a prize for outstanding work	▬
b	shout abusive words	▬
c	what the papers report	▬
d	be carefully and closely examined	▬
e	ambitions	▬
f	left out	▬

FILE 24 Unit 10, Part A, Task 2B → Page 135

Complete the sentences with the most suitable collocation from 2A. The German words in brackets will help you.

1 The ▬ (*verurteilter Straftäter*) was taken from court and driven to prison to start his sentence.
2 Because she was a ▬ (*Ersttäterin*), Rachel was given a suspended sentence for possessing drugs.
3 The number of offenders under the age of 18 has risen sharply, so the new government has made tackling ▬ (*Jugendkriminalität*) its top priority.
4 Binge-drinking, vandalism, hooliganism and graffiti-spraying are all examples of ▬ (*unsoziales Verhalten*).
5 The young offender became involved in petty crime because there was no proper ▬ (*elterliche Aufsicht*) at home after school and too much ▬ (*Gruppenzwang*) from the group of friends that he hung around with.
6 One alternative to a prison sentence or probation is some form of ▬ (*gemeinnützige Arbeit*), where offenders work for the benefit of society.
7 Dealing, trafficking and other ▬ (*Drogendelikte*) are on the increase in many developed countries.
8 ▬ (*Wirtschaftsverbrechen*), such as tax evasion, bribery and fraud, are often considered less serious than violent crime, although the victims often suffer huge losses.
9 Drugs offenders are often sent on a ▬ (*Rehabilitationsprogramm*) to try to get them to break their drug addiction.

FILE 25 Unit 10, Part C, Task 4B → Page 143

Complete these sentences with the correct prepositions. Use your dictionary if necessary.

The majority in / of / on [1] young people have a positive attitude about / of / towards [2] obeying the law, although there are a few juveniles who have no sense at / for / of [3] morality. In one recent example at / for / of [4] delinquency, two youths admitted at / by / to [5] the police that they were responsible for / of /

with[6] vandalizing a bus stop. The police charged them about / as / with[7] vandalism, but a charge for / of / on[8] possessing drugs was dropped because for / of / with[9] a lack for / of / with[10] evidence. By / In / On[11] another incident, the police questioned a well-known drug addict about / as / with[12] a robbery by / for / in[13] which a masked man threatened an old lady by / for / with[14] a baseball bat. The addict recently went for / in / on[15] trial for / of / with[16] the attack and he was jailed at / for / to[17] 18 months. The judge also ordered him to take part at / in / with[18] a rehabilitation programme. One way to get a grip in / on / to[19] the problem as / of / with[20] juvenile delinquency is to put more emphasis at / in / on[21] teaching young people about / of / to[22] moral boundaries. We could deal in / to / with[23] the problem more effectively as / by / in[24] focussing at / in / on[25] education and giving people a second chance. By / In / With[26] this way, offenders could learn to see crime as / at / in[27] being wrong.

FILE 26 Unit 11, Part B, Task 5

→ Page 153

A Match the English phrases on the right (A–J) to the German sentence beginnings (1–10). The phrases are all from the text.

1	[Es] zeichnet sich durch … aus.	**A**	[It] is characterized by …
2	Es gibt drei Gründe, warum …	**B**	At the same time, …
3	Im Vergleich zu …	**C**	In addition to …
4	In Zukunft …	**D**	In an ideal world, …
5	Gleichzeitig …	**E**	In the future, …
6	Zusätzlich zu …	**F**	More than 30 percent of …
7	Das Ergebnis ist …	**G**	The result is …
8	Dies erklärt, weshalb …	**H**	There are three reasons why …
9	Mehr als 30 Prozent des/der …	**I**	This helps explain why …
10	Idealerweise, …	**J**	When compared with …

B Complete these sentences with the most suitable phrases in the box below, taken from 5A.

it is characterized by … ▪ there are three reasons why … ▪ this helps explain why … ▪ when compared with …

1. ▬ the Fourth Industrial Revolution is more than just an extension of the Third Industrial Revolution: its speed, its scope and the number of areas it will affect.
2. Moreover, ▬ a mixture of physical, digital and biological technologies.
3. ▬ previous technological changes, the Fourth Industrial Revolution is developing at a speed that has never been seen before in history.
4. ▬ many people feel uneasy about the effects the changes could have on the way we work, live and interact with others.

C Write four more sentences describing some of the positive and negative effects of the Fourth Industrial Revolution, using one of the phrases from 5A in each sentence. The ideas on p. 157 will help you.

Positive effects

- rise in global income levels
- increase in the quality of life
- long-term gains in efficiency and productivity
- decrease in transport and communication costs

Negative effects

- workers replaced by automation/robots
- stagnation in income levels for most people
- less demand for low-skilled workers
- disillusioned middle classes and social tensions

FILE 27 Unit 11, Part D, Task 1

→ Page 158

23

A Listen to the first part of the interview and choose the correct answers.

1 Which of the following are the BRIC countries?

a Brazil **b** Britain **c** China **d** India **e** Indonesia **f** Romania **g** Russia

2 What happened to the two branches of Standard Chartered bank in India that were set up for and staffed entirely by women?

a They were closed down.
b They became the most profitable branches.

3 How many CEOs of top companies in the USA are women?

a 3% **b** 11% **c** 12%

4 How many CEOs of top companies in Brazil are women?

a 11% **b** 12% **c** 14%

5 In which of the countries mentioned do women seem to be the most ambitious?

a Brazil **b** China **c** India **d** USA

6 In which of the countries mentioned do women seem to be the least ambitious?

a Brazil **b** China **c** India **d** USA

24

B Copy the table below and read the questions. Listen to the second part of the interview and complete the notes with the correct items from the box.

2.3 ▪ 6 ▪ 18 ▪ excited ▪ families ▪ high ▪ losing heart ▪ low-cost ▪ many ▪ not a problem

	USA	BRIC countries
How much is the economy growing?	▪ *flat-line / nothing*	▪ ___ *% per year*
What are the employment opportunities?	▪ ___ *unemployment*	▪ ___ *job opportunities*
How do professional women feel about their career chances?	▪ ___	▪ ___ *by the opportunities*
What are the options for childcare / maternal leave?	▪ *inadequate options*	▪ *extended* ___ ▪ ___ *domestic help*
How does this affect women's career chances?	▪ *average* ___ *year break* ▪ *lose* ___ *% of earning power*	▪ ___

Files for group discussion

FILE 1 Unit 1, Part D, Task 2 → Page 18

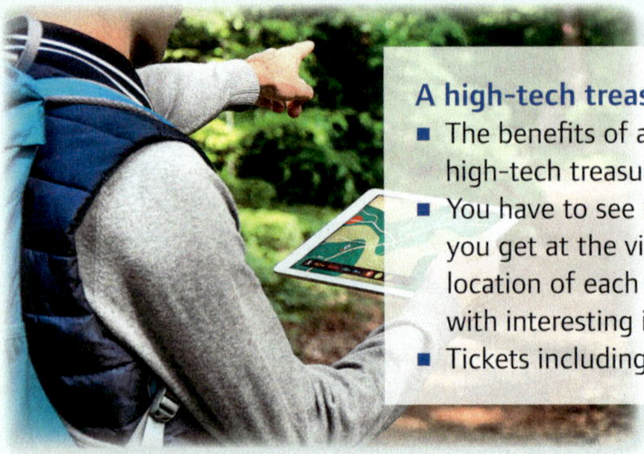

A high-tech treasure hunt in May Hall in Surrey

- The benefits of a good walk, the thrill of exploring and all the fun of a high-tech treasure hunt – that's geocaching!
- You have to see how many geocaches you can track down, using the clues you get at the visitor reception. You have to solve puzzles to reveal the location of each geocache. The geocaches (a package or container) are filled with interesting information and trinkets.
- Tickets including the GPS device and a map: £20

Muggling through London

- This tour enables you to visit the Harry Potter Film locations in Central London. You will find the entrance to *Gringotts Bank*, board a train at the underground station that featured in *The Order of the Phoenix*; stroll along *Diagon Alley* in the footsteps of Harry and Hagrid; see the entrance to Platform Nine-and-three-quarters, where a luggage trolley is embedded in a wall.
- The tour also enables you to explore some of London's hidden away and most fascinating places, which tourists rarely see.
- The beauty of this tour is that you download it for free, and you do it at your own pace with your friends. You are provided with maps and directions and will be set tasks to do. But you can decide when to stop for a coffee or a bite to eat.

Husky trekking on the moors

- If you love dogs, this is for you. If you love huskies, even better!
- A two-hour trek pulled by huskies through some of England's best scenery.
- You get your own team of sled dogs, pulling a two-wheeled scooter around Pesky Husky's purpose-built trail. Trekking gives you the opportunity to see this amazing breed in action.
- It includes a visit to the kennels to meet the friendly dogs and find out about the amazing qualities of the oldest breed on the planet.
- Price: £40. It also includes full training and safety equipment.

Open skies in Northumberland

- A night camping trip at the slick and modern Kielder Observatory to see the night sky far from light pollution.
- With experts you will learn to recognize the planets, stars and galaxies.
- There are pizzas from the outdoor stone-baked oven, while toasted marshmallows and hot chocolate are made over a fire.
- You stay overnight in a yurt or tipi.
- Tickets, including food: £28

Destination 1:

Cuba (10-day holiday in an all-inclusive club)

Accommodation

- 4* hotel 20km from the centre of Varadero, directly on the soft white sands of Varadero beach
- 7 bars, 4 restaurants, spa section for adults only

All inclusive package

- buffet-style breakfast, lunch and dinner
- three à la carte restaurants (dinner), 8 snack bars (24/7), ice cream (24/7)
- drinks (alcoholic, non-alcoholic 24/7), minibar restocked daily
- activities: aquaerobics, pedaloes, table tennis, volleyball, water polo, pool and beach games, dance classes, entertainment shows, gym, sauna

Destination 2:

Extreme coasteering in Wales

Accommodation

- 3* private B&B cottages
- breakfast, dinner at typical local pubs

All-in-one experience on eco-adventure playground at the ocean

- aquatic nature trail, rock pooling, shore scrambling, swell riding, cave exploring, cliff jumping
- discover wildlife and coastline at close quarters, learn about geology
- experienced guides teach you the techniques to go coasteering
- wetsuit and buoyancy aid, safety helmet provided
- requirement: you need to be able to swim

Destination 3:

Sustainable city holiday in Barcelona

Accommodation

- Hostel Gaudí, non-profit, quiet, green neighbourhood
- only clean energy is used, hot water and heating work from biomass boiler
- 24h restaurant, 99% of staff is mentally disabled

Activities

- Paella Experience – buy ingredients at local food market, team up with other guests and cook the dish in the hostel's kitchen
- Segway Experience – using zero carbon emissions, tour the city
- Slow Food Experience – *Ranchos* Restaurant: Catalan cuisine (leftover food is vacuum packed and distributed among the less privileged)

Destination 4:

Myanmar experience **(see Further activities, Task 1, p. 74)**

FILE 3 Unit 6, Part C, Task 5 → Page 87

- **Biofuel** makes a significant contribution to today's renewable energy supply on the European level. It is a renewable energy source based on the carbon cycle, unlike other natural resources such as petroleum, coal, and nuclear fuels. Another source includes animal waste, which is a pollutant produced by animals kept in industrial-sized farms.

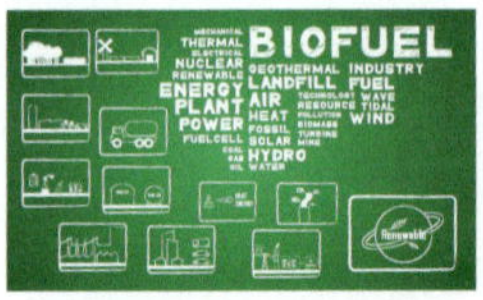

- **Photovoltaics** (also known as **solar energy**) play a key role in Europe's sustainable energy future and are already one of the most important renewable energy sources for the supply of electricity and heating.

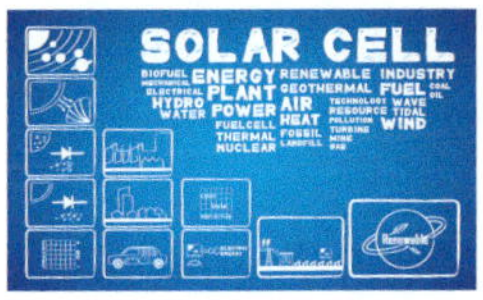

- Europe's **wind energy** industry is one of the world's largest, is at the forefront of technological development in the world and helps profoundly to become independent of conventional forms of energy.

- Europe's **wave power** is in its infancy. Through the harnessing of wave energy one can achieve electricity generation, water desalination, or the pumping of water (into reservoirs).

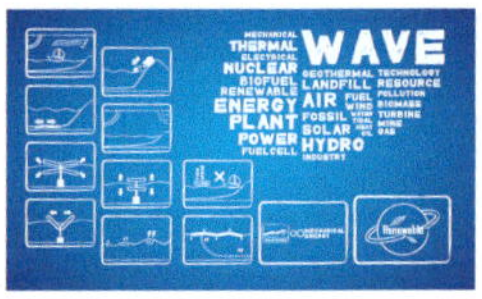

- Europe is acknowledged as a global leader of **green buildings** and energy efficiency. Energy upgrades for existing buildings and energy-efficient new buildings and appliances can make a significant contribution towards reducing Europe's energy consumption.

- **Smart mobility** promises a global mobility revolution. Clean energy will not only fuel the drive technology of the future, it will also provide the opportunity to introduce new kinds of vehicles and develop alternative transport schemes, which will help to save energy.

Here are five cartoons you can use for your poster.

A

B

"The beef has been genetically modified to taste like a more expensive cut."

C

"If we just perfect the self-driving car, we can build the entire interior around distracting communication and entertainment gadgets!"

D

E

Mit unbekannten Wörtern umgehen

Wenn Sie einen Text lesen, werden Sie sicherlich auf Wörter stoßen, die Sie nicht kennen, zumal die Texte im Laufe der Oberstufe immer anspruchsvoller werden. Obwohl Hilfsmittel wie ein einsprachiges Lexikon immer zu Hand sein sollten, sollten Sie nicht unbedingt jedes unbekannte Wort sofort nachschlagen. Man kann auch andere Arbeitstechniken verwenden.

1 Arbeitstechniken zur Erschließung unbekannter Wörter:

1 Schauen Sie zunächst immer unter der Rubrik **Anmerkungen** (*annotations*) nach. Hier werden schwierige Wörter sofort erklärt.

2 Fragen Sie sich, ob das Wort zum Verständnis des Satzsinnes **nötig** ist. Es ist dabei wichtig zu erkennen, ob das Wort zur Beantwortung einer Text- oder Wortfrage notwendig ist. Haben Sie Mut zur Lücke!

3 Beachten Sie den **Kontext**, in dem das Wort benutzt wird.
BEISPIEL: *The average amount of time spent in front of the computer playing games **soared** from 8.5 minutes in 2004 to 17.8 minutes in 2014.*
Die ansteigende Minutenzahl lässt erkennen, dass das Verb „ansteigen" bedeutet. Die Verdoppelung der Zahl legt nahe, dass es sich um ein „starkes Ansteigen" handelt.
BEISPIEL: *About 3.2 million deaths each year are caused by our **sedentary lifestyle**, which means the lack of physical activity undertaken by people.*
Ausdrücke, die eine übergeordnete Bedeutung haben, werden häufig im Text erklärt. Die Bedeutung von *sedentary lifestyle* wird im Relativsatz erklärt. Die „sitzende Lebensweise" – also zu wenig Bewegung – wird direkt erklärt.

4 Achten Sie darauf, ob das Wort mit einem Großbuchstaben beginnt. Dann handelt es sich in der Regel um einen **Eigennamen**. Manchmal wird die Person oder Institution sofort näher erklärt.
BEISPIEL: *… according to **Eurostats**, the European statistics office, …*

5 **Internationale Wörter** sind in mehreren Sprachen ähnlich. Überlegen Sie, ob ein solches Wort vorliegt und wie es auf Deutsch lauten würde.
BEISPIEL: *combine* = kombinieren; *counterproductive* = kontraproduktiv
Aber vorsicht bei sogenannten *false friends*: *eventually*, *actually*, *gymnasium*

6 Oft ist ein Wort ein **Fremdwort**, das aus dem Lateinischen oder Griechischen stammt, und in beiden Sprachen (Englisch und Deutsch) existiert.
BEISPIEL: *phenomenon* = Phänomen; *criterion* = Kriterium; *result* = Resultat, Ergebnis

7 Beachten Sie die Grundlagen der Wortbildung. Worte können sich aus einer Vorsilbe (*prefix*) + Kernwort + Nachsilbe (*suffix*) zusammensetzen.
BEISPIEL: Vorsilbe + Kernwort + Nachsilbe: *inaudible*
in- = Vorsilbe *un-/in-* (negativ)
-ble = adjektivische Endung (z. B. *responsible*)
audi(o) = Fremdwort (vgl. Punkt 6: *audio* ≈ hören)
→ *inaudible* = unhörbar

AUFGABE 1
Versuchen Sie die Bedeutung der hervorgehobenen Wörter mittels einer der oben beschriebenen Techniken zu erschließen.

The average American adult spends 2.5 hours of the day watching TV. This does not correspond with the myth of the overworked American. This high rate of inactivity is alarming. Studies show that it is during childhood that habits are formed. Children must be encouraged to play outdoors regularly. The evolution of technology has enabled people to shop, learn or work from the comfort of their homes. Active free-time activities have become the exception rather than the rule. In Germany health insurance companies often offer bonuses if their members take part in active leisure time such as cycling, jogging or swimming. This has boosted the numbers of local sports clubs to an unprecedented level.

2 Umgang mit dem Wörterbuch

Haben alle diese Überlegungen nichts genutzt, ist das Wörterbuch eine weiteres Hilfsmittel. Um das Wörterbuch sinnvoll nutzen zu können, sollten Sie Folgendes tun:

1 Schauen Sie nach, was die im Wörterbuch benutzten Abkürzungen bedeuten. (z. B. IDM = *idioms*; [U] = *uncountable noun* usw.)

2 Machen Sie sich klar, dass Worteinträge nach Wortart und Grobbedeutung „vorstrukturiert" sind (vgl. cold: TEMPERATURE; UNFRIENDLY; die Kategorien und Grobbedeutungen sind durch Großbuchstaben hervorgehoben). Überlegen Sie, zu welcher Wortart das gesuchte Wort gehört.

3 Beachten Sie, dass in den Einträgen außer den Übersetzungen oft noch Synonyme (SYN), *opposites* (OPP), idiomatische Redewendungen (IDM) und *phrasal verbs* (PHRV) genannt werden.

4 Nicht immer ist der erste Eintrag im Lexikon der passende: Beachten Sie unbedingt den Kontext!

5 Lesen Sie auch die Beispielsätze, die den Wortdefinitionen im Wörterbuch folgen. Sie erleichtern das Erkennen, in welchem Kontext eine Bedeutung gebraucht wird.

AUFGABE 2
Lesen Sie den Text und bearbeiten Sie anschließend die untenstehenden Aufgaben.

Young people bring fresh, innovative approaches to campaigning, which as charities we shouldn't be afraid of adopting. [...] Big-budget charities can't always replicate this authenticity. But it would be wise, when designing campaigns, to consult with young people from the outset. [...] Young people are frank, undiplomatic, even blunt, giving them media and political appeal that few adults can replicate. [...] There's a moral duty here, too; many organisations readily act on behalf of certain groups but often fail to give those same people meaningful opportunities to speak for themselves. Giving young people a sense of empowerment at an early age can create a great sense of loyalty. (from: *The Guardian*, 7 April 2014)

1 a Entscheiden Sie, zu welcher Wortart das erste hervorgehobene Wort (*approaches*) gehört:
1 Substantiv 2 Verb 3 Adjektiv

b Sie finden die folgenden Definitionen in einem einsprachigen Wörterbuch. Welches ist hier die richtige?
1 movements nearer to sb/sth in distance or time
2 ways of dealing with sb/sth; ways of doing or thinking about sth such as a problem or a task
3 the act of speaking to sb about sth, especially when making an offer or a request

3 Schlagen Sie alle hervorgehobenen Wörter in einem Wörterbuch nach und wählen Sie für jedes Wort die am ehesten zutreffende Bedeutung.

Wie man aus seinen Fehlern lernt

Sie kennen diese Situation: Wenn ein bestimmter Wortschatz, der zu lernen war, abgefragt wird, oder wenn Sätze zu einem gerade gelernten Grammatikstoff zu bilden sind, dann erzielen Sie gute Ergebnisse. Wenn Sie sich aber spontan und zusammenhängend zu einem Thema äußern sollen, dann geraten die grammatischen Formen durcheinander, dann fällt Ihnen ein Wort nicht ein oder Sie verwenden ein falsches. Im schlimmsten Fall versteht dann niemand, was Sie sagen wollten. Und wenn es sich um eine schriftliche Arbeit handelt, ist vieles rot angestrichen.

1 Der Grund für so viele Fehler

Sie machen so viele Fehler, wenn Sie zusammenhängend sprechen oder schreiben müssen, weil Sie versuchen, all Ihre Sprachkenntnisse auf einmal abzurufen – nicht nur den Wortschatz oder den Grammatikstoff, der gerade durchgenommen wurde, sondern alles, was Sie seit Ihrer ersten Englischstunde gelernt haben. Oder besser: was Sie glauben, gelernt zu haben. Denn leider setzen sich im Laufe der Jahre, in denen man eine Sprache lernt, mancherlei Fehler im Kopf fest – weil sie Ihnen nicht deutlich gemacht wurden oder weil sie für Anfänger und etwas Fortgeschrittenere als lässliche Fehler gegolten haben.

2 Heben Sie Ihr Englisch auf ein höheres Niveau

Um ein Sprachniveau zu erreichen, das über den mittleren Schulabschluss hinausgeht, müssen Sie sich deutlich verbessern. Je weiter man in eine Sprache eindringt, desto komplexer wird sie, und deshalb stellt sich eine fortgeschrittene Sprachkompetenz nicht alleine dadurch ein, dass man Wörter und Grammatikregeln paukt. Sie müssen zum Beispiel wissen,

a welche Wörter miteinander kombiniert werden können und welche nicht,
b wann welche grammatische Form sinnvoll ist und wann nicht, und
c dass es klare Unterschiede zwischen beiden Sprachen (Deutsch und Englisch) gibt.

Diese Art von Wissen und Kompetenz entwickelt sich langsam und über Jahre hinweg, und zwar durch *trial and error* im Sprachalltag, d. h. dadurch, dass man zunächst versucht, das zu sagen, was man ausdrücken möchte, und dass man dann darauf achtet, wie der Gesprächspartner reagiert und man das Gesagte gegebenenfalls umformuliert, um sich deutlicher und richtiger auszudrücken.

3 Fehler machen gehört zum Lernen

Man lernt vor allem aus den Fehlern, die man macht. Sie dürfen, ja Sie müssen sogar Fehler machen. Aber diese Fehler müssen Ihnen bewusst gemacht werden, und Sie müssen daraus lernen. Das heißt, Sie müssen erkennen, warum Sie den Fehler gemacht haben, und ganz bewusst versuchen, ihn in Zukunft zu vermeiden.

4 Ein *Personal Learning Diary* (PLD) führen

Ein PLD ist ein persönliches Lerntagebuch, das Sie regelmäßig und sorgfältig führen sollten. Es ist *personal*, weil jeder Schüler andere Fehler macht und weil jeder nur aus seinen eigenen Fehlern lernt. Es ist fürs *learning*, weil es Ihnen hilft, in Englisch besser zu werden, denn – wie bereits erwähnt – in der Oberstufe reicht das bloße Lernen von Wortschatz und Grammatikregeln nicht mehr aus.

5 Was man in ein PLD einträgt

Immer wenn Sie auf einen Fehler aufmerksam gemacht werden, z. B. wenn Sie im Unterricht verbessert werden oder wenn Sie einen Aufsatz verbessert zurückbekommen, haben Sie neuen Stoff für Ihr PLD.

6 Wie ein PLD aussieht

Folgende Struktur hat sich als hilfreich erwiesen: Zunächst wird die fehlerhafte Formulierung (what I said) eingetragen; anschließend das, was Sie auf Deutsch (oder in Ihrer Muttersprache) ausdrücken wollten (what I wanted to say); und schließlich das, was Sie in richtigem Englisch hätten sagen sollen (what I should have said). In den Spalten 1 oder 3 notieren Sie zusätzlich, worin genau Ihr Fehler bestand.
Und so könnte eine Tabelle in Ihrem PLD aussehen:

what I said	what I wanted to say	what I should have said
Drugs are ~~spread out to~~ every part of the world spread out = sich ausstrecken, erstrecken über	Drogen sind auf der ganzen Welt weit verbreitet.	Drugs are prevalent/widespread in every part of the world
~~We see~~ this ~~everytime~~ in Hollywood everytime = jedes Mal	Wir sehen (= können beobachten) das überall in Hollywood.	We can see this everywhere in Hollywood.
First ~~there is to say~~ that … deutsche Struktur	Als erstes ist zu sagen, dass …	First, it has to be said that …
There are many things we ~~cannot oversee~~. oversee = kontrollieren, überwachen	Es gibt viele Dinge, die wir nicht übersehen dürfen. ODER Es gibt viele Dinge, die man gar nicht übersehen kann.	There are many things we mustn't overlook. OR There are many things that are impossible to overlook.
I ~~go tonight to the cinema~~ dt. Satzbau; dt. grammat. Zeit	Ich gehe heute Abend ins Kino.	I'm going to the cinema tonight. engl. Satzbau: Ort vor Zeit

Die zweite Spalte ist wichtig, weil viele Fehler sogenannte Interferenzfehler sind, die dadurch entstehen, dass Sie Ihre Muttersprache wortwörtlich ins Englische übertragen und so der englischen Sprache eine fremde Struktur überstülpen.

7 Nachfragen und nachhaken

Noch sind Sie kein Englisch-Experte. Damit Sie es werden, fragen Sie Ihre Lehrkraft (oder einen Ihrer Mitschüler), ob etwas falsch war und was gegebenenfalls richtig gewesen wäre. Das Ganze ist etwas zeitaufwändig, lohnt sich aber!

8 Wiederholen, wiederholen, wiederholen!

So, wie Sie jeden Tag in Ihr Vokabelheft schauen sollten, sollten Sie täglich einen Blick in Ihr PLD werfen, um neue Einträge hinzuzufügen, Bestehendes zu ergänzen und alles immer wieder zu wiederholen. Auf diese Weise werden Sie rasch erhebliche Fortschritte machen!

Mit Hör-/Sehverstehensaufgaben umgehen

Üblicherweise werden Hör- und Sehverstehensaufgaben oder Videos zweimal abgespielt. Der erste Durchgang dient dazu, eine allgemeine Vorstellung vom Inhalt zu bekommen und die Kernaussage zu erfassen. Beim zweiten Hören oder Sehen sollten Sie sich dann auf bestimmte Details konzentrieren.

1 Vorgehensweise bei Hörverstehensaufgaben

1 **Listening for gist.** Denken Sie beim ersten Hören daran, dass Sie nicht jedes einzelne Wort verstehen müssen. Konzentrieren Sie sich lieber ganz bewusst auf das, was Sie verstehen, und geraten Sie nicht in Panik.

2 **Listening for details.** Lesen Sie sich die Fragen vor dem zweiten Hören noch einmal durch. Konnten Sie alles beantworten? Falls nicht, merken Sie sich (oder notieren Sie sich), auf welche Schlüsselwörter und Aussagen Sie beim erneuten Hören achten müssen.

3 **Note taking.** Machen Sie sich beim Hören nur kurze Notizen auf einem Extrablatt. Überlegen Sie sich dann gut, was genau in den Antwortbogen eingetragen gehört.

BEISPIELAUFGABE

27

Sie hören einen Text über Migration in Deutschland. Die Aufnahme wird zweimal abgespielt. Lesen Sie die Fragen und hören Sie aufmerksam zu. Beantworten Sie danach die Fragen.

1 Warum fliegt Francesco nach Italien?
2 Wie lange war Francesco arbeitslos?
3 Wie hat Francesco den Job in Deutschland bekommen?
4 Welche Sprache verwendet Francesco vorwiegend bei der Arbeit?
5 Aus welchem Grund ziehen so viele junge Menschen von Italien nach Deutschland?
6 Was denkt Francesco über das Leben in Deutschland?

Vor dem ersten Hören. Der Titel, das Thema und der Inhalt können Ihnen einen Hinweis über den zu erwartenden Wortschatz geben. Notieren Sie sich ein paar dieser erwartbaren Wörter.

Thema: *Migration in Germany*

Möglicher Wortschatz: *asylum seekers, (un)employment, job market, migrants, moving, migration, population, racism, reasons*

Die Fragen verstehen. Lesen Sie sich die Aufgabe sorgfältig durch und halten Sie Ausschau nach Schlüsselwörtern. Ist Ihnen im Einzelnen klar, welche Informationen Sie benötigen? Lesen Sie sich hierzu die Fragen nochmals genau durch. Sehen Sie sich im Folgenden die hervorgehobenen Schlagworte in den Fragen an: Was wissen Sie bereits über diese Themen? Worüber könnten die Personen sprechen?

1 **Warum** fliegt Francesco nach Italien?
Überlegen Sie sich schon vor dem Hören mögliche Gründe. Achten Sie beim Hören auf Wörter wie „because ...“ oder „(in order) to ...“, die die Antwort einleiten könnten.

2 **Wie lange** war Francesco **arbeitslos**?
Achten Sie auf die bestimmte Zeitdauer, die er ohne Arbeitsplatz war. Hören Sie beim Wort „unemployed“ genau hin.

3 **Wie** hat Francesco den **Job** in Deutschland **bekommen**?
Denken Sie an Wege, wie man eine neue Arbeitsstelle findet, zum Beispiel durch Bewerbung (application) *auf eine Stellenanzeige* (job advertisement).

4 Welche **Sprache** verwendet Francesco vorwiegend bei der **Arbeit**?
Hören Sie genau hin, wenn Fremdsprachen genannt werden z. B. „English“ *oder* „French“.

5 Aus welchem **Grund ziehen** so viele **junge Menschen** von **Italien nach Deutschland**?
Achten Sie auf Schlagworte und Aussagen bei den Wörtern „young people“, „moving“, „Italy“ *und* „Germany“.

6 Was **denkt** Francesco über das **Leben in Deutschland**?
Seien Sie aufmerksam bei Wörtern, die sich auf Gefühle beziehen, oder bei der Beschreibung seiner jetzigen Situation.

AUFGABE

28

The businesswoman Helen Constantin has received three voicemail messages. Listen to the information and complete the form on the right. You will hear the messages twice.

2 Umgang mit Sehverstehensaufgaben

Wenden Sie beim Ansehen eines Videos die gleichen Kriterien an wie beim Hören einer Aufnahme. Stellen Sie sich beim Zusehen folgende Fragen und bedenken Sie den Effekt der Aufnahme auf die Zuschauer.

1 **Figuren/Personen.** Wie viele Personen treten auf? Welche Figuren treten auf? Wie sehen sie aus? Wie verhalten sie sich? Wie würden Sie ihre Körpersprache beschreiben? Gibt es einen *voice-over* Kommentar?

2 **Schauplatz.** Was ist der Schauplatz? Welche Elemente zeigt der Regisseur, um der Schauplatz zu verdeutlichen? Wie wird das Licht verwendet – ist es dunkel oder hell? Sind die Aufnahmen draußen oder drinnen?

3 **Kameraeinstellungen.** Stellen Sie fest, auf wen oder was die Kamera eingestellt wird. Wird die Aufnahme von weitem oder nahem gemacht, oder wechselt die Kamera zwischen beiden Einstellungen hin und her?

4 **Musik.** Wird Musik eingesetzt? Wie würden Sie die Musik beschreiben? Welche Gefühle und Bilder löst sie in Ihnen aus?

Wie man an Mediationsaufgaben herangeht

Bei dieser Aufgabenform geht es um die Umschreibung und Wiedergabe bestimmter, aus einem englischen Originaltext entnommener Informationen in deutscher Sprache. Die Frage wird auf Deutsch gestellt.

1 Das Ziel von Mediationsaufgaben

Mediationsaufgaben sollen überprüfen, ob Sie die Bedeutung einer bestimmten Textpassage, eines Satzteils oder eines bestimmten Ausdrucks richtig verstanden haben. Dabei kommt es darauf an, dass Sie die betreffende Textstelle **nicht einfach wortwörtlich übersetzen**, sondern in ein sinnvolles, grammatikalisch korrektes und sprachlich natürliches Deutsch umwandeln.

2 Die verschiedenen Arten von Mediationaufgaben

1 Ein schwieriger Satz oder ein idiomatischer Ausdruck des englischen Textes soll auf Deutsch erläutert werden. Dabei wird eine sinngemäße Erklärung und keine wortwörtliche Übersetzung erwartet. Meist wird ein Ausdruck speziell aus dem vorliegenden Textzusammenhang abgefragt. Die Textstelle wird hier stets in der Frage angegeben.

2 Es sollen mehrere Inhalte einer (unter Umständen längeren) Textpassage wiedergegeben werden. Die Anzahl der benötigten Aspekte wird in der Frage angegeben oder ist aus der Anzahl der Spiegelstriche oder aus anderen Aufzählungszeichen (z. B. a, b, c usw.) ersichtlich. Bei dieser Aufgabenform reicht meistens eine stichwortartige Beantwortung in deutscher Sprache.

3 Manchmal wird ein tieferes Textverständnis dadurch abgefragt, dass Sie zwischen den Zeilen lesen oder eine logische Schlussfolgerung ziehen sollen und dies anschließend korrekt auf Deutsch darstellen. Diese Aufgabenform eignet sich eher für fiktionale Texte als für Sachtexte.

3 Vorgehensweise

1 Lesen Sie sich die Frage sorgfältig durch. In der Regel soll ein Ausdruck in einem ganz bestimmten Zusammenhang erklärt werden.

2 Suchen Sie Schlüsselwörter oder Ausdrücke im englischen Originaltext, die den deutschen Formulierungen in der Fragestellung entsprechen könnten.

3 Verwenden Sie Ihr einsprachiges Wörterbuch, um unbekannte Ausdrücke der zu übertragenden Passage nachzuschlagen. Achten Sie aber darauf, dass der Ausdruck im Textzusammenhang gegebenenfalls eine ganz spezielle Bedeutung haben kann.

4 Obwohl Sie nicht wortwörtlich übersetzen sollen, ist dennoch Genauigkeit gefragt. Denken Sie also daran, keine relevanten Informationen zu übersehen.
BEISPIEL: Bei an ever increasing number of women sollte man von einer „ständig steigenden Zahl von Frauen" sprechen und nicht unspezifisch von „Frauen" oder „vielen Frauen".

5 Achten Sie darauf, wortwörtliche oder nicht idiomatische Übertragungen zu vermeiden.

BEISPIEL painkiller

Schmerztöter oder *schmerztötendes Medikament* (wortwörtlich)
Schmerzstiller (unnatürlich bzw. weniger gebräuchlich)
schmerzstillendes Mittel oder *Schmerztablette* (idiomatisch)

BEISPIELAUFGABE

Anbei finden Sie Beispiele aus einem Text, der sich mit der übermäßigen Nutzung des Internets beschäftigt:

Originaltext	Aufgabe und ihre Bearbeitung
The survey also found that constantly being connected was having a negative impact on our manners. A quarter of those surveyed said someone bumped into them at least once a week because they were looking at their smartphones. More than a quarter said they had texted or used a messaging service to communicate with someone in the same room at home while 40% felt they had been "smart snubbed" – ignored by a friend or relative too engrossed in their smartphone or tablet.	**1 Was meint der Autor mit dem Ausdruck "smart snubbed"?** Es geht hier nicht um eine Übersetzung des Begriffs, welche hier auch gar nicht zu leisten wäre, da es sich um ein Wortspiel handelt. Vielmehr geht es darum, die – hier hervorgehobenen – Informationen zu finden und ins Deutsche zu übertragen, um die Bedeutung des Begriffs zu erklären. Der Autor meint damit, dass sich jemand nicht beachtet fühlt, weil ein Freund oder Verwandter zu sehr in sein Smartphone oder seinen Tabletcomputer vertieft ist.
Ways of disconnecting vary. Three in 10 said they had gone on some form of digital detox holiday, with 16% saying they had chosen a location with no internet access and 13% that they had deliberately left their phone at home. Almost one in 10 went further and visited a place without even a telephone line. […] Those aged 16 to 24 were most likely to have taken a digital detox at some point, with more than half having done so in the last year. (from: *The Guardian*, 4 August 2016)	**2 Erläutern Sie, was die Leute gemacht haben, um sich vom Internet zu lösen?** Hier gilt es den hervorgehobenen Teil in einem größeren Textzusammenhang zu finden und ins Deutsche zu übertragen. Nur diese Aussage verlangt eine genauere Erläuterung (die weiteren Aussagen sind nur Beispiele). Wenn Sie „detox" nachschlagen, werden Sie eine Erklärung finden, die Ihnen klar macht, dass es sich um „Entzug" oder „Entgiftung" handelt. Die Digitalisierung wird dabei mit einem Suchtmittel verglichen, von dem man sich ähnlich wie bei einer Entziehungs- oder Entgiftungskur erholen muss. Sie sollten nun aber nicht nur „digitale Entgiftungskur" schreiben, sondern auch erklären, was mit diesem Ausdruck gemeint ist: Sie haben versucht, sich in einer Art Urlaub ganz ohne Medien vom digitalen Stress zu erholen.

AUFGABE

Wie würden Sie an die folgende Mediationsaufgabe herangehen?

Those who took a digital detox generally said it was a positive experience, with a third saying they were more productive and a quarter saying they enjoyed life more. However, some found the experience disturbing, with 16% saying they felt like they were missing out and 8% saying they felt anxious. However, of those who had never deliberately disconnected, 34% said they definitely would not like to give it a go.	**Nennen Sie die unterschiedlichen Reaktionen auf die Versuche, sich vom digitalen Stress zu erholen.**

Wie man an *multiple-matching*-Aufgaben, *short-answer questions* und *sentence completion* herangeht

Multiple matching, _short-answer questions_ und _sentence completion_ sind unterschiedliche Aufgaben zur Überprüfung des Textverständnisses.

1 *Multiple matching*

Bei dieser Aufgabenart müssen Sie bestimmte Aussagen bzw. Begriffe einander zuordnen oder bestimmte Satzteile in einen Text einordnen. Dabei werden mehr Antwortmöglichkeiten als nötig angeboten. Es kommen zwei Varianten vor:

1 Aus dem Originaltext werden Sätze oder Absätze unverändert entnommen und müssen den Lücken zugeordnet werden.

2 Überschriften, kurze Zusammenfassungen, Personen, Fragen usw. müssen Absätzen oder Passagen aus dem Originaltext zugeordnet werden.

BEISPIELAUFGABE

The alternative-energy sector has the potential to employ many more people, but it could initially lead to economic difficulties, as consumers and industry would have to pay higher costs. The US government is aiming to reduce the nation's carbon emissions in order to halt climate change, yet hopes to leave the economy undented, which on paper looks like a near impossible task. To liberal economists, the best climate policies are those that are pushed by market forces, while the most disastrous are those pushed by governmental dictates. "Telling companies what they have to do, what rules they must follow and what equipment they need to buy has always been a recipe for disaster," says David Kaplan, an economist adviser to one of the leading oil companies in the USA. "Instead of forcing everyone to follow the same directives, government should be allowing companies to find the solution that is cheapest and best for them." Financing research is one way the government can try to slow climate change without harming economic growth. According to the Brookings Institution, a non-profit organization in Washington, the US government is going to have to spend at least $5 billion a year on clean energy research and development, money that is needed to experiment with solutions before they are put into practice. Of course, no matter what the White House wants, it seems unlikely that Congress will vote in favour of additional financing to support alternative energy. Scientists argue that the strongest economic argument for an appropriate response to climate change is the fact that the economy won't be booming in a world of droughts, hurricanes and excessive heat waves.

A Which statement (1–7) relates to which person or institution (A–E)? There are two more statements than needed.

A US government
B liberal economists
C David Kaplan
D Brookings Institution
E scientists

1 More needs to be spent on research to slow climate change.
2 The government has conflicting goals: to combat climate change and to continue economic output.
3 It's effective to introduce a carbon tax for additional financing.
4 The worst climate policies are those which are imposed by the government.
5 To help the environment, governments should raise the energy costs for every household.
6 There is no one solution to alternative energy for every company.
7 Since climate change will soon harm the economy, it is better to act now.

Vorgehensweise:

1 Machen Sie alle Personen oder Institutionen im Text ausfindig und lesen Sie genau, welche Aussagen diese machen.

2 Suchen Sie im Text Aussagen, die gleiche oder ähnliche Ideen wie in den Statements ausdrücken.

3 Überprüfen Sie, ob die übrig gebliebenen Aussagen (Distraktoren) nicht zu einer der anderen Personen oder Institutionen passen.

2 *Short-answer questions* und *sentence completion*

Bei dieser Aufgabenart werden entweder Fragen zum Text gestellt, die in englischer Sprache beantwortet werden müssen, oder es sollen unvollständige Sätze mit Informationen aus dem Text vervollständigt werden. Gehen Sie folgendermaßen vor:

1 Lesen Sie die Fragen bzw. unvollständigen Sätze sorgfältig durch.

2 Suchen Sie nach Schlüsselwörtern und Ausdrücken im Text, die auch in den Fragen bzw. unvollständigen Sätzen vorkommen.

3 Verwenden Sie zur Vervollständigung der Lücken bzw. zur Beantwortung der Fragen die Wörter aus dem Text, ohne diese zu verändern oder zu umschreiben.

4 Halten Sie sich an die Wortzahl der Antwort, falls eine solche vorgegeben wird.

BEISPIELAUFGABE

Beachten Sie die Übereinstimmungen zwischen den Wörtern (entweder rosa oder gelb hervorgehoben) im Originaltext und in den Aufgaben.

It's time to act on climate change

There are several reasons why an energy revolution is essential. First, a switch to cleaner energy would make tackling other green concerns a lot easier. That is because dealing with many of these energy concerns, e.g. burning waste material, is an energy-intensive task. Task 1
The second reason is that burning fossil fuels rich in carbon is having a massive effect on Task 2
climate change. The most sensible way for governments to tackle this problem is to send a Task 3
powerful signal that the world must move towards a low-carbon future. That would lead to all sorts of clean energy innovations.
One good idea is for governments to impose a tax based on carbon emissions. That would make Task 4
it absolutely clear that the time has come to stop burning dirty fuels such as coal, as it would hit the pockets of consumers and industry.

Answer the following questions or complete the sentences with words/expressions from the text.

1 Which energy concern is given as an example in the text? ___
2 The burning of oil, gas and coal contributes so much to climate change because they are ___.
3 What would be the result if governments decided to significantly reduce carbon emissions? ___
4 An effective way of holding producers and users of energy responsible would be for the government to ___.

Wie man eine *gapped summary* löst

Bei einer *gapped summary* handelt es sich um eine Zusammenfassung (*summary*) des Originaltextes, in der Lücken gelassen sind, die Sie mit relevanten Begriffen aus dem Originaltext füllen sollen. Diese Art von Aufgabe wird eingesetzt, um Ihr Lese- bzw. Hörverstehen zu überprüfen. Je nachdem, wie viele Leerstellen die Lücke hat, müssen Sie diese mit einem einzigen Wort oder mit einem Ausdruck (bestehend aus 2 oder 3 Wörtern) füllen. Dabei dürfen Sie an den Wörtern bzw. Ausdrücken aus dem Originaltext keinerlei Veränderung vornehmen, also kein Plural-s, keine *ed*-Endung, keine *ly*-Endung usw. weglassen oder hinzufügen.

1 Als Hörverstehensaufgabe

Bei einer *gapped summary* zu einem Hörtext müssen Sie zuhören und gleichzeitig die Zusammenfassung lesen. Dabei müssen Sie erkennen, an welcher Stelle des Hörtextes Sie gerade angekommen sind, wenn im *gapped summary* eine Lücke auftaucht, und diese mit dem entsprechenden Wort oder Ausdruck füllen. Dies ist eine anspruchsvolle Hörverstehensaufgabe, die Ihre volle Konzentration erfordert.

2 Als Leseverstehensaufgabe

Zur Überprüfung des Leseverstehens ist die *gapped summary* ebenfalls eine der schwierigeren Aufgabenarten, bei der es sehr auf die richtige Vorgehensweise ankommt. Dies wird Ihnen im Folgenden erläutert und mit Ihnen geübt.

1 **Originaltext durchlesen.** Weil es darauf ankommt, die korrespondierenden Passagen im Text und in der *gapped summary* zu finden, lesen Sie am besten nur den Originaltext einmal konzentriert durch (ohne dabei viel im Wörterbuch zu blättern) und verschaffen Sie sich damit einen Überblick über das Thema insgesamt, über wichtige Aussagen und vor allem über die Reihenfolge, in der sie getroffen werden. Arbeiten Sie dazu mit Unterstreichungen und Randnotizen.

2 **Richtige Textpassage aussuchen.** Die Aufgabenstellung lautet: *Fill the gaps in the summary with words or expressions from the corresponding passages of the text*. Aus dieser Aufgabenstellung ergibt sich, dass nur in der bestimmten Textpassage, auf die sich ein Satz in der *gapped summary* bezieht, sich das gesuchte Wort findet, das in die Lücke gehört. Auch wenn Sie an anderer Stelle im Originaltext ein Wort finden, das die Lücke sinnvoll schließt, dürfen Sie es nicht verwenden.

3 **Reihenfolge der Aussagen erkennen.** Wenn Sie sich anschließend die *gapped summary* durchlesen, dürften Sie beim Lesen schon erkennen, ob die Aussagen in der *gapped summary* der Reihenfolge des Textes folgen. Dies ist nicht immer der Fall, da in einer Zusammenfassung eines Textes manchmal Umstellungen nötig sind.

4 **Die Umschreibung des Originaltexts in der Zusammenfassung erkennen.** Bei einer *gapped summary* können Sie davon ausgehen, dass jeder Satz den Inhalt einer bestimmten Textstelle des Originaltextes wiedergibt, allerdings kürzer und damit in anderen Worten. Es ist Ihre Aufgabe, in dieser Umschreibung die entsprechende Originaltextpassage zu erkennen.

BEISPIELAUFGABE

Sehen wir uns dazu ein paar Beispiele aus einem Text über seltene Tierarten an. Die **fett** und ***fett-kursiv*** gedruckten Passagen in beiden Texten zeigen, wie sich der Originaltext und die Zusammenfassung aufeinander beziehen.

Originaltext	*gapped summary*
The ***threatened*** extinction of **the tiger** in India, the perilous existence of the **orangutan** in Indonesia, the plight of the **panda**: these are wildlife emergencies with which we have become familiar. But now scientists fear the real impact of declining **wildlife** could be **closer to home**, with the threat to creatures such as ladybirds posing the harshest danger to biodiversity.	Whereas previously the ***possible*** ▬ (= das Aussterben) of **wildlife species** (= tiger, organutan, panda) was limited to faraway countries, scientists warn that more and more **creatures in our immediate vicinity** (= closer to home), such as the ladybirds, are under ▬ (= in Gefahr sein; „danger" ist ausgeschlossen, weil man „to be in danger" sagt).

AUFGABE

Lesen Sie die folgende Passage aus einem Text über Jugendarbeitslosigkeit in Europa und die dazu gehörende Passage aus einer *gapped summary*. Finden Sie die Wörter, die in die Lücken gehören und markieren Sie mit grüner Farbe die Übereinstimmungen zwischen der *gapped summary* und dem Originaltext.

Originaltext	*gapped summary*
Almost 8m young Europeans are not in work, education or training; one young person in seven. Compared with the scale of the problem, the funds on offer are puny. The pledge of €8 billion over two years is the equivalent of €850 a year for every young European in those countries who is neither in work, nor training nor education. Apprenticeships are a good idea, but they will do little to help Europe's young jobless unless governments also succeed in boosting growth. The main reason youth unemployment has soared in southern Europe is the depth of the recessions in those countries. The young have been hit harder than older people. Apprenticeship schemes may help at the margins by making youngsters more employable, but they will not substitute for economic recovery. Prospects for this potentially "lost" generation will not improve until the European economy gets better. (From: *The Economist*, 20 July 2013)	Considering the staggering number of youngsters in Europe with little hope for the future, the ▬ are far too small to be effective. The writer criticizes the fact that EU leaders focus too much on ▬ and too little on the economy. While he argues that some young people will become more ▬ by undertaking training, the ▬ for the majority of young people will remain bad unless the EU governments implement the right economic policies.

3 Was Sie noch machen können

Gapped summaries sind Zusammenfassungen von Originaltexten. Dabei werden Inhalte umgeschrieben. Damit Sie sich daran gewöhnen, wie solche Umschreibungen aussehen, legen Sie eine Tabelle nach folgendem Muster an, in die Sie nach jeder *gapped summary*, Inhalte des Originaltextes und die Umformulierungen in der Aufgabe einander gegenüberstellen.

Formulierung in der Aufgabe	Originaltext
the murder rate increased	the number of murders in the city continued to rise

Wie man *multiple-choice*-Aufgaben löst

Eine *multiple-choice*-Aufgabe besteht aus einer Frage mit mehreren Antwortoptionen bzw. aus einem unvollständigen Satz mit mehreren Vervollständigungsmöglichkeiten. Nur eine der angebotenen Lösungen ist richtig.

1 Als Hörverstehensaufgabe

Bei Hörtexten gibt es in der Regel bei jeder *multiple-choice*-Aufgabe drei Optionen, aus denen Sie die richtige auswählen müssen. Die drei Optionen sind relativ kurz gehalten, damit Sie nicht zu viel lesen und behalten müssen und sich auf das Zuhören konzentrieren können.

2 Als Leseverstehensaufgabe

Zur Überprüfung des Leseverstehens werden bei den *multiple-choice*-Aufgaben vier Optionen zur Auswahl gestellt. Sie müssen extrem viel Text verarbeiten und dabei herausfinden, welche Aussagen in Originaltext und Aufgabe inhaltlich übereinstimmen und welche nicht.

3 Vorgehensweise

1 **Text lesen.** Sie dürfen angesichts der vielen möglichen Aussagen in *multiple-choice*-Aufgaben den Originaltext nicht aus den Augen verlieren! Deshalb ist es wichtig, sich zu allererst nur den Originaltext einmal konzentriert durchzulesen. Verschaffen Sie sich dabei einen Überblick über das Thema insgesamt sowie über die wichtigsten Einzelaussagen und deren Reihenfolge. Arbeiten Sie mit Unterstreichungen und/oder Randnotizen.

2 **Die *multiple-choice*-Aufgaben lesen.** Die Aufgaben können sich auf einzelne Aussagen, ganze Passagen oder den gesamten Text und die Meinung des Verfassers beziehen. Die Fragen folgen der Struktur des Textes, und die Frage zum Gesamttext steht in der Regel an letzter Stelle. Gern wird auch danach gefragt, was nicht im Text steht.

3 **Die richtigen Textstellen finden.** Die Frage oder der Satzanfang verweisen Sie auf die Textstelle(n), die Sie sich ansehen müssen, um die richtige Lösung zu finden. Diese Textstelle(n) werden Sie rasch finden, wenn Sie sich einen Überblick über den Text verschafft haben.

4 **Die Wörter verstehen.** Hier müssen Sie nun mit dem Wörterbuch arbeiten und als erstes sicherstellen, dass Sie die Wörter, die in der Aufgabe und den vier Optionen verwendet werden, verstehen. Andernfalls können Sie die vier Optionen nicht richtig voneinander unterscheiden.

5 **Die richtigen Lösungen erkennen.** Die richtigen Lösungen erkennen Sie daran, dass die Passagen des Originaltextes mit anderen Worten wiedergegeben sind.

BEISPIELAUFGABE

Sehen wir uns dazu als Beispiel die *multiple-choice*-Aufgabe zu einem Text über Lehrmethoden an. Hier wurden Aufgabe und Teile des Originaltexts einander gegenübergestellt, damit Sie nachvollziehen können, wie die richtige Lösung zustande kommt. Die entsprechenden Ausdrücke im Originaltext und in den Aufgaben sind farblich hervorgehoben.

Multiple-choice-Aufgabe		Originaltext
1	When the author was a student and had to copy something, he would spend the remaining lesson …	When I went to school, it was common place for a teacher to place a textbook in front a set of students and offer the simple yet daunting line, "copy that".
a b c d	totally focused on the text in front of him. Keine Erwähnung im Text. listening intently to the teacher's stories. Keine Erwähnung im Text. chatting busily about the text with the people sitting next to him. in silent boredom.	There would be no talking (= Gegenteil von "chatting busily") to either the teacher or fellow pupils. For me lessons seemed to drag so much that I wasn't engaged (= die Stunden zogen sich hin und der Autor entwickelte kein Interesse = Langeweile → d ist die richtige Lösung) in the subject material.
2	The author became a teacher …	I'm proud to say that I became a teacher
a b c d	because (= weil) he had received a very poor education himself. **despite** (= obwohl) receiving a poor education himself. in order to (= um zu) find out what good education is all about. for reasons (= aus Gründen) that had nothing to do with his own education.	**in spite of** (= trotz) the education I received; I believed that **I could and would do a better job** (= Grund für die Berufswahl → stimmt weder mit a, noch c noch d überein). This task was made easier through the use of technology in the classroom. *despite/in spite* of bezeichnen beide einen Gegensatz. Dass die Erziehung des Autors *poor* war ergibt sich aus dem 1. Textabsatz (Langeweile). (From: *The Guardian*, 18 June 2013)

AUFGABE

Lesen Sie die folgende Passage aus einem Text über Drogenkriminalität und finden Sie die richtige Antwort zur *multiple-choice*-Aufgabe. Schreiben Sie den Text ab und markieren Sie sich die Übereinstimmungen zwischen den Optionen und dem Text und auch die Unterschiede.

Multiple-choice-Aufgabe		Originaltext
1	Due to the influx of Asian supplies in the 1970s and 1980s, drugs in New York City …	Things began to change in the 1970s and 1980s. In New York, the Italian-American mafia lost its control over the heroin trade as new drug supply routes were opened up from Asia. Increased competition led to a sharp jump in the purity of their goods but also meant that gangsters had to be better connected. In the late 1970s access to sources of heroin created close-knit gangs which then tried to control territory to sell it. (From: *The Economist*, 15 August 2013)
a b c d	became harder to obtain. suddenly improved in quality. were much more in demand than before. were sold via modern means of communication.	

4 Was Sie zusätzlich tun können

Multiple-Choice-Aufgaben arbeiten mit Umschreibungen des Originaltextes. Um diese Umschreibungs-Strategien besser in den Griff zu bekommen, legen Sie sich eine Tabelle an, in der Sie Originaltext und Frageformulierungen einander gegenüberstellen.

Formulierung in der Aufgabe	Originaltext
lessons seemed to drag so much	boredom

An die unterschiedlichen Arten von *argumentative writing* herangehen

Beim *argumentative writing* geht es darum, sich zu einem gestellten Thema differenziert zu äußern. Dabei wird bewertet, ob Sie das Thema inhaltlich korrekt erfassen sowie interessant bearbeiten können und ob Sie Ihre Gedanken strukturiert entwickeln können. Zudem fließen die Verständlichkeit und die Natürlichkeit der sprachlichen Ausgestaltung in die Bewertung ein. Ein solcher Aufsatz sollte in der Regel mindestens 200 Wörter umfassen.

1 Der Aufbau einer *composition*

Eine *composition* besteht aus den drei Teilen Einleitung, Hauptteil und Schluss. Mehr zum Aufbau eines Absatzes finden Sie unter „Einen Absatz strukturieren" (S. 208).

a **Einleitung:** Der Einleitungsabsatz sollte den Leser zu dem Thema hinführen. Hierfür eignet sich zum Beispiel eine aktuell in der Öffentlichkeit viel diskutierte Frage, ein gesellschaftliches Problem, ein schockierendes Ereignis, ein Zitat, Sprichwort oder eine Ihnen bekannte aktuelle Statistik. Die Einleitung sollte mit der Themenfrage enden, die zum Hauptteil überleitet.

b **Hauptteil:** In diesem Teil entwickeln Sie Ihre Argumentation. Als Faustregel hat es sich bewährt, drei Absätze (= drei Argumente) zu verfassen. Beginnen Sie für jedes neue Argument einen neuen Absatz. Sie dürfen allerdings im Hauptteil auch zwei oder vier Argumente präsentieren, solange diese überzeugend und konkret ausgeführt werden.

c **Schluss:** Dieser Teil rundet die Argumentation ab. Geben Sie spätestens hier eine klare Antwort auf die Themafrage. Wiederholen Sie nicht die Argumente des Hauptteils, sondern ordnen Sie das Thema in einen größeren Zusammenhang ein. Dies kann zum Beispiel durch einen Appell, einen Ausblick in die Zukunft, ein Fazit oder einen Kompromissvorschlag geschehen. Achten Sie hierbei jedoch darauf, dass im Schlussteil genauso wie in der Einleitung keine neuen Argumente präsentiert werden dürfen.

2 Die unterschiedlichen Arten von *composition*

Es gibt mehrere Arten von *composition*. Achten Sie zu deren Unterscheidung auf die Operatoren in der Fragestellung:

a **Discussion:** *Discuss …, Weigh up the pros / benefits and cons / drawbacks of …* usw.:
Das Thema muss von beiden Seiten beleuchtet werden, aber mit der Seite schließen, der Sie persönlich eher anhängen. Bei dieser dialektischen Herangehensweise beginnen Sie den Hauptteil mit der Position (pro oder contra), die Sie eher nicht teilen. Nachdem Sie hierzu ein bis zwei Argumente vorgebracht haben, wechseln Sie zur Position (contra oder pro), die Sie selbst vertreten. Schreiben Sie hierzu drei Argumente, die diese Position untermauern. Wenn Ihr Hauptteil also aus drei Absätzen besteht, führen Sie ein Argument, das für Sie weniger stark ist, und anschließend zwei Argumente, die für Sie persönlich überzeugender sind. Wichtig: Schließen Sie nicht mit einem Argument für die Position, die Sie selbst nicht vertreten.

b **Comments:** *Comment on …, What is your opinion of …?, Do you agree …?, What do you think …?* usw.: Sie sollen Ihre Meinung zu einem Thema oder einer Äußerung abgeben und diese mit Erläuterungen oder Beispielen untermauern. Dies kann nun auch in steigernder Form geschehen, d. h. Sie eröffnen den Hauptteil mit der Darlegung Ihres Standpunktes und stützen diesen mit Hilfe von – in der Regel – drei Argumenten. Dabei beginnen Sie mit dem Ihrer Meinung nach schwächsten Aspekt und enden mit Ihrem stärksten Argument. Wichtig: Sie dürfen dialektisch vorgehen wie bei einer *discussion*, wenn Sie keine klare Meinung zu einem Thema haben.

c **Andere:** Daneben gibt es noch einen weiteren Aufgabentyp, bei dem Sie sich zur **Ursache** für ein Problem, **Maßnahmen** gegen ein Problem oder **Folgen** einer Situation äußern sollen. Achten Sie genau auf die Fragestellung, denn hier sind verschiedenste Formulierungen denkbar, z. B. *What are the reasons …, Why …?* (Ursachen), *What measures could be taken …?, What could be done to …?* (Maßnahmen) oder *What are the consequences …?* (Folgen). Schreiben Sie im Hauptteil drei Absätze: Beginnen Sie mit dem für Sie am wenigsten wichtigen Aspekt und schließen Sie mit dem überzeugendsten Punkt. Anstelle von Argumenten nennen Sie nun je nach Aufgabenstellung Gründe, Maßnahmen oder Folgen und erläutern diese oder geben Sie Beispiele. Achten Sie bei diesem Aufgabentyp darauf, dass Sie bestimmte Floskeln nicht verwenden können. Sie können etwa den Schluss nicht mit einem Satz wie *All in all, one can say the benefits outweigh the drawbacks.* beginnen, denn es wird hier nicht nach Vor- und Nachteilen, sondern eben nach Hintergründen, Lösungen oder Folgen gefragt.

d **Materialgestützter Aufsatz:** Darüber hinaus ist es möglich, dass Sie sich mit Hilfe von Material zu einer Fragestellung äußern sollen. Dies bedeutet, dass Ihnen Bilder, Karikaturen, Statistiken, Zitate oder kurze Textstellen (auf Englisch oder Deutsch) angeboten werden, mit deren Hilfe Sie ein Thema untersuchen sollen. Dieses Hintergrundmaterial müssen Sie (teilweise oder vollständig) in Ihre Ausführungen einbauen. Sie könnten also zum Beispiel ein Zitat für Ihre Einleitung verwenden oder die Aussage einer Statistik zur Untermauerung eines Ihrer Argumente gebrauchen.

Ein paar nützliche Tipps und Schritte, die Sie bei der Bearbeitung der *composition* beachten sollten:

1 Analysieren Sie das Thema: Versuchen Sie alle Begriffe in der Themenstellung genau zu verstehen und schlagen Sie unbekannte Begriffe im Wörterbuch nach.
2 Führen Sie ein Brainstorming von Argumenten sowie möglichen Beispielen oder Erklärungen durch. Dann überlegen Sie, welche Inhalte zum Thema gehören und welche Aspekte weggelassen werden können. Halten Sie diese auf einem Notizpapier mit einer Mindmap oder einer anderen Methode fest.
3 Überlegen Sie sich eine Gliederung für Ihren Text. Je präziser Sie diese bereits auf Ihrem Notizpapier festhalten, desto einfacher werden Sie später vorankommen und typische Fehler, wie etwa das Auftauchen mehrerer Argumente in einem Absatz, vermeiden.
4 Verfassen Sie den Text und legen Sie dem Leser einen roten Faden durch Ihren Aufsatz, indem Sie Strukturwörter wie *moreover*, *therefore*, *on the other hand* verwenden.
5 Überprüfen Sie Ihren Text auf Rechtschreibfehler oder typische Grammatikfehler.

AUFGABE

Um welche Art von *composition* handelt es sich bei den folgenden Aufgaben?

- "There should be zero tolerance for athletes who dope." Do you agree with this viewpoint?
- "Travelling and doing good belong together". Discuss.
- A lot of people will do anything for fame. What are the attractions and dangers of fame?

Einen Absatz strukturieren

Ein guter Aufsatz besteht aus klar definierten Absätzen (= *paragraphs*). Ein Absatz ist eine Gruppe von zusammenhängenden Sätzen, die ein Thema oder Argument behandeln.

1 Der Aufbau eines Absatzes

A Verschiedene Teile eines Absatzes: Ein Aufsatz besteht aus Einleitung, Hauptteil und Schluss. Man kann jeden Absatz genauso aufbauen, sozusagen als eine Art „mini-essay".

1 **Topic sentence.** Generell sollte ein Absatz mit einem Satz beginnen, der den wesentlichen Gedanken, i.d.R. ein Argument, ausdrückt.

2 **Supporting sentences.** Dieser Gedanke wird durch zwei oder drei Sätze untermauert, in denen relevante Tatsachen oder Details genannt werden.

3 **Concluding sentence.** Am Ende des Absatzes sollten Sie Ihr Argument nochmals nennen und mit dem Thema in Verbindung setzen.

Jeder Absatz sollte nur einen Hauptgedanken oder ein Hauptargument behandeln. Verschiedene Aspekte eines Arguments können erläutert werden, solange sie in direktem Zusammenhang zueinander stehen. Jeder *supporting sentence* sollte direkt zum Hauptthema beitragen. Es ist auch möglich, zuerst ein Gegenargument (= *counter-argument*) anzuführen, um dieses anschließend zu entkräften.

B Der Zusammenhalt eines Absatzes. Versuchen Sie stets, die Sätze eines Absatzes mit *linking words and phrases* (vgl. die hintere Umschlagklappe des Buches) zu verbinden, um ein logisches und verständliches Ganzes zu schaffen. Schreiben Sie niemals einen Satz, ohne zu überlegen, wie man schlüssig und folgerichtig zum nächsten überleiten kann. So vermeiden Sie Gedankensprünge, die den Leser verwirren und Ihre Argumentation schwächen.

2 Vorbereitung

Bevor Sie Ihren Absatz niederschreiben, sollten Sie Argumente und Fakten stichpunktartig in eine logische Struktur bringen. Dies könnte folgendermaßen aussehen:
1. Satz – *topic sentence* – Hauptthese
2. Satz – *supporting sentence* – Tatsachen oder Details, die die Hauptthese untermauern
3. Satz – *supporting sentence* – Tatsachen oder Details, die die Hauptthese untermauern
4. Satz – *concluding sentence* – Rückbezug der These auf das Thema

AUFGABE 1
Ein Schüler hat drei Absätze eines Aufsatzes zum folgenden Thema verfasst:

"I love food and feel that it is something that should be enjoyed. I eat whatever I want. I just don't overeat." (Tyra Banks, model and actress)

Do you think that this is the secret to a healthy and happy life?

A In general, people who eat a healthy diet have fewer health problems than people who overeat. Vegetarians, for example, are usually less overweight than people who eat too much junk food. However, they may find that they are not getting enough essential vitamins and minerals if they are too careful about their diet. Their diet might also be very boring and in the end they won't enjoy eating at all.

B Food plays a big part in most people's lives and most people in our society are able to enjoy food and not just eat to live. However, obesity is a big problem and a lot of people are worried about staying fit and having a good figure.

C People who consume too many calories and don't do enough physical activity are often overweight. Obesity is also a common cause of diabetes, heart disease and strokes. But, it is not just how much food we consume but the type of food that is important for our health. Someone who eats lots of junk food, such as hamburgers and chips, will have greater health problems than someone who eats a lot of fruit and vegetables.

1 Ordnen Sie die Absätze A, B und C dem Einleitungsmotto zu.
2 Schreiben Sie den Text ab und ordnen Sie jedem Satz innerhalb des Absatzes eine im Kästchen genannte Funktion zu.

topic sentence ▪ supporting argument ▪ example ▪ contradictory argument

3 Bringen Sie die drei Absätze in die richtige Reihenfolge.
4 Schreiben Sie einen den Aufsatz abschließenden Absatz.

AUFGABE 2

Vervollständigen Sie den Text mit den passenden *linking words and phrases* aus dem Kästchen. Manchmal ist mehr als eine Lösung möglich.

according to ▪ although ▪ and ▪ for example ▪ for instance ▪ furthermore ▪ however ▪ in addition ▪ in conclusion ▪ on the one hand ▪ on the other hand ▪ while

Are Americans overweight? There is no easy answer to this question, ___[1] there are some unsettling statistics that support this view. ___[2], 13% of the world's obese population live in the United States, a country which accounts for only 5% of the world's population, ___[3] a recent analysis of data from 188 countries. ___[4], an estimated 160 million Americans are either obese or overweight, ___[5] nearly three-quarters of American men and more than 60% of women are obese or overweight. ___[6], America's children are also growing up to be obese: ___[7], nearly 30% of boys and girls under age 20 are either obese or overweight, up from 19% in 1980.
Overweight is defined as having a Body Mass Index (BMI), or weight-to-height ratio, greater than or equal to 25 and lower than 30, ___[8] obesity is defined as having a BMI equal to or greater than 30. ___[9] the percentage of people worldwide who are either overweight or obese has risen substantially over the last 30 years, there have been considerable differences across regions and countries. ___[10], increases in obesity in developed countries that began in the 1980s and accelerated from 1992 to 2002 have slowed since 2006. ___[11], in developing countries, where almost two-thirds of the world's obese people currently live, increases are likely to continue.
In 2010, obesity and overweight were estimated to have caused 3.4 million deaths globally, most of which were from cardiovascular causes. ___[12], the research indicates that if the rise in obesity continues, it could lead to future declines in life expectancy in countries worldwide.

An Gruppendiskussionen teilnehmen

Es gehört zu den grundlegenden kommunikativen Kompetenzen des Lebens, aktiv an Meetings und Diskussionen teilzunehmen, dabei die eigenen Standpunkte fundiert zu vertreten, aber auch die Meinungen der anderen Teilnehmer zu akzeptieren und wertzuschätzen, um letztendlich auf ein für alle zufriedenstellendes Diskussionsresultat zu kommen. Bei der *group discussion* kommt es darauf an, mit Hilfe des individuell zur Verfügung gestellten Materials entweder eine Lösung oder einen Kompromiss zu finden, oder aber eine Art Ranking auszuarbeiten.

1 Allgemeine Vorbereitung

- Lernen Sie eine Auswahl der *Language for discussion* Phrasen (vgl. hintere Umschlagklappe). Diese Wendungen helfen Ihnen, Ihre Gedanken strukturiert zu äußern und den reibungslosen Sprecherwechsel (*turn-taking*) in der Gruppe zu bewältigen.
- Bereiten Sie sich durch die Wiederholung relevanten Vokabulars auf die möglichen Themengebiete vor (z. B. *Words in context*).
- Lesen Sie englischsprachige Zeitschriftenartikel zu den Lehrplanthemen, um über neueste Entwicklungen informiert zu sein, Themenbereiche zu vertiefen, Verknüpfungen zu erkennen und das im Unterricht eingeführte Vokabular zu vertiefen.

2 Individuelle Vorbereitungsphase: die Fragestellung überprüfen

Markieren Sie in der Fragestellung, welche Situation vorliegt, was von Ihnen in der Diskussion erwartet wird und was das Resultat der Diskussion sein soll. Weitere für Sie hilfreiche Hinweise sowohl in der Fragestellung als auch im Material unterstreichen Sie je nach Bedarf.

BEISPIELAUFGABE

The alumni association of your school is planning a motivational seminar for current students who often get demotivated due to the heavy workload and the fear of failure. Failure as a fact of life needs to be pointed out, and you are planning to put together a booklet for them containing life stories of people who failed before they became big successes. Members of the alumni association are getting together to look into such life stories, discuss them and draw up a ranking list. Their lists are the basis of the final decisions that will be made by an editorial board. You have been given J.K. Rowling as your example.

Preparation phase

Prepare for the discussion by thinking about your person:

- How seriously did he/she fail?
- How big was his/her staying power?
- Is he/she suitable to serve as a role model for students like yourselves?

Interaction phase

Conduct the discussion according to the rules of the oral group exam. Your task is to decide on one person who definitely should (and another one who really doesn't need to) be included in the planned booklet.

3 Individuelle Vorbereitungsphase: Material vorbereiten

Wenn Sie Material erhalten haben oder Informationen durch Recherchen gefunden haben, erarbeiten Sie das Material in Hinblick auf die vorliegende Fragestellung und notieren Sie die dafür relevanten Punkte.

- Machen Sie sich Ihre Notizen ausschließlich auf Englisch. Notieren Sie sich mögliche Stichworte in übersichtlicher Form.
- Schlagen Sie eventuell benötigtes Vokabular nach, aber berücksichtigen Sie auch, dass dieses auch von den anderen Teilnehmern verstanden werden muss.
- Das Ihnen vorliegende Material gibt Ihnen erste Anhaltspunkte für die Diskussion. Sie dürfen aber jederzeit eigene Ideen in die Diskussion miteinbringen, solange diese zum Thema gehören. So könnten Ihre Notizen nach der Recherche aussehen:

J.K. Rowling: UK's best-selling living author – middle class background – difficult childhood – average student – despite hardships in her life – lived off state benefits – did not give up – nowadays: one of the most famous novelists of her time

4 Die Gruppendiskussion

1 Geben Sie zunächst in der Präsentationsphase, in der jeder Teilnehmer in der Gruppe ein erstes Statement (Dauer ca. 1 Minute) abgibt, einen groben Überblick über Ihr mitgebrachtes Material in Hinblick auf die Fragestellung (Ihre Diskussionspartner kennen ja Ihr Material nicht). Für die Aufgabe nicht relevante Details lassen Sie weg.

2 Erst jetzt beginnt die Diskussion, an der sich jedes Gruppenmitglied ausgewogen beteiligt. Besprechen Sie in der Diskussionsphase einzelne Gesichtspunkte strukturiert und in logischer Form. Vermeiden Sie ein chaotisches Hin- und Herspringen zwischen unterschiedlichen Aspekten! Mögliche Strukturierungsansätze wären:

Is it helpful for the readers of the booklet to know the person in question?
What parallels are there between the famous people's lives and students' lives?
What kind of failures are we talking about?
What could the readers of the booklet learn from these persons?

Bei der Diskussion sollten Sie folgendes beachten:

- Gehen Sie nicht allzu früh einen Kompromiss ein, um wertvolle Argumente nicht zu früh auszuschließen.
- Versuchen Sie, an das bereits Gesagte anzuknüpfen, Verbindungen herzustellen oder den bisherigen Stand der Diskussion zusammenzufassen, um die Übersicht zu behalten. Auf diese Weise tragen Sie aktiv zur Entscheidungsfindung bei.
- Artikulieren Sie klar, deutlich und möglichst akzentfrei.
- Unterstreichen Sie das Gesagte mit Ihrer Körperhaltung.
- Orientieren Sie sich an einer offen-freundlichen Arbeitsatmosphäre, in der kreative Gedanken ausgetauscht und wohlwollend diskutiert werden.
- Die Gruppendiskussion ist eine Teamleistung, in der Sie individuell beurteilt werden, von der aber durch das Unterstützen ruhigerer Teilnehmer, das Aushelfen mit Vokabular und das Voranbringen der gesamten Diskussion das Team als Ganzes profitiert. Am Ende der Diskussion einigen Sie sich als Gruppe je nach Fragestellung auf eine Lösung, einen Kompromiss oder ein Ranking.

5 Beurteilung

Die Beurteilung erfolgt nach folgenden Kriterien: *language competence* (sprachliche Kompetenz), *contribution to task achievement* (inhaltliche Qualität des Beitrags), *strategic competence* (interaktive Kompetenz).

Eine Präsentation vorführen

Die Fähigkeit, wirkungsvolle Präsentationen vor Publikum zu halten, ist in fast jedem Lebensstadium von Bedeutung – von der Schule bis zum Arbeitsleben. Dabei ist nicht nur der Inhalt einer Präsentation wichtig, sondern auch, wie klar und verständlich dieser vorgetragen wird.

BEISPIELAUFGABE
Halten Sie eine Präsentation über das Thema „Have fun while getting fit".

1 Bereiten Sie Ihr Thema sorgfältig vor und vergewissern Sie sich, dass die Webseiten, die Sie zitieren, als glaubwürdige Quellen gelten können.

Überlegen Sie sich, welche Suchbegriffe Ihnen am effektivsten zuverlässige Informationen verschaffen. Verlassen Sie sich bei der Suche im Internet nicht auf die erstbesten Suchergebnisse, die Ihnen angezeigt werden. Verwenden Sie grundsätzlich englischsprachige Quellen!

- How to get fit while you have fun
- "get fit" "have fun" family
- "get fit" "have fun" workplace
- "get fit" "have fun" "young people"

Wenn eine URL auf .org, .edu oder .gov endet, ist sie wahrscheinlich eine glaubwürdige Quelle. Prüfen Sie auch den „About us"-Link und finden Sie heraus, wer für den Inhalt verantwortlich ist.

2 Verfassen Sie die Notizen, die Sie für Ihre Präsentation verwenden, auf Englisch.

Kopieren Sie nie ganze Textabschnitte von Webseiten oder aus Büchern. Bauen Sie die wichtigen Formulierungen daraus so in Ihren eigenen Text ein, dass Sie ihn natürlich und frei vortragen können.

Fitness – things to think about are:
- *age / weight / general health*
- *What is realistic?*
- *What sort of sport / fitness training is fun?*

3 Prüfen Sie die Korrektheit Ihrer Notizen in Bezug auf Informationsgehalt und Sprache.

Es ist sehr wichtig, dass Sie alle Wörter richtig aussprechen. Wenn Sie sich nicht sicher sind, hören Sie sich Aussprachebeispiele in einem Online-Wörterbuch an oder suchen Sie Videos, die diesen Begriff enthalten.

Substantive	
calisthenics espAE / callisthenics espBE used with pl. verb [sport.]	die Fitness-Übungen
calisthenics espAE / callisthenics espBE [sport.]	die Freiübung Pl.: die Freiübungen
Aussprache anhören espAE / callisthenics espBE used with pl. verb [sport.]	die Freiübungen Pl.

Video: Trainer explains callisthenics

4 Verwenden Sie geeignetes Anschauungsmaterial, um Ihre Präsentation fesselnder und einprägsamer zu gestalten.

- Wenn Sie ein Flipchart oder Whiteboard benutzen: Überlegen Sie, wie dieses am Ende der Präsentation aussehen soll, und denken Sie daran, sauber und ordentlich zu schreiben.

- Wenn Sie Ihre Präsentation in einem Präsentationsprogramm wie PowerPoint erstellen, überfrachten Sie die Folien nicht mit zu vielen Informationen, Farben usw. Die Aufmerksamkeit sollte auf Ihnen liegen, nicht auf den Folien. Ihre Folien dienen der Veranschaulichung, nicht zum Ablesen oder Vorlesen, d. h. ein Bild unterstützt Ihre Präsentation mehr als tausend Worte.

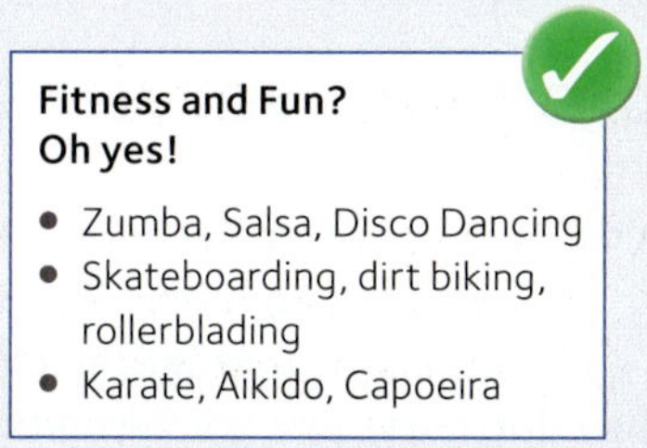

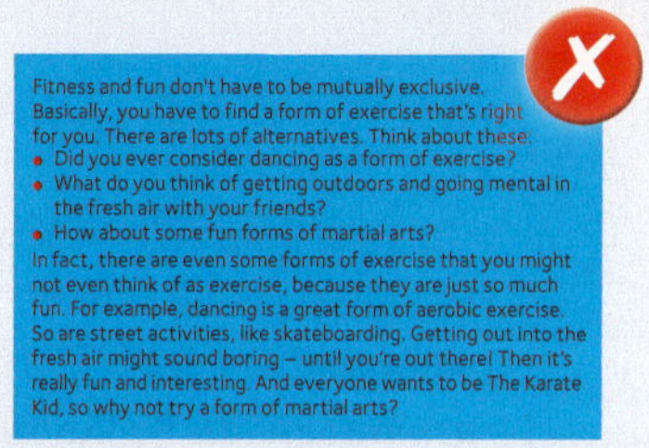

- Auch Gegenstände können effektives Anschauungsmaterial sein. Wenn möglich, besorgen Sie sich für Ihre Präsentation anschauliche Gegenstände wie Souvenirs, Flyer usw.

5 Machen Sie Ihre Präsentation lebendig und interessant.

Erzählen Sie eine Geschichte, einen Witz oder ein persönliches Erlebnis.

→ *As for me, the last thing I want to do in my free time is get sweaty with a group of total strangers in a gym. However, I really love animals, so I found a place where I can ride horses.*

Überhäufen Sie Ihre Zuhörer/innen nicht mit Zahlen und Daten. Verwenden Sie so wenige wie möglich, und entlasten Sie Ihr Publikum, indem Sie sie in schriftlicher Form zeigen.

Interagieren Sie mit Ihrem Publikum. Halten Sie Blickkontakt und stellen Sie ab und zu Fragen.

→ *Think about something you loved doing as a child. Did you like climbing on the monkey bars in the playground, or chasing your friends in the park? Why not do something like that now?*

6 Üben Sie so oft wie möglich.

Üben Sie, ruhig auf beiden Beinen zu stehen, ohne sich dabei unnötig zu bewegen. Proben Sie Ihre Präsentation möglichst oft (vor dem Spiegel oder vor Freunden), um einem Blackout vorzubeugen. Achten Sie dabei auf eine ruhige Haltung und vermeiden Sie hektische Bewegungen. Nehmen Sie die Präsentation auf, um Aussprache und Sprachmelodie zu überprüfen.

Giving a presentation

Introducing yourself and your topic
- Good morning/afternoon. My name is …
- Today I am going to talk about …
- The subject of my talk is …
- My topic today is …
- I'd like to ask you to save your questions for the end of the presentation.

Beginning your first point
- I'd like to begin by saying something about …
- I want to start by explaining …

Guiding your audience through your presentation
- There are a number of points I'd like to make.
- I'll start with … . Then I'll talk about …
- And now, moving on to …
- The next topic I'd like to focus on is …
- Now I'd like to discuss …
- Now we'll move on to …
- Let's look at …
- Why is this important? Because …
- The significance of this is …

Ending your presentation
- Let's summarize briefly what we've looked at.
- Let me remind you of some of the issues we've covered.
- In conclusion, …
- I would like to finish by saying …
- If you have any questions, I'm happy to answer them now.

Letzte Vorbereitungen vor den Prüfungen

Obwohl Englisch nicht zu der Kategorie von Fächern gehört, in denen Sie noch kurz vor der Prüfungsphase schnell Wissen anhäufen können, gibt es neben der kontinuierlichen Arbeit während des Schuljahres durchaus ein paar Möglichkeiten, in den Wochen vor der Prüfung grundlegende Fehlerquellen durch gezielte Wiederholung auszuschließen. Sie sollten mit dieser Wiederholung spätestens vier Wochen vor den mündlichen Prüfungen beginnen.

1 Prüfungsmodalitäten

Zunächst sollten Sie sich mit den Prüfungsmodalitäten (Zeitrahmen, Anforderungen, Art der Aufgabenstellungen, Hilfsmittel) vertraut machen. Im Fach Englisch legen Sie eine verpflichtende mündliche Gruppenprüfung und eine verpflichtende schriftliche Prüfung (*reading*, *writing*) ab. Ihre Lehrkraft ist mit den jeweils aktuellen Prüfungsmodalitäten und Terminen vertraut und hilft Ihnen sicherlich gerne weiter.

2 Wiederholung von Vokabular

1 **Themenwortschatz:** Zunächst sollten Sie das Grundvokabular der Lehrplanthemen wiederholen. Hierbei helfen Ihnen zum einen die Seiten *Words in context* in diesem Buch. Zum anderen gibt es eine Fülle von Zusatzmaterialien, die Ihnen eine gezielte Vokabelwiederholung erleichtern. Je kontinuierlicher Sie während des gesamten Schuljahres Ihr Repertoire an Vokabeln erweitert haben, desto einfacher wird Ihnen die Wiederholung kurz vor der Prüfung fallen. Verwenden Sie vier Wochen vor den Prüfungen mindestens 30–45 Minuten täglich für die aufgeführten Vokabelwiederholungen. Behalten Sie auch die englischsprachige Presse im Auge (z. B. *The Economist*, *TIME Magazine*, *the BBC*), um Ihr Vokabular zu den Lehrplaninhalten in der Praxis zu vertiefen und zu erweitern.

2 **False friends:** Eine häufige Fehlerquelle sind sogenannte *false friends*, d. h. englische Wörter, die in Schrift und Aussprache dem Deutschen so ähnlich sind, dass man dazu verleitet wird, die englische Bedeutung der deutschen gleichzusetzen. Leider ist die Bedeutung aber meist völlig unterschiedlich und führt bei Verwechslung zu erheblichen Missverständnissen. Daher sollten Sie großen Wert auf die Vermeidung solcher typischer Fehler legen. (Siehe S. 234 für die häufigsten *false friends*).
Sollten Sie während des Schuljahres bereits eine individuelle Liste von häufig benötigten Wörtern/Phrasen geführt haben, wiederholen Sie diese, zum Beispiel.

3 **Linking words and phrases:** Um Ihre *writing* Aufgabe in verständlicher und schlüssiger Form zu präsentieren, helfen Ihnen *linking words and phrases*. Diese finden Sie unter „Language for writing" auf der hinteren Umschlagklappe dieses Buchs. Wiederholen Sie diese und machen Sie sich ihre korrekte Verwendungsweise klar.

4 **Nützliche Wörter:** Ein sehr hilfreicher Ausdruck ist *the fact that*, um Konstruktionen zu bilden, die im Deutschen mit einem einfachen „dass" gebildet werden können.

Despite the fact that many people want to spend a year abroad, …
Due to the fact that we could not communicate well, …

She was happy **apart from the fact that** she could not return home.
I hate **the fact that** you are leaving.
I could no longer ignore **the fact that** she did not love me.
How do you account for **the fact that** unemployment is still rising?
It is time to accept **the fact that** you may not get the job you want.
The fact that everything changes is a one of the basic rules of life.

5 Zu häufig verwendete Wörter: Schauen Sie Ihre Aufsätze der letzten Jahre durch und überprüfen Sie, wie häufig Sie bestimmte Wörter wie „says", „writes", „good", „bad", „thinks" verwenden. Legen Sie eine Liste mit häufig verwendeten Wörtern und ihren Ersatzmöglichkeiten an, um mehr Abwechslung und Vielfalt beim Schreiben zu erreichen. Hier einige Beispiele:

also	→	**in addition**, **moreover**, **furthermore**
bad for	→	**detrimental/harmful** to the environment
good	→	a **convincing** argument,
get	→	**obtain/acquire** information, **achieve/attain** a good mark
get better	→	**improve**
get worse	→	**deteriorate**, **worsen**
great	→	some **tremendous** help
like	→	I don't **approve of** these tactics, I **adore** ice cream, I **relish** a good discussion
write about	→	the author **calls attention to** / **points out** …

6 Typische unnötige Fehler vermeiden: Versuchen Sie auf jeden Fall, die für viele Schüler so typischen Fehler zu vermeiden. Beispiele für sogenannte *howlers* sind:

much	~~much people~~ → **a lot of people**
man/men	~~mans/mens~~
information, one piece of information	~~informations, an information~~
he/she/it + „s" in simple present: **does, likes**	~~he do, she like~~ → **he does, she likes**
choose – chose – chosen	~~chose – chosed – choosed~~
lose (verb: *verlieren*), **loose** (adjective: *locker*)	I always ~~loose~~ the game, my shoe is ~~lose~~
NIE **if** + conditional/future im Hauptsatz	If he ~~would/will come,~~ …
something, anything	Have you bought ~~something~~? No, I haven't bought ~~something~~. → Have you bought **anything**? No, I have**n't** bought **anything**. I did buy **something** yesterday.
I can't	I ~~don't can~~
We can also buy … (Adverb folgt Hilfsverb)	We ~~also can~~ buy
There are …	~~It gives~~ animals in the zoo.

3 Grammatik

Wiederholen Sie mit Hilfe der Grammatikübersicht (S. 216) die wichtigsten Formen und Verwendungsweisen grammatischer Strukturen, die Sie häufig in Ihrer *writing* Aufgabe benötigen (z. B. *present perfect vs. past tense, if-clauses, ways of expressing the future*). Übungen werden zu zahlreichen grammatischen Aspekten im ganzen Buch angeboten.

- Um das Subjekt des that-Satzes zu betonen, kann man folgendes Muster benutzen:
  Subjekt + *is/was/...* + 3. Form + *to be* + andere Satzteile (2):
  Aktiv *Many **believe** that the minister is thinking of raising fuel taxes.*
  Passiv *The minister **is believed to be** thinking of raising fuel taxes.*
  ! Der *by agent* wird in solchen Passivsätzen folgendermaßen verwendet:
  Aktiv *The speaker felt that the idea was too radical.*
  Passiv *The idea was felt to be too radical **by** the speaker.*

IF-SENTENCES

1 If we **invest** in new technology, a lot of people **will lose** their jobs.
2 A lot of people **will lose** their jobs if we **invest** in new technology.
3 If more people **took part** in retraining schemes, they **wouldn't have to worry** about finding new employment.
4 We **won't have** political censorship if we **don't start** to censor the internet.
5 **Will** we soon **have** political censorship if we **start** to censor the internet?

- Ein **Konditionalsatz** besteht aus zwei Teilen: dem ***if*-Teil** und dem **Hauptteil**.
  Der ***if*-Teil** drückt eine **Bedingung** aus, der **Hauptteil** eine **Folge**.
- Bei **Konditionalsätzen** kommen folgende **Zeitmuster** am häufigsten vor:
  Typ I *If + simple present* + *will*-Futur
  Typ II *If + simple past* + *would* + Infinitiv
  Typ III *If + past perfect* + *would have* + 3. Form des Verbs
- Der *if*-Teil kann hinter dem Hauptteil stehen. In diesem Fall steht kein Komma dazwischen (2, 4, 5).
- Je nach Sinn kann der *if*-Teil, der Hauptteil oder beide Teile des Satzes **verneint** werden (3, 4).
- Bei **Fragen** kann nur der **Hauptteil** zu einer Frage geformt werden. Dann steht normalerweise dieser Teil **an erster Stelle** (5).
- *if*-Sätze werden gemäß der **Wahrscheinlichkeit** der zu erwartenden Folge eingesetzt:
  Typ I: Folge (fast) sicher.
  *If we **invest** in new technology, a lot of people **will lose** their jobs.*
  D. h. viele Leute werden (vermutlich) ihre Stellen verlieren, da wir (sehr wahrscheinlich) in die neue Technologie investieren werden.
  Typ II: Folge theoretisch möglich, aber kaum wahrscheinlich.
  *If we **invested** in new technology, a lot of people **would lose** their jobs.*
  D. h. es ist kaum zu erwarten, dass viele Leute ihre Stellen verlieren werden, da wir (wahrscheinlich) nicht in die neue Technologie investieren werden.
  Typ III: Folge unmöglich, da die Bedingung nicht erfüllt wurde und bereits in der Vergangenheit liegt.
  *If we **had invested** in new technology, a lot of people **would have lost** their jobs.*
  D. h. der Sprecher weiß schon, dass keiner den Job verloren hat, da wir in die neue Technologie nicht investiert haben.

GERUND/INFINITIVE

1 Max **enjoys reading** in the park.
2 Can you **afford to buy** that new computer software?
3 Cem and Julie **continued to meet** even though they had split up.
4 Cem and Julie **continued meeting** even though they had split up.
5 Alison **normally likes going to** parties, but **today** she **would prefer to stay** at home.

- Nach einigen Verben folgt immer die *-ing*-Form (**gerund**) (1). Am wichtigsten sind:

admit, avoid, consider, deny, enjoy, finish, give up, imagine, mention, (not) mind (etwas/nichts dagegen haben), *miss, practise, recommend, risk, stop, suggest*

- **Nach einigen Verben** folgt immer der Infinitiv (**infinitive**) (2). Die **wichtigsten** Verben dieser Gruppe sind:

afford, choose, decide, expect, hope, manage, mean, plan, promise, refuse, want

! Nach den Verben *begin*, *continue*, *intend* und *start* kann der **Infinitiv** oder die **-*ing*-Form beliebig benutzt werden** (3, 4).

- Einige Verben werden **je nach Bedeutung** entweder mit dem **Infinitiv** oder mit der **-*ing*-Form** benutzt. Die **wichtigsten** Verben dieser Gruppe sind:

like, dislike, love, hate, prefer

- Wenn von einer **allgemeingültigen Situation** die Rede ist, folgt auf diese Verben die **-*ing*-Form**. Handelt es sich aber um eine **Ausnahmesituation**, dann verwendet man den **Infinitiv** (5).

advise, allow, encourage, forbid, permit, recommend
Handelt es sich um einen **konkreten Einzelfall**, wird mit diesen Verben ein **Objekt + Infinitiv** verwendet.
*I strongly **advise you to be** more polite to people.*
Wenn es sich aber um eine **allgemeine Situation** handelt, dann steht das nachfolgende Verb in der **-*ing*-Form**.
*Most firms don't **allow smoking** in their offices.*

forget/remember
Die Struktur ***forget/remember* + -*ing*-Form** bezieht sich auf die Vergangenheit. Sie drückt etwa die Idee „Ich werde nie vergessen …" aus.
! „Vergangenheit" bezieht sich hier nicht auf *forget/remember*, sondern auf das nachfolgende Verb.
*I still **remember getting** my first job.*
*I'll never **forget going** to the Japanese headquarters last year.*

Die Struktur ***forget/remember* + Infinitiv** dagegen bezieht sich auf die Zukunft. Sie drückt etwa die Idee aus „Ich darf nicht vergessen, etwas zu tun" bzw. „Ich habe noch etwas zu tun, weil ich es bis jetzt vergessen habe".
*Dad, please **remember / don't forget to pick me up** from the station.*
*Oh dear. I **forgot / didn't remember to pick Sally up** from the station.*

regret

Die Struktur **regret + *-ing*-Form** drückt Bedauern über eine vergangene Situation bzw. einen vergangenen Vorfall aus. Häufig geht es dabei um verpasste Chancen.
*I really **regret leaving** school without any qualifications.*
*I know they will **regret buying** such a big, expensive car.*

Die Struktur ***regret* + Infinitiv** – fast immer mit einem Verb des Mitteilens wie *inform, say, tell* kombiniert – drückt eine schlechte Nachricht aus.
*I **regret to say** that I can't attend the meeting tomorrow.*
*We **regret to inform** you that the vacancy has now been filled.*

stop

Bedeutet ***stop*** „aufhören, etwas zu tun", steht das nachfolgende Verb in der ***-ing*-Form**.
Bedeutet ***stop*** aber „kurz anhalten, um etwas anderes zu tun", folgt ein Verb im **Infinitiv**.
*For heaven's sake **stop shouting** at me.*
*I'm a little late because I **stopped to give** somebody a lift.*

try

Bedeutet ***try*** „etwas ausprobieren", steht das nachfolgende Verb in der ***-ing*-Form**.
Bedeutet ***try*** aber „sich anstrengen, etwas zu tun", folgt ein Verb im **Infinitiv**.
*I **tried phoning** Ellie, but she wasn't at home.*
*We**'ll try to repair** your computer by the weekend.*

ADJECTIVES AND ADVERBS

1 John has a **new** printer.
2 He always buys **expensive** equipment.
3 My computer has become **very slow**.
4 That CD sounds **terrible**.
5 We can make printouts **quickly** and **cheaply**.

- Um **Personen** oder **Sachen** näher zu beschreiben, benutzt man **Adjektive** (1–4).
- Adjektive stehen **unmittelbar** vor Substantiven oder **unmittelbar nach** einer Form von *be* (bzw. *become* oder *seem*, die *be* ersetzen können) (3).
- **Adjektive** können mit Verben wie *feel, look* (aussehen), *sound, smell* und *taste* eine **sinnliche Wahrnehmung** ausdrücken (4).
- Um einen **Tätigkeitsverb** näher zu beschreiben, setzt man ein **Adverb unmittelbar hinter das Verb** bzw. Verb + Objekt (5).
  ! Im Englischen können ein Verb und sein Objekt – anders als im Deutschen – nicht durch ein Adverb getrennt werden. Also NICHT: ~~We can make quickly printouts.~~ (siehe **word order** auf S. 227)
- Adverbien werden auch benutzt, um **Adjektive**, **andere Adverbien** und **ganze Sätze** näher zu bestimmen:
  *MP3 players have become **surprisingly cheap**.* (Adverb + Adjektiv)
  *My fax machine prints out **terribly slowly**.* (Adverb + Adverb)
  ***Luckily** Gerd left a message on my mailbox.* (Satzadverb)
- Die meisten Adverbien werden durch Anhängen von *-ly* an das Adjektiv gebildet (5). Eine kleine Anzahl von Adverbien hat dieselbe Form wie Adjektive; die häufigsten sind:

fast, hard, early, late, long, daily

COMPARISON OF ADJECTIVES AND ADVERBS

1 A hundred years ago life was **slower** and people may have been **happier**.
2 Which technological innovation is the **most/least important**?
3 Today you can copy data **more easily than** ever before.

- **Einsilbige** und **zweisilbige Adjektive**, die auf *-y* enden – zum Beispiel *easy*, *happy* und *lucky* –, werden mit *-(i)er/-(i)est* gesteigert (1).
- **Mehrsilbige Adjektive** und **Adverbien**, die auf *-ly* enden, werden mit *more/most* gesteigert (2, 3).
  ! Die Adverbien, die dieselbe Form wie das entsprechende Adjektiv haben (*fast*, *hard*, *early* usw.), werden mit *-er/-est* gesteigert.
- Um Personen oder Sachen im Satz miteinander zu vergleichen, gibt es folgende Möglichkeiten:

Kein Unterschied	***as*** *good* ***as***	genau so gut wie
Unterschied	***not as*** *good* ***as***	nicht so gut wie
Unterschied	*better* ***than***	besser als

WORD ORDER

positions of adverbs of time, place and frequency

1 She goes shopping **every week**.
2 Their school is located in a small town **outside of Frankfurt**.
3 **Last year** we went to Italy for our holidays.
4 Paul and Emily went to **the USA last year**.
5 She **always finishes** school early on Fridays.
6 He **is never** at home when I call.
7 I like to stay at home **now and then**.
8 Gina acted **strangely during the presentation last week**.

- Zeitangaben (Wann?) und Ortsangaben (Wo?, Wohin?) stehen in der Regel am Satzende (1, 2).
- Um die Zeit eines bestimmten Ereignisses hervorzuheben, kann man die Zeitangabe an die erste Stelle setzen (3).
- Stehen eine Zeitangabe und eine Ortsangabe zusammen am Satzende, dann gilt die Reihenfolge Ort vor Zeit (alphabetisch merken: O vor Z!) (4).
- Besteht eine Häufigkeitsangabe aus einem Wort, z. B. *always*, *often*, *sometimes*, steht sie unmittelbar vor dem Vollverb (5).
- Lautet das Vollverb *to be*, steht das Adverb direkt dahinter (6).
- Besteht die Häufigkeitsangabe aus mehreren Wörtern, z. B. *every day*, *now and then*, steht sie wie eine Zeitangabe am Satzende (7).
- Adverbien der Art und Weise stehen in der Regel am Satzende. Kommen noch Zeit- oder Ortsadverbien hinzu, lautet die Reihenfolge: Art und Weise – Ort – Zeit (AOZ) (8).

RELATIVE CLAUSES AND CONTACT CLAUSES

1 Car manufacturers are designing cars **which/that** can use hydrogen fuel cells.
2 Wildernesses are being spoiled by tourists **who/that** want to go to 'unspoiled' places.
3 Tony filled in a job satisfaction questionnaire (**which/that**) he found on the internet.
4 Fred Foley is an artist **whose** fortune amounts to over €400 million.
5 Call centre employees, most **of whom** come from India, work long hours.
6 Some non-GM crops are attacked by pests **against which** they have no resistance.

- Relativsätze werden benutzt, um den Hauptsatz durch zusätzliche Informationen genauer zu bestimmen.
- Für **Sachen** benutzt man das Relativpronomen *which* bzw. *that* (1) und für Personen *who* bzw. *that* (2).
- Steht das Relativpronomen für das **Objekt des Hauptsatzes**, dann kann man es weglassen (3). Solche Relativsätze heißen **contact clauses**.
- Um **Besitz** bzw. **Zugehörigkeit** anzuzeigen, gebraucht man whose unmittelbar vor dem Substantiv bei Personen und Sachen (4).
- Steht eine **Präposition** vor dem **Relativpronomen**, wird *whom* für Personen und *which* für Sachen benutzt (5, 6). In solchen Fällen ist der Gebrauch von *that* nicht möglich.

DEFINING AND NON-DEFINING RELATIVE CLAUSES

1 The first Europeans **who** settled in Australia came from Britain.
2 Sydney, **which** is famous for its unusually designed opera house, is situated on the south-eastern coast of Australia.

- Im **ersten Beispielsatz** ist der Sinn des Hauptsatzes *The first Europeans came from Britain* ohne den Relativsatz *who settled in Australia* offensichtlich falsch bzw. unvollständig. Relativsätze dieser Art – die wesentlich für das Verständnis des gesamten Satzes sind – nennt man **defining relative clauses** (notwendige oder bestimmende Relativsätze).
- Im **zweiten Beispielsatz** ist die Aussage des Hauptsatzes *Sydney is situated on the south-eastern coast of Australia* ohne den Relativsatz völlig verständlich, weil der Relativsatz *which is famous for its unusually designed opera house* eine zusätzliche, also nebensächliche, Information enthält. Daher werden solche Relativsätze ***non-defining relative clauses*** (nicht notwendige oder nicht bestimmende Relativsätze) genannt.
  ! Notwendige Relativsätze werden immer **ohne** trennende **Kommas** benutzt. Dies signalisiert, dass sie fester Bestandteil der Hauptaussage sind.

PARTICIPLE CONSTRUCTIONS

1 Malaria, preventable with a treated bed net **costing** less than one pound, is endemic.
2 Many men believe that any work **involving** cooking is a woman's chore.
3 **Losing** more and more people to AIDS, Africa now needs effective help more urgently than ever before.
4 **Burdened** with declining life expectancy, large parts of Africa are caught in a poverty trap.
5 **Having fetched** water from a river for many years, some women in developing countries are now happy to be able to use the Hippo Roller.
6 **When facing** extreme destitution, many people give up hope.

7 Donors should invest in projects that help local inhabitants become self-supporting, **thereby making** sure that the money isn't wasted.
8 Poor infrastructure is a key barrier to economic growth in Nepal, **thus causing** huge additional costs to the transport of commercial goods.
9 Life is becoming hard in the developing countries, **with** many small farmers **going** out of business.
10 AIDS represents a major challenge to sub-Saharan Africa, currently **killing** more than two million people every year.

Die englische Sprache ist geprägt durch die häufige Verwendung von Partizipialkonstruktionen. Diese ermöglichen einen eleganteren Sprachfluss.

- Partizipialkonstruktionen verkürzen Relativsätze; dabei kann entweder das **present participle** (1) oder das **past participle** (2) verwendet werden.
- Sie werden auch verwendet, um adverbiale Nebensätze zu vekürzen. In diesen Fällen unterscheidet man zwischen Partizipialkonstruktionen ohne Konjunktion (3–5) und solchen mit Konjunktion (6–9). In Sätzen ohne Konjunktion ist der Inhalt des Satzes auch ohne eine solche klar. Dagegen sind Konjunktionen nötig, um zu verhindern, dass der logische Zusammenhang des Satzes verloren geht. Zum Beispiel wird der Inhalt von Satz 6 unklar, wenn die Konjunktion *despite* ausgelassen wird.
- Wie bei der Verkürzung von Relativsätzen kommen auch bei der Verkürzung von adverbialen Nebensätzen das **present participle** (3, 6–9) und das **past participle** (4) zur Anwendung. Darüber hinaus wird hier auch noch das **perfect participle** verwendet (5), und zwar um die Vorzeitigkeit der Handlung im Nebensatz auszudrücken. *(Nachdem sie jahrelang Wasser aus dem Fluss geholt hatten, …)*
- Schließlich verknüpft man mit einer Partizipialkonstruktion zwei Hauptsätze zu einem einzigen Satz, und zwar ausnahmslos mittels **present participle** (10).

COUNTABLE AND UNCOUNTABLE NOUNS

1	Visit our website for more **information** on our firm.	NICHT ~~informations~~
2	Have you read the paper today? The political **news** is interesting.	NICHT ~~news are~~
3	Where can I get some **advice**?	NICHT ~~an advice~~

- Einige wichtige **Substantive** sind **zählbar im Deutschen, nicht jedoch im Englischen**. Diese Substantive können also nicht ohne weiteres mit dem unbestimmten Artikel *a/an* oder mit einem Zahlwort benutzt werden. Bei diesen Substantiven muss *some, a bit of* bzw. *a piece of* hinzugefügt werden (3).
  Hier ist eine Liste solcher Wörter, die Sie auswendig lernen sollten:

advice, baggage, damage, data, equipment, evidence, furniture, information, knowledge, luck, luggage, machinery, news, progress, research, rubbish, work (housework, homework)

SOME AND *ANY*

1 **Some** head teachers prefer to hold regular weekly meetings with their staff.
2 They haven't got **any** women working in their company.
3 Have you got **any** information about arrival times?
4 Can I have **some** more coffee, please?
5 Would you like **some** mineral water?
6 There's **something** I need to do but I can't remember what it is.
7 He can't find that letter **anywhere**. Maybe **somebody** took it.

- Wir verwenden *some* in **bejahten Aussagen** (1) und *any* in **verneinten Aussagen** (2) und **„echten" Fragen** (3).
- Drückt die Frage eine höfliche **Bitte** (4) bzw. ein **Angebot** (5) aus, worauf eine positive Antwort erwartet wird, verwenden wir ebenfalls *some*.
- Wir verwenden die Zusammensetzungen von *some* and *any* – also *somebody/someone, something, somewhere, anybody/anyone, anything* und *anywhere* – in genau derselben Art und Weise (6–7).

THE DEFINITE ARTICLE

1 **Sociologists** say that **violence** is increasing among young people.
2 Is **the current trend** partly caused by **the violent films** they watch?
3 **Most sentences** are not tough enough.
4 Nearly **half the prisoners** in **British prisons** are under 25.
5 **Spring** is my favourite season but **the spring** we're having this year is more like **winter**.
6 We had **breakfast** late this morning so we came to work **by car** instead of **by bus**.
7 They are thinking of legalizing soft drugs in **the Netherlands**.

- Hat ein Substantiv eine allgemeine, uneingeschränkte Bedeutung – also „alle ohne Ausnahme" – dann steht es ohne Artikel (1, 5).
- Ist die Bedeutung eines Substantives auf bestimmte Fälle eingeschränkt, benutzt man den Artikel (2, 5).
- Ferner wird der Artikel in den folgenden Fällen und Wendungen im Englischen – z.T. anders als im Deutschen – nicht gebraucht:
  - bei *most* in der Bedeutung „die meisten" (3),
  - bei öffentlichen Gebäuden im allgemeinen Sinn (4),
  - bei Mahlzeiten (6),
  - bei Verkehrsmitteln (6),
  - bei Straßennamen,
  - bei Tageszeiten, Wochentagen, Monaten und Jahreszeiten im allgemeinen Sinn (5).
- Der Artikel wird verwendet nach *all* und *half* (4) und mit den Pluralnamen von Staaten (7).
  ! Der bestimmte Artikel steht im Englischen (viel) seltener als im Deutschen.
  Daher: *When in doubt, leave it out!*

THE INDEFINITE ARTICLE

1 Yesterday I met **a woman** who works for **a friend** of my father's.
2 We'll have to buy **a** new **computer**.
3 That's **an** interesting **idea**.
4 Jane's **an accountant**? I thought she was **a sales rep**.
5 My father has been **a non-smoker** all his life.
6 How much does petrol cost **a litre**?
7 We give presentations twice **a month**.

- Der unbestimmten Artikel *a/an* steht bei einer einzelnen, nicht näher bestimmten Person (1), einer Sache (2), oder einem Begriff (3).
- Anders als im Deutschen verwenden wir im Englischen den unbestimmten Artikel in folgenden Fällen:
  - bei Berufsangaben (4),
  - bei Angaben über Nationalität, Religion, Politik oder Gruppenzugehörigkeit (5)
  - bei Maß- (6), Verpackungs-, und Zeitangaben (7)
  - bei den folgenden Wendungen:

to be in a hurry	in Eile sein, es eilig haben
to come to an end	enden
to have a bath/shower/...	sich baden/duschen/...
to have a go	es ausprobieren
to have a turn at (+ -ing-Form)	an der Reihe sein, etwas zu tun
to make a noise	Lärm machen
to take a seat	Platz nehmen
for a change	zur Abwechslung
for a long/short time	lange/kurze Zeit
in a loud/quiet voice	mit lauter/ruhiger Stimme
What a pity!	Wie schade!
without a break	ohne Pause

! Bei *half, quite, rather* und *such* wird der unbestimmte Artikel nachgestellt:
- The meeting starts in half **an** hour.
- We had quite **a** successful year in 2005.
- Jack can be rather **an** idiot sometimes.
- We've never had such **a** big order.

Irregular verbs

arise	arose	arisen	*entstehen*
be	was/were	been	*sein*
beat	beat	beaten	*schlagen*
become	became	become	*werden*
begin	began	begun	*starten, anfangen*
bind	bound	bound	*fesseln, binden*
break	broke	broken	*brechen, kaputtmachen*
bring	brought	brought	*bringen*
broadcast	broadcast	broadcast	*senden, ausstrahlen*
build	built	built	*bauen*
burn	burnt/burned	burnt/burned	*brennen*
buy	bought	bought	*kaufen*
catch	caught	caught	*fangen*
choose	chose	chosen	*wählen*
come	came	come	*kommen*
cost	cost	cost	*kosten*
cut	cut	cut	*schneiden*
deal	dealt	dealt	*handeln, sich beschäftigen mit*
dig	dug	dug	*graben, bohren*
do	did	done	*tun, machen*
draw	drew	drawn	*zeichnen*
dream	dreamt/dreamed	dreamt/dreamed	*träumen*
drink	drank	drunk	*trinken*
drive	drove	driven	*fahren*
eat	ate	eaten	*essen*
fall	fell	fallen	*fallen*
feel	felt	felt	*fühlen*
fight	fought	fought	*(be)kämpfen*
find	found	found	*finden*
fly	flew	flown	*fliegen*
forget	forgot	forgotten	*vergessen*
freeze	froze	frozen	*frieren*
get	got	got	*bekommen*
give	gave	given	*geben*
go	went	gone	*gehen*
grow	grew	grown	*wachsen*
have	had	had	*haben*
hear	heard	heard	*hören*
hide	hid	hidden	*(sich) verstecken*
hit	hit	hit	*schlagen*
hold	held	held	*halten*
hurt	hurt	hurt	*weh tun*
input	input	input	*eingeben*
keep	kept	kept	*behalten*
know	knew	known	*wissen, kennen*
lay	laid	laid	*legen*
lead	led	led	*führen*
learn	learnt/learned	learnt/learned	*lernen*
leave	left	left	*(weg)gehen, (ver)lassen*
let	let	let	*lassen, erlauben*
light	lit	lit	*erleuchten, entzünden*
lose	lost	lost	*verlieren*
make	made	made	*machen, tun*

mean	**meant**	**meant**	*bedeuten*
meet	**met**	**met**	*treffen*
pay	**paid**	**paid**	*bezahlen*
put	**put**	**put**	*legen, stellen*
read	**read**	**read**	*lesen*
ride	**rode**	**ridden**	*fahren, reiten*
rise	**rose**	**risen**	*steigen, sich erheben*
ring	**rang**	**rung**	*klingeln, anrufen*
run	**ran**	**run**	*laufen, verwalten*
say	**said**	**said**	*sagen*
see	**saw**	**seen**	*sehen*
seek	**sought**	**sought**	*suchen*
sell	**sold**	**sold**	*verkaufen*
send	**sent**	**sent**	*senden*
set	**set**	**set**	*setzen, stellen, legen*
shake	**shook**	**shaken**	*schütteln*
show	**showed**	**shown**	*zeigen*
shut	**shut**	**shut**	*schließen*
sing	**sang**	**sung**	*singen*
sink	**sank**	**sunk**	*(ver)senken*
sit	**sat**	**sat**	*sitzen*
sleep	**slept**	**slept**	*schlafen*
smell	**smelt/smelled**	**smelt/smelled**	*riechen*
speak	**spoke**	**spoken**	*sprechen*
speed	**sped**	**sped**	*rasen*
spell	**spelt/spelled**	**spelt/spelled**	*buchstabieren*
spend	**spent**	**spent**	*ausgeben, verbringen*
stand	**stood**	**stood**	*stehen*
steal	**stole**	**stolen**	*stehlen*
swim	**swam**	**swum**	*schwimmen*
take	**took**	**taken**	*nehmen*
teach	**taught**	**taught**	*unterrichten*
tear	**tore**	**torn**	*zerreißen*
tell	**told**	**told**	*erzählen*
think	**thought**	**thought**	*denken, meinen*
throw	**threw**	**thrown**	*werfen*
understand	**understood**	**understood**	*verstehen*
wake	**woke**	**woken**	*wecken*
wear	**wore**	**worn**	*tragen*
win	**won**	**won**	*gewinnen*
write	**wrote**	**written**	*schreiben*

Problem words and false friends

Fremdsprachenlernen ist faszinierend. Man stolpert immer wieder über erstaunliche Dinge.
So gibt es im Englischen etwa eine Reihe von Wörtern, die mehrere Bedeutungen haben können (ähnlich wie im Deutschen). Solche Wörter kann man als Problemwörter sehen. Es gibt auch deutsche und englische Wörter, die zwar gleich oder ähnlich aussehen, gleich oder ähnlich klingen, die jedoch ganz verschiedene Bedeutungen haben. Solche Wörter nennt man *false friends* – man kann sich auf sie nicht verlassen.
Hier ist eine kleine Auswahl von Problemwörtern und falschen Freunden. Machen Sie sich eine Notiz, wenn Sie derartigen Wörtern begegnen, und ergänzen Sie die Liste. Dann werden Sie diese Wörter gut beherrschen.

NOUNS

brochure	Prospekt, Faltblatt
prospect	(Zukunfts-)Aussicht
chef	(Chef-)Koch/Köchin
boss	Chef/Chefin (einer Firma)
look	Blick, Aussehen
to watch (v)	ansehen
meaning	Bedeutung
opinion	Meinung
mobile phone (BE) **/ cell phone** (AE)	Handy
handy (adj)	praktisch, nützlich, geschickt

ADJECTIVES

actual	eigentlich, tatsächlich
current	aktuell
the latest	die neueste
the last	der/die/das Letzte
last	letzte(r, s), am Ende
at last	endlich, schließlich
sensible	vernünftig
sensitive	sensibel

ADVERBS

actually	eigentlich
currently	zurzeit, momentan
for (two days)	seit (zwei Tagen)
(two days) ago	vor (zwei Tagen)
least	am wenigsten
at least	wenigstens, zumindest
possibly	möglicherweise, vielleicht
eventually	schließlich, endlich

PREPOSITIONS

beside	neben
besides (adv)	außerdem
next	nächste(r, s)
nearly (adv)	fast, beinahe

VERBS AND VERB PHRASES

to be lucky	Glück haben
to be happy	glücklich sein
to become	werden
to get	bekommen
to blame sb for	jdm die Schuld geben an, für
to disgrace sb/oneself	jdn/sich blamieren
to borrow	borgen, ausleihen
to lend	verleihen
to bring sb/sth	jdn/etwas mitbringen
to take sb/sth	jdn/etwas irgendwohin bringen
to discuss sth	etwas besprechen
to get up	aufstehen
to stand up	sich erheben
keep (working)	(an der Arbeit) bleiben
stay (working)	dranbleiben
to look	aussehen
to look at	anschauen
to look after sb/sth	sich um jdn/etwas kümmern
to look for sb/sth	nach jdm/etwas suchen
to look into sth	etwas untersuchen
to lose	verlieren
to loosen	locker machen, lösen
loose (adj)	locker, nicht fest
to make sth	etwas machen, herstellen
to make sth of ~	etwas herstellen aus ~
to make out	etwas ausschreiben, entwickeln, entziffern
to mean	bedeuten
to think, to believe	meinen, glauben
to prove	beweisen, sich erweisen als
to check (on)	überprüfen, nachprüfen, kontrollieren
to raise	heben
to rise	hochgehen, aufgehen
to rob	(aus)rauben
to steal	stehlen, entwenden
to start off	etwas anfangen
to take off	starten, abheben
to wonder (if ...)	sich fragen (ob ...)
to be surprised	überrascht sein

Unit word list

Der im Vokabelverzeichnis angegebene Wortschatz dient der Festigung des ggf. bereits vorhandenen Aufbauwortschatzes der Schüler und Schülerinnen und erweitert diesen auf die dem Fachabitur in Englisch entsprechende Niveaustufe. Die Wörter erscheinen in der Reihenfolge ihres Auftretens in **Focus on Success Plus**. Nicht aufgeführt sind internationale Wörter wie *hotel*, *email* usw.
Wörter, die in den Audio- und Videotexten vorkommen, sind mit einem blauen Balken, und Wörter, die in den *Files* vorkommen, mit einem orangefarbenen Balken gekennzeichnet

pl = Plural *AE* = amerikanisches Englisch *BE* = britisches Englisch *fml* = formell *infml* = informell, umgangssprachlich

UNIT 1

page 7

to **make the most of sth** [ˌmeɪk ðə 'məʊst əv]	das Beste aus etw machen
leisure ['leʒə]	Freizeit, Muße
psychiatrist [saɪ'kaɪətrɪst]	Psychiater/in
precious ['preʃəs]	wertvoll, kostbar
to **slow down** [ˌsləʊ 'daʊn]	(sich) verlangsamen
worthwhile [ˌwɜːθ'waɪl]	lohnend
to **represent sth** [ˌreprɪ'zent]	etw ausmachen, etw darstellen
to **illustrate sth** ['ɪləstrəɪt]	etw zeigen, etw veranschaulichen
quote [kwəʊt]	Zitat
to **justify sth** ['dʒʌstɪfaɪ]	etw begründen, etw rechtfertigen
to **be prepared to do sth** [prɪ'peəd tə]	bereit sein, etw zu tun

page 8

doubt [daʊt]	Zweifel
vacation *(AE)* [və'keɪʃn]	Urlaub
indispensable [ˌɪndɪ'spensəbl]	unentbehrlich, unverzichtbar
well-being ['wel biːɪŋ]	Wohl(befinden)
to **unwind** [ˌʌn'waɪnd]	sich entspannen
to **recover** [rɪ'kʌvə]	sich erholen
to **pursue sth** [pə'sjuː]	einer Sache nachgehen, etw verfolgen
passion ['pæʃn]	Leidenschaft
advocate ['ædvəkət]	Befürworter/in
(work) ethic ['eθɪk]	(Arbeits-)Ethik, Moral
idle ['aɪdl]	ungenutzt, müßig, faul
to **require sth** [rɪ'kwaɪə]	etw erfordern, etw benötigen
equilibrium [ˌiːkwɪ'lɪbriəm]	Gleichgewicht
poll [pəʊl]	Umfrage
annual ['ænjuəl]	jährlich
satisfaction [ˌsætɪs'fækʃn]	Zufriedenheit
amount [ə'maʊnt]	Menge, Ausmaß, Umfang
paradoxically [ˌpærə'dɒksɪkli]	paradoxerweise
fairly ['feəli]	ziemlich, recht
to **subscribe to sth** [səb'skraɪb tə]	einer Sache beipflichten, sich *(einer Meinung, Aussage etc.)* anschließen
basically ['beɪsɪkli]	grundsätzlich, im Grunde
sedentary ['sedntri]	sitzend
issue ['ɪʃuː]	Streitpunkt, Frage, Problem, Thema
couch potato [ˌkaʊtʃ pə'teɪtəʊ]	Stubenhocker/in, Dauerglotzer/in
pursuit [pə'sjuːt]	Betätigung, Beschäftigung
board game ['bɔːd geɪm]	Brettspiel
to your heart's content [tə jə ˌhɑːts kən'tent]	nach Herzenslust
to **develop (sth)** [dɪ'veləp]	(sich/etw) entwickeln
doer ['duə]	Macher/in
sobering ['səʊbərɪŋ]	ernüchternd
to **be keen on sth** [bi 'kiːn ɒn]	auf etw versessen/scharf sein, etw gerne haben/tun
to **limit sth** ['lɪmɪt]	etw begrenzen, etw einschränken
imagination [ɪˌmædʒɪ'neɪʃn]	Phantasie, Vorstellungskraft
to **participate (in sth)** [pɑː'tɪsɪpeɪt]	(an etw) teilnehmen, sich (an etw) beteiligen
to **take part (in sth)** [ˌteɪk 'pɑːt ɪn]	(an etw) teilnehmen
to **exchange sth** [ɪks'tʃeɪndʒ]	etw austauschen, etw eintauschen, etw umtauschen
to **volunteer** [ˌvɒlən'tɪə]	freiwillig/ehrenamtlich arbeiten *(unbezahlt)*
voluntary ['vɒləntri]	freiwillig, ehrenamtlich
charity ['tʃærəti]	Wohltätigkeit(s-), wohltätige Zwecke
to **enhance sth** [ɪn'hɑːns]	etw verbessern, etw aufbessern
self-esteem [ˌself ɪ'stiːm]	Selbstachtung, Selbstwertgefühl
to **encourage sb/sth** [ɪn'kʌrɪdʒ]	jdn/etw fördern, jdn/etw unterstützen
outlook ['aʊtlʊk]	(Zukunfts-)Aussicht(en)
physical ['fɪzɪkl]	körperlich, physisch
to **indulge in sth** [ɪn'dʌldʒ]	sich etw gönnen, genehmigen
after all [ˌɑːftər 'ɔːl]	schließlich (doch), immerhin
All work and no play makes Jack a dull boy. [ɔːl wɜːk ən nəʊ ˌpleɪ meɪks dʒæk ə dʌl 'bɔɪ]	Arbeit alleine macht (auch) nicht glücklich. *(Sprichwort)*
dull [dʌl]	langweilig
indeed [ɪn'diːd]	tatsächlich, in der Tat
to **highlight sth** ['haɪlaɪt]	etw hervorheben

page 9

term [tɜːm]	Begriff
collocation [ˌkɒlə'keɪʃn]	Kollokation *(inhaltliche Kombinierbarkeit sprachlicher Einheiten)*
aspect ['æspekt]	Gesichtspunkt, Aspekt
occasional [ə'keɪʒənl]	gelegentlich
bracket ['brækɪt]	Klammer
participation (in) [pɑːˌtɪsɪ'peɪʃn]	Teilnahme, Beteiligung (an)
rewarding [rɪ'wɔːdɪŋ]	lohnend, erfüllend
passionate ['pæʃənət]	leidenschaftlich
to **underestimate sb/sth** [ˌʌndər'estɪmeɪt]	jdn/etw unterschätzen
to **guarantee sth** [ˌgærən'tiː]	etw garantieren

to **satisfy sb** ['sætɪsfaɪ]	jdn zufriedenstellen, jdn befriedigen
to **fool around** [ˌfuːl ə'raʊnd]	herumblödeln, Unsinn machen
to **derive** [dɪ'raɪv]	gewinnen, beziehen
pleasure ['pleʒə]	Vergnügen, Freude
charitable ['tʃærətəbl]	wohltätig, gemeinnützig
as well as [əz 'wel əz]	sowohl … als auch …, ebenso wie, sowie
choir ['kwaɪə]	Chor
wasteful ['weɪstfl]	verschwenderisch
to **facilitate sth** [fə'sɪlɪteɪt]	etw ermöglichen, etw vermitteln, etw vereinfachen
equivalent [ɪ'kwɪvələnt]	Äquivalent, Entsprechung
to **foster sth** ['fɒstə]	etw fördern
it is known to be/do … [nəʊn]	man weiß, dass es … ist/tut
to **mention sth** ['menʃn]	etw erwähnen, etw nennen
to **add sth** [æd]	etw hinzufügen, etw addieren

page 10

exchange [ɪks'tʃeɪndʒ]	Austausch(-)
attitude ['ætɪtjuːd]	Einstellung, (Geistes-) Haltung
therefore ['ðeəfɔː]	daher, deshalb, demzufolge
gallery walk ['gæləri wɔːk]	Galerierundgang
to **display sth** [dɪ'spleɪ]	etw zeigen, etw ausstellen, etw präsentieren
intended [ɪn'tendɪd]	gedacht, vorgesehen
to **appeal to sb** [ə'piːl tə]	für jdn attraktiv sein, jdn ansprechen
to **brainstorm** ['breɪnstɔːm]	Ideen (ungeordnet) sammeln
individual [ˌɪndɪ'vɪdʒuəl]	einzeln, individuell
to **skim (a text)** [skɪm]	(einen Text) überfliegen
findings *(pl)* ['faɪndɪŋz]	Ergebnisse
actually ['æktʃuəli]	eigentlich, wirklich, in der Tat
impact ['ɪmpækt]	Einfluss, Auswirkung
to **tend to do sth** ['tend tə]	dazu neigen, etw zu tun
mental ['mentl]	geistig, psychisch, seelisch
to **revitalize sb/sth** [ˌriː'vaɪtəlaɪz]	jdn/etw wieder beleben
spirit ['spɪrɪt]	Geist, Seele
release [rɪ'liːs]	Befreiung
to **remain** [rɪ'meɪn]	bleiben
disciplined ['dɪsəplɪnd]	diszipliniert
valuable ['væljuəbl]	wertvoll
demanding [dɪ'mɑːndɪŋ]	anstrengend, anspruchsvoll
long-term [ˌlɒŋ 'tɜːm]	langfristig, Langzeit-
confidence ['kɒnfɪdəns]	(Selbst-)Vertrauen, Zuversicht
fiction ['fɪkʃn]	Belletristik, Prosa(literatur)
non-fiction [ˌnɒn 'fɪkʃn]	Sachliteratur, Sachbücher
to **introduce sb to sb/sth** [ˌɪntrə'djuːs]	jdm jdn/etw vorstellen
character ['kærəktə]	Figur, Person *(in Roman, Film usw.)*
similarly ['sɪmələli]	in ähnlicher Weise, ebenso

page 11

career [kə'rɪə]	Karriere, Laufbahn
college ['kɒlɪdʒ]	Fach(hoch)schule
to **restrict (to)** [rɪ'strɪkt]	einschränken, beschränken (auf)
commitment (to) [kə'mɪtmənt]	Engagement (für), Bekenntnis (zu)
to **incorporate sth (in/into)** [ɪn'kɔːpəreɪt]	etw einbeziehen (in)
résumé *(AE)* ['rezjumeɪ]	Lebenslauf
instructional [ɪn'strʌkʃənl]	Lehr-, Schulungs-
particularly [pə'tɪkjələli]	besonders, insbesondere
era ['ɪərə]	Ära, Epoche
value ['væljuː]	Wert
no matter what/how/who [ˌnəʊ 'mætə]	(ganz) egal, was/wie/wer
beneficial [ˌbenɪ'fɪʃl]	nützlich, vorteilhaft
to **go a long way toward(s) doing sth** [ˌgəʊ ə lɒŋ 'weɪ təwɔːdz]	zu einer Sache viel beitragen
one way or another [ˌwʌn weɪ ɔːr ən'ʌðə]	so oder so, auf die eine oder andere Art
to **drive sth** [draɪv]	etw vorantreiben, etw stärken
to **focus on sth** ['fəʊkəs ɒn]	sich auf etw konzentrieren
exclusively [ɪk'skluːsɪvli]	ausschließlich *(Adv.)*
fast track [ˌfɑːst 'træk]	Überholspur, der schnellste Weg
to **distract sb** [dɪ'strækt]	jdn ablenken
to **funnel** ['fʌnl]	strömen (lassen), fließen (lassen)
effort ['efət]	Anstrengung, Bemühung(en)
approach [ə'prəʊtʃ]	Ansatz, Herangehensweise
nasty ['nɑːsti]	gemein, hässlich, böse
downside ['daʊnsaɪd]	Nachteil
to **stress sb out** [ˌstres 'aʊt]	jdn stressen
to **set sb up** [ˌset 'ʌp]	jdm eine Falle stellen
to **prevent sb from doing sth** [prɪ'vent]	jdn davon abhalten, etw zu tun
to **relieve sth** [rɪ'liːv]	etw erleichtern, *(Druck)* verringern, etw lindern
to **put sth in perspective** [ˌpʊt ɪn pə'spektɪv]	etw relativieren, etw ins rechte Licht rücken
grounded ['graʊndɪd]	geerdet, vernünftig, selbstsicher
opportunity [ˌɒpə'tjuːnəti]	Gelegenheit, Möglichkeit, Chance
to **imply sth** [ɪm'plaɪ]	etw andeuten, etw nahelegen
to **prioritize sth** [praɪ'ɒrətaɪz]	etw der Wichtigkeit nach ordnen, etw priorisieren
bond [bɒnd]	Bindung, Verbindung
to **neglect sb/sth** [nɪ'glekt]	jdn/etw vernachlässigen
source [sɔːs]	Quelle

page 12

to **select sb/sth** [sɪ'lekt]	jdn/etw (aus)wählen
role model ['rəʊl mɒdl]	Vorbild
to **consider sth** [kən'sɪdə]	über etw nachdenken, sich etw überlegen, etw in Erwägung ziehen
grid [grɪd]	Schema, Tabelle
to **serve (as)** [sɜːv]	dienen (als)
to **design sth** [dɪ'zaɪn]	etw entwerfen, etw gestalten
item ['aɪtəm]	Artikel, Gegenstand, Punkt *(auf einer Liste)*
to **present sth** [prɪ'zent]	etw vorstellen, etw präsentieren
to **come up with sth** [ˌkʌm 'ʌp wɪð]	sich etw ausdenken, sich etw einfallen lassen

ranking (list) ['ræŋkɪŋ]	Rangliste
to **boost sth** [buːst]	etw stärken, etw ankurbeln, einer Sache Auftrieb geben
word power ['wɜːd paʊə]	Wortverständnis, Wortschatz, Wortgewandtheit
to **contain sth** [kən'teɪn]	etw enthalten
to **make sth your own** [ˌmeɪk jər 'əʊn]	sich etw aneignen, sich etw zu eigen machen
to **replace sth** [rɪ'pleɪs]	etw ersetzen, etw austauschen
powerful ['paʊəfl]	stark, mächtig, kräftig

page 13

gym [dʒɪm]	Sportstudio, Fitnessstudio
to **keep to sth** ['kiːp tə]	sich an etw halten, etw einhalten, bei etw bleiben
secure [sɪ'kjuə]	sicher
ability [ə'bɪləti]	Fähigkeit, Befähigung
there is no doing sth [ðər ɪz 'nəʊ]	man kann etw nicht tun, es ist unmöglich etw zu tun
to **deny sth** [dɪ'naɪ]	etw leugnen, etw bestreiten
sensible ['sensəbl]	vernünftig, sinnvoll
outcome ['aʊtkʌm]	Ergebnis, Resultat
paraphrase ['pærəfreɪz]	Umschreibung
explanation [ˌeksplə'neɪʃn]	Erläuterung, Erklärung
illness ['ɪlnəs]	Krankheit
graph [grɑːf]	Diagramm, Kurve
to **visualize sth** ['vɪʒuəlaɪz]	etw bildlich darstellen, etw visualisieren
specific [spə'sɪfɪk]	bestimmt, speziell, spezifisch
loudspeaker [ˌlaʊd'spiːkə]	Lautsprecher
to **evaluate sth** [ɪ'væljueɪt]	etw bewerten, etw beurteilen
to **arise** [ə'raɪz]	sich ergeben, entstehen, auftreten

page 14

to **claim** [kleɪm]	behaupten
waking hours *(pl)* ['weɪkɪŋ aʊəz]	die Stunden, in denen man wach ist
engaged [ɪn'geɪdʒd]	eingestellt, beschäftigt
despite [dɪ'spaɪt]	trotz
to **consider sth sth** [kən'sɪdə]	etw für etw halten, etw als etw betrachten
over time [ˌəʊvə 'taɪm]	im Laufe der Zeit
outdoor (play/sport) ['aʊtdɔː]	(Spiel/Sport) im Freien, draußen
to **socialize (with)** ['səʊʃəlaɪz]	sich treffen (mit), unter Leute gehen
to **modify sth** ['mɒdɪfaɪ]	etw (ver)ändern, etw modifizieren
to **modify sth beyond recognition** [bɪˌjɒnd rekəg'nɪʃn]	etw so verändern, dass es nicht wiederzuerkennen ist
accusation [ˌækju'zeɪʃn]	Vorwurf, Anschuldigung
merely ['mɪəli]	bloß, nur
a variety of [ə və'raɪəti əv]	eine Vielzahl (von)
entire [ɪn'taɪə]	ganz, vollständig
to **glow** [gləʊ]	leuchten
thus [ðʌs]	daher, deshalb, somit
medium, *pl* **media** ['miːdiəm, 'miːdiə]	Medium, Medien
to **lead (to)** [liːd]	führen (zu), leiten
creation [kri'eɪʃn]	Schaffung
classic ['klæsɪk]	klassisch
to **change for the worse** [ˌfə ðə 'wɜːs]	(sich) zum Schlechteren wandeln, (sich) verschlechtern
increasingly [ɪn'kriːsɪŋli]	zunehmend, in zunehmendem Maße
...-based [beɪst]	auf der Basis von ..., ...-basiert
overly ['əʊvəli]	allzu
concerned [kən'sɜːnd]	besorgt, beunruhigt
concern [kən'sɜːn]	Sorge, Befürchtung
to **note sth** [nəʊt]	etw zur Kenntnis nehmen, etw feststellen, etw beachten
to **survey sb** [sə'veɪ]	jdn befragen
(not/no) at all [ət 'ɔːl]	überhaupt (nicht/kein/keine)

page 15

survey ['sɜːveɪ]	(Meinungs-)Umfrage
to **point sth out** [ˌpɔɪnt 'aʊt]	auf etw hinweisen
to **seek sth** [siːk]	(nach) etw suchen, etw anstreben
to **establish sth** [ɪ'stæblɪʃ]	etw herstellen, etw einrichten
educational [ˌedʒu'keɪʃənl]	schulisch, Bildungs-
equally ['iːkwəli]	gleichermaßen, genauso
laziness ['leɪzinəs]	Faulheit, Trägheit
solitary ['sɒlətri]	einsam, solitär, Einzel-
connectedness [kə'nektɪdnəs]	Vernetzung, Verflechtung
adverse ['ædvɜːs]	nachteilig, ungünstig
intrusion [ɪn'truːʒn]	Eindringen, Störung
deterioration [dɪˌtɪəriə'reɪʃn]	Verschlechterung
no longer [nəʊ 'lɒŋgə]	nicht mehr
to **hang from** ['hæŋ frəm]	hängen an
wall bars *(pl)* ['wɔːl bɑːz]	Sprossenwand
branch [brɑːntʃ]	Zweig
contradictory [ˌkɒntrə'dɪktəri]	widersprüchlich
according to [ə'kɔːdɪŋ tə]	entsprechend, nach, gemäß
to **raise sth** [reɪz]	etw erhöhen, etw (an)heben, etw steigern
to **meet sth** [miːt]	*(Bedarf, Norm etc.)* erfüllen, etw befriedigen, einer Sache entsprechen
guideline ['gaɪdlaɪn]	Richtlinie
moderate ['mɒdərət]	gemäßigt, maßvoll
intensity [ɪn'tensəti]	Intensität
conflicting [kɒn'flɪktɪŋ]	widersprüchlich, gegensätzlich
psychiatric [saɪki'ætrɪk]	psychiatrisch
as well [əz 'wel]	auch (noch), ebenfalls
to **overdo (sth)** [ˌəʊvə'duː]	(es) übertreiben (mit etw)
to **be likely to do sth** [bi 'laɪkli tə]	etw wahrscheinlich tun (werden)
to **suffer (from sth)** ['sʌfə frəm]	(an etw) leiden
attention-span disorder [əˌtenʃn spæn dɪs'ɔːdə]	Aufmerksamkeitsstörung
boundary ['baʊndri]	Grenze, Trennlinie
to **remove sth** [rɪ'muːv]	etw entfernen, etw beseitigen
barrier ['bæriə]	Barriere, Schranke, Grenze
the former ['fɔːmə]	Ersteres

to **transform** [træns'fɔːm]	umwandeln, (sich) verwandeln
such as ['sʌtʃ əz]	wie (zum Beispiel)
to **exacerbate sth** [ɪg'zæsəbeɪt]	etw verschärfen, etw verschlimmern
impatience [ɪm'peɪʃns]	Ungeduld
anxiety (about/over) [æŋ'zaɪəti]	Angst, Sorge (wegen), Ängstlichkeit
in that … [ɪn 'ðət]	insofern, als …
to **be on call** [ɒn 'kɔːl]	in Bereitschaft sein, Bereitschaftsdienst haben
not … anymore [nɒt ˌeni 'mɔː]	nicht mehr
unrest [ʌn'rest]	Unruhe(n)
tool [tuːl]	Werkzeug, Instrument
hands-on [ˌhændz 'ɒn]	praktisch, praxisnah
parental [pə'rentl]	Eltern-, elterlich
guidance ['gaɪdəns]	Anleitung, Hilfestellung
gadget ['gædʒɪt]	Gerät, technischer Krimskrams
it is up to sb (to do sth) ['ʌp tə]	es ist jds Sache / es liegt an jdm (etw zu tun)
-driven ['drɪvn]	-betrieben, -gesteuert
accordingly [ək'ɔːdɪŋli]	(dem)entsprechend
completion [kəm'pliːʃn]	Fertigstellung, Vervollständigung
to **refer to sth** [rɪ'fɜː tə]	sich auf etw beziehen

page 16

corresponding [ˌkɒrɪ'spɒndɪŋ]	entsprechend, passend
youngster ['jʌŋstə]	Jugendliche/r
to **distinguish (between)** [dɪ'stɪŋgwɪʃ]	unterscheiden (zwischen)
to **weigh sth up** [ˌweɪ 'ʌp]	etw abwägen, etw einschätzen, etw beurteilen
enormous [ɪ'nɔːməs]	enorm, gewaltig
various ['veəriəs]	verschieden, mehrere, allerlei
to **have a game of …** [ˌhəv ə 'geɪm əv]	… (zusammen) spielen
to **be back in the game** [ˌbæk ɪn ðə 'geɪm]	wieder dabei sein, wieder im Geschäft sein
to **stick to sth** ['stɪk tə]	bei etw bleiben, sich an etw halten
to **take effect** [ˌteɪk ɪ'fekt]	wirken, Wirkung zeigen
to no effect [tə nəʊ ɪ'fekt]	ohne Erfolg
on and off [ˌɒn ənd 'ɒf]	mit Unterbrechungen, hin und wieder
on average [ɒn 'ævərɪdʒ]	im Durchschnitt
pretty much [ˌprɪti 'mʌtʃ]	(so) ziemlich, fast
to **act your age** [ˌækt jər 'eɪdʒ]	sich altersgemäß verhalten
to **age** [eɪdʒ]	altern
neither … nor … [ˌnaɪðə 'nɔː]	weder … noch …
giant ['dʒaɪənt]	Riese/Riesin
to **get the message across** [get ðə ˌmesɪdʒ ə'krɒs]	die Botschaft rüberbringen
a happy medium [hæpi 'miːdiəm]	ein goldener Mittelweg

page 17

(in) bold [bəʊld]	fett(gedruckt)
commonly ['kɒmənli]	häufig, üblicherweise
idiom ['ɪdiəm]	Redewendung
to **glorify sth** ['glɔːrɪfaɪ]	etw verherrlichen, etw glorifizieren
… which is why … [ˌwɪtʃ ɪz 'waɪ]	…, weswegen …
biking ['baɪkɪŋ]	Radfahren
deplorable *(fml)* [dɪ'plɔːrəbl]	erbärmlich, beklagenswert
exactly [ɪg'zækt]	exakt, genau
based on ['beɪst ɒn]	basierend auf, auf der Grundlage von
to **contradict** [ˌkɒntrə'dɪkt]	widersprechen
to **bring sb/sth along** [ˌbrɪŋ ə'lɒŋ]	jdn/etw mitbringen
to **help sb out** [ˌhelp 'aʊt]	jdm (aus)helfen

page 18

psychologist [saɪ'kɒlədʒɪst]	Psychologe/-in
to **affect sth** [ə'fekt]	etw beeinflussen, sich auswirken auf etw
to **kick back** [ˌkɪk 'bæk]	abschalten, relaxen
stationary ['steɪʃənri]	ruhend, bewegungslos
to **sew** [səʊ]	nähen
to **ruminate (on/over/about)** ['ruːmɪneɪt]	grübeln, nachsinnen (über)
to **back sth up** [ˌbæk 'ʌp]	etw untermauern, etw bekräftigen, etw belegen
antidote (to) ['æntidəʊt]	Gegenmittel, Gegengift (gegen)
unequivocal [ˌʌnɪ'kwɪvəkl]	eindeutig, unzweideutig
to **add up (to)** [ˌæd 'ʌp]	sich summieren (auf)
suitable ['suːtəbl]	geeignet, passend
to **lessen sth** ['lesn]	etw mindern, etw verringern
to **turn out** [ˌtɜːn 'aʊt]	sich herausstellen
puzzle ['pʌzl]	Rätsel, Puzzle
prayer [preə]	Gebet
absorption [əb'sɔːpʃn]	Aufgehen
to **measure** ['meʒə]	messen
to **record sth** [rɪ'kɔːd]	etw dokumentieren, etw verzeichnen, etw aufzeichnen
evidence ['evɪdəns]	Beweise, Beweismittel
blood vessel ['blʌd vesl]	Blutgefäß
blood pressure ['blʌd preʃə]	Blutdruck
to **gain sth** [geɪn]	etw erwerben, etw erlangen
enjoyable [ɪn'dʒɔɪəbl]	angenehm, schön
absorbed (in) [əb'sɔːbd]	vertieft, versunken (in)
monotonous [mə'nɒtənəs]	eintönig, monoton
to **take sth into consideration** [kənˌsɪdə'reɪʃn]	etw berücksichtigen
gender ['dʒendə]	Geschlecht
ethnic ['eθnɪk]	ethnisch, Volks-
data *(pl)* ['deɪtə]	Daten
electronic tag [ɪlekˌtrɒnɪk 'tæg]	elektronische Fußfessel
to **lower sth** ['ləʊə]	etw senken, etw herabsetzen
heart rate ['hɑːt reɪt]	Herzfrequenz, Puls
as far as … go(es) [əz 'fɑːr əz]	was … betrifft/angeht
short-term [ʃɔːt 'tɜːm]	kurzfristig, Kurzzeit-
in the long run [ɪn ðə 'lɒŋ rʌn]	auf lange Sicht, langfristig
proposal [prə'pəʊzl]	Vorschlag
to **convince sb** [kən'vɪns]	jdn überzeugen
to **be willing to do sth** [bi 'wɪlɪŋ tə]	bereit sein, etw zu tun

to **compromise** ['kɒmprəmaɪz]	Kompromisse eingehen
thrill [θrɪl]	Nervenkitzel, (aufregendes) Gefühl
package *(AE)* ['pækɪdʒ]	Schachtel, Verpackung, Paket
container [kən'teɪnə]	Behälter
trinket ['trɪŋkɪt]	Modeschmuck, *(kleines, billiges)* Schmuckstück
to **enable sb to do sth** [ɪ'neɪbl]	es jdm ermöglichen / jdn befähigen, etw zu tun
to **board** [bɔːd]	einsteigen (in), an Bord gehen
to **stroll** [strəʊl]	spazieren, bummeln
in sb's footsteps ['fʊtsteps]	in jds Fußstapfen
luggage ['lʌgɪdʒ]	Gepäck
trolley ['trɒli]	(Hand-)Wagen
to **embed sth** [ɪm'bed]	etw integrieren, etw einbetten, etw einbauen
the beauty of … ['bjuːti]	das Schöne/Schönste an …
pace [peɪs]	Tempo, Schritt, Geschwindigkeit
to **provide sb with sth** [prə'vaɪd]	jdn mit etw versorgen, ausstatten
moors *(pl)* [mɔːz]	Heide(landschaft)
sled [sled]	Schlitten
purpose-built [ˌpɜːpəs 'bɪlt]	eigens dafür gebaut, speziell entwickelt
breed [briːd]	Züchtung, Rasse
kennels *(pl)* ['kenlz]	(Hunde-)Zuchtbetrieb
slick [slɪk]	glatt, raffiniert (gebaut)
pollution [pə'luːʃn]	(Umwelt-)Verschmutzung
stone-baked oven [ˌstəʊn beɪkt 'ʌvn]	Steinbackofen

page 19

economic [ˌiːkə'nɒmɪk]	wirtschaftlich
burden ['bɜːdn]	Last, Belastung, Bürde
ill health [ˌɪl 'helθ]	schlechter Gesundheitszustand
billion, bn ['bɪliən]	Milliarde
poor [pʊə]	schlecht, mangelhaft
diet ['daɪət]	Ernährung, Kost, Diät(-)
overweight [ˌəʊvə'weɪt]	Übergewicht, übergewichtig
obesity [əʊ'biːsəti]	Fettleibigkeit
inactivity [ˌɪnæk'tɪvəti]	Untätigkeit, Trägheit, Inaktivität
rate [reɪt]	Rate, Quote, Anteil
in favour of sb/sth [ɪn 'feɪvər əv]	zugunsten von jdm/etw, für jdn/etw
belief [bɪ'liːf]	Glaube, Überzeugung
depressing [dɪ'presɪŋ]	deprimierend

page 20

to **spot sb/sth** [spɒt]	jdn/etw entdecken
to **dig** [dɪg]	graben
hole [həʊl]	Loch
otherwise ['ʌðəwaɪz]	ansonsten, andernfalls
wilderness ['wɪldənəs]	Wildnis
valley ['væli]	Tal
to **frame sb/sth** [freɪm]	jdn/etw (um)rahmen
mountain range ['maʊntən reɪndʒ]	Gebirge, Gebirgszug
to **blow sth up** [ˌbləʊ 'ʌp]	etw aufblasen
mattress ['mætrəs]	Matratze
to **inflate sth** [ɪn'fleɪt]	etw aufpumpen, etw aufblasen
determined [dɪ'tɜːmɪnd]	(fest) entschlossen
judging by … ['dʒʌdʒɪŋ baɪ]	… nach zu urteilen, … nach zu schließen
to **appear** [ə'pɪə]	(er)scheinen
annoyed [ə'nɔɪd]	verärgert
to **watch out (for sth)** [ˌwɒtʃ 'aʊt]	(auf etw) aufpassen, (auf etw) achten
to **donate** [dəʊ'neɪt]	spenden
to **make a contribution** [ˌmeɪk ə ˌkɒntrɪ'bjuːʃn]	einen Beitrag leisten
single ['sɪŋgl]	einzelne/r/s
injury ['ɪndʒəri]	Verletzung
fatty ['fæti]	fetthaltig, fett

UNIT 2

page 21

connected to [kə'nektɪd tə]	verbunden mit
to **come to mind** [ˌkʌm tə 'maɪnd]	einem einfallen
apart from [ə'pɑːt frəm]	abgesehen von, außer

page 22

compulsory [kəm'pʌlsəri]	Pflicht-, obligatorisch
developing country [dɪˌveləpɪŋ 'kʌntri]	Entwicklungsland
equal ['iːkwəl]	gleich(berechtigt), ebenbürtig
access ['ækses]	Zugang
primary education ['praɪməri edʒʊkeɪʃn]	Primarstufe, Grundschulausbildung
secondary education ['sekəndri edʒʊkeɪʃn]	Sekundarstufe 1 und 2
tertiary ['tɜːʃəri]	tertiär
further education [ˌfɜːðər edʒʊ'keɪʃn]	Weiterbildung
technical college ['teknɪkl kɒlɪdʒ]	Technische Universität
vocational school [vəʊˌkeɪʃənl 'skuːl]	Berufsschule, berufsbildende Schule
particular [pə'tɪkjələ]	bestimmt, speziell
widespread ['waɪdspred]	(weit) verbreitet, allgemein, groß
working life [ˌwɜːkɪŋ 'laɪf]	Arbeitsleben
work placement ['wɜːk pleɪsmənt]	Praktikum
course [kɔːs]	Weg, Vorgehensweise
apprentice [ə'prentɪs]	Lehrling, Auszubildende/r
to **attend sth** [ə'tend]	etw besuchen
apprenticeship [ə'prentɪʃɪp]	Ausbildung, Lehre
curriculum [kə'rɪkjələm]	Lehrplan
to **state sth** [steɪt]	etw darlegen, etw festlegen
mixture ['mɪkstʃə]	Mischung, Gemisch
range [reɪndʒ]	Bereich, Bandbreite, Palette
elective subject [ɪ'lektɪv sʌbdʒɪkt]	Wahlfach
depending on [dɪ'pendɪŋ ɒn]	je nach(dem)
period ['pɪəriəd]	(Unterrichts-)Stunde
independent study [ɪndɪˌpendənt 'stʌdi]	Selbststudium
homeschooling [ˌhəʊm'skuːlɪŋ]	Heimunterricht
assessment [ə'sesmənt]	Beurteilung, Einstufung

to **progress** [prə'gres]	vorankommen, weiterkommen
assessed coursework [əˌsest 'kɔːswɜːk]	*bewertete Projektarbeit/ Mitarbeit in einer Unterrichtseinheit*
either ['aɪðə]	eine/r/s (von beiden)
case [keɪs]	Fall
to **determine sth** [dɪ'tɜːmɪn]	etw ermitteln, etw feststellen
knowledge ['nɒlɪdʒ]	Wissen, Kenntnis(se)
whatever [wɒt'evə]	was auch immer
to **interact** [ˌɪntər'ækt]	interagieren, aufeinander eingehen
admission [əd'mɪʃn]	Aufnahme, Zulassung *(z. B. Hochschule)*
degree [dɪ'griː]	Abschluss
profession [prə'feʃn]	Beruf
competition [ˌkɒmpə'tɪʃn]	Wettbewerb, Wettkampf
process ['prəʊses]	Ablauf, Vorgang, Prozess
to **apply (for sth)** [ə'plaɪ]	sich (um/auf etw) bewerben
to **revise sth** [rɪ'vaɪz]	*(Lernstoff)* wiederholen
application [ˌæplɪ'keɪʃn]	Bewerbung
to **consist of sth** [kən'sɪst əv]	aus etw bestehen
CV (curriculum vitae) *(BE)* [ˌsiː 'viː]	Lebenslauf
cover letter ['kʌvə letə]	Anschreiben, Begleitschreiben
personal statement [ˌpɜːsənl 'steɪtmənt]	Selbstbeschreibung
applicant ['æplɪkənt]	Bewerber/in
to **stand out** [ˌstænd 'aʊt]	auffallen, herausstechen
volunteer [ˌvɒlən'tɪə]	freiwillig, ehrenamtlich
work experience ['wɜːk ɪkspɪəriəns]	Praktikum
to **thrive on sth** ['θraɪv ɒn]	bei etw (richtig) aufblühen
to **fit in** [ˌfɪt 'ɪn]	sich anpassen, sich einfügen
victim ['vɪktɪm]	Opfer
childhood ['tʃaɪldhʊd]	Kindheit
to **make sure** [ˌmeɪk 'ʃʊə]	sicherstellen

page 23

to **be related to sth** [bi rɪ'leɪtɪd tə]	mit etw in Zusammenhang stehen
to **assess sth** [ə'ses]	etw beurteilen
assessor [ə'sesə]	Prüfer/in; Gutachter/in
examiner [ɪg'zæmɪnə]	Prüfer/in
examinee [ɪgˌzæmɪ'niː]	Prüfling
trainee [treɪ'niː]	Auszubildende/r
purpose ['pɜːpəs]	Absicht, Zweck
rather than ['rɑːðə ðən]	anstatt
to **undergo sth** [ˌʌndə'gəʊ]	sich einer Sache unterziehen
unfortunately [ʌn'fɔːtʃənətli]	leider
grade *(AE)* [greɪd]	Note
employer [ɪm'plɔɪə]	Arbeitgeber/in
proper ['prɒpə]	ordentlich, angemessen
to **acquire sth** [ə'kwaɪə]	etw erwerben
candidate ['kændɪdət]	Bewerber/in

page 24

to **feature sth** ['fiːtʃə]	etw zeigen
performance [pə'fɔːməns]	Vorstellung, Aufführung
extra-curricular [ˌekstrə kə'rɪkjulə]	außerschulisch
to **base sth on sth** ['beɪs ɒn]	etw auf etw gründen, etw als Grundlage benutzen für etw
to **research sth** [rɪ'sɜːtʃ]	etw recherchieren, Nachforschungen über etw anstellen
to **come across sth** ['kʌm əkrɒs]	auf etw stoßen, etw (zufällig) finden
extract ['ekstrækt]	Auszug, Ausschnitt
novel ['nɒvl]	Roman
narrator [nə'reɪtə]	Erzähler/in
to **dominate sth** ['dɒmɪneɪt]	etw beherrschen, etw dominieren
affluent ['æfluənt]	wohlhabend

page 25

in order to [ɪn 'ɔːdə tə]	um … zu
premise ['premɪs]	Prämisse, Voraussetzung
to **accept sth** [ək'sept]	etw akzeptieren, etw gutheißen
universal [juːnɪ'vɜːsl]	universell, allgemein, weltweit
to **acknowledge sth** [ək'nɒlɪdʒ]	etw anerkennen, etw zugeben
in fact [ɪn 'fækt]	tatsächlich, eigentlich
basic ['beɪsɪk]	einfach, elementar
existential [ˌegzɪ'stenʃəl]	existenziell
pathetic [pə'θetɪk]	erbärmlich, jämmerlich
period ['pɪəriəd]	Zeit(raum), Periode
senior *(AE)* ['siːniə]	Schüler/in der Abschlussklasse *(US High School)*
border ['bɔːdə]	Grenze
to **draw** [drɔː]	(an)ziehen
to **assert control** [ə'sɜːt]	Kontrolle ausüben
genuine ['dʒenjuɪn]	echt, wirklich, aufrichtig
to **impose sth on sb** [ɪm'pəʊz]	jdm etw auferlegen
order ['ɔːdə]	Reihenfolge, Rangordnung
plentiful ['plentɪfl]	reichlich, im Überfluss (vorhanden)
definitely ['defɪnətli]	absolut, ganz sicher
domination [dɒmɪ'neɪʃn]	Dominanz
will [wɪl]	Wille
cookie *(AE)* ['kʊki]	Keks, Plätzchen
off [ɒf]	seltsam, eigentümlich, befremdlich
eventually [ɪ'ventʃuəli]	letztendlich, schließlich
creepy ['kriːpi]	unheimlich
to **be a good bet** [ə gʊd 'bet]	ein heißer Anwärter sein
to **ascend** [ə'send]	aufsteigen, hochsteigen, ansteigen
smart [smɑːt]	intelligent, pfiffig, geschickt
to **attract sb** [ə'trækt]	jdn anlocken, jdn anziehen
to **escape from sth** [ɪ'skeɪp frəm]	einer Sache entkommen
to **mock sb** [mɒk]	sich über jdn lustig machen
bloody ['blʌdi]	blutig
to **beat sb** [biːt]	jdn schlagen, jdn besiegen

page 26

a bunch of [ə 'bʌntʃ əv]	eine Menge
consequently ['kɒnsɪkwəntli]	folglich, demzufolge
to **murder sb** ['mɜːdə]	jdn ermorden
insane [ɪn'seɪn]	irrsinnig, verrückt

to **flick** [flɪk]	schnippen, schnipsen
to **accomplish sth** [ə'kʌmplɪʃ]	etw erreichen, etw leisten
to **adapt** [ə'dæpt]	*(Text)* bearbeiten; (sich) anpassen
in charge [ɪn 'tʃɑːdʒ]	verantwortlich, (feder)führend

page 27

to **behave** [bɪ'heɪv]	sich benehmen, sich verhalten
to **include sb/sth** [ɪn'kluːd]	jdn/etw einbeziehen, jdn/etw einschließen
everyday ['evrideɪ]	alltäglich, Alltags-
outsider [ˌaʊt'saɪdə]	Außenseiter/in
canteen [kæn'tiːn]	Kantine, Mensa, Cafeteria
to **be faced with sth** [bi 'feɪst wɪð]	mit etw konfrontiert werden
to **react (to)** [ri'ækt]	reagieren (auf)
to **act sth out** [ˌækt 'aʊt]	etw spielen, etw vorspielen
to **vote on sth** ['vəʊt ɒn]	über etw abstimmen
to **enter a competition** [ˌentər ə kɒmpə'tɪʃn]	an einem Wettkampf/Wettbewerb teilnehmen

page 28

to **top sth up** [ˌtɒp 'ʌp]	etw vollständig machen, etw ergänzen
tan [tæn]	Sonnenbräune
to **envy sb** ['envi]	jdn beneiden
ahead [ə'hed]	voraus, vorausliegend
carefree ['keəfriː]	unbekümmert, sorgenfrei
enviable ['enviəbl]	beneidenswert
responsibility [rɪˌspɒnsə'bɪləti]	Aufgabe, Zuständigkeit
to **conjure sth up** ['kʌndʒə]	etw (herauf)beschwören
mind [maɪnd]	Geist, Verstand, Gedanken, Denkweise
to **put the record straight** ['rekəd streɪt]	etw gerade rücken, etw klarstellen
to **concentrate on sth** ['kɒnsntreɪt ɒn]	sich auf etw konzentrieren
to **curate sth** [kjʊə'reɪt]	etw zusammenstellen (um es zu präsentieren)
to **chill out** [ˌtʃɪl 'aʊt]	sich entspannen, abhängen
tops *(slang)* [tɒps]	super, toll
big time ['bɪg taɪm]	so richtig
mate [meɪt]	Kumpel, Freund/in
cleaner ['kliːnə]	Reinigungskraft
rejection [rɪ'dʒekʃn]	Ablehnung
glum [glʌm]	verdrießlich
to **urge sb** [ɜːdʒ]	jdn drängen
suitability [ˌsuːtə'bɪləti]	Eignung
critical ['krɪtɪkl]	kritisch
to **review sth** [rɪ'vjuː]	etw bewerten, etw prüfen
to **vary** ['veəri]	variieren, schwanken
borderline ['bɔːdəlaɪn]	grenzwertig
slightly ['slaɪtli]	leicht, geringfügig
tutor ['tjuːtə]	Lehrer/in, Dozent/in, Kursleiter/in
to **reflect upon sth** [rɪ'flekt]	etw reflektieren, über etw nachdenken
to **demonstrate** ['demənstreɪt]	vorstellen, vorführen
advice [əd'vaɪs]	(guter) Rat, Ratschläge
a load of sth *(infml)* [ə 'ləʊd]	eine Menge (von etw)
to **pile sth on** [paɪl]	etw aufstapeln
spokesman ['spəʊksmən]	Sprecher

page 29

part-time [ˌpɑːt'taɪm]	Teilzeit-
to **scrap sth** [skræp]	etw aufgeben, etw wegwerfen
stuff [stʌf]	Zeug, Sache(n)
obvious ['ɒbviəs]	offensichtlich, klar
daunting ['dɔːntɪŋ]	einschüchternd, entmutigend, beängstigend
ain't *(slang)* [eɪnt]	= am not / isn't / aren't
to **turn into sth** ['tɜːn ɪntə]	zu etw werden (lassen)

page 30

frightening ['fraɪtnɪŋ]	beängstigend
confident ['kɒnfɪdənt]	(selbst)sicher
refusal [rɪ'fjuːzl]	Ablehnung, Verweigerung
to **advise sb** [əd'vaɪz]	jdn beraten, jdm etw raten
possession [pə'zeʃn]	Besitz, Besitztum
to **wonder** ['wʌndə]	sich fragen
impression [ɪm'preʃn]	Eindruck
string [strɪŋ]	Kette, Reihe

page 31

GCSE (= General Certificate of Secondary Education) [ˌdʒiː siː es 'iː]	Prüfung für Schüler/innen ab 15, mittlerer Schulabschluss
to **polish sth** ['pɒlɪʃ]	etw (auf)polieren
to **favour sb/sth** ['feɪvə]	jdn/etw bevorzugen
fire brigade ['faɪə brɪgeɪd]	Feuerwehr
tuition [tju'ɪʃn]	Unterricht, Anleitung
to **broaden sth** ['brɔːdn]	etw erweitern
to **reach an agreement** [ˌriːtʃ ən ə'griːmənt]	übereinkommen

page 32

scramble (for sth) ['skræmbl]	Gerangel (um etw)
to **have a crush** [krʌʃ]	verknallt sein
and so forth [ənd səʊ fɔːθ]	und so weiter
distinct [dɪ'stɪŋkt]	deutlich, unterschiedlich
preference ['prefrəns]	Präferenz, Vorliebe
principle ['prɪnsəpl]	Grundsatz, Prinzip
retail ['riːteɪl]	Einzelhandel(s-)
curiosity [ˌkjʊəri'ɒsəti]	Neugier
sensitive ['sensətɪv]	heikel
unemployment [ˌʌnɪm'plɔɪmənt]	Arbeitslosigkeit
assumption [ə'sʌmpʃn]	Annahme
to **refer sb to sb/sth** [rɪ'fɜː]	jdm jdn überweisen, jdn an etw verweisen
economy [ɪ'kɒnəmi]	Wirtschaft
pushy ['pʊʃi]	penetrant, Druck ausübend
drop [drɒp]	Rückgang, Abfall
internship ['ɪntɜːnʃɪp]	Praktikum
mostly ['məʊstli]	meistens, hauptsächlich
to **drop sth off** [ˌdrɒp 'ɒf]	etw abliefern
Latino [læ'tiːnəʊ]	US-Amerikaner/in lateinamerikanischer Abstammung

retiring [rɪ'taɪrɪŋ]	zurückhaltend
to **fold your arms** [ˌfəʊld jər 'ɑːmz]	die Arme verschränken
to **convey sth** [kən'veɪ]	etw vermitteln, etw übermitteln
to **tilt** [tɪlt]	kippen, sich neigen
repetitive [rɪ'petətɪv]	sich ständig wiederholend, *(z. B. Arbeit)* monoton
ceiling ['siːlɪŋ]	(Zimmer-)Decke
devious ['diːviəs]	hinterhältig, verschlagen, unaufrichtig
apprehensive [ˌæprɪ'hensɪv]	besorgt
plain [pleɪn]	einfach, schlicht
steady ['stedi]	kontinuierlich, stabil
intense [ɪn'tens]	intensiv
serial killer [ˌsɪəriəl 'kɪlə]	Serienmörder/in
imaginary [ɪ'mædʒɪnəri]	imaginär, (frei) erfunden
triangle ['traɪæŋgl]	Dreieck
gaze [geɪz]	Blick
intimate ['ɪntɪmət]	intim, eng, persönlich
agreeable [ə'griːəbl]	angenehm, akzeptabel
to **maintain sth** [meɪn'teɪn]	etw aufrecht erhalten
attire *(fml)* [ə'taɪə]	Kleidung
manner ['mænə]	Art, Wesen
sense [sens]	Sinn
to **astound sb** [ə'staʊnd]	jdn verblüffen
gesture ['dʒestʃə]	Geste
grip [grɪp]	Griff
vibes *(pl)* [vaɪbz]	Ausstrahlung, Atmosphäre
to **slouch** [slaʊtʃ]	sich lümmeln
subconscious [ˌsʌb'kɒnʃəs]	unterbewusst
to **brush sb/sth** [brʌʃ]	jdn/etw streifen
to **tweak sth** [twiːk]	etw optimieren
tool shed [ˌtuːl 'ʃed]	Geräteschuppen, „Kuhstall"
to **caress sb/sth** [kə'res]	jdn/etw streicheln, jdn/etw liebkosen
to **scratch sth** [skrætʃ]	etw (zer)kratzen
to **interlock sth (with sth)** [ˌɪntə'lɒk]	etw (mit etw) verbinden
lap [læp]	Schoß
neat [niːt]	ordentlich, sauber
rendition [ren'dɪʃn]	Vortrag
distraction [dɪ'strækʃn]	Ablenkung
to **channel sth into sth** ['tʃænl]	etw auf etw richten
to **groom sth** [gruːm]	etw bürsten, etw putzen, etw striegeln
garment *(fml)* ['gɑːmənt]	Kleidungsstück
distrust [dɪs'trʌst]	Misstrauen
speck [spek]	Fleck
shape [ʃeɪp]	Form
to **exaggerate sth** [ɪg'zædʒəreɪt]	etw übertreiben
to **motion (to sb)** ['məʊʃn]	(jdm) ein Zeichen geben
palm [pɑːm]	Hand(fläche)
to **signify sth** ['sɪgnɪfaɪ]	etw bedeuten, etw bezeichnen
awkward ['ɔːkwəd]	unangenehm, peinlich
clumsy ['klʌmzi]	ungeschickt, schwerfällig
You nailed it! [ju 'neɪld ɪt]	Du hast es geschafft
to **hang tight** [ˌhæŋ 'taɪt]	ruhig abwarten
dos and don'ts *(pl)* [ˌduːz ən 'dəʊnts]	*Hinweise, was man tun und lassen sollte*
to **greet sb** [griːt]	jdn (be)grüßen
interviewer ['ɪntəvjuːə]	Person, die ein Vorstellungsgespräch führt
firm [fɜːm]	fest, sicher
handshake ['hændʃeɪk]	Händedruck
to **fidget** ['fɪdʒɪt]	zappeln
to **fiddle** ['fɪdl]	(an etw) herumfummeln
to **pick at sth** [pɪk]	an etw herumzupfen
facing sb/sth ['feɪsɪŋ]	gegen etw, jdm gegenüber, mit dem Gesicht zu jdm/etw

page 33

closely ['kləʊsli]	genau, näher
worries *(pl)* ['wʌriz]	Sorgen, Bedenken
queue [kjuː]	Warteschlange
waiting staff ['weɪtɪŋ stɑːf]	Servicepersonal, Bedienung
hospitality [ˌhɒspɪ'tæləti]	Hotel- und Gaststättengewerbe
currently ['kʌrəntli]	zurzeit
to **recruit sb** [rɪ'kruːt]	jdn anwerben, jdn neu einstellen
located in/on [ləʊ'keɪtɪd]	in/an (... gelegen)
premier ['premiə]	führend; erstklassig
previous ['priːviəs]	vorherig, früher
to **deal with sb/sth** ['diːl wɪð]	mit jdm/etw zurechtkommen, mit jdm/etw umgehen
shift [ʃɪft]	Schicht
on-site [ɒn 'saɪt]	vor Ort, im Betrieb
accommodation [əˌkɒmə'deɪʃn]	Unterkunft
available [ə'veɪləbl]	verfügbar
summer camp ['sʌmə kæmp]	(Sommer-)Ferienlager
counsellor ['kaʊnsələ]	Berater/in, Betreuer/in
to **involve sth** [ɪn'vɒlv]	etw mit sich bringen, etw umfassen
camper ['kæmpə]	Lagerbewohner/in, Teilnehmer/in an einem Campingurlaub
to **care for sb** ['keə fə]	für jdn sorgen, sich um jdn kümmern, auf jdn aufpassen
to **supervise sb** ['suːpəvaɪz]	jdn beaufsichtigen
bunk [bʌŋk]	Schlafkabine, Koje
a host of [həʊst]	eine Menge
waterfront ['wɔːtəfrʌnt]	Ufer
return flight [rɪˌtɜːn 'flaɪt]	(Hin- und) Rückflug
medical insurance [ˌmedɪkl ɪn'ʃʊərəns]	Krankenversicherung
visa ['viːzə]	Visum
assistance [ə'sɪstəns]	Hilfe, Unterstützung
sponsorship ['spɒnsəʃɪp]	Förderung
requirement [rɪ'kwaɪəmənt]	Voraussetzung, Bedingung, Anforderung
fluent ['fluːənt]	*(Sprache:)* fließend
to **depart** [dɪ'pɑːt]	abreisen, abfahren, abfliegen
prior to ['praɪə]	vor *(zeitlich)*

page 34

to **receive sth** [rɪ'siːv]	etw erhalten, etw empfangen
up to date [ˌʌp tə 'deɪt]	aktuell, auf dem/den neuesten Stand
altogether [ˌɔːltə'geðə]	insgesamt, zusammen

literal ['lɪtərəl]	wörtlich, buchstäblich
electrician [ɪˌlek'trɪʃn]	Elektriker/in

UNIT 3

page 35

to **take it in turns** [ˌteɪk ɪt ɪn 'tɜːnz]	sich abwechseln
dice, *pl* **dice** [daɪs]	Würfel
counter ['kaʊntə]	Spielstein, Spielmarke
square [skweə]	(Spiel-)Feld
Lent [lent]	(die) Fastenzeit
to **break down** [ˌbreɪk 'daʊn]	eine Panne haben, kaputtgehen
to **drown sb/sth** [draʊn]	jdn/etw ertränken
sorrow ['sɒrəʊ]	Kummer, Leid
tub [tʌb]	Becher, Packung *(z. B. Eiscreme)*
chocolate chips *(pl)* ['tʃɒklət tʃɪps]	Schokoladenstückchen
afterwards ['ɑːftəwədz]	danach, hinterher
awake [ə'weɪk]	wach
slope [sləʊp]	(Ab-)Hang, Piste
desperation [ˌdespə'reɪʃn]	Verzweiflung
to **lose weight** [ˌluːz 'weɪt]	abnehmen *(Körpergewicht reduzieren)*
to **cut back on sth** [ˌkʌt 'bæk ɒn]	etw verringern, (bei) etw zurückschrauben
addicted (to) [ə'dɪktɪd]	süchtig (nach), abhängig (von)
juicy ['dʒuːsi]	saftig
chewing gum ['tʃuːɪŋ gʌm]	Kaugummi
basement ['beɪsmənt]	Keller, Untergeschoss
finish ['fɪnɪʃ]	Ende, Ziel

page 36

balanced ['bælənst]	ausgeglichen, ausgewogen, im Gleichgewicht
to **depend on sb/sth** [dɪ'pend ɒn]	von jdm/etw abhängen
to **consume sth** [kən'sjuːm]	etw verbrauchen, etw konsumieren, *(Kalorien)* aufnehmen
to **correspond to/with sth** [ˌkɒrə'spɒnd]	einer Sache entsprechen, mit etw übereinstimmen
to **put on weight** [ˌpʊt ɒn 'weɪt]	zunehmen *(Körpergewicht erhöhen)*
obese [əʊ'biːs]	fettleibig
fluid ['fluːɪd]	Flüssigkeit
to **stop sth** [stɒp]	etw verhindern
dehydration [ˌdiːhaɪ'dreɪʃn]	Austrocknung
vigorous ['vɪgərəs]	kräftig, energisch
mood [muːd]	Stimmung, Laune
stroke [strəʊk]	Schlaganfall
starchy ['stɑːtʃi]	stärkehaltig
carbohydrate [ˌkɑːbəʊ'haɪdreɪt]	Kohle(n)hydrat
to **make sth up** [ˌmeɪk 'ʌp]	etw erfinden, sich etw ausdenken
wholegrain ['həʊlgreɪn]	Vollkorn-
variety [və'raɪəti]	Sorte, Art, Variante
fibre ['faɪbə]	Ballaststoffe
fattening ['fætnɪŋ]	dick machend
to **provide sth** [prə'vaɪd]	etw (an)bieten, etw zur Verfügung stellen
fat [fæt]	dick, fett, Fett
nutritionist [nju'trɪʃənɪst]	Ernährungswissenschaftler/in, Ernährungsberater/in
unsweetened [ˌʌn'swiːtnd]	ungesüßt
…, as do vegetables … [æz, əz]	…, wie es auch Gemüse tut/macht …
dish [dɪʃ]	Gericht, Speise
protein ['prəʊtiːn]	Eiweiß, Protein
lean [liːn]	schlank, hager, mager *(Fleisch)*
visible ['vɪzəbl]	sichtbar
nutrition [nju'trɪʃn]	Nahrung, Ernährung
mineral ['mɪnərəl]	Mineral(stoff)
oily ['ɔɪli]	ölig, fett
salmon, *pl* **salmon** ['sæmən]	Lachs
trout, *pl* **trout** [traʊt]	Forelle
tuna ['tjuːnə]	Thunfisch
to **prevent sth** [prɪ'vent]	etw (ver)hindern, einer Sache vorbeugen
(un)saturated fat [ˌsætʃəreɪtɪd 'fæt, ʌnˌsætʃəreɪtɪd 'fæt]	(un)gesättigte Fettsäure
cholesterol [kə'lestərɒl]	Cholesterin
sugary ['ʃʊgəri]	zuckerhaltig, süß(lich)
fizzy drink ['fɪzi drɪŋk]	Erfrischungsgetränk (mit Kohlensäure)
pastry ['peɪstri]	Teig, Gebäck(stück)
high in … ['haɪ ɪn]	reich an …, mit hohem …-Gehalt
to **contribute (to)** [kən'trɪbjuːt]	beitragen (zu)
(weight) gain [geɪn]	(Gewichts-)Zunahme
to **cause sth** [kɔːz]	etw verursachen
tooth decay ['tuːθ dɪkeɪ]	Karies, Zahnfäule
intake ['ɪnteɪk]	Zufuhr, Aufnahme
vital ['vaɪtl]	lebensnotwendig, unerlässlich
processed food ['prəʊsest]	industriell verarbeitete Lebensmittel

page 37

medical condition [ˌmedɪkl kən'dɪʃn]	Leiden, Erkrankung
starch [stɑːtʃ]	Stärke *(in Lebensmitteln)*
major ['meɪdʒə]	Haupt-, wesentlich, größer
cause [kɔːz]	Ursache, Grund
wheat [wiːt]	Weizen
to **saturate sth** ['sætʃəreɪt]	etw sättigen *(chemisch)*
to **process sth** ['prəʊses]	etw (weiter)verarbeiten
packet soup ['pækɪt suːp]	Tütensuppe

page 38

vending machine ['vendɪŋ məʃiːn]	(Verkaufs-)Automat
close [kləʊs]	eingehend, genau
soft drink ['sɒft drɪŋk]	alkoholfreies Getränk
to **put sth into practice** [ˌpʊt ɪntə'præktɪs]	etw in die Praxis umsetzen
to **persuade sb** [pə'sweɪd]	jdn überreden, jdn überzeugen
fellow ['feləʊ]	Mit-, andere
to **change people's minds** [ˌtʃeɪndʒ piːplz 'maɪndz]	die Menschen zum Umdenken bewegen
to **fade into the background** [ˌfeɪd ɪntə ðə 'bækgraʊnd]	in den Hintergrund rücken

page 39

to **advise against sth** [əd,vaɪz ə'genst] — von etw abraten
dire ['daɪə] — ernst *(z. B. Warnung)*
to **lose your touch** [ˌluːz jə 'tʌtʃ] — nachlassen
grocery store *(AE)* ['grəʊsəri stɔː] — Lebensmittelgeschäft
legislator ['ledʒɪsleɪtə] — Mitglied der Legislative, Abgeordnete/r
weapon ['wepən] — Waffe
to **dissuade sb from doing sth** [dɪ'sweɪd] — jdn davon abbringen, etw zu tun
beverage ['bevərɪdʒ] — Getränk
to **propose sth** [prə'pəʊz] — etw vorschlagen, etw unterbreiten, etw darlegen
calorie-count label ['kæləri kaʊnt leɪbl] — Brennwerttabelle *(auf Produktetiketten)*
layer ['leɪə] — Schicht, Ebene
lead researcher [ˌliːd rɪ'sɜːtʃə] — Forschungsleiter/in
researcher [rɪ'sɜːtʃə] — Forscher/in, Wissenschaftler/in
public health [ˌpʌblɪk 'helθ] — öffentliches Gesundheitswesen
to **publish sth** ['pʌblɪʃ] — etw veröffentlichen
to **join sb/sth** [dʒɔɪn] — sich jdm/einer Sache anschließen
body of research [ˌbɒdi əv rɪ'sɜːtʃ] — Forschungsmaterial, Forschungsarbeiten
to **demonstrate sth** ['demənstreɪt] — etw zeigen, etw demonstrieren
to **package sth** ['pækɪdʒ] — etw (ver)packen
it ought to make … ['ɔːt tə] — es sollte … machen
anniversary [ˌænɪ'vɜːsəri] — Jahrestag
acting ['æktɪŋ] — stellvertretend
pack [pæk] — Packung
yet [jet] — (und) doch, dennoch
to **estimate** ['estɪmeɪt] — schätzen
preventable [prɪ'ventəbl] — vermeidbar
to **indicate** ['ɪndɪkeɪt] — (an)zeigen, darauf hindeuten, hinweisen auf
since [sɪns] — weil, da, seit
shock [ʃɒk] — Schock

page 40

drastically ['dræstɪkli] — drastisch
to **weaken** ['wiːkən] — (sich) (ab)schwächen, nachlassen
virtually ['vɜːtʃuəli] — praktisch, nahezu
meaningless ['miːnɪŋləs] — unbedeutend, sinnlos
campaign [kæm'peɪn] — Kampagne, Aktion
tobacco [tə'bækəʊ] — Tabak
advocacy (of) ['ædvəkəsi] — Eintreten (für), Befürwortung *(einer Sache)*
moreover [mɔːr'əʊvə] — überdies, zudem
to **become/be habitualized (to sth)** [hə'bɪtʃuəlaɪzd] — sich (an etw) gewöhnen / (an etw) gewöhnt sein
to **go unnoticed** [ˌʌn'nəʊtɪst] — unbemerkt bleiben
to **support sb/sth** [sə'pɔːt] — jdn/etw unterstützen
prevention [prɪ'venʃn] — Prävention, Prophylaxe
act [ækt] — Gesetz
graphic ['græfɪk] — anschaulich
to **accompany sb/sth** [ə'kʌmpəni] — jdn/etw begleiten, mit etw einhergehen
lung [lʌŋ] — Lunge
harm [hɑːm] — (körperlicher) Schaden
ubiquitousness [juː'bɪkwɪtəsnəs] — Allgegenwart
effectiveness [ɪ'fektɪvnəs] — Wirksamkeit, Effektivität
grocery bag ['grəʊsəri bæg] — Einkaufstasche
(printer) cartridge ['kɑːtrɪdʒ] — (Drucker-)Patrone
explicit [ɪk'splɪsɪt] — klar, deutlich, ausdrücklich
to **have second thoughts** [həv ˌsekənd 'θɔːts] — es sich anders überlegen
thought [θɔːt] — Gedanke
to **shock sb** [ʃɒk] — jdn schockieren
disturbing [dɪ'stɜːbɪŋ] — verstörend, erschütternd, unheimlich, bedrohlich
worth (millions) [wɜːθ] — (Millionen) wert
bar [bɑː] — Riegel *(z. B. Schokolade)*
measure ['meʒə] — Maßnahme

page 41

to **stick sth** [stɪk] — etw (an)kleben, etw (an)hängen
to **hang sth up** [ˌhæŋ 'ʌp] — etw aufhängen
cover flap ['kʌvə flæp] — Umschlagklappe
unless [ən'les] — es sei denn, außer wenn
course of action [ˌkɔːs əv 'ækʃn] — Vorgehen, Maßnahmen
alert [ə'lɜːt] — Warnung, Alarm
caution ['kɔːʃn] — Vorsicht, Warnung

page 42

grain [greɪn] — Getreide
maize [meɪz] — Mais
dairy ['deəri] — Molkerei, Milch-, Molkerei-
reformed [rɪ'fɔːmd] — geläutert, ehemalig
starvation [stɑː'veɪʃn] — Hunger
treadmill ['tredmɪl] — Tretmühle
bright [braɪt] — hell, strahlend, freundlich *(Wetter)*
amazing [ə'meɪzɪŋ] — erstaunlich
ancestor ['ænsestə] — Vorfahr/in
crisis, *pl* **crises** ['kraɪsɪs, 'kraɪsiːz] — Krise
lentil ['lentl] — Linse *(Lebensmittel)*
six weeks in [ɪn] — sechs Wochen nach Beginn *(von etw)*
unbelievable [ˌʌnbɪ'liːvəbl] — unglaublich
desperate ['despərət] — verzweifelt
tiredness ['taɪədnəs] — Müdigkeit
craving ['kreɪvɪŋ] — Verlangen
to **programme sth** ['prəʊgræm] — etw programmieren
thesis, *pl* **theses** ['θiːsɪz, 'θiːsiːz] — These
berry ['bəri] — Beere
seafood ['siːfuːd] — Meeresfrüchte
corn [kɔːn] — Getreide, *(AE)* Mais
agricultural [ˌægrɪ'kʌltʃərəl] — landwirtschaftlich, Landwirtschafts-
to **cultivate sth** ['kʌltɪveɪt] — etw bewirtschaften, *(Getreide, Gemüse)* anbauen
caveman, *pl* **cavemen** ['keɪvmæn, 'keɪvmən] — Höhlenmensch
seed [siːd] — Samen, Saat(gut), *(AE)* Kern

along with [ə'lɒŋ wɪð] (zusammen) mit, neben
prehistoric [ˌpriːhɪ'stɒrɪk] vorgeschichtlich, prähistorisch
primal ['praɪml] ursprünglich, Ur-, urweltlich
supporter [sə'pɔːtə] Anhänger/in
to **fossilize** ['fɒsəlaɪz] fossilisieren (lassen), versteinern (lassen)
remains *(pl)* [rɪ'meɪnz] (Über-)Reste, Relikte
agriculture ['ægrɪkʌltʃə] Landwirtschaft
remarkably [rɪ'mɑːkəbli] erstaunlicherweise
hunter-gatherer [ˌhʌntə 'gæðərə] Jäger und Sammler
absence ['æbsəns] Abwesenheit
trial ['traɪəl] Versuch, Test, Probe
loss [lɒs] Verlust
participant [pɑː'tɪsɪpənt] Teilnehmer/in

page 43

large-scale [ˌlɑːdʒ 'skeɪl] groß, groß angelegt
to **be opposed to sth** [bi ə'pəʊzd tə] gegen etw sein
spokeswoman ['spəʊkswʊmən] Sprecherin
dietetic [ˌdaɪə'tetɪk] diätetisch, Ernährungs-
to **exclude sb/sth** [ɪk'skluːd] jdn/etw ausschließen
essential (to) [ɪ'senʃl] wesentlich, unerlässlich (für)
dietician [ˌdaɪə'tɪʃn] Ernährungsberater/in, Ernährungswissenschaftler/in
harmfulness ['hɑːmflnəs] Schädlichkeit
life expectancy ['laɪf ɪkspektənsi] Lebenserwartung
to **make sense** [ˌmeɪk 'sens] Sinn ergeben, sinnvoll sein
to **be a pain (in the arse)** *(infml)* [bi ə ˌpeɪn ɪn ði 'ɑːs] jdm auf die Nerven gehen
to **opt out of sth** [ˌɒpt 'aʊt əv] sich gegen etw entscheiden, bei etw nicht mitmachen
concession [kən'seʃn] Konzession, Zugeständnis
to **lay sth out** [ˌleɪ 'aʊt] etw ausführen, etw niederlegen *(aufschreiben)*
naturopath ['neɪtʃərəpæθ] Naturheilkundige/r
to **cut sth out** [ˌkʌt 'aʊt] etw weglassen, auf etw verzichten
fortnight ['fɔːtnaɪt] zwei Wochen, vierzehn Tage
to **be/go mad on sth** ['mad ɒn] nach etw verrückt sein/werden
torture ['tɔːtʃə] Folter
to **adopt sth** [ə'dɒpt] etw übernehmen, sich für etw entscheiden
to **resemble sth** [rɪ'zembl] einer Sache ähneln, einer Sache gleichen, etw widerspiegeln

page 44

scientific [ˌsaɪən'tɪfɪk] wissenschaftlich
harmful (to) ['hɑːmfl] schädlich, schlecht (für)
current ['kʌrənt] aktuell, derzeitig
amazed [ə'meɪzd] erstaunt
to **overcook sth** [ˌəʊvə'kʊk] etw verkochen *(zu lange kochen)*, etw verbraten
anger ['æŋgə] Zorn, Wut
crop [krɒp] Nutzpflanze, Feldfrucht

page 45

to **adjust (to sth)** [ə'dʒʌst] (sich) anpassen (an etw), (sich) einstellen (auf etw)
I can't/couldn't stand ... [stænd] ich kann/konnte ... nicht ausstehen

page 46

primary school ['praɪməri skuːl] Grundschule
scheme [skiːm] Programm, Projekt
nursery school ['nɜːsəri skuːl] Kindergarten
icy ['aɪsi] eiskalt, eisig, vereist
to **down sth** [daʊn] etw niederlegen
lap [læp] Runde *(Sport)*
random ['rændəm] zufällig, beliebig
apparently [ə'pærəntli] anscheinend
behaviour [bɪ'heɪvjə] Benehmen, Verhalten
scores (of ...) [skɔː] eine Menge (...), viel/e (...)
to **follow suit** [ˌfɒləʊ 'suːt] gleichziehen
(local) authority [ɔː'θɒrəti] (Kommunal-)Behörde
figure ['fɪgə] Zahl, Ziffer
to **launch sth** [lɔːntʃ] etw ins Leben rufen, etw starten
common sense [ˌkɒmən 'sens] gesunder Menschenverstand
to **sustain sth** [sə'steɪn] etw (aufrecht)erhalten, etw (unter)stützen
(bright)-eyed [aɪd] mit (strahlenden) Augen
(rosy)-cheeked [tʃiːkt] mit (rosigen/roten) Wangen
joyous ['dʒɔɪəs] froh, freudig
circuit ['sɜːkɪt] Rundparcours, Rennstrecke
to **suit sb/sth** [suːt] zu jdm/etw passen
track [træk] Rennstrecke, Laufbahn
spokesperson ['spəʊkspɜːsn] Sprecher/in
chair [tʃeə] Vorsitzende/r
extent [ɪk'stent] Umfang, Ausmaß
comparative [kəm'pærətɪv] vergleichend
to **settle in(to sth)** [ˌsetl 'ɪn] sich (in etw) eingewöhnen, (bei/in etw) ankommen
colleague ['kɒliːg] Kollege/-in
to **be committed to sth** [kə'mɪtɪd] sich für etw engagieren, für etw engagiert sein
to **be expected to do sth** [ɪk'spektɪd] etw tun sollen/müssen, es wird erwartet, dass man etw tut
to **deliver sth** [dɪ'lɪvə] etw liefern
to **achieve sth** [ə'tʃiːv] etw erreichen, etw leisten
leadership ['liːdəʃɪp] Führung
supportive [sə'pɔːtɪv] (unter)stützend
tax [tæks] Steuer

page 47

sales *(pl)* [seɪlz] Verkauf, Vertrieb, Verkaufs-
restriction [rɪ'strɪkʃn] Beschränkung, Einschränkung
to **question sth** ['kwestʃən] etw infrage stellen
to **forbid** [fə'bɪd] verbieten, untersagen
premises *(pl)* ['premɪsɪz] Betrieb(sräume), Geschäft(sräume), (Betriebs-)Gelände
merit ['merɪt] Vorzug, Verdienst
to **implement sth** ['ɪmplɪmənt] etw einführen, etw umsetzen, etw einsetzen

page 48

campus ['kæmpəs]	Gelände *(z. B. Schule, Unternehmen)*
straight away [streɪt ə'weɪ]	sofort
right away [ˌraɪt ə'weɪ]	sofort
board [bɔːd]	Gremium, Ausschuss
to **translate** [træns'leɪt]	übersetzen, (sich) übertragen (lassen)

UNIT 4

page 49

to **bounce (sth)** [baʊns]	hüpfen; *(Ball)* prellen
to **dive** [daɪv]	tauchen, einen Kopfsprung machen
equipment [ɪ'kwɪpmənt]	Ausrüstung, Geräte
course [kɔːs]	Rennstrecke, Kurs *(Sport)*
court [kɔːt]	Platz *(Sport)*; Gerichtshof
diamond ['daɪəmənd]	(Innen-)Feld *(Baseball)*
pitch [pɪtʃ]	Platz, Spielfeld
rink [rɪŋk]	Eisbahn, Rollschuhbahn
bat [bæt]	Schläger
boots *(pl)* [buːts]	Stiefel
club [klʌb]	Schläger *(Golf)*
costume *(BE)* ['kɒstjuːm]	Badeanzug
goggles *(pl)* ['gɒglz]	Schutzbrille; Ski-/Taucherbrille
gumshield *(BE)* ['gʌmʃiːld]	Mundschutz, Zahnschutz
mouthguard *(AE)* ['maʊθgɑːd]	Mundschutz, Zahnschutz
racket ['rækɪt]	Schläger *(Tennis, Squash)*
shin pad ['ʃɪn pæd]	Schienbeinschoner
stick [stɪk]	Schläger *(Hockey)*
tee [tiː]	Tee *(Abschlag beim Golf)*
trunks *(pl)* [trʌŋks]	Badehose
athletics *(BE)* [æθ'letɪks]	Leichtathletik

page 50

desire [dɪ'zaɪə]	Wunsch, Verlangen
indoor ['ɪndɔː]	im Haus, Innen-
orienteering [ˌɔːriən'tɪərɪŋ]	Orientierungslauf
archery ['ɑːtʃəri]	Bogenschießen
niche [niːʃ, nɪtʃ]	Nische(n-)
following ['fɒləʊɪŋ]	Anhängerschaft
audience ['ɔːdiəns]	Publikum
spectator [spek'teɪtə]	Zuschauer/in
scarf, *pl* **scarves** [skɑːf, skɑːvz]	Schal, Halstuch
recent ['riːsnt]	jüngst, aktuell
to **combat sth** ['kɒmbæt]	etw bekämpfen
advertiser ['ædvətaɪzə]	Werber/in *(Auftraggeber/in in der Werbung)*, Inserent/in
to **be quoted on the stock exchange** [bi ˌkwəʊtɪd ət ðə 'stɒk ɪkstʃeɪndʒ]	an der Börse notiert werden
corporation [ˌkɔːpə'reɪʃn]	Konzern
sportswear ['spɔːtsweə]	Sportkleidung
brand [brænd]	Marke
to **endorse sth** [ɪn'dɔːs]	für etw werben
to **make a living** [ˌmeɪk ə 'lɪvɪŋ]	seinen Lebensunterhalt verdienen
in your own right [əʊn 'raɪt]	eigenständig
financial reward [faɪˌnænʃl rɪ'wɔːd]	(finanzielle) Entlohnung, Entgelt
temptation [temp'teɪʃn]	Versuchung
to **cheat** [tʃiːt]	schummeln, betrügen, schwindeln
considerable [kən'sɪdərəbl]	erheblich, beträchtlich
endurance [ɪn'djʊərəns]	Ausdauer
athlete ['æθliːt]	Sportler/in, Athlet/in
match-fixing ['mætʃ fɪksɪŋ]	Spielmanipulation
to **uncover sth** [ʌn'kʌvə]	etw aufdecken
to **bet** [bet]	wetten
syndicate ['sɪndɪkət]	Syndikat, Interessensgemeinschaft
to **bribe sb** [braɪb]	jdn bestechen
to **damage sth** ['dæmɪdʒ]	etw beschädigen
to **host sth** [həʊst]	etw ausrichten
priceless ['praɪsləs]	unbezahlbar, von unschätzbarem Wert
official [ə'fɪʃl]	Beamte/r, Funktionär/in
federation [ˌfedə'reɪʃn]	Verband, Föderation
to **accuse sb of sth** [ə'kjuːz]	jdn einer Sache beschuldigen, jdm etw vorwerfen
to **award sth (to sb)** [ə'wɔːd]	(jdm) etw zusprechen, (jdm) etw zuerkennen, (jdm) etw verleihen
to **flourish** ['flʌrɪʃ]	florieren, blühen, gedeihen
at (the) grass-roots level [ˌgrɑːs ruːts 'levl]	an der Basis
enjoyment [ɪn'dʒɔɪmənt]	Freude, Vergnügen
excitement [ɪk'saɪtmənt]	Begeisterung

page 51

endorsement [ɪn'dɔːsmənt]	Werbung, Unterstützung
to **tempt sb** [tempt]	jdn in Versuchung führen, jdn verleiten
to **bend the rules** [ˌbend ðə 'ruːlz]	über die Regeln hinwegsehen, die Vorschriften beugen
to **fix sth** [fɪks]	etw festlegen, etw reparieren
suspicion [sə'spɪʃn]	Verdacht
to **compete** [kəm'piːt]	*(in Wettbewerben)* antreten, teilnehmen
to **spectate** [spek'teɪt]	zuschauen
coverage ['kʌvərɪdʒ]	Berichterstattung, Behandlung *(eines Themas)*
to **invest sth** [ɪn'vest]	etw investieren
airline ['eəlaɪn]	Fluglinie
ranking ['ræŋkɪŋ]	Rangfolge
contract ['kɒntrækt]	Vertrag
to **arrange sth** [ə'reɪndʒ]	etw arrangieren, etw vereinbaren
gambler ['gæmblə]	Spieler/in, Zocker/in
to **gamble** ['gæmbl]	spielen, zocken
office-holder ['ɒfɪs həʊldə]	Amtsinhaber/in
alive and kicking [əˌlaɪv ən 'kɪkɪŋ]	gesund und munter

page 52

tournament ['tʊənəmənt]	Turnier
to **fund sth** [fʌnd]	etw finanzieren
recently ['riːsntli]	kürzlich, in letzter Zeit
letter to the editor [ˌletə tə ði 'edɪtə]	Leserbrief
it's the turn of sth [tɜːn]	etw ist an der Reihe
vanity ['vænəti]	Eitelkeit

misplaced [ˌmɪsˈpleɪst]	fehl am Platz
pride [praɪd]	Stolz
foul [faʊl]	scheußlich, unanständig
narcissistic [ˌnɑːsɪˈsɪstɪk]	narzisstisch
a contradiction in terms [ˌkɒntrədɪkʃn ɪn ˈtɜːmz]	ein Widerspruch in sich

page 53

unchallenged [ʌnˈtʃælɪnʒd]	unwidersprochen
trait [treɪt]	Wesenszug, Eigenschaft
initially [ɪˈnɪʃəli]	anfangs, anfänglich
to **strive** [straɪv]	streben, bemüht sein
excellence [ˈeksələns]	ausgezeichnete Qualität; Spitzenleistung
pointless [ˈpɔɪntləs]	zwecklos, sinnlos
practitioner [prækˈtɪʃənə]	Fachmann/frau, Praktizierende/r
endeavour [ɪnˈdevə]	Bemühung, Unterfangen
vast majority [ˌvɑːst məˈdʒɒrəti]	(bei weitem) größter Teil, Löwenanteil
primarily [praɪˈmerəli]	vorrangig, hauptsächlich
to **condemn sth** [kənˈdem]	etw verdammen, etw verurteilen
involvement (in) [ɪnˈvɒlvmənt]	Engagement (bei), Beteiligung (an), Einbindung (in)
exception [ɪkˈsepʃn]	Ausnahme
skillful [ˈskɪlfl]	geschickt, gut
defiant [dɪˈfaɪənt]	trotzig
to **equal sth** [ˈiːkwəl]	etw bedeuten, einer Sache entsprechen
innocence [ˈɪnəsns]	Unschuld, Arglosigkeit
conkers [ˈkɒŋkəz]	*Kinderspiel, bei dem man Kastanien an Schnüren gegeneinander schlägt*
to **prove** [pruːv]	sich erweisen (als)
impetus [ˈɪmpɪtəs]	Impuls, Anstoß
to **invigorate** [ɪnˈvɪgəreɪt]	stärken, beleben, anregen
supposedly [səˈpəʊzɪdli]	vermeintlich, angeblich

page 54

goalie [ˈgəʊli]	Torwart/in
striker [ˈstrɪkə]	Stürmer/in
dedication (to) [ˌdedɪˈkeɪʃn]	Einsatz, Engagement (für)
to **bust** *(infml)* [bʌst]	zerplatzen
to **breathe down sb's neck** [ˌbriːð daʊn sʌmbədiz ˈnek]	jdm im Nacken sitzen
opponent [əˈpəʊnənt]	Gegner/in
to **clap** [klæp]	(Beifall) klatschen
to **lose graciously** [ˌluːz ˈgreɪʃəsli]	mit Anstand verlieren

page 55

gymnasium [dʒɪmˈneɪziəm]	Sporthalle
to **outline sth** [ˈaʊtlaɪn]	etw skizzieren, etw grob beschreiben
in return [ɪn rɪˈtɜːn]	im Gegenzug, als Ausgleich

page 56

to **tackle sth** [ˈtækl]	etw *(z. B. ein Problem)* angehen, etw bewältigen
agency [ˈeɪdʒənsi]	Behörde, Agentur
to **pose sth** [pəʊz]	etw darstellen
threat [θret]	Bedrohung
to **violate sth** [ˈvaɪəleɪt]	gegen etw verstoßen, etw verletzen
to **date back …** [ˌdeɪt ˈbæk]	… alt sein, stammen aus …
association [əˌsəʊʃiˈeɪʃn]	Verband, Vereinigung
to **govern sth** [ˈgʌvn]	etw regieren, etw verwalten, etw führen
retired [rɪˈtaɪəd]	pensioniert, im Ruhestand
cyclist [ˈsaɪklɪst]	Radfahrer/in
to **admit to sth** [ədˈmɪt]	etw zugeben, (ein)gestehen
to **strip sb of sth** [strɪp]	jdm etw aberkennen
kidney [ˈkɪdni]	Niere
baldness [ˈbɔːldnəs]	Kahlheit, Glatze
sperm count [ˈspɜːm kaʊnt]	Spermienzahl
facial hair [feɪʃl ˈheə]	Bartwuchs, Gesichtsbehaarung
to **deepen sth** [ˈdiːpən]	etw tiefer werden lassen
to **overcome sth** [ˌəʊvəˈkʌm]	etw überwinden
fatigue [fəˈtiːg]	Müdigkeit
addictive [əˈdɪktɪv]	süchtig machend
heart failure [ˈhɑːt feɪljə]	Herzversagen
competitor [kəmˈpetɪtə]	Konkurrent/in, Konkurrenz, Wettbewerbsteilnehmer/in

page 57

bulk [bʌlk]	(Körper-)Masse
to **inject sth** [ɪnˈdʒekt]	etw injizieren, etw (ein)spritzen
oxygen [ˈɒksɪdʒən]	Sauerstoff
unique [juˈniːk]	einzigartig
fingerprint [ˈfɪŋgəprɪnt]	Fingerabdruck
to **detect sth** [dɪˈtekt]	etw wahrnehmen, etw entdecken
capable of [ˈkeɪpəbl əv]	fähig zu, imstande zu
to **aid sth** [eɪd]	bei etw helfen, etw unterstützen
detection [dɪˈtekʃn]	Entdeckung, Aufdeckung
throughout [θruːˈaʊt]	überall, in der ganzen Zeit … hindurch
confession [kənˈfeʃn]	Beichte, Geständnis
in disgrace [ɪn dɪsˈgreɪs]	unehrenhaft
guilty [ˈgɪlti]	schuldig
compatriot [kəmˈpætriət]	Landsmann/Landsmännin
to **fail sth** [feɪl]	etw nicht bestehen, bei etw durchfallen
to **rid sth of sth** [rɪd]	etw von etw befreien
to **pledge** [pledʒ]	sich verpflichten
abuse [əˈbjuːs]	Missbrauch
vigilance [ˈvɪdʒɪləns]	Wachsamkeit
punishment [ˈpʌnɪʃmənt]	Strafe, Bestrafung
approved [əˈpruːvd]	anerkannt, genehmigt
to **double** [ˈdʌbl]	(sich) verdoppeln

page 58

addiction (to) [əˈdɪkʃn]	Sucht (nach), Abhängigkeit (von)
inspector [ɪnˈspektə]	Kontrolleur/in
high-profile [ˌhaɪ ˈprəʊfaɪl]	prominent, mit hohem Bekanntheitsgrad

page 59

hatred [ˈheɪtrɪd]	Hass, Abscheu
to **result in sth** [rɪˈzʌlt ɪn]	zu etw führen
syringe [sɪˈrɪndʒ]	(Injektions-)Spritze
to **suspect sth** [səˈspekt]	etw vermuten

page 60

birth [bɜːθ]	Geburt
mine [maɪn]	Bergwerk, Mine
mill [mɪl]	Fabrik *(insbesondere Textilfabrik)*
to **last** [lɑːst]	dauern, andauern, so bleiben
working conditions *(pl)* [ˌwɜːkɪŋ kənˈdɪʃnz]	Arbeitsbedingungen
slot [slɒt]	Platz, Zeitfenster
recreation [ˌrekriˈeɪʃn]	Freizeit, Erholung
to **found sth** [faʊnd]	etw gründen
invincible [ɪnˈvɪnsəbl]	unbesiegbar
shareholder [ˈʃeəhəʊldə]	Aktionär/in, Teilhaber/in, Gesellschafter/in
fee [fiː]	Gebühr
steel [stiːl]	Stahl
iron [ˈaɪən]	Eisen
to **punish sb** [ˈpʌnɪʃ]	jdn bestrafen
to **announce sth** [əˈnaʊns]	etw verkünden, etw ankündigen
rumour [ˈruːmə]	Gerücht
unexpected [ˌʌnɪkˈspektɪd]	unerwartet

page 61

to **deter sb** [dɪˈtɜː]	jdn abschrecken, jdn (von etw) abhalten
to **deserve sth** [dɪˈzɜːv]	etw verdienen
deliberate [dɪˈlɪbərət]	absichtlich, (ganz) bewusst, vorsätzlich
fraud [frɔːd]	Betrug

page 62

illicit [ɪˈlɪsɪt]	illegal, verboten
lifetime [ˈlaɪftaɪm]	lebenslang, (ganzes) Leben

UNIT 5

page 63

to **cater for sb/sth** [ˈkeɪtə fə]	jdm/einer Sache gerecht werden, auf jdn/etw eingestellt sein
agritourism [ˈæɡrɪtʊərɪzəm]	Agrotourismus, Landtourismus
poverty [ˈpɒvəti]	Armut

page 64

in pursuit of sth [pəˈsjuːt]	beim Streben nach etw, auf der Suche nach etw
provision [rəˈvɪʒn]	Bereitstellung, Versorgung
to **coin sth** [kɔɪn]	etw prägen
to **flock** [flɒk]	strömen
holy [ˈhəʊli]	heilig
advent (of sth) [ˈædvent]	Ankunft, Beginn (einer Sache)
affordable [əˈfɔːdəbl]	erschwinglich
due to sth [ˈdjuː tə]	wegen etw
to **cater to sb/sth** [ˈkeɪtə tə]	auf jdn/etw ausgerichtet sein, jdm/etw gerecht werden
package tour [ˈpækɪdʒ tʊə]	Pauschalreise
to **take advantage of sth** [ˌteɪk ədˈvɑːntɪdʒ əv]	sich etw zunutze machen, etw ausnutzen
thanks to [ˈθæŋks tə]	dank
carrier [ˈkæriə]	Fluggesellschaft
emergence [iˈmɜːdʒəns]	Entstehen, Aufkommen
culinary [ˈkʌlɪnəri]	kulinarisch, Koch-
stag party [ˈstæɡ pɑːti]	Junggesellenabschied (des Bräutigams)
itinerary [aɪˈtɪnərəri]	Reiseroute, Reiseplan
gross domestic product (GDP) [ˌɡrəʊs dəˌmestɪk ˈprɒdʌkt]	Bruttosozialprodukt
rental [ˈrentl]	Verleih, Vermietung
amusement park [əˈmjuːzmənt pɑːk]	Vergnügungspark, Freizeitpark
retailer [ˈriːteɪlə]	Einzelhändler/in
income [ˈɪnkʌm]	Einkommen
means, *pl* **means** [miːnz]	Möglichkeit, Mittel
to **overuse sth** [ˌəʊvəˈjuːz]	etw überstrapazieren, etw übermäßig beanspruchen
destruction [dɪˈstrʌkʃn]	Zerstörung, Vernichtung
habitat [ˈhæbɪtæt]	natürlicher Lebensraum
not necessarily [nɒt ˌnesəˈserəli]	nicht unbedingt
to **promote sth** [prəˈməʊt]	etw fördern, etw unterstützen
globe [ɡləʊb]	Globus
local [ˈləʊkl]	Einheimische/r
oxymoron [ˌɒksɪˈmɔːrɒn]	Oxymoron, Widerspruch in sich
to **compensate for sth** [ˈkɒmpənseɪt fə]	etw ausgleichen
in the vicinity (of …) [vəˈsɪnəti]	in der Nähe (von …), in der näheren Umgebung (von …)
bicycle [ˈbaɪsɪkl]	Fahrrad

page 65

formation [fɔːˈmeɪʃn]	Entwicklung, Bildung

page 66

indecision [ˌɪndɪˈsɪʒn]	Unentschlossenheit
entitled [ɪnˈtaɪtld]	mit dem Titel
session [ˈseʃn]	Sitzung, Termin, Treffen, (Unterrichts-)Stunde
subgroup [ˈsʌbɡruːp]	Untergruppe

page 67

for ages [fər ˈeɪdʒɪz]	eine Ewigkeit (lang), sehr lange
adolescence [ˌædəˈlesns]	Jugend, jugendliches Alter
nevertheless [ˌnevəðəˈles]	trotzdem, dennoch
on sb's behalf [ɒn sʌmbədiz bɪˈhɑːf]	in jds Namen
to **rely on sb/sth** [rɪˈlaɪ ɒn]	sich auf jdn/etw verlassen
to **end up doing sth** [ˌend ˈʌp]	am Ende / schließlich etw tun
once [wʌns]	sobald, wenn (erst)
to **value sth** [ˈvæljuː]	etw (wert)schätzen
reserved [rɪˈzɜːvd]	reserviert, zurückhaltend
to **figure sth out** [ˌfɪɡər ˈaʊt]	etw herausfinden
to **liberate sb** [ˈlɪbəreɪt]	jdn befreien
to **exude sth** [ɪɡˈzjuːd]	vor etw strotzen, etw ausströmen
maturity [məˈtʃʊərəti]	Reife
worldly [ˈwɜːldli]	welterfahren, weltlich
to **set sb back sth** [ˌset ˈbæk]	jdn etw kosten
to **master sth** [ˈmɑːstə]	etw meistern, etw bewältigen

frugal [ˈfruːgl]	genügsam, bescheiden
conscious (of sth) [ˈkɒnʃəs]	(sich einer Sache) bewusst
to **haggle (with sb over sth)** [ˈhægl]	(mit jdm um etw) feilschen
to **rob sb** [rɒb]	jdn be-/ausrauben
to **be/get exposed to sth** [ɪkˈspəʊzd tə]	einer Sache ausgesetzt sein, mit etw in Berührung kommen
to **presume sth** [prɪˈzjuːm]	etw annehmen, etw vermuten, etw voraussetzen
to **enrich (sb's life)** [ɪnˈrɪtʃ]	(jds Leben) bereichern
custom [ˈkʌstəm]	Gewohnheit, Brauch, Sitte
sensitivity [ˌsensəˈtɪvəti]	Sensibilität, Einfühlungsvermögen
to **dip** [dɪp]	(ein)tauchen
to **immerse yourself in sth** [ɪˈmɜːs]	in etw eintauchen, sich in etw vertiefen

page 68

to **pick sth up** [ˌpɪk ˈʌp]	etw aufschnappen, sich etw aneignen
the … the … [ðə]	je … desto …
prospect [ˈprɒspekt]	Aussicht, Perspektive
to **have a (good) grasp of sth** [grɑːsp]	etw (gut) beherrschen
insight (into) [ˈɪnsaɪt]	Einblick (in), Verständnis (von)
to **further sth** [ˈfɜːðə]	etw fördern
(competitive) edge [kəmˌpetətɪv ˈedʒ]	(Wettbewerbs-)Vorteil, Vorsprung
to **turn out to be …** [ˌtɜːn ˈaʊt tə bi]	sich erweisen/herausstellen als …
to **come in handy** [ˌkʌm ɪn ˈhændi]	sich als nützlich erweisen, gelegen kommen
keyword [ˈkiːwɜːd]	Schlagwort, Schlüsselwort
initial [ɪˈnɪʃl]	anfänglich, erste(r,s)
cf. [ˌsiː ˈef]	vgl.

page 69

to **brush sth up** [ˌbrʌʃ ˈʌp]	etw auffrischen
on a day-to-day basis [ɒn ə ˌdeɪ tə deɪ ˈbeɪsɪs]	im Alltag, tagtäglich
wisdom [ˈwɪzdəm]	Weisheit, Klugheit
to **refute** [rɪˈfjuːt]	widerlegen, zurückweisen, bestreiten
to **find your way around** [faɪnd jə ˌweɪ əˈraʊnd]	sich zurechtfinden (in)
i.e. (= that is) [ˌaɪ ˈiː]	d. h. (= das heißt)

page 70

carbon [ˈkɑːbən]	Kohlenstoff
aviation [ˌeɪviˈeɪʃn]	Luftfahrt
to **reuse** [ˌriːˈjuːz]	wiederverwenden
composting toilet [ˌkɒmpɒstɪŋ ˈtɔɪlət]	Trockentoilette, Komposttoilette
notion [ˈnəʊʃn]	Vorstellung, Auffassung
to **fall short of sth** [fɔːl ˈʃɔːt əv]	etw nicht erreichen, etw nicht erfüllen, hinter etw zurückbleiben
to **step off the beaten track** [step ˌɒf ðə biːtn ˈtræk]	ausgetretene Pfade verlassen
to **preserve sth** [prɪˈzɜːv]	etw bewahren, etw erhalten
gain [geɪn]	Gewinn, Vorteil
overcrowded [ˌəʊvəˈkraʊdɪd]	überfüllt, übervölkert
comparatively [kəmˈpærətɪvli]	vergleichsweise, relativ, verhältnismäßig
unspoilt [ʌnˈspɔɪlt]	unverdorben, unberührt *(Landschaft)*
agent [ˈeɪdʒənt]	Instrument, Mittel
conservation [ˌkɒnsəˈveɪʃn]	(Natur-)Schutz, Erhaltung, Bewahrung
temporary [ˈtemprəri]	vorübergehend, befristet
to **resolve sth** [rɪˈzɒlv]	etw (auf)lösen
developer [dɪˈveləpə]	Bauträger/in, Bauunternehmer/in
to **vanish** [ˈvænɪʃ]	verschwinden, aussterben
to **employ sb** [ɪmˈplɔɪ]	jdn beschäftigen, jdn einstellen *(Personal)*
lease [liːs]	Mietvertrag, Pachtvertrag
property [ˈprɒpəti]	Grundstück, Eigentum an Grund und Boden

page 71

rocket stove [ˈrɒkɪt stəʊv]	Raketenofen/-herd (der Brennstoff besonders effizient verbrennt)
thereby [ˌðeəˈbaɪ]	dabei, dadurch
deforestation [diːˌfɒrɪˈsteɪʃn]	Waldzerstörung
renewable [rɪˈnjuːəbl]	erneuerbar
surrounding area [səˌraʊndɪŋ ˈeərɪə]	Umgebung
boost [buːst]	(schnelle) Steigerung, Auftrieb
to **mitigate sth** [ˈmɪtɪgeɪt]	etw (ab)mildern
to **overstate sth** [ˌəʊvəˈsteɪt]	etw übertreiben
to **account for sth** [əˈkaʊnt fə]	etw ausmachen
… and the like [ˌənd ðə ˈlaɪk]	… und dergleichen
to **kick against sth** *(infml)* [ˌkɪk əˈgenst]	gegen etw aufmucken, sich gegen etw wehren
patron [ˈpeɪtrən]	Gast *(z. B. Hotel)*, Besucher/in *(z. B. Konzert)*, Kunde/Kundin
air conditioning [ˈeə kəndɪʃnɪŋ]	Klimaanlage
key card [ˈkiː kɑːd]	Schlüsselkarte
to **override sth** [ˌəʊvəˈraɪd]	sich über etw hinwegsetzen, etw außer Kraft setzen
to **insert sth (in)** [ɪnˈsɜːt]	etw einführen (in), etw (hin)einstecken (in)
slot [slɒt]	Schlitz, (Karten-)Einzug
portable [ˈpɔːtəbl]	tragbar
to **put up with sth** [ˌpʊt ˈʌp wɪð]	sich mit etw abfinden, etw ertragen
stuffy [ˈstʌfi]	stickig
overall [ˌəʊvərˈɔːl]	allgemein, insgesamt, im Großen und Ganzen
to **outweigh sth** [ˌaʊtˈweɪ]	schwerer als etw wiegen
businessfolk *(pl)* [ˈbɪznəsfəʊk]	Geschäftsleute
toe-touch meeting [ˌtəʊ tʌtʃ ˈmiːtɪŋ]	kurzer Vor-Ort-Termin, geschäftliche „Stippvisite"
to **occur** [əˈkɜː]	stattfinden, passieren, geschehen
executive [ɪgˈzekjətɪv]	leitende/r Angestellte/r
incentive [ɪnˈsentɪv]	Anreiz
economist [ɪˈkɒnəmɪst]	Volkswirt/in, Wirtschaftswissenschaftler/in

page 72

adjustment [ə'dʒʌstmənt]	Anpassung, Veränderung
vicious circle [ˌvɪʃəs 'sɜːkl]	Teufelskreis
force [fɔːs]	Kraft, Macht
decade ['dekeɪd]	Jahrzehnt
to **expire** [ɪk'spaɪə]	ablaufen, verfallen
environmentally friendly [ɪnˌvaɪrənˌmentəli 'frendli]	umweltfreundlich
consumption [kən'sʌmpʃn]	Verbrauch, Konsum
revenue ['revənjuː]	Einkünfte, Einnahmen

page 73

to **safeguard sth** ['seɪfgɑːd]	etw schützen
culprit ['kʌlprɪt]	Schuldige/r, Übeltäter/in
to **consult sth** [kən'sʌlt]	in etw nachsehen, in etw nachlesen
mandatory ['mændətəri]	verpflichtend, vorgeschrieben, obligatorisch
panel discussion ['pænl dɪskʌʃn]	Podiumsdiskussion
entrepreneur [ˌɒntrəprə'nɜː]	Unternehmer/in

page 74

sewage ['suːɪdʒ]	Abwasser
sustainability [səˌsteɪnə'bɪləti]	Nachhaltigkeit
subtitles *(pl)* ['sʌbtaɪtlz]	Untertitel
investment [ɪn'vestmənt]	Investition
reminder [rɪ'maɪndə]	Erinnerung, Mahnung
to **sacrifice sth** ['sækrɪfaɪs]	etw opfern
vulnerable ['vʌlnərəbl]	verletzlich, verwundbar
to **regard sth (as)** [rɪ'gɑːd]	etw ansehen, etw betrachten (als)
feasible ['fiːzəbl]	machbar, möglich
to **aim at / for / to do sth** ['eɪm ət]	zielen auf, sich richten an
stunning ['stʌnɪŋ]	phantastisch, umwerfend
double-edged [ˌdʌbl 'edʒd]	zweischneidig, zwiespältig
runoff ['rʌnɒf]	Abfluss, abfließendes Wasser
fertilizer ['fɜːtəlaɪzə]	Dünger, Düngemittel
to **pioneer sth** [ˌpaɪə'nɪə]	etw zum ersten Mal anwenden, etw entwickeln
surroundings *(pl)* [sə'raʊndɪŋz]	Umgebung
financial viability [faɪˌnænʃl vaɪə'bɪləti]	finanzielle Realisierbarkeit, Durchführbarkeit
panel ['pænl]	Platte, Tafel, Kollektor
solid waste [ˌsɒlɪd 'weɪst]	Feststoffabfall, Hausmüll
to **treat sth** [triːt]	etw behandeln, *(Abwasser)* klären
wastewater ['weɪstwɔːtə]	Abwasser
artisan [ˌɑːtɪ'zæn]	Handwerker/in
to **revive sth** [rɪ'vaɪv]	etw wieder beleben, etw wieder aufleben lassen
to **weave** [wiːv]	weben
to **reintroduce sth** [ˌriːɪntrə'djuːs]	etw wieder einführen, etw wieder heimisch machen
endemic (to) [en'demɪk]	einheimisch (in), verbreitet (in)
species, *pl* **species** ['spiːʃiːz]	Art *(Biologie)*
to **conserve sth** [kən'sɜːv]	etw erhalten, etw schonen
it is feared lost [fɪəd]	es wird befürchtet, dass er/sie/es verloren ist
invasive [ɪn'veɪsɪv]	eindringend, invasiv
to **be able to afford sth** [ˌeɪbl tu ə'fɔːd]	sich etw leisten können
to **subsidize sb/sth** ['sʌbsɪdaɪz]	jdn finanziell unterstützen, etw subventionieren
corporate ['kɔːpərət]	Unternehmens-, von Unternehmen
root [ruːt]	Wurzel
recognizable (by) ['rekəgnaɪzəbl]	(wieder)erkennbar (an)
clothing ['kləʊðɪŋ]	Bekleidung, Kleidung
mythical ['mɪθɪkl]	mythisch, legendär
dragon ['drægən]	Drachen
it is said that … [ɪt ɪz 'sed ðət]	man sagt, dass …
headdress ['heddres]	Kopfschmuck
to **inhabit (a region)** [ɪn'hæbɪt]	(eine Region) bewohnen
priority [praɪ'ɒrəti]	Priorität, Vorrang
funds *(pl)* [fʌndz]	Gelder
vineyard ['vɪnjəd]	Weinberg
to **overlook sth** [ˌəʊvə'lʊk]	etw überblicken
breathtaking ['breθteɪkɪŋ]	atemberaubend, hinreißend
to **contract sth** [kən'trækt]	etw vertraglich regeln
farming ['fɑːmɪŋ]	Anbau (landwirtschaftlicher Produkte), Landwirtschaft
grape [greɪp]	(Wein-)Traube
vine [vaɪn]	Weinrebe
compound fertilizer [ˌkɒmpaʊnd 'fɜːtəlaɪzə]	Komplexdünger, Mehrnährstoffdünger
to **pollute sth** [pə'luːt]	etw verschmutzen
table water ['teɪbl wɔːtə]	Grundwasser
contract farming [ˌkɒntrækt 'fɑːmɪŋ]	Vertragsanbau
small-scale [ˌsmɔːl 'skeɪl]	Klein-, klein angelegt
to **be inclusive of sb** [ɪn'kluːsɪv əv]	jdn miteinbeziehen
spa [spɑː]	Wellnessbereich
to **restock sth** [ˌriː'stɒk]	etw wieder auffüllen
pedalo ['pedələʊ]	Tretboot
coasteering [ˌkəʊst'ɪərɪŋ]	*Klettern an steilen Küsten mit Sprüngen ins Wasser*
aquatic [ə'kwætɪk]	Wasser-
rock pooling ['rɒk puːlɪŋ]	*bei Ebbe Gezeitentümpel untersuchen/nach Tieren absuchen*
to **scramble** ['skræmbl]	klettern, krabbeln
swell [swel]	Woge, Seegang
coastline ['kəʊstlaɪn]	Küste
wetsuit ['wetsuːt]	Tauchanzug, Surfanzug
buoyancy aid ['bɔɪənsi eɪd]	Schwimmhilfe
non-profit [ˌnɒn 'prɒfɪt]	gemeinnützig, nicht auf Gewinn ausgerichtet
to **team up with sb** [ˌtiːm 'ʌp wɪð]	mit jdm zusammenarbeiten, sich mit jdm zusammentun
to **distribute sth** [dɪ'strɪbjuːt]	etw verteilen, etw austeilen

page 75

window dressing ['wɪndəʊ dresɪŋ]	Schönfärberei, Augenwischerei
to **forgo sth** [fɔː'gəʊ]	auf etw verzichten
adventurous [əd'ventʃərəs]	abenteuerlich, abenteuerlustig
fan [fæn]	Ventilator
to **ventilate sth** ['ventɪleɪt]	etw belüften

cabin ['kæbɪn] – Hütte
bedlinen ['bedlɪnɪn] – Bettwäsche

page 76

pint [paɪnt] – Glas Bier (ca. ein halber Liter), Halbe
to **bother with sth** ['bɒðə wɪð] – sich um etw kümmern, sich mit etw befassen
somewhat ['sʌmwɒt] – etwas, ziemlich
to **be starved of sth** ['stɑːvd əv] – unter (…-)Mangel leiden, nicht genug von etw bekommen/haben
nervous breakdown [ˌnɜːvəs 'breɪkdaʊn] – Nervenzusammenbruch
to **hold on** [ˌhəʊld 'ɒn] – warten
travel agent ['trævl eɪdʒənt] – Reisebüro(angestellte/r)
to **crash** [kræʃ] – abstürzen, zusammenbrechen

UNIT 6

page 77

underlying [ˌʌndə'laɪɪŋ] – zugrunde liegend
urgent ['ɜːdʒənt] – dringend

page 78

power station ['paʊə steɪʃn] – Kraftwerk
to **emit sth** [ɪ'mɪt] – etw emittieren, etw ausstoßen, etw abstrahlen
toxic ['tɒksɪk] – giftig, Gift-
acid ['æsɪd] – sauer
fuel ['fjuːəl] – Brennstoff
coal [kəʊl] – Kohle
soil [sɔɪl] – Erde, Boden
to **contaminate sth** [kən'tæmɪneɪt] – etw verunreinigen, etw kontaminieren
greenhouse ['griːnhaʊs] – Treibhaus
carbon dioxide [ˌkɑːbən daɪ'ɒksaɪd] – Kohlendioxid
detrimental (to) [ˌdetrɪ'mentl] – schädlich (für)
to **expand sth** [ɪk'spænd] – etw erweitern, etw expandieren
to **ensure sth/that** [ɪn'ʃʊə] – etw sicherstellen, dafür sorgen, dass
economical [ˌiːkə'nɒmɪkl] – sparsam, wirtschaftlich
pulp [pʌlp] – *(Papier-, Holz-)* Brei
to **store** [stɔː] – speichern
to **release sth/sb** [rɪ'liːs] – etw freisetzen, jdn entlassen
carbon (dioxide) capture [ˌkɑːbən daɪ'ɒksaɪd kæptʃə] – Kohlenstoffbindung
climate change ['klaɪmət tʃeɪndʒ] – Klimawandel
extinction [ɪk'stɪŋkʃn] – Vernichtung, Ausrottung, Aussterben
glacier ['glæsiə] – Gletscher
to **melt** [melt] – schmelzen, abschmelzen
sea level ['siː levl] – Meeresspiegel
waste [weɪst] – Müll
reflection [rɪ'flekʃn] – Spiegelbild
inhabitant [ɪn'hæbɪtənt] – Einwohner/in, Bewohner/in
landfill site ['lændfɪl saɪt] – Mülldeponie
sophisticated [sə'fɪstɪkeɪtɪd] – raffiniert, anspruchsvoll
disposal [dɪ'spəʊzl] – Entsorgung
domestic waste [dəˌmestɪk 'weɪst] – Hausmüll
returnable bottle [rɪˌtɜːnəbl 'bɒtl] – Mehrwegflasche
jar [dʒɑː] – Glas, Gefäß
cardboard ['kɑːdbɔːd] – Pappe
reusable [ˌriː'juːzəbl] – wiederverwendbar
household ['haʊshəʊld] – Haushalt, Haushalts-
to **incinerate sth** [ɪn'sɪnəreɪt] – etw verbrennen
hazardous waste [hæzədəs 'weɪst] – Sondermüll
for instance [fə'rɪnstəns] – zum Beispiel
to **dispose of sth** [dɪ'spəʊz əv] – etw beseitigen, etw entsorgen
humanity [hjuː'mænəti] – Menschheit, Menschlichkeit

page 79

to **bury sth** ['beri] – etw vergraben, etw begraben
impure [ɪm'pjʊə] – unrein, unanständig
poisonous ['pɔɪzənəs] – giftig
preservation [ˌprezə'veɪʃn] – Erhaltung, Bewahrung
protection [prə'tekʃn] – Schutz

page 80

self-sufficient [ˌself sə'fɪʃnt] – autark
intern ['ɪntɜːn] – Praktikant/in
foundation [faʊn'deɪʃn] – Stiftung
grid [grɪd] – Versorgungsnetz
to **operate sth** ['ɒpəreɪt] – etw unterhalten, etw bedienen
fleet [fliːt] – Flotte
excess [ɪk'ses] – Überschuss
cooperative [kəʊ'ɒpərətɪv] – Genossenschaft
simultaneous [ˌsɪml'teɪniəs] – gleichzeitig
manure [mə'njʊə] – Dung, Mist

page 81

livestock ['laɪvstɒk] – Vieh
enclosure [ɪn'kləʊʒə] – Gehege, Einfriedung
additional [ə'dɪʃənl] – zusätzlich
to **supply sth** [sə'plaɪ] – etw liefern, etw bieten, etw bereitstellen
opposite ['ɒpəzɪt] – gegenüber (von), gegenüberliegend
dependent on sth [dɪ'pendənt ɒn] – von etw abhängig
to **raise your eyebrows (at sth)** [ˌreɪz jər 'aɪbraʊz] – (über etw) die Stirn runzeln
remainder [rɪ'meɪndə] – Rest(bestand)
bill [bɪl] – Rechnung
plant [plɑːnt] – Fabrik, Werk, Anlage, Kraftwerk
construction [kən'strʌkʃn] – (Auf-)Bau
to **comprise sth** [kəm'praɪz] – etw umfassen, aus etw bestehen
installation [ˌɪnstə'leɪʃn] – Anlage
to **rejuvenate sth** [rɪ'dʒuːvəneɪt] – etw verjüngen
to **dismantle sth** [dɪs'mæntl] – etw abbauen, etw abreißen
to **restore sth** [rɪ'stɔː] – etw restaurieren, etw wieder aufbauen
transition [træn'zɪʃn] – Übergang, Umstellung

page 82

disused	[ˌdɪsˈjuːzd]	stillgelegt
to **intend sth**	[ɪnˈtend]	etw beabsichtigen

page 83

furthermore	[ˌfɜːðəˈmɔː]	darüber hinaus
to **pronounce sth**	[prəˈnaʊns]	etw aussprechen
delivery	[dɪˈlɪvəri]	Vortrag

page 84

to **degrade sth**	[dɪˈgreɪd]	etw abbauen
freshwater	[ˈfreʃwɔːtə]	Süßwasser-
vast	[vɑːst]	riesig, sehr groß
to **pinpoint sth**	[ˈpinpɔɪnt]	etw genau lokalisieren, etw feststellen
liveable	[ˈlɪvəbl]	lebenswert, bewohnbar
to **underpin sth**	[ˌʌndəˈpɪn]	etw (ab)stützen, etw untermauern
to **exceed sth**	[ɪkˈsiːd]	etw übersteigen
nitrogen	[ˈnaɪtrədʒən]	Stickstoff
core	[kɔː]	Kern-, Haupt-
baseline	[ˈbeɪslaɪn]	Basis, Ausgangspunkt
unprecedented	[ʌnˈpresɪdentɪd]	beispiellos, einmalig
stable	[ˈsteɪbl]	stabil, konstant
to **advance**	[ədˈvɑːns]	voranschreiten, Fortschritte machen
to **become extinct**	[bɪˌkʌm ɪkˈstɪŋkt]	aussterben
primary	[ˈpraɪməri]	Haupt-, hauptsächlich
to **soar**	[sɔː]	steigen
to **quadruple**	[kwɒˈdruːpl]	(sich) vervierfachen
to **shift**	[ʃɪft]	(sich) verlagern, (sich) verändern
hospitable	[hɒˈspɪtəbl]	gastfreundlich
resilience	[rɪˈzɪliəns]	Widerstandsfähigkeit
to **go into overdrive**	[gəʊ ɪntə ˈəʊvədraɪv]	hochaktiv werden
confined (to)	[kənˈfaɪnd]	beengt, begrenzt, beschränkt (auf)
scale	[skeɪl]	Ausmaß, Umfang
to **be down to sth**	[ˈdaʊn tə]	auf etw zurückzuführen sein, an etw liegen
variability	[ˌveəriəˈbɪləti]	Schwankung, Unbeständigkeit
carbonic acid	[kɑːˌbɒnɪk ˈæsɪd]	Kohlensäure
depletion	[dɪˈpliːʃn]	Verringerung, Abbau
to **cope with sth**	[ˈkəʊp wɪð]	etw bewältigen, mit etw klarkommen, mit etw fertig werden
to **fence sth in**	[ˌfens ˈɪn]	etw einzäunen
soot	[sʊt]	Ruß
compound	[ˈkɒmpaʊnd]	Verbindung

page 85

disruption	[dɪsˈrʌpʃn]	Störung, Behinderung, Unterbrechung
nutrient	[ˈnjuːtriənt]	Nährstoff
predator	[ˈpredətə]	Raubtier
marine	[məˈriːn]	Meeres-
to **reverse sth**	[rɪˈvɜːs]	etw umkehren
tipping point	[ˈtɪpɪŋ pɔɪnt]	Kipppunkt, kritischer Punkt, Wendepunkt
to **cross sth**	[krɒs]	etw überqueren
mammal	[ˈmæml]	Säugetier
to **evolve**	[ɪˈvɒlv]	sich weiter entwickeln
flawed	[flɔːd]	fehlerhaft, mangelhaft
to **collapse**	[kəˈlæps]	zusammenbrechen, kollabieren

page 86

diversified	[daɪˈvɜːsɪfaɪd]	diversifiziert, gefächert, gestreut
beforehand	[bɪˈfɔːhænd]	vorher, im Voraus
exceptional	[ɪkˈsepʃənl]	außergewöhnlich
to **hint at sth**	[hɪnt]	auf etw hindeuten
to **accelerate**	[əkˈseləreɪt]	beschleunigen
whereas	[ˌweərˈæz]	während, wohingegen
raw material	[ˌrɔː məˈtɪəriəl]	Rohstoff
clearance	[ˈklɪərəns]	Räumung, Abholzung

page 87

to **devour sth**	[dɪˈvaʊə]	etw verschlingen
ravenous	[ˈrævənəs]	ausgehungert
intent on doing sth	[ɪnˈtent]	entschlossen sein, etw zu tun
selfish	[ˈselfɪʃ]	egoistisch, selbstsüchtig
urbanization	[ˌɜːbənaɪˈzeɪʃn]	Verstädterung, Urbanisierung
settlement	[ˈsetlmənt]	Siedlung, Kolonie
capability	[ˌkeɪpəˈbɪləti]	Fähigkeit, Potenzial
to **trigger sth**	[ˈtrɪgə]	etw auslösen
biofuel	[ˌbaɪəʊˈfjuːəl]	Biokraftstoff
petroleum	[pəˈtrəʊliəm]	Erdöl
pollutant	[pəˈluːtənt]	Schadstoff
at the forefront	[ˈfɔːfrʌnt]	an der Spitze, in vorderster Reihe
profound	[prəˈfaʊnd]	tief greifend, tief gehend, fundiert
conventional	[kənˈvenʃənl]	konventionell, herkömmlich
infancy	[ˈɪnfənsi]	(frühe) Kindheit
to **harness**	[ˈhɑːnɪs]	an-/einspannen, nutzen
desalination	[ˌdiːˌsælɪˈneɪʃn]	Entsalzung
reservoir	[ˈrezəvwɑː]	Stausee, Staubecken
efficiency	[ɪˈfɪʃnsi]	Leistungsfähigkeit, Wirksamkeit, Wirkungsgrad
appliance	[əˈplaɪəns]	Gerät, Haushaltsgerät

page 88

pricey	[ˈpraɪsi]	kostspielig, teuer
distribution	[ˌdɪstrɪˈbjuːʃn]	Versorgung
hamlet	[ˈhæmlət]	Weiler, kleines Dorf
powerhouse	[ˈpaʊəhaʊs]	treibende Kraft
to **surround sth**	[səˈraʊnd]	etw umgeben
dozen	[ˈdʌzn]	Dutzend
to **trickle**	[ˈtrɪkl]	tropfen, tröpfeln
sufficient	[səˈfɪʃnt]	ausreichend, hinreichend
pipe	[paɪp]	Rohr(leitung), Röhre
beneath	[bɪˈniːθ]	unterhalb, unter
blade	[bleɪd]	Rotorblatt, Turbinenschaufel
mist	[mɪst]	Nebel, Dunst
voltage	[ˈvəʊltɪdʒ]	Spannung
to **involve sb**	[ɪnˈvɒlv]	jdn (mit) einbeziehen
lease	[liːs]	Miete, Pacht
foreigner	[ˈfɒrənə]	Ausländer/in
impressive	[ɪmˈpresɪv]	beeindruckend, eindrucksvoll

page 89

man-made ['mæn meɪd]	künstlich, menschlichen Ursprungs
geothermal power [dʒiːəʊˌθɜːml 'paʊə]	Erdwärme

page 90

to **insulate sth** ['ɪnsjuleɪt]	etw isolieren
endangered [ɪn'deɪndʒəd]	bedroht
italics *(pl)* [ɪ'tælɪks]	Kursivschrift
to **decompose** [ˌdiːkəm'pəʊz]	sich zersetzen, zerfallen
fermentation [ˌfɜːmen'teɪʃn]	Gärung
storage ['stɔːrɪdʒ]	Speicherung, Speicher-
residue ['rezɪdjuː]	Rückstand
to **utilize sth** ['juːtəlaɪz]	etw einsetzen, etw (be)nutzen
to **criticize sb/sth** ['krɪtɪsaɪz]	jdn/etw kritisieren
housing ['haʊzɪŋ]	Wohnungsbau, Wohnungen
to **absorb sth** [əb'sɔːb]	etw aufnehmen, etw absorbieren
solid ['sɒlɪd]	fest, solide
thermal ['θɜːml]	thermisch, Wärme-
footprint ['fʊtprɪnt]	Fußabdruck
nuclear power station [ˌnjuːkliə 'paʊə steɪʃn]	Kernkraftwerk

UNIT 7

page 91

privacy ['prɪvəsi]	Privatsphäre
surveillance [sɜː'veɪləns]	Überwachung

page 92

broadsheet ['brɔːdʃiːt]	*(großformatige, seriöse)* Zeitung
tabloid ['tæblɔɪd]	Boulevardzeitung
daily ['deɪli]	Tageszeitung
to **break the news (to sb)** [ˌbreɪk ðə 'njuːz]	(jdm) die Nachricht(en) überbringen
on the decline [ˌɒn ðə dɪ'klaɪn]	rückläufig
to **downsize sth** ['daʊnsaɪz]	etw verkleinern, etw gesundschrumpfen
edition [ɪ'dɪʃn]	Ausgabe *(z. B. einer Zeitschrift)*
subscriber [səb'skraɪbə]	Abonnent/in
to **decline** [dɪ'klaɪn]	zurückgehen, fallen, sinken
demographic [ˌdemə'græfɪk]	Bevölkerungsgruppe, Altersgruppe
shift [ʃɪft]	Verschiebung, Verlagerung, Wandel
millennials *(pl)* [mɪ'leniəlz]	Generation Y *(Generation der zwischen 1980 und 1999 Geborenen)*
adulthood ['ædʌlthʊd]	Erwachsenenalter
to **abandon sth** [ə'bændən]	etw aufgeben, etw sein lassen, etw hinter sich lassen
roughly ['rʌfli]	ungefähr, etwa
doomed [duːmd]	todgeweiht, dem Untergang geweiht
divide [dɪ'vaɪd]	Kluft
to **reflect sth** [rɪ'flekt]	etw reflektieren, etw widerspiegeln
to **edit sth** ['edɪt]	etw redigieren, etw bearbeiten *(Text)*
to **alter sth** ['ɔːltə]	etw (ab)ändern
content(s) ['kɒntent]	Inhalt
to **jump on the bandwagon** [ˌdʒʌmp ɒn ðə 'bændwægən]	auf den fahrenden Zug aufspringen
to **go viral** [ˌgəʊ 'vaɪrəl]	sich *(im Internet)* rasend schnell verbreiten
proficiency [prə'fɪʃnsi]	Können, Kenntnisse, Fähigkeiten
generation gap [dʒenə'reɪʃn gæp]	Generationsunterschied, Generationenkonflikt
concerning [kən'sɜːnɪŋ]	betreffend, hinsichtlich
indelible [ɪn'deləbl]	unlöschbar, nicht entfernbar, unauslöschlich
harassment ['hærəsmənt]	Schikane, Mobbing, Belästigung
to **invent sth** [ɪn'vent]	etw erfinden, sich etw ausdenken
theft [θeft]	Diebstahl
to **take care** [teɪk 'keə]	vorsichtig sein, aufpassen

page 93

commonplace ['kɒmənpleɪs]	alltäglich, gewöhnlich
deletion [dɪ'liːʃn]	Löschung, Tilgung
to **harass sb** ['hærəs]	jdn schikanieren, jdn belästigen
pope [pəʊp]	Papst

page 94

budding ['bʌdɪŋ]	aufkeimend, angehend
to **fast forward** [ˌfɑːst 'fɔːwəd]	vorspulen
elementary age kid [elɪˌmentri eɪdʒ 'kɪd]	Grundschulkind, Kind im Grundschulalter
stunned [stʌnd]	fassungslos
dumbfounded [dʌm'faʊndɪd]	sprachlos, verblüfft
to **conceive (of) sth** [kən'siːv]	sich etw vorstellen
unsightly [ʌn'saɪtli]	unschön, hässlich
occasion [ə'keɪʒn]	Anlass, Gelegenheit
uprising ['ʌpraɪzɪŋ]	Aufstand
elsewhere [ˌels'weə]	woanders, anderswo
to **raid a place** [reɪd]	einen Ort überfallen, durchsuchen
fortress ['fɔːtrəs]	Festung
observation [ˌɒbzə'veɪʃn]	Beobachtung
shortage (of) ['ʃɔːtɪdʒ]	Mangel, Knappheit (an)
to **draw a conclusion** [ˌdrɔː ə kən'kluːʒn]	eine Schlussfolgerung ziehen
dial ['daɪəl]	Wählscheibe *(Telefon)*
answering machine ['ɑːnsərɪŋ məʃiːn]	Anrufbeantworter

page 95

to **catch up with sb** [ˌkætʃ 'ʌp wɪð]	mit jdm Nachrichten austauschen
to **assume** [ə'sjuːm]	annehmen, davon ausgehen
a mere … [mɪə]	bloß …, lediglich …
to **recall sth** [rɪ'kɔːl]	sich an etw erinnern
to **rant (about sth)** [rænt]	(über etw) schimpfen
to **rave** [reɪv]	toben, phantasieren, wirres Zeug reden

to **mingle (with)** ['mɪŋgl]	(sich) (ver)mischen (mit), Umgang haben (mit)
to **grab hold of ab/sth** [ˌgræb 'həʊld əv]	jdn/etw ergreifen, jdn/etw packen
noticeable ['nəʊtɪsəbl]	erkennbar, auffällig
short-sighted [ˌʃɔːt 'saɪtɪd]	kurzsichtig
ad nauseam [ˌæd 'nɔːziæm]	bis zum Überdruss, bis zum Abwinken
to **flex (your muscles)** [fleks]	(die Muskel) spielen lassen
judgment ['dʒʌdʒmənt]	Urteilsvermögen, Urteil, Einschätzung
to **be stuck with sth** [stʌk]	etw am Hals haben, etw nicht wieder loswerden
to **get sth** [get]	etw verstehen, etw kapieren
to **come** [kʌm]	erhältlich sein, geliefert werden
passer-by ['pɑːsə baɪ]	Passant/in
to **brag about sth** [ˌbræg ə'baʊt]	mit etw angeben
contentious [kən'tenʃəs]	*(Debatte etc.)* hitzig, *(Person)* streitlustig
to **defend sb/sth** [dɪ'fend]	jdn/etw verteidigen
to **cave in to sth** [ˌkeɪv 'ɪn]	einer Sache nachgeben
delicate ['delɪkət]	sensibel, heikel
to **mask sth** [mɑːsk]	etw verdecken, etw verbergen
outright ['aʊtraɪt]	total, völlig, offen, direkt
habitual [hə'bɪtʃuəl]	gewohnheitsmäßig, Gewohnheits-
prankster [præŋkstə]	Witzbold
offensive [ə'fensɪv]	beleidigend, anstößig
cowardly ['kaʊədli]	feige
lack (of) [læk]	Mangel (an)
bucket ['bʌkɪt]	Eimer
to **challenge sb (to sth)** ['tʃælɪndʒ]	jdn (zu etw) herausfordern
to **be crawling with sth** ['krɔːlɪŋ wɪð]	von etw wimmeln
to **vent on sb/sth** ['vent ɒn]	sich über jdn/etw auslassen
to **stir the pot** [ˌstɜː ðə 'pɒt]	Bewegung in die Sache bringen
ups and downs [ˌʌps ən 'daʊnz]	Höhen und Tiefen
truly ['truːli]	wahrhaftig, wirklich, tatsächlich

page 96

topical ['tɒpɪkl]	thematisch
readership ['riːdəʃɪp]	Leserschaft
turn of the century [ˌtɜːn əv ðə 'sentʃəri]	Jahrhundertwende

page 97

to **get sick of sth** [get 'sɪk əv]	von etw zuviel bekommen
reasonable ['riːznəbl]	vernünftig
to **speak volumes** [ˌspiːk 'vɒljuːmz]	Bände sprechen
turn of events [ˌtɜːn əv ɪ'vents]	Wende der Ereignisse/des Schicksals
to **overwhelm sb** [ˌəʊvə'welm]	jdn überwältigen, jdn überschütten
to **oppose sth** [ə'pəʊz]	gegen etw opponieren, sich gegen etw widersetzen
sound [saʊnd]	solide, vernünftig

page 98

bi-weekly [baɪ 'wiːkli]	alle zwei Wochen (erscheinend)
at a rate of … [ət ə 'reɪt əv]	mit einer Geschwindigkeit von …
speedy [spiːdi]	schnell, zügig
to **insist** [ɪn'sɪst]	darauf bestehen, beteuern
perception [pə'sepʃn]	Wahrnehmung
to **back sth** [bæk]	etw unterstützen
to **take sth into account** [ˌteɪk ɪntu ə'kaʊnt]	etw (mit) berücksichtigen
to **be aware of sth** [bi ə'weər əv]	etw wissen, sich einer Sache bewusst sein
rise [raɪz]	Aufschwung, Aufstieg
to **owe sb sth** [əʊ]	jdm etw schulden
law enforcement ['lɔː ɪnfɔːsmənt]	Gesetzesvollzug, Polizeigewalt
to **keep sb at bay** [ˌkiːp sʌmbədi ət 'beɪ]	jdn fernhalten, sich jdn vom Leib halten

page 99

at your fingertips ['fɪŋgətɪps]	zur Hand
current affairs *(pl)* [ˌkʌrənt ə'feəz]	Tagespolitik, aktuelle Ereignisse
… is a matter of choice [ə ˌmætər əv 'tʃɔɪs]	… hat man selbst in der Hand, … liegt im eigenen Ermessen
to **take steps** [teɪk 'steps]	Schritte unternehmen
to **go on strike** [ˌgəʊ ɒn 'straɪk]	streiken
reasoning ['riːzənɪŋ]	Argumentation, Logik
to **investigate sth** [ɪn'vestɪgeɪt]	etw ermitteln, etw untersuchen
to **serve a purpose** [ˌsɜːv ə 'pɜːpəs]	einem Zweck dienen
to **feed sb (with) information** [ˌfiːd sʌmbədi wɪð ɪnfə'meɪʃn]	jdn mit Informationen versorgen
associate professor [əˌsəʊʃiət prə'fesə]	Hochschuldozent
to **become engaged with sth** [ˌbɪkʌm ɪn'geɪdʒd wɪð]	sich mit etw auseinandersetzen, sich mit etw beschäftigen
laughable ['lɑːfəbl]	lächerlich
a drop in the bucket [ˌdrɒp ɪn ðə 'bʌkɪt]	ein Tropfen auf den heißen Stein
to **be fond of sb/sth** ['fɒnd əv]	jdn gernhaben, etw mögen
head start [ˌhed 'stɑːt]	Vorsprung
to **bemoan sth** [bɪ'məʊn]	etw beklagen, etw betrauern

page 100

predecessor ['priːdɪsesə]	Vorgänger/in, Vorläufer/in
unreliable [ˌʌnrɪ'laɪəbl]	unzuverlässig
factual ['fæktʃuəl]	Sach-, sachlich
to **retain sb/sth** [rɪ'teɪn]	jdn/etw behalten, etw beibehalten, etw bewahren
broadcaster ['brɔːdkɑːstə]	Moderator/in
entertaining [ˌentə'teɪnɪŋ]	unterhaltsam
…, no doubt, … [ˌnəʊ 'daʊt]	… zweifellos …
to **hold sb accountable (for sth)** [ˌhəʊld sʌmbədi ə'kaʊntəbl]	jdn (für etw) zur Rechenschaft ziehen
to **perceive sth** [pə'siːv]	etw wahrnehmen, etw erkennen

instantly ['ɪnstənt]	sofort, unmittelbar
exposure [ɪk'spəʊʒə]	Ausgesetztsein

page 101

crossword puzzle ['krɒswɜːd pʌzl]	Kreuzworträtsel
to **emerge** [ɪ'mɜːdʒ]	entstehen
investigation [ɪnˌvestɪ'geɪʃn]	Untersuchung, Nachforschung
freelance ['friːlɑːns]	freiberuflich
unbearable [ʌn'beərəbl]	unerträglich, *(Mensch)* unausstehlich
improvement (in/to) sth [ɪm'pruːvmənt]	Verbesserung bei etw

page 102

eager ['iːgə]	bestrebt, darauf aus
newsroom ['njuːzruːm]	Nachrichtenredaktion
mutual ['mjuːtʃuəl]	gegenseitig
cycle ['saɪkl]	Zyklus, Kreislauf
to **apply sth** [ə'plaɪ]	etw anwenden, etw ausüben
to **engage sb** [ɪn'geɪdʒ]	jdn fesseln
to **engage with sth** [ɪn'geɪdʒ wɪð]	sich mit etw befassen
bump [bʌmp]	Erhöhung, Unebenheit
oppression [ə'preʃn]	Unterdrückung
to **complement sth** ['kɒmplɪmənt]	etw ergänzen
collaboration [kəˌlæbə'reɪʃn]	Zusammenarbeit, Gemeinschaftsprodukt(ion)
peace [piːs]	Frieden
laureate ['lɒriət]	Preisträger/in
to **jumble sth up** [ˌdʒʌmbl 'ʌp]	etw (kunterbunt) durcheinanderwerfen
adequate ['ædɪkwət]	ausreichend, angemessen
to **commit (a crime)** [kə'mɪt]	(ein Verbrechen) begehen
suicide ['suːɪsaɪd]	Selbstmord
incident ['ɪnsɪdənt]	Vorfall, Begebenheit

page 103

blessing ['blesɪŋ]	Segen
curse [kɜːs]	Fluch
to **access sth** ['ækses]	auf etw zugreifen, Zugang haben zu etw
to **exploit sb** [ɪk'splɔɪt]	jdn ausnutzen, jdn ausbeuten
to **pin sth (to a place)** [pɪn]	etw (an einem Ort) befestigen, etw (an einen Ort) heften, stecken
refrigerator [rɪ'frɪdʒəreɪtə]	Kühlschrank
to **cut down on sth** [ˌkʌt 'daʊn ɒn]	sich bei etw einschränken
to **put sth forward** [ˌpʊt 'fɔːwəd]	(Argument/Vorschlag) vorbringen, etw zur Diskussion stellen
council ['kaʊnsl]	Rat, Versammlung
to **split (into)** [splɪt]	(sich) aufteilen (in)
detox *(infml)* ['diːtɒks]	Entzug, Entgiftung (sbehandlung)

page 104

to **refuse to do sth** [rɪ'fjuːz]	sich weigern etw zu tun
to **do without sth** [ˌduː wɪ'ðaʊt]	ohne etw auskommen
spare time [ˌspeə 'taɪm]	Freizeit
negligent (about) ['neglɪdʒənt]	nachlässig (bei), fahrlässig
to **be on the alert (for sth)** [ˌbi ɒn ði ə'lɜːt]	(vor etw) auf der Hut sein
to **resist sth** [rɪ'zɪst]	einer Sache widerstehen
taxpayer ['tækspeɪə]	Steuerzahler/in
to **waste sth** [weɪst]	etw verschwenden, etw vergeuden
to **fail** [feɪl]	versagen, scheitern
to **follow sth up (with sth)** [ˌfɒləʊ 'ʌp]	(etw) einer Sache folgen lassen, etw weiterverfolgen (mit etw)
hardly ['hɑːdli]	kaum
to **disgrace yourself** [dɪs'greɪs]	sich blamieren
flatmate ['flætmeɪt]	Mitbewohner/in *(in einer WG)*
chef [ʃef]	Chefkoch/-köchin, Küchenchef/in
bench [bentʃ]	Bank *(zum Sitzen)*
pension ['penʃn]	Rente, Pension

UNIT 8

page 105

to **huddle** ['hʌdl]	sich zusammendrängen
to **hang on to sth** [ˌhæŋ 'ɒn tə]	sich an etw festhalten, sich an etw festklammern
shiny ['ʃaɪni]	glänzend
to **say grace** [ˌseɪ 'greɪs]	das Tischgebet sprechen
to **unfurl sth** [ˌʌn'fɜːl]	etw entfalten, etw auseinanderrollen
liberty ['lɪbəti]	Freiheit
to **pen sb in** [ˌpen 'ɪn]	jdn einpferchen, jdn einsperren
to **flee (from sb/sth)** [fliː]	(vor jdm/etw) flüchten, (vor jdm/etw) fliehen
compassionate [kəm'pæʃənə]	mitfühlend, mitleidig
indifferent [ɪn'dɪfrənt]	gleichgültig

page 106

to **merge sth** [mɜːdʒ]	etw verschmelzen, etw mischen
persecution [ˌpɜːsɪ'kjuːʃn]	Verfolgung
drove [drəʊv]	Schar, Herde
to **displace sb** [dɪs'pleɪs]	jdn vertreiben
beyond [bɪ'jɒnd]	jenseits, außerhalb
human trafficker [ˌhjuːmən 'træfɪkə]	Schleuser/in, Menschenhändler/in
xenophobia [ˌzenə'fəʊbiə]	Fremdenfeindlichkeit, Ausländerhass
resentment [rɪ'zentmənt]	Unmut, Groll, Ressentiment
wealthy ['welθi]	wohlhabend, reich
drain on sb/sth [dreɪn]	Belastung für jdn/etw
to **shrink** [ʃrɪŋk]	schrumpfen
workforce ['wɜːkfɔːs]	Erwerbstätige, Erwerbsbevölkerung
pensioner ['penʃənə]	Rentner/in
menial ['miːniəl]	niedere(r,s), untergeordnet *(Arbeit)*
right-wing [ˌraɪt 'wɪŋ]	rechtsgerichtet
racial ['reɪʃl]	rassisch, Rassen-
tension ['tenʃn]	Spannung
shelter ['ʃeltə]	Unterkunft
to **introduce** *(a law)* [ˌɪntrə'djuːs]	*(ein Gesetz)* einbringen
quota ['kwəʊtə]	Kontingent, Quote

to **curb sth** [kɜːb]	etw begrenzen, etw einschränken
influx [ˈɪnflʌks]	Zustrom
citizenship [ˈsɪtɪzənʃɪp]	Staatsbürgerschaft, Staatsbürgerkunde
onus [ˈəʊnəs]	Pflicht, Verpflichtung
to **be an asset to sb** [bi ən ˈæset tə]	für jdn eine Bereicherung sein
to **be torn between A and B** [tɔːn]	zwischen A und B hin und her gerissen sein
alienation [ˌeɪliəˈneɪʃn]	Entfremdung
uncertainty [ʌnˈsɜːtnti]	Ungewissheit, Unsicherheit

page 107

ruthless [ˈruːθləs]	rücksichtslos, skrupellos
erroneously [ɪˈrəʊniəsli]	irrtümlicherweise
outdated [ˌaʊtˈdeɪtɪd]	veraltet, nicht mehr aktuell
to **appreciate sth** [əˈpriːʃieɪt]	etw schätzen, etw zu schätzen wissen
offspring, *pl* **offspring** [ˈɒfsprɪŋ]	Sprössling, Nachwuchs
despair [dɪˈspeə]	Verzweiflung
to **stir sth up** [ˌstɜːr ˈʌp]	etw schüren

page 108

hostility [hɒˈstɪləti]	Feindseligkeit
awareness [əˈweənəs]	Bewusstsein
descent [dɪˈsent]	Herkunft, Abstammung
account [əˈkaʊnt]	Bericht, Beschreibung
to **be at odds with sb** [ət ˈɒdz]	mit jdm uneinig sein, sich mit jdm streiten
harvest [ˈhɑːvɪst]	Ernte
to **set about sth** [ˌset əˈbaʊt]	sich über etw hermachen, sich auf etw stürzen
pad [pæd]	Notizblock
in a flurry [ˈflʌri]	hektisch, aufgeregt
painful [ˈpeɪnfl]	schmerzhaft, schmerzlich
meticulous [məˈtɪkjələs]	sorgfältig, gewissenhaft, gründlich
doorstep [ˈdɔːstep]	Tür(schwelle)
to **bend down** [ˌbend ˈdaʊn]	sich herunterbeugen
genial [ˈdʒiːniəl]	freundlich, herzlich
to **dash** [dæʃ]	stürmen, (los)stürzen
to **usher sb** [ˈʌʃə]	jdn führen, jdn geleiten
chess [tʃes]	Schach
snub [snʌb]	Abfuhr, Brüskierung
replacement [rɪˈpleɪsmənt]	Ersatz, Ersetzung, Austausch
glorious [ˈglɔːriəs]	ruhmreich, herrlich, fantastisch
to **yell** [jel]	schreien, brüllen
to **whip** [wɪp]	flitzen
bullet [ˈbʊlɪt]	(Gewehr-)Kugel

page 109

RAF (= Royal Air Force) [ˌɑːr eɪ ˈef]	*britische Luftwaffe*
the forces *(pl)* [ˈfɔːsɪz]	die Streitkräfte
labour exchange [ˈleɪbər ɪkstʃeɪndʒ]	Arbeitsvermittlung
storeman [ˈstɔːmən]	Lagerist
to **pinch sb** [pɪntʃ]	jdn kneifen
to **acquaint sb with sb/sth** [əˈkweɪnt]	jdn mit jdm/etw bekannt machen
shrewd [ʃruːd]	klug, scharfsinnig, geschickt
accidentally [ˌæksɪˈdentəli]	versehentlich, unabsichtlich
courteous [ˈkɜːtiəs]	höflich
to **assure sb** [əˈʃʊə]	jdm versichern
all hell would break loose [ɑːl ˌhel wʊd breɪk ˈluːs]	hier wäre der Teufel / die Hölle los
to **not stand for sth** [ˈstænd fə]	sich etw nicht gefallen lassen
backside [ˈbæksaɪd]	Hintern, Po
serviceman [ˈsɜːvɪsmən]	Militärangehöriger
to **pray** [preɪ]	beten
blotting pad [ˈblɒtɪŋ pæd]	Schreibunterlage
the Almighty [ɔːlˈmaɪti]	der Allmächtige
to **bless sb/sth** [bles]	jdn/etw segnen
opposition [ˌɒpəˈzɪʃn]	Widerstand
to **campaign for/against sth** [kæmˈpeɪn]	sich für/gegen etw einsetzen
filing cabinet [ˈfaɪlɪŋ kæbɪnət]	Aktenschrank
estate agent [ɪˈsteɪt eɪdʒənt]	Immobilienmakler/in
thoroughly [ˈθʌrəli]	gründlich, aufmerksam
odd [ɒd]	gelegentlich
mind you [ˌmaɪnd ˈjuː]	allerdings
upset [ˌʌpˈset]	verstimmt, verärgert
to **stack sth** [stæk]	etw stapeln
alien [ˈeɪliən]	Ausländer/in

page 111

riot [ˈraɪət]	Aufstand, Aufruhr
to **associate sth with sth** [əˈsəʊʃiət]	etw mit etw verbinden, etw mit etw assoziieren
unpleasant [ʌnˈpleznt]	unangenehm, unschön
annoying [əˈnɔɪɪŋ]	ärgerlich, lästig, störend

page 112

to **assimilate** [əˈsɪmɪleɪt]	sich anpassen
barely [ˈbeəli]	kaum
faithful [ˈfeɪθfl]	treu, loyal; originalgetreu
tribute (to) [ˈtrɪbjuːt]	Würdigung, Anerkennung
homeland [ˈhəʊmlənd]	Heimat(land)
maker [ˈmeɪkə]	Hersteller/in
loo *(infml)* [luː]	Klo
founder [ˈfaʊndə]	Gründer/in
ancestry [ˈænsestri]	Abstammung
to **trace sth** [treɪs]	etw (zurück)verfolgen
to **outnumber sth** [ˌaʊtˈnʌmbə]	etw *(zahlenmäßig)* übertreffen
to **flavour sth** [ˈfleɪvəd]	etw aromatisieren, etw würzen
cinnamon [ˈsɪnəmən]	Zimt
Easter bunny [ˈiːstə bʌni]	Osterhase

page 113

historian [hɪˈstɔːriən]	Historiker/in
to **brew sth** [bruː]	etw brauen
trade [treɪd]	Branche, Gewerbe
fertile [ˈfɜːtaɪl]	fruchtbar
to **rename sb/sth** [ˌriːˈneɪm]	jdn/etw umbenennen, jdn/etw umtaufen
cabbage [ˈkæbɪdʒ]	Kohl, Kraut
dachshund [ˈdæksnd]	Dackel
war bonds *(pl)* [ˈwɔː bɒndz]	Kriegsanleihen
predominantly [prɪˈdɒmɪnəntli]	überwiegend
the draft *(AE)* [ðə ˈdræft]	die Einberufung
to **appoint sb** [əˈpɔɪnt]	jdn ernennen, jdn berufen

axis, *pl* **axes** ['æksɪs, 'æksi:z]	Achse
median ['mi:diən]	mittlere/r/s, durchschnittlich
to **prosper** ['prɒspə]	florieren, gedeihen
tailored ['teɪləd]	maßgeschneidert
ambassador [æm'bæsədə]	Botschafter/in
caucus ['kɔ:kəs]	Gremium, Ausschuss
craftsmanship ['krɑ:ftsmənʃɪp]	Handwerkskunst
chancellor ['tʃɑ:nsələ]	(Bundes-)Kanzler/in
to **wobble** ['wɒbl]	schwanken, wackeln
summit ['sʌmɪt]	Gipfel(treffen)

page 114

wherever [weər'evə]	wo (auch) immer
ploughshare ['plaʊʃeə]	Pflugschar
plumbing ['plʌmɪŋ]	Klempnerei, Sanitär
Hispanic [hɪ'spænɪk]	Amerikaner/in lateinamerikanischer oder spanischer Herkunft
prominent ['prɒmɪnənt]	bekannt, bedeutend
ambition [æm'bɪʃn]	Ehrgeiz, Ziel, Ambition
drunkard ['drʌŋkəd]	Trinker/in, Säufer/in
skilled [skɪld]	qualifiziert, Fach-

page 115

faint [feɪnt]	schwach, matt
memory (of) ['meməri]	Erinnerung (an)
goods *(pl)* [gʊdz]	Waren, Güter
scapegoat ['skeɪpgəʊt]	Sündenbock
to **originate from** [ə'rɪdʒɪneɪt frəm]	kommen aus
to **inherit sth** [ɪn'herɪt]	etw erben
ambitious [æm'bɪʃəs]	ehrgeizig
prosperity [prɒ'sperəti]	Wohlstand
arts and crafts *(pl)* [ˌɑ:ts ən 'krɑ:fts]	Kunsthandwerk

page 116

percentage [pə'sentɪdʒ]	Prozentsatz, Anteil
remedial class [rɪ'mi:diəl klɑ:s]	Förderklasse
to **catch up with sb** [ˌkætʃ 'ʌp wɪð]	jdn einholen
the ebb and flow [ði ˌeb ən 'fləʊ]	das Auf und Ab, das Kommen und Gehen
aka *(= also known as)* [ˌeɪ keɪ 'eɪ]	alias

page 117

Dust Bowl ['dʌst baʊl]	Trockengebiet; *Naturkatastrophe in den USA in den 1930er Jahren*
famine ['fæmɪn]	Hungersnot

page 118

to **swear sb in** [ˌsweər 'ɪn]	jdn vereidigen
to **outdo sb** [ˌaʊt'du:]	jdn übertreffen
to **enroll** [ɪn'rəʊl]	sich einschreiben, sich anmelden
to **monitor** ['mɒnɪtə]	überwachen
presidency ['prezɪdensi]	Präsidentschaft
overhaul ['əʊvəhɔ:l]	Überholung, Revision
to **opt for sth** ['ɒpt fə]	sich für etw entscheiden
actual ['æktʃuəl]	tatsächlich, konkret
misleading [ˌmɪs'li:dɪŋ]	irreführend

UNIT 9

page 119

in our day and age [ɪn ɑ: ˌdeɪ ən 'eɪdʒ]	in unserer Zeit
venue ['venju:]	Veranstaltungsort, Veranstaltungsstätte
to **decorate sth** ['dekəreɪt]	etw schmücken, etw verzieren

page 120

to **gain ground** [ˌgeɪn 'graʊnd]	Boden gutmachen
nuclear family [ˌnju:kliə 'fæməli]	Kernfamilie, Kleinfamilie
to **go way back** *(infml)* [gəʊ ˌweɪ 'bæk]	schon lange bestehen
extended family [ɪkˌstendɪd 'fæməli]	Großfamilie
outward ['aʊtwəd]	äußere/r/s, äußerlich
dress code ['dres kəʊd]	Kleiderordnung
whichever [wɪtʃ'evə]	wer/was (auch immer), egal welche/r/s
willingly ['wɪlɪŋli]	bereitwillig, gern
to **befriend sb** [bɪ'frend]	sich mit jdm anfreunden
contraception [ˌkɒntrə'sepʃn]	Empfängnisverhütung
marriage ['mærɪdʒ]	Ehe, Heirat
to **consent** *(fml)* [kən'sent]	zustimmen, einwilligen
regardless of sth [rɪ'gɑ:dləs əv]	ungeachtet einer Sache
registered partnership [ˌredʒɪstəd 'pɑ:tnəʃɪp]	eingetragene Partnerschaft
cohabitation [ˌkəʊˌhæbɪ'teɪʃn]	Zusammenleben, eheähnliche Gemeinschaft
common practice [ˌkɒmən 'præktɪs]	gängige/übliche Praxis
ongoing ['ɒngəʊɪŋ]	laufend
minor ['maɪnə]	weniger bedeutend, gering(er)
to **conform** [kən'fɔ:m]	sich anpassen
code of conduct [ˌkəʊd əv 'kɒndʌkt]	Verhaltenskodex, -regeln
to **raise (children)** [reɪz]	(Kinder) erziehen, aufziehen
to **take care to do sth** [teɪk 'keə]	(sorgfältig) darauf achten, etw zu tun
exclusion [ɪk'sklu:ʒn]	Ausschluss, Ausschließung
to **prevail** [prɪ'veɪl]	(vor)herrschen
first and foremost [ˌfɜ:st ən 'fɔ:məʊst]	vor allem, in erster Linie
obedience [ə'bi:diəns]	Gehorsam
to **comply with sth** [kəm'plaɪ wɪð]	etw erfüllen, etw befolgen, sich an etw halten
to **stain sth** [steɪn]	etw beschmutzen, *(Ruf)* (be)schädigen
honour ['ɒnə]	Ehre
elders *(pl)* ['eldəz]	ältere Generation, die Erwachsenen
to **take sth for granted** [ˌteɪk fə 'grɑ:ntɪd]	etw als selbstverständlich betrachten
by no means [baɪ 'nəʊ mi:nz]	keineswegs
suppression [sə'preʃn]	Unterdrückung
liberation [lɪbə'reɪʃn]	Befreiung

page 121

to **annoy sb** [ə'nɔɪ]	jdn ärgern
in terms of … [ɪn 'tɜːmz əv]	was … betrifft/angeht
decoration [ˌdekə'reɪʃn]	Schmuck, Verzierung

page 122

(oil) rig [rɪg]	(Öl-)Bohrinsel, Förderturm

page 123

closet *(AE)* ['klɒzɪt]	(Wand-)Schrank
diehard ['daɪhɑːd]	hartnäckig, eingefleischt
to **frequent (a place)** [fri'kwent]	(einen Ort) häufig besuchen, frequentieren
gathering ['gæðərɪŋ]	Versammlung, Treffen
to **be to do sth** ['bi tə]	etw tun sollen
attempt [ə'tempt]	Versuch
footloose and fancy-free [ˌfʊtluːs ənd fænsi 'friː]	frei und ungebunden
to **sign up for sth** [ˌsaɪn 'ʌp fə]	sich für/bei etw anmelden
chorus ['kɔːrəs]	Sing- und Tanzgruppe, Tänzer/innen
commercial (time) slot [kəˌmɜːʃl 'slɒt]	Sendezeit für Werbung *(Radio/TV)*
to **anticipate sth** [æn'tɪsɪpeɪt]	mit etw rechnen, etw erwarten
follow-up ['fɒləʊ ʌp]	Folge-, Nachfolger
iconic [aɪ'kɒnɪk]	kultig, Kult-
populous ['pɒpjələs]	bevölkerungsreich
to **bond** [bɒnd]	eine Bindung aufbauen
to **dread sth** [dred]	etw fürchten
sequin ['siːkwɪn]	Paillette
embarrassment [ɪm'bærəsmənt]	Verlegenheit, Peinlichkeit
come May [kʌm]	wenn der Mai kommt, im Mai
to **harmonize** ['hɑːmənaɪz]	harmonieren, in Einklang stehen, mehrstimmig singen
to **chew sth** [tʃuː]	etw kauen
button ['bʌtn]	Knopf
utter ['ʌtə]	völlig, vollkommen
flashy ['flæʃi]	auffällig, protzig
convertible [kən'vɜːtəbl]	Cabrio(let) *(Auto)*
junior *(AE)* ['dʒuːniə]	*Schüler/in im vorletzten Schuljahr*
open-heart surgery [ˌəʊpən hɑːt 'sɜːdʒəri]	Operation am offenen Herzen
to **update sb** [ˌʌp'deɪt]	jdn auf den neusten Stand bringen
to **flip** [flɪp]	(sich) umdrehen
to **stumble over your words** [ˌstʌmbl əʊvə jə 'wɜːdz]	stottern
to **spit sth out** [ˌspɪt 'aʊt]	etw ausspucken

page 124

to **resent sth** [rɪ'zent]	sich über etw ärgern
do-over *(AE, infml)* ['du əʊvə]	erneuter Versuch
thankful ['θæŋkfl]	dankbar
to **not give a damn** *(infml)* [ˌnɒt gɪv ə 'dæm]	sich einen Dreck scheren
conspicuous [kən'spɪkjuəs]	auffällig, auffallend
(the task) at hand [ət 'hænd]	die vorliegende Aufgabe

page 125

anxious (about) ['æŋkʃəs]	besorgt, beunruhigt, ängstlich (wegen)
horrified ['hɒrɪfaɪd]	entsetzt
ridiculous [rɪ'dɪkjələs]	lächerlich, unglaublich
more often than not [mɔːr ˌɒfn ðən 'nɒt]	meistens
to **exhibit sth** [ɪg'zɪbɪt]	etw zeigen, etw ausstellen
communal [kə'mjuːnl]	Gemeinschafts-, gemeinschaftlich, gemeinsam

page 126

notable ['nəʊtəbl]	bedeutend, bemerkenswert
recognition [ˌrekəg'nɪʃn]	(An-)Erkennung, (Wieder-)Erkennen
recipient [rɪ'sɪpiənt]	Empfänger/in
to **stage sth** [steɪdʒ]	etw inszenieren, etw veranstalten, etw aufführen
to **hurl insults (at sb)** [ˌhɜːl 'ɪnsʌlts]	(jdn) beschimpfen, (jdn) beleidigen
delight [dɪ'laɪt]	Vergnügen, Freude
to **negotiate sth** [nɪ'gəʊʃieɪt]	über etw verhandeln, etw aushandeln
to **publicise sth** ['pʌblɪsaɪz]	auf etw aufmerksam machen
to **be centred on sth** ['sentəd ɒn]	sich um etw drehen, sich auf etw konzentrieren
penchant ['pentʃənt]	Vorliebe, Schwäche
outspoken [aʊt'spəʊkən]	freimütig, direkt, unverblümt
predictable [prɪ'dɪktəbl]	voraussagbar, vorhersehbar
duchess ['dʌtʃəs]	Herzogin
offender [ə'fendə]	Straftäter/in, Übeltäter/in

page 127

obsessed with [əb'sest wɪð]	besessen von
discourse ['dɪskɔːs]	Diskurs, Erörterung
in this vein [ˌɪn ðɪs 'veɪn]	dieser Art
under scrutiny [ˌʌndə 'skruːtəni]	auf dem/den Prüfstand
routinely [ruː'tiːnli]	routinemäßig, regelmäßig
sense of agency [ˌsens əv 'eɪdʒənsi]	Handlungsbewusstsein, Handlungskompetenz
to **impact on/upon sth** [ɪm'pækt]	sich auf etw auswirken
eating disorder ['iːtɪŋ dɪsɔːdə]	Essstörung
mental health [ˌmentl 'helθ]	psychische/seelische Gesundheit
glorification [ˌglɔːrɪfɪ'keɪʃn]	Verherrlichung
to **cite sth** [saɪt]	etw zitieren, etw angeben
to **ridicule sb** ['rɪdɪkjuːl]	jdn lächerlich machen
continual [kən'tɪnjuəl]	ständig, ununterbrochen, kontinuierlich
to what degree [tə ˌwɒt dɪ'griː]	in welchem (Aus-)Maß, bis zu welchem Grad
wayward *(fml)* ['weɪwəd]	ungehörig
aspiration [ˌæspə'reɪʃn]	Ambition, Bestreben
to **omit sth** [ə'mɪt]	etw auslassen, etw weglassen
to **position sb/sth** [pə'zɪʃn]	jdn/etw platzieren, jdn/etw (auf)stellen
race [reɪs]	Abstammung, Rasse
sweeping ['swiːpɪŋ]	pauschal, umfassend, weit reichend

Unit word list

generalisation [ˌdʒenrəlaɪ'zeɪʃn]	Verallgemeinerung
to **eliminate sth** [ɪ'lɪmɪneɪt]	etw eliminieren, etw unterbinden
to **make sense of sth** [ˌmeɪk 'sens]	etw verstehen, aus etw schlau werden

page 128

for once [fə 'wʌns]	ausnahmsweise, dieses eine Mal
row [raʊ]	Streit, Krach
to **come up with sth** [ˌkʌm 'ʌp wɪð]	auf etw kommen *(Lösung)*, etw erbringen
handling ['hændlɪŋ]	Umgang, Handhabung
to **misrepresent sb/sth** [ˌmɪsˌreprɪ'zent]	jdn/etw falsch darstellen, etw verfälschen
respective [rɪ'spektɪv]	jeweilig

page 129

to **dismiss sth as sth** [dɪs'mɪs]	etw als etw abtun
disagreeable [ˌdɪsə'griːəbl]	unangenehm, unliebsam, unsympathisch
to **play people off against each other** [ˌpleɪ piːpl 'ɒf əgenst iːtʃ ʌðə]	Menschen gegeneinander ausspielen
outstanding [aʊt'stændɪŋ]	hervorragend, überragend, außergewöhnlich
abusive [ə'bjuːsɪv]	beleidigend, ausfallend
translation [træns'leɪʃn]	Übersetzung
siblings *(pl)* ['sɪblɪŋz]	Geschwister

page 130

to **model sth** ['mɒdl]	etw vorführen *(z. B. als Fotomodell)*
buzzword ['bʌzwɜːd]	Modewort, Schlagwort
underwear ['ʌndəweə]	Unterwäsche
to **hire sb** ['haɪə]	jdn engagieren, jdn anstellen
top-notch [ˌtɒp 'nɒtʃ]	erstklassig
pussy bow ['pʊsi bəʊ]	Schleifenkragen (an Blusen)
to **unveil sb/sth** [ˌʌn'veɪl]	jdn vorstellen, etw enthüllen
measurement ['meʃəmənt]	Abmessung, Maß
to **purchase sth** *(fml)* ['pɜːtʃəs]	etw kaufen
expectation [ˌekspek'teɪʃn]	Erwartung
societal [sə'saɪətl]	gesellschaftlich, sozial
twist [twɪst]	*(überraschende)* Wendung, *(überraschende)* (Geschmacks-)Note
to **challenge sth** ['tʃælɪndʒ]	etw infrage stellen, etw anzweifeln
preconception [ˌpriːkən'sepʃn]	vorgefasste Meinung, Vorstellung
casual ['kæʒuəl]	leger, zwanglos
easy-fitting [ˌiːzi 'fɪtɪŋ]	lässig sitzend *(Kleidung)*
division [dɪ'vɪʒn]	Trennung
to **come across as …** [ˌkʌm 'əkrɒs əz]	… wirken, einen … Eindruck machen
sombre [sɒmbə]	traurig, düster, betrübt
prompt [prɒmpt]	Stichwort, Vorgabe
to **have the makings of sth** ['meɪkɪŋz]	das Zeug zu etw haben

page 131

alumni *(pl)* [ə'lʌmnaɪ]	Ehemalige
workload ['wɜːkləʊd]	Arbeitsbelastung
booklet ['bʊklət]	Broschüre
to **draw sth up** [ˌdrɔː 'ʌp]	etw erstellen
editorial board [edɪˌtɔːriəl 'bɔːd]	Redaktionsleitung
to **allocate sth to sb** ['æləkeɪt]	jdm etw zuweisen, jdm etw zuteilen
staying power ['steɪɪŋ paʊə]	Ausdauer, Durchhaltevermögen

page 132

inevitably [ɪn'evɪtəbli]	zwangsläufig
earnest ['ɜːnɪst]	ernsthaft
to **make a fuss** [fʌs]	sich anstellen, Umstände machen
just about *(infml)* ['dʒʌst əbaʊt]	nahezu, so ziemlich
to **sport sth** [spɔːt]	etw (stolz) tragen *(z. B. Kleidungsstück)*
seaside ['siːsaɪd]	(Meeres-)Küste, Strand

UNIT 10

page 133

arson ['ɑːsn]	Brandstiftung
burglary ['bɜːgləri]	Einbruch
manslaughter ['mænslɔːtə]	Totschlag
rape [reɪp]	Vergewaltigung
robbery ['rɒbəri]	Raub, Überfall
shoplifting ['ʃɒplɪftɪŋ]	Ladendiebstahl
poison ['pɔɪzn]	Gift
handbag ['hændbæg]	Handtasche
drunken ['drʌŋkən]	betrunken
railway ['reɪlweɪ]	Eisenbahn
carriage ['kærɪdʒ]	Waggon
thief, *pl* **thieves** [θiːf, θiːvz]	Dieb/in
to **injure sb** ['ɪndʒə]	jdn verletzen
to **rank sb/sth** [ræŋk]	jdn/etw einstufen, jdn/etw (ein-)ordnen

page 134

juvenile ['dʒuːvənaɪl]	Jugend-, jugendlich
delinquency [dɪ'lɪŋkwənsi]	Straffälligkeit
to **sentence sb (to sth)** ['sentəns]	jdn (zu etw) verurteilen
to **convict sb** [kən'vɪkt]	jdn verurteilen *(für schuldig befinden)*
judge [dʒʌdʒ]	Richter/in
humane [hjuː'meɪn]	human, menschenwürdig
parole [pə'rəʊl]	Bewährung
assault [ə'sɔːlt]	Körperverletzung
offence [ə'fens]	Straftat, Vergehen
drug trafficking ['drʌg træfɪkɪŋ]	Drogenhandel
custody ['kʌstədi]	Gewahrsam
on bail [ɒn 'beɪl]	gegen Kaution
lenient ['liːniənt]	milde, nachsichtig
to **suspend sth** [sə'spend]	etw zeitweilig aufheben, etw aussetzen
sentence ['sentəns]	Haftstrafe

petty crime [ˌpeti 'kraɪm] — Kleinkriminalität, Bagatelldelikt
convict ['kɒnvɪkt] — Sträfling
prosecutor ['prɒsɪkjuːtə] — Staatsanwalt/-anwältin, Ankläger/in
deterrent [dɪ'terənt] — Abschreckung(smittel)
in the first place [ɪn ðə 'fɜːst pleɪs] — überhaupt (erst mal), am Anfang (schon), an erster Stelle
white-collar crime ['waɪt kɒlə kraɪm] — Wirtschaftskriminalität
bribery ['braɪbəri] — Bestechung
tax evasion [ˌtækx i'veɪʒn] — Steuerhinterziehung
greed [griːd] — Gier, Habgier
big time ['bɪg taɪm] — ganz groß
to **make ends meet** [meɪk ˌendz 'miːt] — über die Runden kommen
to **lack sth** [læk] — etw nicht haben
truancy ['truːənsi] — Schwänzen, unentschuldigtes Fernbleiben
to **binge drink** ['bɪndʒ drɪŋk] — komasaufen
to **project sth** [prə'dʒekt] — etw vermitteln
to **differentiate** [ˌdɪfə'renʃieɪt] — unterscheiden
probation [prə'beɪʃn] — Bewährung
ordeal [ɔː'diːl] — Qual, Tortur
counselling ['kaʊnsəlɪŋ] — (professionelle) Beratung
to **be eligible for early parole** [ˌelɪdʒəbl fər ɜːli pə'rəʊl] — für eine vorzeitige, bedingte Haftentlassung infrage kommen

page 135

to **possess sth** [pə'zes] — etw besitzen
sharp [ʃɑːp] — stark

page 136

to **smuggle sth** ['smʌgl] — etw schmuggeln
innocent ['ɪnəsnt] — unschuldig
to **trick sb into doing sth** ['trɪk ɪntə] — jdn mit List / mit einem Trick dazu bringen, etw zu tun
to **imprison sb** [ɪm'prɪzn] — jdn inhaftieren
broadcast ['brɔːdkɑːst] — Rundfunk-

page 137

booze [buːz] — Alkohol
misunderstanding [ˌmɪsʌndə'stændɪŋ] — Missverständnis
to **shiver** ['ʃɪvə] — zittern
behind bars [bɪˌhaɪnd 'bɑːz] — hinter Gittern
to **sort sth out** [ˌsɔːt 'aʊt] — etw klären, etw lösen
magistrate ['mædʒɪstreɪt] — (US) Untersuchungsrichter/in, (GB) Laienrichter/in
to **await sth** [ə'weɪt] — etw erwarten, etw abwarten
trial ['traɪəl] — Verfahren, Prozess
to **clear out sth** [ˌklɪə 'aʊt] — etw ausräumen
bank account [ˌbæŋk ə'kaʊnt] — Bankkonto
jury ['dʒʊəri] — die Geschworenen
lawyer ['lɔːjə] — (Rechts-)Anwalt/Anwältin
jail [dʒeɪl] — Gefängnis
the sheer enormity [ˌʃɪə ɪ'nɔːməti] — das ungeheure Ausmaß
to **not register** ['redʒɪstə] — nicht wahrgenommen werden

page 138

crack [kræk] — Sprung, Riss
interrogation [ɪnˌterə'geɪʃn] — Befragung, Verhör
to **change your mind** [ˌtʃeɪndʒ jə 'maɪnd] — seine Meinung ändern
terrifying ['terɪfaɪɪŋ] — Furcht erregend
verdict ['vɜːdɪkt] — Urteil
to **not sleep a wink** [nɒt ˌsliːp ə 'wɪŋk] — kein Auge zutun
justice ['dʒʌstɪs] — Gerechtigkeit
to **speculate about sth** ['spekjuleɪt] — sich über etw Gedanken machen
magistrates' court ['mædʒɪstreɪts kɔːt] — Amtsgericht
prisoner ['prɪzənə] — Strafgefangene/r

page 139

to **fall apart** [ˌfɔːl ə'pɑːt] — auseinanderfallen, platzen
legal proceedings *(pl)* [ˌliːgl prə'siːdɪŋz] — Gerichtsverfahren, gerichtliche Schritte

page 140

morality [mə'ræləti] — Moral *(Wertesystem)*
to **police sth** [pə'liːs] — etw überwachen, etw kontrollieren
armed [ɑːmd] — bewaffnet
attempted [ə'temptɪd] — versucht
bladed article ['bleɪdɪd ɑːtɪkl] — scharfer Gegenstand *(mit einer Klinge)*
accomplice [ə'kʌmplɪs] — Komplize/Komplizin
rusty ['rʌsti] — rostig
to **punch sb** [pʌntʃ] — jdn schlagen
pregnant ['pregnənt] — schwanger
wallet ['wɒlɪt] — Brieftasche, (Herren-)Portemonnaie

page 141

insight (into) ['ɪnsaɪt] — Einblick (in), Verständnis (von)
notably ['nəʊtəbli] — insbesondere
rampage [ræm'peɪdʒ] — Randale
comprehensive [ˌkɒmprɪ'hensɪv] — umfassend
averse *(fml)* [ə'vɜːs] — abgeneigt
to **run counter to sth** [ˌrʌn 'kaɪntə tə] — im Widerspruch zu etw stehen
emphasis, *pl* **emphases** ['emfəsɪs] — Betonung, Schwerpunkt, Akzent
to **lecture sb** ['lektʃə] — jdm einen Vortrag halten
to **observe sth** [əb'zɜːv] — etw beobachten
to **preach sth** [priːtʃ] — etw predigen
reduction [rɪ'dʌkʃn] — Verringerung, Senkung

page 142

underage ['ʌndəreɪdʒ] — minderjährig
deprived [dɪ'praɪvd] — benachteiligt
residential area [reziˌdenʃl 'eəriə] — Wohngebiet
amoral [ˌeɪ'mɒrəl] — amoralisch *(sich über die Moral hinwegsetzend)*
burglar ['bɜːglə] — Einbrecher/in

page 143

to **obey sth** [ə'beɪ] — etw beachten, etw befolgen
drug addict ['drʌg ədɪkt] — Drogenabhängige/r

page 144

compensation [ˌkɒmpən'seɪʃn]	(finanzieller) Ausgleich
conviction [kən'vɪkʃn]	Verurteilung
reparation [ˌrepə'reɪʃn]	Entschädigung, Wiedergutmachung
amends *(pl)* [ə'mendz]	Schadensersatz
penalty ['penəlti]	Strafe
curfew ['kɜːfjuː]	Ausgangssperre
attendance [ə'tendəns]	Anwesenheit
detention [dɪ'tenʃn]	Haft
to **liaise** [li'eɪz]	zusammenarbeiten, Bindeglied sein
guardian ['gɑːdiən]	Vormund
representative [ˌreprɪ'zentətɪv]	Vertreter/in, Beauftragte/r
whilst [waɪlst]	während
defendant [dɪ'fendənt]	Angeklagte/r
knowledgeable ['nɒlɪdʒəbl]	bewandert, kenntnisreich
district ['dɪstrɪkt]	Bezirk
starter ['stɑːtə]	Eingangs-
goal [gəʊl]	Ziel, Absicht
CCTV (closed-circuit television) [ˌsiː siː tiː 'viː]	Videoüberwachung
brick [brɪk]	Backstein
to **truant** ['truːənt]	Schule schwänzen
to **aggravate sth** ['ægrəveɪt]	etw verschlimmern, etw erschweren
to **emphasise sth** ['emfəsaɪz]	etw betonen, etw hervorheben
footage ['fʊtɪdʒ]	Film-/Bildmaterial
to **victimise sb** ['vɪktɪmaɪz]	jdn schikanieren
in mitigation [ɪn ˌmɪti'geɪʃn]	zur Entlastung
immature [ˌɪmə'tjʊə]	unreif
to **plead guilty** [pliːd 'gɪlti]	sich schuldig bekennen
to **lead sb astray** [ˌliːd ə'streɪ]	jdn vom rechten Weg abbringen
youth custodial sentence [ˌjuːθ kʌˌstəʊdiəl 'sentəns]	Jugendstrafe
harmful ['hɑːmfl]	schädlich
to your credit ['kredɪt]	zu Ihren Gunsten
electronic tag [ɪlekˌtrɒnɪk 'tæg]	elektronische Fessel
to **conclude sth** [kən'kluːd]	etw (ab)schließen

page 145

panel ['pænl]	Gremium, Jury
to **sleep rough** [ˌsliːp 'rʌf]	im Freien übernachten, auf der Straße leben
illiteracy [ɪ'lɪtərəsi]	Analphabetismus
self esteem [ˌself ɪ'stiːm]	Selbstachtung, Selbstwertgefühl

page 146

MP (Member of Parliament) [ˌem 'piː, ˌmembər əv 'pɑːləmənt]	Parlamentsabgeordnete/r
patrol [pə'trəʊl]	Streife, Rundgang
nightmare ['naɪtmeə]	Albtraum

UNIT 11

page 147

paycheck *(AE)* ['peɪtʃek]	Gehalt(sscheck)
to **provide for sb/sth** [prə'vaɪd fə]	für jdn/etw sorgen
welfare ['welfeə]	Wohl, Wohlergehen
retirement [rɪ'taɪəmənt]	Ruhestand, Rente
consideration [kənˌsɪdə'reɪʃn]	Erwägung, Überlegung

page 148

steam [stiːm]	(Wasser-)Dampf
employment [ɪm'plɔɪmənt]	Anstellung, Beschäftigung, Arbeit
the course of ... [kɔːs]	der (Ver-)Lauf von ...
to **fall on hard times** [ˌfɔːl ɒn hɑːd 'taɪmz]	schwere Zeiten durchleben
production line [prə'dʌkʃn laɪn]	Fließband, Fertigungsband
to **man sth** [mæn]	etw *(mit Personal)* besetzen, etw bemannen
manual ['mænjuəl]	handbetrieben, Hand-, manuell
unskilled [ˌʌn'skɪld]	ungelernt
to **relocate** [ˌriːləʊ'keɪt]	umziehen, umsiedeln
sought after ['sɔːt ɑːftə]	begehrt, gefragt
to **occupy sth** ['ɒkjupaɪ]	etw einnehmen, etw besetzen, etw innehaben
post [pəʊst]	(Arbeits-)Stelle, Posten
counterpart ['kaʊntəpɑːt]	Gegenstück, Gegenüber, Pendant

page 149

in demand [ɪn dɪ'mɑːnd]	(nach)gefragt, gesucht
mining ['maɪnɪŋ]	Bergbau
manufacturing [ˌmænju'fæktʃərɪŋ]	Fertigung, Herstellung
retailing ['riːteɪlɪŋ]	Einzelhandel
to **leave a lot to be desired** [liːv ə ˌlɒt tə bi dɪ'zaɪəd]	sehr/viel zu wünschen übrig lassen
cut [kʌt]	(Ver-)Kürzung, Senkung

page 150

executive [ɪg'zekjətɪv]	leitend, Vorstands-, Führungs-
chairman, *pl* **chairmen** ['tʃeəmən]	Vorsitzende/r
on the brink of [brɪŋk]	an der Schwelle zu
to **relate to sb/sth** [rɪ'leɪt tə]	einen Bezug zu jdm/etw haben, mit jdm/etw in Zusammenhang stehen
one another [ˌwʌn ə'nʌðə]	einander, sich (gegenseitig)
humankind [ˌhjuːmən'kaɪnd]	(die) Menschheit
to **blur sth** [blɜː]	etw verwischen
prolongation [ˌprəʊlɒŋ'geɪʃn]	Verlängerung
velocity [və'lɒsəti]	Geschwindigkeit
scope [skəʊp]	Rahmen, Umfang
breakthrough ['breɪkθruː]	Durchbruch
precedent ['presɪdənt]	Präzedenzfall, Beispiel, Tradition
to **disrupt sth** [dɪs'rʌpt]	etw stören, etw behindern
breadth [bredθ]	Breite
depth [depθ]	Tiefe

to **herald sth** ['herəld] — etw ankündigen, etw einläuten
capacity [kə'pæsəti] — Kapazität, Leistung
artificial [ˌɑːtɪ'fɪʃl] — künstlich
robotics [rəʊ'bɒtɪks] — Robotertechnik
materials science [mə'tɪəriəlz saɪəns] — Werkstoffkunde, -wissenschaft
to **precede sth** [prɪ'siːd] — einer Sache vorausgehen, einer Sache vorangehen
to date [tə 'deɪt] — bis heute, bislang
cab [kæb] — Taxi
to **make a payment** [ˌmeɪk ə 'peɪmənt] — eine Zahlung vornehmen, leisten
remotely [rɪ'məʊtli] — aus der Ferne
supply-side [sə'plaɪ saɪd] — angebotsorientiert, was das Angebot betrifft
miracle ['mɪrəkl] — Wunder

page 151

to **diminish** [dɪ'mɪnɪʃ] — (sich) verringern, abnehmen
to **yield sth** [jiːld] — etw erzielen, etw hervorbringen, etw einbringen
to **substitute for sb/sth** ['sʌbstɪtjuːt fə] — jdn/etw ersetzen
net [net] — netto, Netto-
displacement [dɪs'pleɪsmənt] — Verdrängung
return [rɪ'tɜːn] — Ertrag, Rendite
to **foresee sth** [fɔː'siː] — etw voraussehen, etw vorhersehen
in turn [ɪn 'tɜːn] — wiederum, seiner-/ihrerseits
beneficiary [ˌbenɪ'fɪʃəri] — Nutznießer/in
innovator ['ɪnəveɪtə] — Neuerer, Neuerin
wealth [welθ] — Wohlstand, Reichtum
versus ['vɜːsəs] — gegen
to **decrease** [dɪ'kriːs] — abnehmen, zurückgehen
fearful ['fɪəfl] — ängstlich
pervasive [pə'veɪsɪv] — um sich greifend, durchdringend
dissatisfaction [ˌdɪsˌsætɪs'fækʃn] — Unzufriedenheit
discontent [ˌdɪskən'tent] — Unzufriedenheit
to **fuel sth** ['fjuːəl] — etw anheizen, etw anfachen
pervasiveness [pə'veɪsɪvnəs] — Verbreitung
information sharing [ˌɪnfə'meɪʃn ʃeərɪŋ] — Informationsaustausch
to **typify sth** ['tɪpɪfaɪ] — etw verkörpern, für etw typisch sein
cohesion [kəʊ'hiːʒn] — Zusammenhalt
to **propagate sth** *(fml)* ['prɒpəgeɪt] — etw propagieren, etw verbreiten
to **constitute sth** *(fml)* ['kɒnstɪtjuːt] — etw darstellen, etw ausmachen, etw bilden

page 152

uneasiness [ʌn'iːzinəs] — Unbehagen, Unwohlsein

page 153

inequality [ˌɪnɪ'kwɒləti] — Ungleichheit
improbability [ɪmˌprɒbə'bɪləti] — Unwahrscheinlichkeit
uneasy [ʌn'iːzi] — besorgt, unbehaglich, mulmig
decline [dɪ'klaɪn] — Rückgang

page 154

to **juggle sth** ['dʒʌgl] — etw miteinander vereinbaren, (mit) etw jonglieren
sth is anyone's guess [ˌeniwʌnz 'ges] — etw wissen die Götter
to **pamper sb** ['pæmpə] — jdn verwöhnen
to **jam sth somewhere** [dʒæm] — etw an einen Ort klemmen, (fest) drücken
to **conduct sth** [kən'dʌkt] — etw (durch)führen, etw leiten
seamless ['siːmləs] — nahtlos
no big deal [ˌnəʊ bɪg 'diːl] — nichts Besonderes
driven ['drɪvn] — besessen, ehrgeizig
to **customise sth** ['kʌstəmaɪz] — etw anpassen, etw individuell gestalten
to **put it** [pʊt] — es formulieren, es ausdrücken
to **marshal sth** *(fml)* ['mɑːʃl] — etw (an)ordnen, etw arrangieren, etw kontrollieren
to **extend sth** [ɪk'stend] — etw erweitern, etw ausdehnen
to **request sth** *(fml)* [rɪ'kwest] — etw (an)fordern, etw erbitten, um etw bitten
timely ['taɪmli] — zeitgerecht, zur rechten Zeit
to **tap (into) sth** [tæp] — etw erschließen, sich etw zunutze machen
to **reinvent sth** [ˌriːɪn'ven] — etw wieder/neu erfinden
broadband ['brɔːdbænd] — Breitband(-)
sth is the game-changer ['geɪm tʃeɪndʒə] — etw bringt die (Spiel-) Wende
to **dissolve sth** *(fml)* [dɪ'zɒlv] — etw auflösen, etw verschwinden lassen
to **catch on** [ˌkætʃ 'ɒn] — sich durchsetzen, populär werden
... was still a twinkle in sb's eyes ['twɪŋkl] — ... war für jdn noch Zukunftsmusik
to **jostle** ['dʒɒsl] — (sich) drängeln
indistinguishable [ˌɪndɪ'stɪŋgwɪʃəbl] — nicht unterscheidbar
to **bring sth up** [ˌbrɪŋ 'ʌp] — etw auf den Bildschirm holen

page 155

clickbait ['klɪkbeɪt] — Klickfang, Klickköder
ostensibly [ɒ'stensəbli] — angeblich, scheinbar
breaking news [ˌbreɪkɪŋ 'njuːz] — Sondermeldung, Kurzmeldung *(Nachrichten)*
given (that) ... ['gɪvn] — vorausgesetzt, dass ... / angesichts der Tatsache, dass ...
to **suck sb into sth** [sʌk] — jdn in etw hineinziehen
to **speed sth up** [ˌspiːd 'ʌp] — etw beschleunigen
frantic ['fræntɪk] — hektisch, fieberhaft
to **be short on sth** ['ʃɔːt ɒn] — etw nicht haben, von etw zu wenig haben
businesswoman, *pl* **businesswomen** ['bɪznəswʊmən, 'bɪznəswɪmɪn] — Geschäftsfrau
to **knock off** *(infml)* [ˌnɒk 'ɒf] — Feierabend machen
school run ['skuːl rʌn] — „Elterntaxi" zur/von der Schule
to **reconcile sth (with sth)** ['rekənsaɪl] — etw (mit etw) vereinbaren

gear change ['gɪə tʃeɪndʒ]	Gangwechsel *(Schaltvorgang beim Auto/Fahrrad)*
(well-)suited to/for sb/sth ['suːtɪd]	für jdn/etw (gut) geeignet
to **blend sth** [blend]	etw (ver)mischen
domestic [də'mestɪk]	Haushalts-, Familien-
to **nip** *(infml)* [nɪp]	schnell irgendwo hingehen, huschen, flitzen
panacea [ˌpænə'siːə]	Allheilmittel, Patentlösung
fixed [fɪkst]	feste(r,s), festgelegte(r,s)
binman, *pl* **binmen** *(infml)* ['bɪnmæn]	Müllmann
surgeon ['sɜːdʒən]	Chirurg/in
downright ['daʊnraɪt]	ausgesprochen, geradezu, regelrecht
miserable ['mɪzrəbl]	erbärmlich, trostlos
achievable [ə'tʃiːvəbl]	erreichbar, realisierbar
to **throw in the towel** *(infml)* [ˌθrəʊ ɪn ðə 'taʊəl]	das Handtuch werfen
to **submerge** [səb'mɜːdʒ]	untertauchen
to **drown** [draʊn]	ertrinken, untergehen, im Meer versinken
guilt [gɪlt]	Schuld(gefühle)

page 156

to **tear sth down** [ˌteə 'daʊn]	etw abreißen, etw einreißen
to **fulfil sth** [fʊl'fɪl]	etw erfüllen, etw ausführen
preferable to sth ['prefrəbl tə]	besser als etw

page 157

colloquial [kə'ləʊkwiəl]	umgangssprachlich
axe [æks]	Axt, Beil
drawing board ['drɔːɪŋ bɔːd]	Reißbrett
to **slice bread** [ˌslaɪs 'bred]	Brot in Scheiben schneiden
competitive [kəm'petətɪv]	umkämpft, wettbewerbsintensiv
client ['klaɪənt]	Kunde/Kundin
partner ['pɑːtnə]	Gesellschafter/in, Teilhaber/in
to **lose out to sb/sth** *(infml)* [ˌluːz 'aʊt tə]	von jdm/etw verdrängt werden
recreational [ˌrekri'eɪʃənl]	Freizeit-, Erholungs-

page 158

to **staff sth** [stɑːf]	etw *(mit Personal)* besetzen
swift [swɪft]	schnell, rasch
to **set sth up** [ˌset 'ʌp]	etw eröffnen, etw einrichten
advisor [əd'vaɪzə]	Berater/in
holistic [həʊ'lɪstɪk]	ganzheitlich
rung [rʌŋ]	Sprosse *(einer Leiter)*
oftentimes *(AE)* ['ɒfntaɪmz]	oftmals
to **be stuck** [stʌk]	stecken bleiben, festsitzen, nicht weiterkommen
head of state [ˌhed əv 'steɪt]	Staatsoberhaupt
to **shoot for sth** *(AE, infml)* ['ʃuːt fə]	auf etw aus sein
startling ['stɑːtlɪŋ]	alarmierend, erschreckend, erstaunlich
maternal leave [məˌtɜːnl 'liːv]	Mutterschaftsurlaub
to **flatline** ['flætlaɪn]	stagnieren
inadequate [ɪn'ædɪkwət]	mangelhaft, unzureichend
to **lose heart** [luːz 'hɑːt]	den Mut verlieren
to **disengage from sth** *(fml)* [ˌdɪsɪn'geɪdʒ frəm]	sich von etw lösen, sich von/aus etw zurückziehen

page 159

carer ['keərə]	Betreuer/in, Pfleger/in
respondent [rɪ'spɒndənt]	Befragte/r
convenient [kən'viːniənt]	günstig, praktisch, angenehm
to **be made redundant** [bi ˌmeɪd rɪ'dʌndənt]	entlassen werden, den Arbeitsplatz verlieren

page 160

to **gather pace** [ˌgæðə 'peɪs]	Fahrt aufnehmen

UNIT 12

page 161

catchy ['kætʃi]	eingängig *(Lied, Slogan)*

page 162

leap [liːp]	Sprung
to **shape sth** [ʃeɪp]	etw formen
disruptive [dɪs'rʌptɪv]	(zer)störend, zerreißend
lifespan ['laɪfspæn]	Lebensdauer
genetic engineering [dʒəˌnetɪk endʒɪ'nɪərɪŋ]	Gentechnik, Gentechnologie
to **transmit sth** [træns'mɪt]	etw übertragen
elimination [ɪˌlɪmɪ'neɪʃn]	Ausrottung, Ausschaltung
tailor-made ['teɪlə meɪd]	maßgeschneidert
desirable [dɪ'zaɪərəbl]	wünschenswert
GM (genetically modified) [ˌdʒiː 'em]	genmanipuliert
transgenic [ˌtrænz'dʒnɪk]	transgen, genmanipuliert

page 163

reasonably priced [ˌriːznəbli 'praɪst]	zu einem vernünftigen Preis
to **handle sth** ['hændl]	mit etw umgehen, etw handhaben
to **condense sth** [kən'dens]	etw zusammenfassen, etw kürzen
resistant to sth [rɪ'zɪstənt tə]	resistent gegen etw
accessible [ək'sesəbl]	zugänglich, erreichbar, offen
to **innovate (sth)** ['ɪnəveɪt]	Neuerungen einführen, (etw neu) einführen

page 164

to **lose out on sth** [ˌluːz 'aʊt]	bei etw schlecht wegkommen
exasperation [ɪgˌzæspə'reɪʃn]	Verzweiflung
to **cut power** [ˌkʌt 'paʊə]	den Strom abstellen
to **be stranded** ['stændɪd]	festsitzen, gestrandet sein
to **coordinate sth** [kəʊ'ɔːdɪneɪt]	etw koordinieren
coalition [ˌkəʊə'lɪʃn]	Bündnis, Zusammenschluss
congestion [kən'dʒestʃən]	Stauung, Überlastung
laboratory [lə'bɒrətri]	Labor
to **undertake sth** [ˌʌndə'teɪk]	etw unternehmen, etw in Angriff nehmen
online connectivity [ˌɒnlaɪn kɒnek'tɪvəti]	Online-Anbindung
malfunction [ˌmæl'fʌŋkʃn]	Fehlfunktion
prospective [prə'spektɪv]	(zu)künftig, potenziell
realm [relm]	Bereich

to **obtain sth** [əb'teɪn]	etw erhalten, an etw gelangen
incapacitated [ˌɪnkə'pæsɪteɪtɪd]	arbeitsunfähig, behindert

page 165

to **secure sth** [sɪ'kjuə]	(sich) etw sichern, etw sicherstellen
memorandum, *pl* **memoranda** [ˌmemə'rændəm]	Absichtserklärung
to **stimulate sth** ['stɪmjuleɪt]	etw anregen, etw stimulieren
receptive (to sth) [rɪ'septɪv]	(etw gegenüber) aufgeschlossen
relation [rɪ'leɪʃn]	Beziehung, Verhältnis
leakage ['li:kɪdʒ]	Leck, Austreten
failure ['feɪljə]	Versagen, Ausfall, Zusammenbruch
plenty (of) ['plenti]	reichlich, viel
limitation [ˌlɪmɪ'teɪʃn]	Einschränkung
benign [bɪ'naɪn]	gutartig
to **set off an alarm** [ˌset 'ɒf ən əlɑ:m]	Alarm auslösen
to **concede sth** [kən'si:d]	etw zugeben, etw einräumen
severe [sɪ'vɪə]	ernst, schwer
to **address sth** [ə'dres]	etw angehen, sich mit etw befassen
collection [kə'lekʃn]	Sammlung

page 166

novelty ['nɒvlti]	Neuheit
to **permit sth** [pə'mɪt]	etw erlauben

page 168

tight [taɪt]	eng
moon [mu:n]	Mond
abundant *(fml)* [ə'bʌndənt]	reich, reichlich (vorhanden)
to **slow sth** [sləʊ]	etw verlangsamen, etw eindämmen
simulated ['sɪmjuleɪtɪd]	simuliert
to **prevail** [prɪ'veɪl]	siegen, sich durchsetzen

page 169

to **calculate sth** ['kælkjuleɪt]	etw berechnen
weirdness ['wɪədnəs]	Verrücktheit
to **crunch sth** [krʌntʃ]	etw verarbeiten *(Computer)*
generic [dʒə'nerɪk]	generisch, allgemein, typisch
self-fulfilling prophecy [ˌself fʊlfɪlɪŋ 'prɒfəsi]	selbsterfüllende Prophezeiung
demise [dɪ'maɪz]	Ende, Untergang

page 170

availability [əˌveɪlə'bɪləti]	Verfügbarkeit
slowdown ['sləʊdaʊn]	Verlangsamung
to **disguise sth** [dɪs'gaɪz]	etw verschleiern, etw tarnen
to **strengthen** ['streŋθn]	kräftigen, stärken
inexorable [ɪn'eksərəbl]	unaufhaltsam
to **fade** [feɪd]	nachlassen, schwächer werden
to **outplay sb** [ˌaʊt'pleɪ]	besser als jd spielen, jdn an die Wand spielen

page 171

to **initiate sth** [ɪ'nɪʃieɪt]	etw einleiten, etw initiieren
dependable [dɪ'pendəbl]	zuverlässig, verlässlich
breakneck ['breɪknek]	halsbrecherisch

page 172

combat ['kɒmbæt]	Kampf
to **attribute sth to sth** [ə'trɪbju:t]	etw einer Sache zuschreiben, etw einer Sache zuweisen
to **match sth** [mætʃ]	zu etw passen, mit etw übereinstimmen
to **insult sb** [ɪn'sʌlt]	jdn beleidigen
forceful ['fɔ:sfl]	überzeugend, eindringlich
light-hearted [ˌlaɪt 'hɑ:tɪd]	heiter, unbekümmert
lively ['laɪvli]	lebendig, lebhaft, munter
human rights *(pl)* [ˌhju:mən 'raɪts]	Menschenrechte
to **be of relevance** [ˌbi əv 'reləvəns]	von Bedeutung sein
to **hand sth over** [ˌhænd 'əʊvə]	etw übergeben, etw überantworten
to **fire on sb/sth** ['faɪə]	auf jdn/etw schießen
ant [ænt]	Ameise
battlefield ['bætlfi:ld]	Schlachtfeld
defence [dɪ'fens]	Verteidigung
in harm's way [ɪn ˌhɑ:mz 'weɪ]	in Gefahr
civilian [sə'vɪliən]	Zivilist/in
to **judge** [dʒʌdʒ]	(be)urteilen, ermessen
to **have a valid point** [həv ə ˌvælɪd 'pɔɪnt]	ganz Recht haben, einen berechtigtes Argument vorbringen
to **direct sb/sth** [də'rekt]	etw leiten, jdm den Weg sagen/zeigen
warfare ['wɔ:feə]	Krieg(führung)
dignity ['dɪgnət]	Würde
to **come up** [ˌkʌm 'ʌp]	auftauchen, vorkommen
to **decrease sth** [dɪ'kri:s]	etw senken, etw reduzieren
violation [ˌvaɪə'leɪʃn]	Verstoß, Verletzung *(von Gesetzen, Rechten)*

page 173

to **worsen sth** ['wɜ:sn]	verschlechtern
astigmatism [ə'stɪgmətɪzəm]	Hornhautverkrümmung, Stabsichtigkeit
fair [feə]	Messe
cut (of meat) [kʌt]	Stück (Fleisch)
drongo *(AustE, infml)* ['drɒŋgəʊ]	Schwachkopf
to **grasp sth** [grɑ:sp]	etw begreifen, etw (er)greifen, etw beim Schopf packen

page 174

dental ['dentl]	Zahn-
treatment ['tri:tmənt]	Behandlung
to **manufacture sth** [ˌmænju'fæktʃə]	etw fertigen, etw herstellen
aircraft, *pl* **aircraft** ['eəkrɑ:ft]	Flugzeug
to **confront sb with sb/sth** [kən'frʌnt]	jdn mit jdm/etw konfrontieren
permission [pə'mɪʃn]	Erlaubnis, Genehmigung
cancer ['kænsə]	Krebs *(Krankheit, Sternzeichen)*

A–Z word list

Dieses Wörterverzeichnis enthält alle Wörter aus **Focus on Success Plus** in alphabetischer Reihenfolge. Nicht aufgeführt sind internationale Wörter wie *hotel, email* usw. Wörter, die in den Audio- und Videotexten vorkommen, sind mit einem *T*, und Wörter, die in den *Files* vorkommen, mit einem *F* hinter der Seitenzahl gekennzeichnet.

A

to **abandon sth** *92* etw aufgeben, etw sein lassen, etw hinter sich lassen
ability *13* Fähigkeit, Befähigung
absence *42* Abwesenheit
to **absorb sth** *90* etw aufnehmen, etw absorbieren
absorbed (in) *18T* vertieft, versunken (in)
absorption *18T* Aufgehen
abundant *(fml)* *168* reich, reichlich (vorhanden)
abuse *57* Missbrauch
abusive *129* beleidigend, ausfallend
to **accelerate** *86* beschleunigen
to **accept sth** *25* etw akzeptieren, etw gutheißen
access *22* Zugang; to **~ sth** *103* auf etw zugreifen, Zugang haben zu etw
accessible *163* zugänglich, erreichbar, offen
accidentally *109* versehentlich, unabsichtlich
accommodation *33* Unterkunft
to **accompany sb/sth** *40* jdn/etw begleiten, mit etw einhergehen
accomplice *140* Komplize/Komplizin
to **accomplish sth** *26* etw erreichen, etw leisten
according to *15* entsprechend, nach, gemäß
accordingly *15* (dem)entsprechend
account *108* Bericht, Beschreibung; to **~ for sth** *71* etw ausmachen; **bank ~** *137* Bankkonto; to **take sth into ~** *98* etw (mit) berücksichtigen
accountable: to **hold sb ~ (for sth)** *100* jdn (für etw) zur Rechenschaft ziehen
accusation *14* Vorwurf, Anschuldigung
to **accuse sb of sth** *50* jdn einer Sache beschuldigen, jdm etw vorwerfen
achievable *155* erreichbar, realisierbar
to **achieve sth** *46T* etw erreichen, etw leisten
acid *78* sauer; **carbonic ~** *84* Kohlensäure
to **acknowledge sth** *25* etw anerkennen, etw zugeben
to **acquaint sb with sb/sth** *109* jdn mit jdm/etw bekannt machen
to **acquire sth** *23* etw erwerben
across: to **come ~ as …** *130* … wirken, einen … Eindruck machen; to **come ~ sth** *24* auf etw stoßen, etw (zufällig) finden; to **get the message ~** *16* die Botschaft rüberbringen
act: to **~ sth out** *27* etw spielen, etw vorspielen; to **~ your age** *16* sich altersgemäß verhalten
act *40* Gesetz
acting *39* stellvertretend
action: course of ~ *41* Vorgehen, Maßnahmen
actual *118* tatsächlich, konkret
actually *10* eigentlich, wirklich, in der Tat
ad nauseam *95* bis zum Überdruss, bis zum Abwinken
to **adapt** *26* *(Text)* bearbeiten; (sich) anpassen
add: to **~ sth** *9* etw hinzufügen, etw addieren; to **~ up (to)** *18* sich summieren (auf)
addict: drug ~ *143* Drogenabhängige/r
addicted (to) *35* süchtig (nach), abhängig (von)
addiction (to) *58* Sucht (nach), Abhängigkeit (von)
addictive *56* süchtig machend
additional *81* zusätzlich
to **address sth** *165* etw angehen, sich mit etw befassen
adequate *102F* ausreichend, angemessen
to **adjust (to sth)** *45* (sich) anpassen (an etw), (sich) einstellen (auf etw)
adjustment *72* Anpassung, Veränderung
admission *22* Aufnahme, Zulassung *(z. B. Hochschule)*
to **admit to sth** *56* etw zugeben, (ein)gestehen
adolescence *67* Jugend, jugendliches Alter
to **adopt sth** *43* etw übernehmen, sich für etw entscheiden
adulthood *92* Erwachsenenalter
to **advance** *84* voranschreiten, Fortschritte machen
advantage: to **take ~ of sth** *64* sich etw zunutze machen, etw ausnutzen
advent (of sth) *64* Ankunft, Beginn (einer Sache)
adventurous *75* abenteuerlich, abenteuerlustig
adverse *15* nachteilig, ungünstig
advertiser *50* Werber/in *(Auftraggeber/in in der Werbung)*, Inserent/in
advice *28* (guter) Rat, Ratschläge
advise: to **~ against sth** *39* von etw abraten; to **~ sb** *30* jdn beraten, jdm etw raten
advisor *158T* Berater/in
advocacy (of) *40* Eintreten (für), Befürwortung *(einer Sache)*
advocate *8* Befürworter/in
affairs: current ~ *(pl)* *99* Tagespolitik, aktuelle Ereignisse
to **affect sth** *18* etw beeinflussen, sich auswirken auf etw
affluent *24* wohlhabend
afford: to **be able to ~ sth** *74T* sich etw leisten können
affordable *64* erschwinglich
after all *8* schließlich (doch), immerhin
afterwards *35* danach, hinterher
age: for ~s *67* eine Ewigkeit (lang), sehr lange; **in our day and ~** *119* in unserer Zeit; to **act your ~** *16* sich altersgemäß verhalten
to **age** *16* altern
agency *56* Behörde, Agentur; **sense of ~** *127* Handlungsbewusstsein, Handlungskompetenz
agent *70* Instrument, Mittel
to **aggravate sth** *144T* etw verschlimmern, etw erschweren
agreeable *32T* angenehm, akzeptabel
agreement: to **reach an ~** *31* übereinkommen
agricultural *42* landwirtschaftlich, Landwirtschafts-
agriculture *42* Landwirtschaft
agritourism *63* Agrotourismus, Landtourismus
ahead *28* voraus, vorausliegend
to **aid sth** *57* bei etw helfen, etw unterstützen
to **aim at / for / to do sth** *74T* zielen auf, sich richten an
ain't *(slang)* *29* = am not / isn't / aren't
air conditioning *71* Klimaanlage
aircraft, *pl* **aircraft** *174* Flugzeug
airline *51* Fluglinie
aka *(= also known as)* *116* alias
alarm: to **set off an ~** *165* Alarm auslösen
alert *41* Warnung, Alarm; to **be on the ~ (for sth)** *104* (vor etw) auf der Hut sein
alien *109* Ausländer/in
alienation *106* Entfremdung
alive and kicking *51* gesund und munter
All work and no play makes Jack a dull boy. *8* Arbeit alleine macht (auch) nicht glücklich. *(Sprichwort)*
to **allocate sth to sb** *131* jdm etw zuweisen, jdm etw zuteilen

the Almighty *109* der Allmächtige
along with *42* (zusammen) mit, neben
to alter sth *92* etw (ab)ändern
altogether *34* insgesamt, zusammen
alumni *(pl) 131* Ehemalige
amazed *44* erstaunt
amazing *42* erstaunlich
ambassador *113* Botschafter/in
ambition *114* Ehrgeiz, Ziel, Ambition
ambitious *115* ehrgeizig
amends *(pl) 144* Schadensersatz
amoral *142* amoralisch *(sich über die Moral hinwegsetzend)*
amount *8* Menge, Ausmaß, Umfang
amusement park *64* Vergnügungspark, Freizeitpark
ancestor *42* Vorfahr/in
ancestry *112* Abstammung
anecdotal evidence *46T* (nur) vereinzelte Hinweise
anger *44* Zorn, Wut
anniversary *39* Jahrestag
to announce sth *60* etw verkünden, etw ankündigen
to annoy sb *121* jdn ärgern
annoyed *20* verärgert
annoying *111* ärgerlich, lästig, störend
annual *8* jährlich
another: one ~ *150* einander, sich (gegenseitig); one way or ~ *11* so oder so, auf die eine oder andere Art
answering machine *94* Anrufbeantworter
ant *172T* Ameise
to anticipate sth *123* mit etw rechnen, etw erwarten
antidote (to) *18* Gegenmittel, Gegengift (gegen)
anxiety (about/over) *15* Angst, Sorge (wegen), Ängstlichkeit
anxious (about) *125* besorgt, beunruhigt, ängstlich (wegen)
anymore: not ... ~ *15* nicht mehr
apart from *21* abgesehen von, außer
apparently *46T* anscheinend
to appeal to sb *10* für jdn attraktiv sein, jdn ansprechen
to appear *20* (er)scheinen
appliance *87F* Gerät, Haushaltsgerät
applicant *22* Bewerber/in
application *22* Bewerbung
apply: to ~ (for sth) *22* sich (um/auf etw) bewerben; to ~ sth *102T* etw anwenden, etw ausüben
to appoint sb *113* jdn ernennen, jdn berufen
to appreciate sth *107* etw schätzen, etw zu schätzen wissen
apprehensive *32T* besorgt
apprentice *22* Lehrling, Auszubildende/r
apprenticeship *22* Ausbildung, Lehre
approach *11* Ansatz, Herangehensweise
approved *57* anerkannt, genehmigt
aquatic *74F* Wasser-
archery *50* Bogenschießen
to arise *13* sich ergeben, entstehen, auftreten
armed *140* bewaffnet
around: to find your way ~ *69* sich zurechtfinden (in)
to arrange sth *51* etw arrangieren, etw vereinbaren
arson *133* Brandstiftung
artificial *150* künstlich
artisan *74T* Handwerker/in
arts and crafts *(pl) 115* Kunsthandwerk
as: ~ far ~ ... go(es) *18* was ... betrifft/angeht; ~ well *15* auch (noch), ebenfalls; ~ well ~ *9* sowohl ... als auch ..., ebenso wie, sowie; ..., as do vegetables ... *36* ..., wie es auch Gemüse tut/macht ...; such ~ *15* wie (zum Beispiel)
to ascend *25* aufsteigen, hochsteigen, ansteigen
aspect *9* Gesichtspunkt, Aspekt
aspiration *127* Ambition, Bestreben
assault *134* Körperverletzung
to assert control *25* Kontrolle ausüben
to assess sth *23* etw beurteilen
assessed coursework *22* *bewertete Projektarbeit/Mitarbeit in einer Unterrichtseinheit*
assessment *22* Beurteilung, Einstufung
assessor *23* Prüfer/in; Gutachter/in
asset: to be an ~ to sb *106* für jdn eine Bereicherung sein
to assimilate *112* sich anpassen
assistance *33* Hilfe, Unterstützung
to associate sth with sth *111* etw mit etw verbinden, etw mit etw assoziieren
associate professor *99* Hochschuldozent
association *56* Verband, Vereinigung
to assume *95* annehmen, davon ausgehen
assumption *32T* Annahme
to assure sb *109* jdm versichern
astigmatism *173* Hornhautverkrümmung, Stabsichtigkeit
to astound sb *32T* jdn verblüffen
astray: to lead sb ~ *144T* jdn vom rechten Weg abbringen
at all: (not/no) ~ *14* überhaupt (nicht/kein/keine)
athlete *50* Sportler/in, Athlet/in
athletics *(BE) 49* Leichtathletik
attempt *123* Versuch
attempted *140* versucht
to attend sth *22* etw besuchen
attendance *144* Anwesenheit
attention-span disorder *15* Aufmerksamkeitsstörung
attire *(fml) 32T* Kleidung
attitude *10* Einstellung, (Geistes-) Haltung
to attract sb *25* jdn anlocken, jdn anziehen
to attribute sth to sth *172* etw einer Sache zuschreiben, etw einer Sache zuweisen
audience *50* Publikum
authority: (local) ~ *46T* (Kommunal-) Behörde
availability *170* Verfügbarkeit
available *33* verfügbar
average: on ~ *16* im Durchschnitt
averse *(fml) 141* abgeneigt
aviation *70* Luftfahrt
to await sth *137* etw erwarten, etw abwarten
awake *35* wach
to award sth (to sb) *50* (jdm) etw zusprechen, (jdm) etw zuerkennen, (jdm) etw verleihen
aware: to be ~ of sth *98* etw wissen, sich einer Sache bewusst sein
awareness *108* Bewusstsein
awkward *32T* unangenehm, peinlich
axe *157* Axt, Beil
axis, *pl* axes *113* Achse

B

back: to be ~ in the game *16* wieder dabei sein, wieder im Geschäft sein; to go way ~ *(infml) 120* schon lange bestehen; to kick ~ *18* abschalten, relaxen
back: to ~ sth *98* etw unterstützen; to back sth up *18* etw untermauern, etw bekräftigen, etw belegen
background: to fade into the ~ *38* in den Hintergrund rücken
backside *109* Hintern, Po
bail: on ~ *134* gegen Kaution
balanced *36* ausgeglichen, ausgewogen, im Gleichgewicht
baldness *56* Kahlheit, Glatze
bandwagon: to jump on the ~ *92* auf den fahrenden Zug aufspringen
bank account *137* Bankkonto
bar *40* Riegel *(z. B. Schokolade)*; behind ~s *137* hinter Gittern
barely *112* kaum
barrier *15* Barriere, Schranke, Grenze
bars: wall ~ *(pl) 15* Sprossenwand
to base sth on sth *24* etw auf etw gründen, etw als Grundlage benutzen für etw
based: ~ on *17F* basierend auf, auf der Grundlage von; ...-~ *14* auf der Basis von ..., ...-basiert
baseline *84* Basis, Ausgangspunkt
basement *35* Keller, Untergeschoss
basic *25* einfach, elementar
basically *8* grundsätzlich, im Grunde
basis: on a day-to-day ~ *69* im Alltag, tagtäglich
bat *49* Schläger
battlefield *172T* Schlachtfeld
bay: to keep sb at ~ *98* jdn fernhalten, sich jdn vom Leib halten
to be to do sth *123* etw tun sollen

to **beat sb** *25* jdn schlagen, jdn besiegen
beaten track: to **step off the ~** *70* ausgetretene Pfade verlassen
beauty: the ~ of … *18F* das Schöne/Schönste an …
to **become engaged with sth** *99* sich mit etw auseinandersetzen, sich mit etw beschäftigen
bedlinen *75* Bettwäsche
beforehand *86* vorher, im Voraus
to **befriend sb** *120* sich mit jdm anfreunden
behalf: on sb's ~ *67* in jds Namen
to **behave** *27* sich benehmen, sich verhalten
behaviour *46T* Benehmen, Verhalten
belief *19F* Glaube, Überzeugung
to **bemoan sth** *99* etw beklagen, etw betrauern
bench *104* Bank *(zum Sitzen)*
bend: to **~ down** *108* sich herunterbeugen; to **~ the rules** *51* über die Regeln hinwegsehen, die Vorschriften beugen
beneath *88T* unterhalb, unter
beneficial *11* nützlich, vorteilhaft
beneficiary *151* Nutznießer/in
benign *165* gutartig
berry *42* Beere
to **bet** *50* wetten
bet: to **be a good ~** *25* ein heißer Anwärter sein
beverage *39* Getränk
beyond *106* jenseits, außerhalb; to **modify sth ~ recognition** *14* etw so verändern, dass es nicht wiederzuerkennen ist
bicycle *64* Fahrrad
big: ~ time *28* so richtig; *134* ganz groß; **no ~ deal** *154* nichts Besonderes
biking *17* Radfahren
bill *81* Rechnung
billion, bn, billion, bn *19* Milliarde
to **binge drink** *134* komasaufen
binman, *pl* **binmen** *(infml)* *155* Müllmann
biofuel *87F* Biokraftstoff
birth *60T* Geburt
bi-weekly *98* alle zwei Wochen (erscheinend)
blade *88T* Rotorblatt, Turbinenschaufel
bladed article *140* scharfer Gegenstand *(mit einer Klinge)*
to **blend sth** *155* etw (ver)mischen
to **bless sb/sth** *109* jdn/etw segnen
blessing *103* Segen
blood pressure *18T* Blutdruck
blood vessel *18T* Blutgefäß
bloody *25* blutig
blotting pad *109* Schreibunterlage
to **blow sth up** *20* etw aufblasen
to **blur sth** *150* etw verwischen
board *48* Gremium, Ausschuss; **~ game** *8* Brettspiel
to **board** *18F* einsteigen (in), an Bord gehen
body: ~ of research *39* Forschungsmaterial, Forschungsarbeiten; **strategic ~** *46T* Organisation, strategisches Organ/Gremium
bold: (in) ~ *17* fett(gedruckt)
bond *11* Bindung, Verbindung; **war ~s** *(pl)* *113* Kriegsanleihen
to **bond** *123* eine Bindung aufbauen
booklet *131* Broschüre
boost *71* (schnelle) Steigerung, Auftrieb
to **boost sth** *12* etw stärken, etw ankurbeln, einer Sache Auftrieb geben
boots *(pl)* *49* Stiefel
booze *137* Alkohol
border *25* Grenze
borderline *28* grenzwertig
to **bother with sth** *76* sich um etw kümmern, sich mit etw befassen
to **bounce (sth)** *49* hüpfen; *(Ball)* prellen
boundary *15* Grenze, Trennlinie
bracket *9* Klammer
to **brag about sth** *95* mit etw angeben
to **brainstorm** *10* Ideen (ungeordnet) sammeln
branch *15* Zweig
brand *50* Marke
bread: to **slice ~** *157* Brot in Scheiben schneiden
breadth *150* Breite
break: to **~ down** *35* eine Panne haben, kaputtgehen; to **~ the news (to sb)** *92* (jdm) die Nachricht(en) überbringen; **all hell would ~ loose** *109* hier wäre der Teufel / die Hölle los
breaking news *155* Sondermeldung, Kurzmeldung *(Nachrichten)*
breakneck *171* halsbrecherisch
breakthrough *150* Durchbruch
to **breathe down sb's neck** *54T* jdm im Nacken sitzen
breathtaking *74T* atemberaubend, hinreißend
breed *18F* Züchtung, Rasse
to **brew sth** *113* etw brauen
to **bribe sb** *50* jdn bestechen
bribery *134* Bestechung
brick *144T* Backstein
brigade: fire ~ *31* Feuerwehr
bright *42* hell, strahlend, freundlich *(Wetter)*
bright-eyed *46T* mit (strahlenden) Augen
bring: to **~ sb/sth along** *17* jdn/etw mitbringen; to **~ sth up** *154* etw auf den Bildschirm holen
brink: on the ~ of *150* an der Schwelle zu
broadband *154* Breitband(-)
broadcast *136* Rundfunk-
broadcaster *100* Moderator/in
to **broaden sth** *31* etw erweitern
broadsheet *92* *(großformatige, seriöse)* Zeitung
brush: to **~ sb/sth** *32T* jdn/etw streifen; to **~ sth up** *69* etw auffrischen
bucket *95* Eimer; **a drop in the ~** *99* ein Tropfen auf den heißen Stein
budding *94* aufkeimend, angehend
bulk *57* (Körper-)Masse
bullet *108* (Gewehr-)Kugel
bump *102T* Erhöhung, Unebenheit
bunch: a ~ of *26* eine Menge
bunk *33* Schlafkabine, Koje
buoyancy aid *74F* Schwimmhilfe
burden *19* Last, Belastung, Bürde
Bureau of Labor Statistics *32T* *(USA)* Agentur für Arbeitsstatistiken
burglar *142* Einbrecher/in
burglary *133* Einbruch
to **bury sth** *79* etw vergraben, etw begraben
businessfolk *(pl)* *71* Geschäftsleute
businesswoman, *pl* **businesswomen** *155* Geschäftsfrau
to **bust** *(infml)* *54T* zerplatzen
button *123* Knopf
buzzword *130T* Modewort, Schlagwort

C

cab *150* Taxi
cabbage *113* Kohl, Kraut
cabin *75* Hütte
to **calculate sth** *169* etw berechnen
call: to **be on ~** *15* in Bereitschaft sein, Bereitschaftsdienst haben
calorie-count label *39* Brennwerttabelle *(auf Produktetiketten)*
camp: summer ~ *33* (Sommer-)Ferienlager
campaign *40* Kampagne, Aktion
to **campaign for/against sth** *109* sich für/gegen etw einsetzen
camper *33* Lagerbewohner/in, Teilnehmer/in an einem Campingurlaub
campus *48* Gelände *(z. B. Schule, Unternehmen)*
cancer *174* Krebs *(Krankheit, Sternzeichen)*
candidate *23* Bewerber/in
canteen *27* Kantine, Mensa, Cafeteria
capability *87* Fähigkeit, Potenzial
capable of *57* fähig zu, imstande zu
capacity *150* Kapazität, Leistung
capture: carbon (dioxide) ~ *78* Kohlenstoffbindung
carbohydrate *36* Kohle(n)hydrat
carbon *70* Kohlenstoff; **~ (dioxide) capture** *78* Kohlenstoffbindung; **~ dioxide** *78* Kohlendioxid
carbonic acid *84* Kohlensäure
card: key ~ *71* Schlüsselkarte
cardboard *78* Pappe
to **care for sb** *33* für jdn sorgen, sich um jdn kümmern, auf jdn aufpassen
care: to **take ~** *92* vorsichtig sein, aufpassen; to **take care to do sth** *120* (sorgfältig) darauf achten, etw zu tun
career *11* Karriere, Laufbahn

carefree *28* unbekümmert, sorgenfrei
carer *159* Betreuer/in, Pfleger/in
to **caress sb/sth** *32T* jdn/etw streicheln, jdn/etw liebkosen
carriage *133* Waggon
carrier *64* Fluggesellschaft
cartridge: (printer) ~ *40* (Drucker-) Patrone
case *22* Fall
casual *130* leger, zwanglos
catch: to **~ on** *154* sich durchsetzen, populär werden; to **~ up with sb** *116* jdn einholen; *95* mit jdm Nachrichten austauschen
catchy *161* eingängig *(Lied, Slogan)*
cater: to **~ for sb/sth** *63* jdm/einer Sache gerecht werden, auf jdn/etw eingestellt sein; to **~ to sb/sth** *64* auf jdn/etw ausgerichtet sein, jdm/etw gerecht werden
caucus *113* Gremium, Ausschuss
cause *37* Ursache, Grund; to **~ sth** *36* etw verursachen
caution *41* Vorsicht, Warnung
to **cave in to sth** *95* einer Sache nachgeben
caveman, *pl* **cavemen** *42* Höhlenmensch
CCTV (closed-circuit television) *144T* Videoüberwachung
ceiling *32T* (Zimmer-)Decke
centred on: to **be ~ sth** *126* sich um etw drehen, sich auf etw konzentrieren
century: turn of the ~ *96* Jahrhundertwende
CEO (Chief Executive Officer) *28* Vorstandsvorsitzende/r
cf. *68* vgl.
chair *46* Vorsitzende/r
chairman, *pl* **chairmen** *150* Vorsitzende/r
challenge: to **~ sb (to sth)** *95* jdn (zu etw) herausfordern; to **~ sth** *130T* etw infrage stellen, etw anzweifeln
chancellor *113* (Bundes-)Kanzler/in
change: to **~ people's minds** *38* die Menschen zum Umdenken bewegen; to **~ your mind** *138* seine Meinung ändern
changer: sth is the game-~ *154* etw bringt die (Spiel-)Wende
to **channel sth into sth** *32T* etw auf etw richten
character *10* Figur, Person *(in Roman, Film usw.)*
charge: in ~ *26* verantwortlich, (feder) führend
charitable *9* wohltätig, gemeinnützig
charity *8* Wohltätigkeit(s-), wohltätige Zwecke
to **cheat** *50* schummeln, betrügen, schwindeln
cheeked: (rosy)-~ *46T* mit (rosigen/ roten) Wangen
chef *104* Chefkoch/-köchin, Küchenchef/in
chess *108* Schach
to **chew sth** *123* etw kauen
chewing gum *35* Kaugummi
childhood *22* Kindheit
to **chill out** *28* sich entspannen, abhängen
chocolate chips *(pl)* *35* Schokoladenstückchen
choice: ... is a matter of ~ *99* ... hat man selbst in der Hand, ... liegt im eigenen Ermessen
choir *9* Chor
cholesterol *36* Cholesterin
chorus *123* Sing- und Tanzgruppe, Tänzer/innen
cinnamon *112* Zimt
circuit *46T* Rundparcours, Rennstrecke
to **cite sth** *127* etw zitieren, etw angeben
citizenship *106* Staatsbürgerschaft, Staatsbürgerkunde
civilian *172T* Zivilist/in
to **claim** *14* behaupten
to **clap** *54T* (Beifall) klatschen
class: remedial ~ *116* Förderklasse
classic *14* klassisch
cleaner *28* Reinigungskraft
to **clear out sth** *137* etw ausräumen
clearance *86* Räumung, Abholzung
clickbait *155* Klickfang, Klickköder
client *157* Kunde/Kundin
climate change *78* Klimawandel
close *38* eingehend, genau
closely *33* genau, näher
closet *(AE)* *123* (Wand-)Schrank
clothing *74T* Bekleidung, Kleidung
club *49* Schläger *(Golf)*
clumsy *32T* ungeschickt, schwerfällig
coal *78* Kohle
coalition *164* Bündnis, Zusammenschluss
coasteering *74F* *Klettern an steilen Küsten mit Sprüngen ins Wasser*
coastline *74F* Küste
code: ~ of conduct *120* Verhaltenskodex, -regeln; **dress ~** *120* Kleiderordnung
cohabitation *120* Zusammenleben, eheähnliche Gemeinschaft
cohesion *151* Zusammenhalt
to **coin sth** *64* etw prägen
collaboration *102T* Zusammenarbeit, Gemeinschaftsprodukt(ion)
to **collapse** *85* zusammenbrechen, kollabieren
colleague *46T* Kollege/-in
collection *165* Sammlung
college *11* Fach(hoch)schule
collocation *9* Kollokation *(inhaltliche Kombinierbarkeit sprachlicher Einheiten)*
colloquial *157* umgangssprachlich
combat *172* Kampf
to **combat sth** *50* etw bekämpfen
to **come** *95* erhältlich sein, geliefert werden; to **~ across as ...** *130* ... wirken, einen ... Eindruck machen; to **~ across sth** *24* auf etw stoßen, etw (zufällig) finden; to **~ to mind** *21* einem einfallen; to **~ up** *172* auftauchen, vorkommen; to **~ up with sth** *12* sich etw ausdenken, sich etw einfallen lassen; *128* auf etw kommen *(Lösung)*, etw erbringen; **~ May** *123* wenn der Mai kommt, im Mai
commercial (time) slot *123* Sendezeit für Werbung *(Radio/TV)*
to **commit (a crime)** *102F* (ein Verbrechen) begehen
commitment (to) *11* Engagement (für), Bekenntnis (zu)
committed: to **be ~ to sth** *46T* sich für etw engagieren, für etw engagiert sein
common practice *120* gängige/ übliche Praxis
common sense *46T* gesunder Menschenverstand
commonly *17* häufig, üblicherweise
commonplace *93* alltäglich, gewöhnlich
communal *125* Gemeinschafts-, gemeinschaftlich, gemeinsam
comparative *46T* vergleichend
comparatively *70* vergleichsweise, relativ, verhältnismäßig
compassionate *105* mitfühlend, mitleidig
compatriot *57* Landsmann/Landsmännin
to **compensate for sth** *64* etw ausgleichen
compensation *144* (finanzieller) Ausgleich
to **compete** *51* *(in Wettbewerben)* antreten, teilnehmen
competition *22* Wettbewerb, Wettkampf; to **enter a ~** *27* an einem Wettkampf/Wettbewerb teilnehmen
competitive *157* umkämpft, wettbewerbsintensiv; **(~) edge** *68* (Wettbewerbs-)Vorteil, Vorsprung
competitor *56* Konkurrent/in, Konkurrenz, Wettbewerbsteilnehmer/in
to **complement sth** *102T* etw ergänzen
completion *15* Fertigstellung, Vervollständigung
to **comply with sth** *120* etw erfüllen, etw befolgen, sich an etw halten
composting toilet *70* Trockentoilette, Komposttoilette
compound *84* Verbindung; **~ fertilizer** *74T* Komplexdünger, Mehrnährstoffdünger
comprehensive *141* umfassend
to **comprise sth** *81* etw umfassen, aus etw bestehen
to **compromise** *18* Kompromisse eingehen
compulsory *22* Pflicht-, obligatorisch
to **concede sth** *165* etw zugeben, etw einräumen
to **conceive (of) sth** *94* sich etw vorstellen
to **concentrate on sth** *28* sich auf etw konzentrieren
concern *14* Sorge, Befürchtung
concerned *14* besorgt, beunruhigt

concerning *92* betreffend, hinsichtlich
concession *43* Konzession, Zugeständnis
to **conclude sth** *144T* etw (ab) schließen
conclusion: to **draw a ~** *94* eine Schlussfolgerung ziehen
to **condemn sth** *53* etw verdammen, etw verurteilen
to **condense sth** *163* etw zusammenfassen, etw kürzen
conditions: working ~ *(pl) 60T* Arbeitsbedingungen
conduct: code of ~ *120* Verhaltenskodex, -regeln
to **conduct sth** *154* etw (durch)führen, etw leiten
confession *57* Beichte, Geständnis
confidence *10* (Selbst-)Vertrauen, Zuversicht
confident *30* (selbst)sicher
confined (to) *84* beengt, begrenzt, beschränkt (auf)
conflicting *15* widersprüchlich, gegensätzlich
to **conform** *120* sich anpassen
to **confront sb with sb/sth** *174* jdn mit jdm/etw konfrontieren
congestion *164* Stauung, Überlastung
to **conjure sth up** *28* etw (herauf) beschwören
conkers *53 Kinderspiel, bei dem man Kastanien an Schnüren gegeneinander schlägt*
connected to *21* verbunden mit
connectedness *15* Vernetzung, Verflechtung
connectivity: online ~ *164* Online-Anbindung
conscious (of sth) *67* (sich einer Sache) bewusst
to **consent** *(fml) 120* zustimmen, einwilligen
consequently *26* folglich, demzufolge
conservation *70* (Natur-)Schutz, Erhaltung, Bewahrung
to **conserve sth** *74T* etw erhalten, etw schonen
consider: to **~ sth** *12* über etw nachdenken, sich etw überlegen, etw in Erwägung ziehen; to **~ sth sth** *14* etw für etw halten, etw als etw betrachten
considerable *50* erheblich, beträchtlich
consideration *147* Erwägung, Überlegung; to **take sth into ~** *18* etw berücksichtigen
to **consist of sth** *22* aus etw bestehen
conspicuous *124* auffällig, auffallend
to **constitute sth** *(fml) 151* etw darstellen, etw ausmachen, etw bilden
construction *81* (Auf-)Bau
to **consult sth** *73F* in etw nachsehen, in etw nachlesen
to **consume sth** *36* etw verbrauchen, etw konsumieren, *(Kalorien)* aufnehmen
consumption *72* Verbrauch, Konsum
to **contain sth** *12* etw enthalten
container *18F* Behälter
to **contaminate sth** *78* etw verunreinigen, etw kontaminieren
content: to your heart's ~ *8* nach Herzenslust
content(s) *92* Inhalt
contentious *95 (Debatte etc.)* hitzig, *(Person)* streitlustig
continual *127* ständig, ununterbrochen, kontinuierlich
contraception *120* Empfängnisverhütung
contract *51* Vertrag
contract farming *74T* Vertragsanbau
to **contract sth** *74T* etw vertraglich regeln
to **contradict** *17F* widersprechen
contradiction: a ~ in terms *52* ein Widerspruch in sich
contradictory *15* widersprüchlich
to **contribute (to)** *36* beitragen (zu)
contribution: to **make a ~** *20* einen Beitrag leisten
control: to **assert ~** *25* Kontrolle ausüben
convenient *159* günstig, praktisch, angenehm
conventional *87F* konventionell, herkömmlich
convertible *123* Cabrio(let) *(Auto)*
to **convey sth** *32T* etw vermitteln, etw übermitteln
convict *134* Sträfling
to **convict sb** *134* jdn verurteilen *(für schuldig befinden)*
conviction *144* Verurteilung
to **convince sb** *18* jdn überzeugen
cookie *(AE) 25* Keks, Plätzchen
cooperative *80* Genossenschaft
to **coordinate sth** *164* etw koordinieren
to **cope with sth** *84* etw bewältigen, mit etw klarkommen, mit etw fertig werden
core *84* Kern-, Haupt-
corn *42* Getreide, *(AE)* Mais
corporate *74T* Unternehmens-, von Unternehmen
corporation *50* Konzern
to **correspond to/with sth** *36* einer Sache entsprechen, mit etw übereinstimmen
corresponding *16* entsprechend, passend
costume *(BE) 49* Badeanzug
couch potato *8* Stubenhocker/in, Dauerglotzer/in
council *103* Rat, Versammlung
counselling *134* (professionelle) Beratung
counsellor *33* Berater/in, Betreuer/in
count: sperm ~ *56* Spermienzahl
counter *35* Spielstein, Spielmarke
counter: to **run ~ to sth** *141* im Widerspruch zu etw stehen
counterpart *148* Gegenstück, Gegenüber, Pendant
course *22* Weg, Vorgehensweise; *49* Rennstrecke, Kurs *(Sport)*; **~ of action** *41* Vorgehen, Maßnahmen; **the ~ of ...** *148* der (Ver-)Lauf von ...
coursework: assessed ~ *22 bewertete Projektarbeit/Mitarbeit in einer Unterrichtseinheit*
court *49* Platz *(Sport)*; Gerichtshof; **magistrates' ~** *138* Amtsgericht
courteous *109* höflich
cover flap *41* Umschlagklappe
cover letter *22* Anschreiben, Begleitschreiben
coverage *51* Berichterstattung, Behandlung *(eines Themas)*
cowardly *95* feige
crack *138* Sprung, Riss
crafts: arts and ~ *(pl) 115* Kunsthandwerk
craftsmanship *113* Handwerkskunst
to **crash** *76* abstürzen, zusammenbrechen
craving *42* Verlangen
crawling: to **be ~ with sth** *95* von etw wimmeln
creation *14* Schaffung
credit: to your ~ *144T* zu Ihren Gunsten
creepy *25* unheimlich
crime: white-collar ~ *134* Wirtschaftskriminalität
crisis, *pl* **crises** *42* Krise
critical *28* kritisch
to **criticize sb/sth** *90* jdn/etw kritisieren
crop *44* Nutzpflanze, Feldfrucht
to **cross sth** *85* etw überqueren
crossword puzzle *101* Kreuzworträtsel
to **crunch sth** *169* etw verarbeiten *(Computer)*
crush: to **have a ~** *32T* verknallt sein
culinary *64* kulinarisch, Koch-
culprit *73* Schuldige/r, Übeltäter/in
to **cultivate sth** *42* etw bewirtschaften, *(Getreide, Gemüse)* anbauen
to **curate sth** *28* etw zusammenstellen (um es zu präsentieren)
to **curb sth** *106* etw begrenzen, etw einschränken
curfew *144* Ausgangssperre
curiosity *32T* Neugier
current *44* aktuell, derzeitig; **~ affairs** *(pl) 99* Tagespolitik, aktuelle Ereignisse
currently *33* zurzeit
curriculum *22* Lehrplan
curse *103* Fluch
custodial: youth ~ sentence *144T* Jugendstrafe
custody *134* Gewahrsam
custom *67* Gewohnheit, Brauch, Sitte
to **customise sth** *154* etw anpassen, etw individuell gestalten
cut *149* (Ver-)Kürzung, Senkung; **~ (of meat)** *173F* Stück (Fleisch)
cut: to **~ back on sth** *35* etw verringern, (bei) etw zurückschrauben;

to **cut down on sth** *103* sich bei etw einschränken; to **cut power** *164* den Strom abstellen; to **cut sth out** *43* etw weglassen, auf etw verzichten

CV (curriculum vitae) *(BE)* *22* Lebenslauf

cycle *102T* Zyklus, Kreislauf

cyclist *56* Radfahrer/in

D

dachshund *113* Dackel

daily *92* Tageszeitung

dairy *42* Molkerei, Milch-, Molkerei-

to **damage sth** *50* etw beschädigen

damn: to **not give a ~** *(infml)* *124* sich einen Dreck scheren

to **dash** *108* stürmen, (los)stürzen

data *(pl)* *18* Daten

date: to ~ *150* bis heute, bislang; **up to ~** *34* aktuell, auf dem/den neuesten Stand

to **date back …** *56* … alt sein, stammen aus …

daunting *29* einschüchternd, entmutigend, beängstigend

day: in our ~ and age *119* in unserer Zeit; **on a ~-to-~ basis** *69* im Alltag, tagtäglich

deal: no big ~ *154* nichts Besonderes

to **deal with sb/sth** *33* mit jdm/etw zurechtkommen, mit jdm/etw umgehen

decade *72* Jahrzehnt

decay: tooth ~ *36* Karies, Zahnfäule

decline *153* Rückgang; **on the ~** *92* rückläufig

to **decline** *92* zurückgehen, fallen, sinken

to **decompose** *90* sich zersetzen, zerfallen

to **decorate sth** *119* etw schmücken, etw verzieren

decoration *121* Schmuck, Verzierung

to **decrease** *151* abnehmen, zurückgehen; to **~ sth** *172* etw senken, etw reduzieren

dedication (to) *54T* Einsatz, Engagement (für)

to **deepen sth** *56* etw tiefer werden lassen

defence *172T* Verteidigung

to **defend sb/sth** *95* jdn/etw verteidigen

defendant *144T* Angeklagte/r

defiant *53* trotzig

definitely *25* absolut, ganz sicher

deforestation *71* Waldzerstörung

to **degrade sth** *84* etw abbauen

degree *22* Abschluss; **to what ~** *127* in welchem (Aus-)Maß, bis zu welchem Grad

dehydration *36* Austrocknung

deletion *93* Löschung, Tilgung

deliberate *61F* absichtlich, (ganz) bewusst, vorsätzlich

delicate *95* sensibel, heikel

delight *126* Vergnügen, Freude

delinquency *134* Straffälligkeit

to **deliver sth** *46T* etw liefern

delivery *83* Vortrag

demand: in ~ *149* (nach)gefragt, gesucht

demanding *10* anstrengend, anspruchsvoll

demise *169* Ende, Untergang

demographic *92* Bevölkerungsgruppe, Altersgruppe

to **demonstrate** *28* vorstellen, vorführen; to **~ sth** *39* etw zeigen, etw demonstrieren

dental *174* Zahn-

to **deny sth** *13* etw leugnen, etw bestreiten

to **depart** *33* abreisen, abfahren, abfliegen

to **depend on sb/sth** *36* von jdm/etw abhängen

dependable *171* zuverlässig, verlässlich

dependent on sth *81* von etw abhängig

depending on *22* je nach(dem)

depletion *84* Verringerung, Abbau

deplorable *(fml)* *17* erbärmlich, beklagenswert

depressing *19* deprimierend

deprived *142* benachteiligt

depth *150* Tiefe

to **derive** *9* gewinnen, beziehen

desalination *87F* Entsalzung

descent *108* Herkunft, Abstammung

to **deserve sth** *61F* etw verdienen

to **design sth** *12* etw entwerfen, etw gestalten

desirable *162* wünschenswert

desire *50* Wunsch, Verlangen

desired: to **leave a lot to be ~** *149* sehr/viel zu wünschen übrig lassen

despair *107* Verzweiflung

desperate *42* verzweifelt

desperation *35* Verzweiflung

despite *14* trotz

destruction *64* Zerstörung, Vernichtung

to **detect sth** *57* etw wahrnehmen, etw entdecken

detection *57* Entdeckung, Aufdeckung

detention *144* Haft

to **deter sb** *61F* jdn abschrecken, jdn (von etw) abhalten

deterioration *15* Verschlechterung

to **determine sth** *22* etw ermitteln, etw feststellen

determined *20* (fest) entschlossen

deterrent *134* Abschreckung(smittel)

detox *(infml)* *103* Entzug, Entgiftung(sbehandlung)

detrimental (to) *78* schädlich (für)

to **develop (sth)** *8* (sich/etw) entwickeln

developer *70* Bauträger/in, Bauunternehmer/in

developing country *22* Entwicklungsland

devious *32T* hinterhältig, verschlagen, unaufrichtig

to **devour sth** *87* etw verschlingen

dial *94* Wählscheibe *(Telefon)*

diamond *49* (Innen-)Feld *(Baseball)*

dice, *pl* **dice** *35* Würfel

diehard *123* hartnäckig, eingefleischt

diet *19* Ernährung, Kost, Diät(-)

dietetic *43* diätetisch, Ernährungs-

dietician *43* Ernährungsberater/in, Ernährungswissenschaftler/in

to **differentiate** *134* unterscheiden

to **dig** *20* graben

dignity *172T* Würde

to **diminish** *151* (sich) verringern, abnehmen

to **dip** *67* (ein)tauchen

dire *39* ernst *(z.B. Warnung)*

to **direct sb/sth** *172T* etw leiten, jdm den Weg sagen/zeigen

disagreeable *129* unangenehm, unliebsam, unsympathisch

disciplined *10* diszipliniert

discontent *151* Unzufriedenheit

discourse *127* Diskurs, Erörterung

to **disengage from sth** *(fml)* *158T* sich von etw lösen, sich von/aus etw zurückziehen

disgrace: in ~ *57* unehrenhaft

to **disgrace yourself** *104* sich blamieren

to **disguise sth** *170* etw verschleiern, etw tarnen

dish *36* Gericht, Speise

to **dismantle sth** *81* etw abbauen, etw abreißen

to **dismiss sth as sth** *129* etw als etw abtun

to **displace sb** *106* jdn vertreiben

displacement *151* Verdrängung

to **display sth** *10* etw zeigen, etw ausstellen, etw präsentieren

disposal *78* Entsorgung

to **dispose of sth** *78* etw beseitigen, etw entsorgen

to **disrupt sth** *150* etw stören, etw behindern

disruption *85* Störung, Behinderung, Unterbrechung

disruptive *162* (zer)störend, zerreißend

dissatisfaction *151* Unzufriedenheit

to **dissolve sth** *(fml)* *154* etw auflösen, etw verschwinden lassen

to **dissuade sb from doing sth** *39* jdn davon abbringen, etw zu tun

distinct *32T* deutlich, unterschiedlich

to **distinguish (between)** *16* unterscheiden (zwischen)

to **distract sb** *11* jdn ablenken

distraction *32T* Ablenkung

to **distribute sth** *74F* etw verteilen, etw austeilen

distribution *88T* Versorgung

district *144T* Bezirk

distrust *32T* Misstrauen

disturbing *40* verstörend, erschütternd, unheimlich, bedrohlich

disused *82* stillgelegt
to **dive** *49* tauchen, einen Kopfsprung machen
diversified *86* diversifiziert, gefächert, gestreut
divide *92* Kluft
division *130* Trennung
dos and don'ts *(pl) 32 Hinweise, was man tun und lassen sollte*
to **do without sth** *104* ohne etw auskommen
doer *8* Macher/in
domestic *155* Haushalts-, Familien-; **~ waste** *78* Hausmüll; **gross ~ product (GDP)** *64* Bruttosozialprodukt
to **dominate sth** *24* etw beherrschen, etw dominieren
domination *25* Dominanz
to **donate** *20* spenden
doomed *92* todgeweiht, dem Untergang geweiht
doorstep *108* Tür(schwelle)
do-over *(AE, infml) 124* erneuter Versuch
to **double** *57* (sich) verdoppeln
double-edged *74T* zweischneidig, zwiespältig
doubt *8* Zweifel; **..., no doubt, ...** *100* ... zweifellos ...
down: to **be ~ to sth** *84* auf etw zurückzuführen sein, an etw liegen
to **down sth** *46T* etw niederlegen
downright *155* ausgesprochen, geradezu, regelrecht
downs: ups and ~ *95* Höhen und Tiefen
downside *11* Nachteil
to **downsize sth** *92* etw verkleinern, etw gesundschrumpfen
dozen *88T* Dutzend
draft: the ~ *(AE) 113* die Einberufung
dragon *74T* Drachen
drain on sb/sth *106* Belastung für jdn/etw
drastically *40* drastisch
to **draw** *25* (an)ziehen; to **~ a conclusion** *94* eine Schlussfolgerung ziehen; to **~ sth up** *131* etw erstellen
drawing board *157* Reißbrett
to **dread sth** *123* etw fürchten
dress code *120* Kleiderordnung
drink: to **binge ~** *134* komasaufen
to **drive sth** *11* etw vorantreiben, etw stärken
driven *154* besessen, ehrgeizig; **-~** *15* -betrieben, -gesteuert
drongo *(AustE, infml) 173F* Schwachkopf
drop *32* Rückgang, Abfall; **a ~ in the bucket** *99* ein Tropfen auf den heißen Stein
to **drop sth off** *32* etw abliefern
drove *106* Schar, Herde
to **drown** *155* ertrinken, untergehen, im Meer versinken; to **~ sb/sth** *35* jdn/etw ertränken
drug: ~ addict *143* Drogenabhängige/r; **~ trafficking** *134* Drogenhandel
drunkard *114* Trinker/in, Säufer/in
drunken *133* betrunken
duchess *126* Herzogin
due to sth *64* wegen etw
dull *8* langweilig; **All work and no play makes Jack a ~ boy.** *8* Arbeit alleine macht (auch) nicht glücklich. *(Sprichwort)*
dumbfounded *94* sprachlos, verblüfft
Dust Bowl *117* Trockengebiet; *Naturkatastrophe in den USA in den 1930er Jahren*

E

eager *102T* bestrebt, darauf aus
earnest *132* ernsthaft
Easter bunny *112* Osterhase
easy-fitting *130* lässig sitzend *(Kleidung)*
eating disorder *127* Essstörung
ebb: the ~ and flow *116* das Auf und Ab, das Kommen und Gehen
economic *19* wirtschaftlich
economical *78* sparsam, wirtschaftlich
economist *71* Volkswirt/in, Wirtschaftswissenschaftler/in
economy *32T* Wirtschaft
edge: (competitive) ~ *68* (Wettbewerbs-)Vorteil, Vorsprung
to **edit sth** *92* etw redigieren, etw bearbeiten *(Text)*
edition *92* Ausgabe *(z. B. einer Zeitschrift)*
editor: letter to the ~ *52* Leserbrief
editorial board *131* Redaktionsleitung
education: secondary ~ *22* Sekundarstufe 1 und 2
educational *15* schulisch, Bildungs-
effect: to no ~ *16* ohne Erfolg; to **take ~** *16* wirken, Wirkung zeigen
effectiveness *40* Wirksamkeit, Effektivität
efficiency *87F* Leistungsfähigkeit, Wirksamkeit, Wirkungsgrad
effort *11* Anstrengung, Bemühung(en)
either *22* eine/r/s (von beiden)
elders *(pl) 120* ältere Generation, die Erwachsenen
elective subject *22* Wahlfach
electrician *34* Elektriker/in
electronic tag *144T* elektronische Fessel; *18* elektronische Fußfessel
elementary age kid *94* Grundschulkind, Kind im Grundschulalter
eligible: to **be ~ for early parole** *134* für eine vorzeitige, bedingte Haftentlassung infrage kommen
to **eliminate sth** *127* etw eliminieren, etw unterbinden
elimination *162* Ausrottung, Ausschaltung
elsewhere *94* woanders, anderswo
embarrassment *123* Verlegenheit, Peinlichkeit
to **embed sth** *18F* etw integrieren, etw einbetten, etw einbauen
to **emerge** *101* entstehen
emergence *64* Entstehen, Aufkommen
to **emit sth** *78* etw emittieren, etw ausstoßen, etw abstrahlen
emphasis, *pl* **emphases** *141* Betonung, Schwerpunkt, Akzent
to **emphasise sth** *144T* etw betonen, etw hervorheben
to **employ sb** *70* jdn beschäftigen, jdn einstellen *(Personal)*
employer *23* Arbeitgeber/in
employment *148* Anstellung, Beschäftigung, Arbeit
to **enable sb to do sth** *18F* es jdm ermöglichen / jdn befähigen, etw zu tun
enclosure *81* Gehege, Einfriedung
to **encourage sb/sth** *8* jdn/etw fördern, jdn/etw unterstützen
end: to **~ up doing sth** *67* am Ende / schließlich etw tun; to **make ~s meet** *134* über die Runden kommen
endangered *90* bedroht
endeavour *53* Bemühung, Unterfangen
endemic (to) *74T* einheimisch (in), verbreitet (in)
to **endorse sth** *50* für etw werben
endorsement *51* Werbung, Unterstützung
endurance *50* Ausdauer
enforcement: law ~ *98* Gesetzesvollzug, Polizeigewalt
engage: to **~ sb** *102T* jdn fesseln; to **~ with sth** *102T* sich mit etw befassen
engaged *14* eingestellt, beschäftigt; to **become ~ with sth** *99* sich mit etw auseinandersetzen, sich mit etw beschäftigen
engineering: genetic ~ *162* Gentechnik, Gentechnologie
to **enhance sth** *8* etw verbessern, etw aufbessern
enjoyable *18T* angenehm, schön
enjoyment *50* Freude, Vergnügen
enormity: the sheer ~ *137* das ungeheure Ausmaß
enormous *16* enorm, gewaltig
to **enrich (sb's life)** *67* (jds Leben) bereichern
to **enroll** *118* sich einschreiben, sich anmelden
to **ensure sth/that** *78* etw sicherstellen, dafür sorgen, dass
to **enter a competition** *27* an einem Wettkampf/Wettbewerb teilnehmen
entertaining *100* unterhaltsam
entire *14* ganz, vollständig
entitled *66* mit dem Titel
entrepreneur *73* Unternehmer/in
enviable *28* beneidenswert
environmentally friendly *72* umweltfreundlich
to **envy sb** *28* jdn beneiden
equal *22* gleich(berechtigt), ebenbürtig

to **equal sth** *53* etw bedeuten, einer Sache entsprechen
equally *15* gleichermaßen, genauso
equilibrium *8* Gleichgewicht
equipment *49* Ausrüstung, Geräte
equivalent *9* Äquivalent, Entsprechung
era *11* Ära, Epoche
erroneously *(fml)* *107* irrtümlicherweise
to **escape from sth** *25* einer Sache entkommen
essential (to) *43* wesentlich, unerlässlich (für)
to **establish sth** *15* etw herstellen, etw einrichten
estate agent *109* Immobilienmakler/in
esteem: self ~ *145* Selbstachtung, Selbstwertgefühl
to **estimate** *39* schätzen
ethic: (work) ~ *8* (Arbeits-)Ethik, Moral
ethnic *18* ethnisch, Volks-
to **evaluate sth** *13* etw bewerten, etw beurteilen
evasion: tax ~ *134* Steuerhinterziehung
events: turn of ~ *97* Wende der Ereignisse/des Schicksals
eventually *25* letztendlich, schließlich
everyday *27* alltäglich, Alltags-
evidence *18T* Beweise, Beweismittel
to **evolve** *85* sich weiter entwickeln
to **exacerbate sth** *15* etw verschärfen, etw verschlimmern
exactly *17* exakt, genau
to **exaggerate sth** *32T* etw übertreiben
examinee *23* Prüfling
examiner *23* Prüfer/in
exasperation *164* Verzweiflung
to **exceed sth** *84* etw übersteigen
excellence *53* ausgezeichnete Qualität; Spitzenleistung
exception *53* Ausnahme
exceptional *86* außergewöhnlich
excess *80* Überschuss
exchange *10* Austausch(-); **labour ~** *109* Arbeitsvermittlung; to **be quoted on the stock ~** *50* an der Börse notiert werden
to **exchange sth** *8* etw austauschen, etw eintauschen, etw umtauschen
excitement *50* Begeisterung
to **exclude sb/sth** *43* jdn/etw ausschließen
exclusion *120* Ausschluss, Ausschließung
exclusively *11* ausschließlich *(Adv.)*
executive *71* leitende/r Angestellte/r; *150* leitend, Vorstands-, Führungs-
to **exhibit sth** *125* etw zeigen, etw ausstellen
existential *25* existenziell
to **expand sth** *78* etw erweitern, etw expandieren
expectation *130T* Erwartung
expected: to **be ~ to do sth** *46T* etw tun sollen/müssen, es wird erwartet, dass man etw tut
experience: work ~ *22* Praktikum
to **expire** *72* ablaufen, verfallen
explanation *13* Erläuterung, Erklärung
explicit *40* klar, deutlich, ausdrücklich
to **exploit sb** *103* jdn ausnutzen, jdn ausbeuten
exposed: to **be/get ~ to sth** *67* einer Sache ausgesetzt sein, mit etw in Berührung kommen
exposure *100* Ausgesetztsein
to **extend sth** *154* etw erweitern, etw ausdehnen
extended family *120* Großfamilie
extent *46T* Umfang, Ausmaß
extinct: to **become ~** *84* aussterben
extinction *78* Vernichtung, Ausrottung, Aussterben
extract *24* Auszug, Ausschnitt
extra-curricular *24* außerschulisch
to **exude sth** *67* vor etw strotzen, etw ausströmen
eyebrows: to **raise your ~ (at sth)** *81* (über etw) die Stirn runzeln
eyed: (bright)-~ *46T* mit (strahlenden) Augen
eyes: … was still a twinkle in sb's ~ *154* … war für jdn noch Zukunftsmusik

F

faced: to **be ~ with sth** *27* mit etw konfrontiert werden
facial hair *56* Bartwuchs, Gesichtsbehaarung
to **facilitate sth** *9* etw ermöglichen, etw vermitteln, etw vereinfachen
facing sb/sth *32* gegen etw, jdm gegenüber, mit dem Gesicht zu jdm/etw
fact: in ~ *25* tatsächlich, eigentlich
factual *100* Sach-, sachlich
to **fade** *170* nachlassen, schwächer werden; to **~ into the background** *38* in den Hintergrund rücken
to **fail** *104* versagen, scheitern; to **~ sth** *57* etw nicht bestehen, bei etw durchfallen
failure *165* Versagen, Ausfall, Zusammenbruch; **heart ~** *56* Herzversagen
faint *115* schwach, matt
fair *173* Messe
fairly *8* ziemlich, recht
faithful *112* treu, loyal; originalgetreu
fall: to **~ apart** *139* auseinanderfallen, platzen; to **~ on hard times** *148* schwere Zeiten durchleben; to **~ short of sth** *70* etw nicht erreichen, etw nicht erfüllen, hinter etw zurückbleiben
famine *117* Hungersnot
fan *75* Ventilator
fancy-free: footloose and ~ *123* frei und ungebunden
far: as ~ as … go(es) *18* was … betrifft/angeht
farming *74T* Anbau (landwirtschaftlicher Produkte), Landwirtschaft
to **fast forward** *94* vorspulen
fast track *11* Überholspur, der schnellste Weg
fat *36* dick, fett, Fett; **(un)saturated ~** *36* (un)gesättigte Fettsäure
fatigue *56* Müdigkeit
fattening *36* dick machend
fatty *20* fetthaltig, fett
favour: in ~ of sb/sth *19F* zugunsten von jdm/etw, für jdn/etw
to **favour sb/sth** *31* jdn/etw bevorzugen
feared: it is ~ lost *74T* es wird befürchtet, dass er/sie/es verloren ist
fearful *151* ängstlich
feasible *74* machbar, möglich
to **feature sth** *24* etw zeigen
federation *50* Verband, Föderation
fee *60T* Gebühr
to **feed sb (with) information** *99* jdn mit Informationen versorgen
fellow *38* Mit-, andere
to **fence sth in** *84* etw einzäunen
fermentation *90* Gärung
fertile *113* fruchtbar
fertilizer *74T* Dünger, Düngemittel; **compound ~** *74T* Komplexdünger, Mehrnährstoffdünger
fibre *36* Ballaststoffe
fiction *10* Belletristik, Prosa(literatur); **non-~** *10* Sachliteratur, Sachbücher
to **fiddle** *32* (an etw) herumfummeln
to **fidget** *32* zappeln
figure *46T* Zahl, Ziffer
to **figure sth out** *67* etw herausfinden
filing cabinet *109* Aktenschrank
financial: ~ reward *50* (finanzielle) Entlohnung, Entgelt; **~ viability** *74T* finanzielle Realisierbarkeit, Durchführbarkeit
findings *(pl)* *10* Ergebnisse
fingerprint *57* Fingerabdruck
fingertips: at your ~ *99* zur Hand
finish *35* Ende, Ziel
fire brigade *31* Feuerwehr
to **fire on sb/sth** *172T* auf jdn/etw schießen
firm *32* fest, sicher
first: ~ and foremost *120* vor allem, in erster Linie; **in the ~ place** *134* überhaupt (erst mal), am Anfang (schon), an erster Stelle
to **fit in** *22* sich anpassen, sich einfügen
to **fix sth** *51* etw festlegen, etw reparieren
fixed *155* feste(r,s), festgelegte(r,s)
fizzy drink *36* Erfrischungsgetränk (mit Kohlensäure)
flashy *123* auffällig, protzig
to **flatline** *158* stagnieren
flatmate *104* Mitbewohner/in *(in einer WG)*
to **flavour sth** *112* etw aromatisieren, etw würzen
flawed *85* fehlerhaft, mangelhaft

to **flee (from sb/sth)** *105* (vor jdm/etw) flüchten, (vor jdm/etw) fliehen
fleet *80* Flotte
to **flex (your muscles)** *95* (die Muskel) spielen lassen
to **flick** *26* schnippen, schnipsen
flight: return ~ *33* (Hin- und) Rückflug
to **flip** *123* (sich) umdrehen
to **flock** *64* strömen
to **flourish** *50* florieren, blühen, gedeihen
flow: the ebb and ~ *116* das Auf und Ab, das Kommen und Gehen
fluent *33* *(Sprache:)* fließend
fluid *36* Flüssigkeit
flurry: in a ~ *108* hektisch, aufgeregt
to **focus on sth** *11* sich auf etw konzentrieren
to **fold your arms** *32T* die Arme verschränken
follow: to **~ sth up (with sth)** *104* (etw) einer Sache folgen lassen, etw weiterverfolgen (mit etw); to **~ suit** *46T* gleichziehen
following *50* Anhängerschaft
follow-up *123* Folge-, Nachfolger
fond: to **be ~ of sb/sth** *99* jdn gernhaben, etw mögen
to **fool around** *9* herumblödeln, Unsinn machen
footage *144T* Film-/Bildmaterial
footloose and fancy-free *123* frei und ungebunden
footprint *90* Fußabdruck
footsteps: in sb's ~ *18F* in jds Fußstapfen
to **forbid** *47* verbieten, untersagen
force *72* Kraft, Macht; **the ~s** *(pl)* *109* die Streitkräfte
forceful *172* überzeugend, eindringlich
forefront: at the ~ *87F* an der Spitze, in vorderster Reihe
foreigner *88T* Ausländer/in
foremost: first and ~ *120* vor allem, in erster Linie
to **foresee sth** *151* etw voraussehen, etw vorhersehen
to **forgo sth** *75* auf etw verzichten
formation *65* Entwicklung, Bildung
former: the ~ *15* Ersteres
forth: and so ~ *32T* und so weiter
fortnight *43* zwei Wochen, vierzehn Tage
fortress *94* Festung
forward: to **put sth ~** *103* (Argument/Vorschlag) vorbringen, etw zur Diskussion stellen
to **fossilize** *42* fossilisieren (lassen), versteinern (lassen)
to **foster sth** *9* etw fördern
foul *52* scheußlich, unanständig
to **found sth** *60T* etw gründen
foundation *80* Stiftung
founder *112* Gründer/in
to **frame sb/sth** *20* jdn/etw (um) rahmen
frantic *155* hektisch, fieberhaft
fraud *61F* Betrug
freelance *101F* freiberuflich
to **frequent (a place)** *123* (einen Ort) häufig besuchen, frequentieren
freshwater *84* Süßwasser-
frightening *30* beängstigend
frugal *67* genügsam, bescheiden
fuel *78* Brennstoff
to **fuel sth** *151* etw anheizen, etw anfachen
to **fulfil sth** *156* etw erfüllen, etw ausführen
to **fund sth** *52* etw finanzieren
funds *(pl)* *74T* Gelder
to **funnel** *11* strömen (lassen), fließen (lassen)
further education *22* Weiterbildung
to **further sth** *68* etw fördern
furthermore *83* darüber hinaus
fuss: to **make a ~** *132* sich anstellen, Umstände machen

G

gadget *15* Gerät, technischer Krimskrams
gain *70* Gewinn, Vorteil; **(weight) ~** *36* (Gewichts-)Zunahme
gain: to **~ ground** *120* Boden gutmachen; to **gain sth** *18T* etw erwerben, etw erlangen
gallery walk *10* Galerierundgang
to **gamble** *51* spielen, zocken
gambler *51* Spieler/in, Zocker/in
game: sth is the ~-changer *154* etw bringt die (Spiel-)Wende; to **be back in the ~** *16* wieder dabei sein, wieder im Geschäft sein; to **have a ~ of …** *16* … (zusammen) spielen
garment *(fml)* *32T* Kleidungsstück
to **gather pace** *160* Fahrt aufnehmen
gathering *123* Versammlung, Treffen
gaze *32T* Blick
GCSE (= General Certificate of Secondary Education) *31* Prüfung für Schüler/innen ab 15, mittlerer Schulabschluss
gear change *155* Gangwechsel *(Schaltvorgang beim Auto/Fahrrad)*
gender *18* Geschlecht
generalisation *127* Verallgemeinerung
generation gap *92* Generationsunterschied, Generationenkonflikt
generic *169* generisch, allgemein, typisch
genetic engineering *162* Gentechnik, Gentechnologie
genetically: GM (~ modified) *162* genmanipuliert
genial *108* freundlich, herzlich
genuine *25* echt, wirklich, aufrichtig
geothermal power *89* Erdwärme
gesture *32T* Geste
get: to **~ sth** *95* etw verstehen, etw kapieren; to **~ the message across** *16* die Botschaft rüberbringen
giant *16* Riese/Riesin
give: to **not ~ a damn** *(infml)* *124* sich einen Dreck scheren
given (that) … *155* vorausgesetzt, dass … / angesichts der Tatsache, dass …
glacier *78* Gletscher
globe *64* Globus
glorification *127* Verherrlichung
to **glorify sth** *17* etw verherrlichen, etw glorifizieren
glorious *108* ruhmreich, herrlich, fantastisch
to **glow** *14* leuchten
glum *28* verdrießlich
GM (genetically modified) *162* genmanipuliert
go: to **~ a long way toward(s) doing sth** *11* zu einer Sache viel beitragen; **as far as … ~(es)** *18* was … betrifft/angeht
goal *144T* Ziel, Absicht
goalie *54T* Torwart/in
goggles *(pl)* *49* Schutzbrille; Ski-/Taucherbrille
goods *(pl)* *115* Waren, Güter
to **govern sth** *56* etw regieren, etw verwalten, etw führen
to **grab hold of ab/sth** *95* jdn/etw ergreifen, jdn/etw packen
grace: to **say ~** *105T* das Tischgebet sprechen
graciously: to **lose ~** *54T* mit Anstand verlieren
grade *(AE)* *23* Note
grain *42* Getreide
granted: to **take sth for ~** *120* etw als selbstverständlich betrachten
grape *74T* (Wein-)Traube
graph *13* Diagramm, Kurve
graphic *40* anschaulich
grasp: to **have a (good) ~ of sth** *68* etw (gut) beherrschen
to **grasp sth** *173F* etw begreifen, etw (er)greifen, etw beim Schopf packen
grass-roots: at (the) ~ level *50* an der Basis
greed *134* Gier, Habgier
greenhouse *78* Treibhaus
to **greet sb** *32* jdn (be)grüßen
grid *12* Schema, Tabelle; *80* Versorgungsnetz
grip *32T* Griff
grocery store *(AE)* *39* Lebensmittelgeschäft
grocery bag *40* Einkaufstasche
to **groom sth** *32T* etw bürsten, etw putzen, etw striegeln
gross domestic product (GDP) *64* Bruttosozialprodukt
ground: to **gain ~** *120* Boden gutmachen
grounded *11* geerdet, vernünftig, selbstsicher
to **guarantee sth** *9* etw garantieren
guardian *144T* Vormund
guess: sth is anyone's ~ *154* etw wissen die Götter

guidance *15* Anleitung, Hilfestellung
guideline *15* Richtlinie
guilt *155* Schuld(gefühle)
guilty *57* schuldig; to **plead ~** *144T* sich schuldig bekennen
gumshield *(BE) 49* Mundschutz, Zahnschutz
gym *13* Sportstudio, Fitnessstudio
gymnasium *55* Sporthalle

H

habitat *64* natürlicher Lebensraum
habitual *95* gewohnheitsmäßig, Gewohnheits-
habitualized: to **become/be ~ (to sth)** *40* sich (an etw) gewöhnen / (an etw) gewöhnt sein
to **haggle (with sb over sth)** *67* (mit jdm um etw) feilschen
hamlet *88T* Weiler, kleines Dorf
hand: (the task) at ~ *124* die vorliegende Aufgabe
to **hand sth over** *172T* etw übergeben, etw überantworten
handbag *133* Handtasche
to **handle sth** *163* mit etw umgehen, etw handhaben
handling *128* Umgang, Handhabung
handshake *32* Händedruck
hands-on *15* praktisch, praxisnah
handy: to **come in ~** *68* sich als nützlich erweisen, gelegen kommen
hang: to **~ from** *15* hängen an; to **~ on to sth** *105T* sich an etw festhalten, sich an etw festklammern; to **~ sth up** *41* etw aufhängen; to **~ tight** *32T* ruhig abwarten
happy: a ~ medium *16* ein goldener Mittelweg
to **harass sb** *93* jdn schikanieren, jdn belästigen
harassment *92* Schikane, Mobbing, Belästigung
hard: to **fall on ~ times** *148* schwere Zeiten durchleben
hardly *104* kaum
harm *40* (körperlicher) Schaden; **in ~'s way** *172T* in Gefahr
harmful (to) *44* schädlich, schlecht (für)
harmfulness *43* Schädlichkeit
to **harmonize** *123* harmonieren, in Einklang stehen, mehrstimmig singen
to **harness** *87F* an-/einspannen, nutzen
harvest *108* Ernte
hatred *59* Hass, Abscheu
hazardous waste *78* Sondermüll
head start *99* Vorsprung
head of state *158T* Staatsoberhaupt
headdress *74T* Kopfschmuck
health: ill ~ *19* schlechter Gesundheitszustand; **mental ~** *127* psychische/seelische Gesundheit
heart: ~ failure *56* Herzversagen; **open-~ surgery** *123* Operation am offenen Herzen; **to your ~'s content** *8* nach Herzenslust; to **lose ~** *158T* den Mut verlieren
heart rate *18* Herzfrequenz, Puls
hell: all ~ would break loose *109* hier wäre der Teufel / die Hölle los
to **help sb out** *17* jdm (aus)helfen
to **herald sth** *150* etw ankündigen, etw einläuten
high in … *36* reich an …, mit hohem …-Gehalt
to **highlight sth** *8* etw hervorheben
high-profile *58* prominent, mit hohem Bekanntheitsgrad
to **hint at sth** *86* auf etw hindeuten
to **hire sb** *130T* jdn engagieren, jdn anstellen
Hispanic *114* Amerikaner/in lateinamerikanischer oder spanischer Herkunft
historian *113* Historiker/in
hold: to **~ on** *76* warten; to **~ sb accountable (for sth)** *100* jdn (für etw) zur Rechenschaft ziehen
hold: to **grab ~ of ab/sth** *95* jdn/etw ergreifen, jdn/etw packen
hole *20* Loch
holistic *158T* ganzheitlich
holy *64* heilig
homeland *112* Heimat(land)
homeschooling *22* Heimunterricht
honour *120* Ehre
horrified *125* entsetzt
hospitable *84* gastfreundlich
hospitality *33* Hotel- und Gaststättengewerbe
host: a ~ of *33* eine Menge
to **host sth** *50* etw ausrichten
hostility *108* Feindseligkeit
hours: waking ~ *(pl) 14* die Stunden, in denen man wach ist
household *78* Haushalt, Haushalts-
housing *90* Wohnungsbau, Wohnungen
to **huddle** *105T* sich zusammendrängen
human trafficker *106* Schleuser/in, Menschenhändler/in
human rights *(pl) 172T* Menschenrechte
humane *134* human, menschenwürdig
humanity *78* Menschheit, Menschlichkeit
humankind *150* (die) Menschheit
hunter-gatherer *42* Jäger und Sammler
to **hurl insults (at sb)** *126* (jdn) beschimpfen, (jdn) beleidigen

I

i.e. (= that is) *69* d. h. (= das heißt)
iconic *123* kultig, Kult-
icy *46* eiskalt, eisig, vereist
idiom *17* Redewendung
idle *8* ungenutzt, müßig, faul
ill health *19* schlechter Gesundheitszustand
illicit *62* illegal, verboten
illiteracy *145* Analphabetismus
illness *13* Krankheit
to **illustrate sth** *7* etw zeigen, etw veranschaulichen
imaginary *32T* imaginär, (frei) erfunden
imagination *8* Phantasie, Vorstellungskraft
immature *144T* unreif
to **immerse yourself in sth** *67* in etw eintauchen, sich in etw vertiefen
impact *10* Einfluss, Auswirkung
to **impact on/upon sth** *127* sich auf etw auswirken
impatience *15* Ungeduld
impetus *53* Impuls, Anstoß
to **implement sth** *47* etw einführen, etw umsetzen, etw einsetzen
to **imply sth** *11* etw andeuten, etw nahelegen
to **impose sth on sb** *25* jdm etw auferlegen
impression *30* Eindruck
impressive *88* beeindruckend, eindrucksvoll
to **imprison sb** *136* jdn inhaftieren
improbability *153* Unwahrscheinlichkeit
improvement (in/to) sth *101F* Verbesserung bei etw
impure *79* unrein, unanständig
in: ~ that … *15* insofern, als …; **six weeks ~** *42* sechs Wochen nach Beginn *(von etw)*
inactivity *19* Untätigkeit, Trägheit, Inaktivität
inadequate *158* mangelhaft, unzureichend
incapacitated *164* arbeitsunfähig, behindert
incentive *71* Anreiz
incident *102F* Vorfall, Begebenheit
to **incinerate sth** *78* etw verbrennen
to **include sb/sth** *27* jdn/etw einbeziehen, jdn/etw einschließen
inclusive: to **be ~ of sb** *74T* jdn miteinbeziehen
income *64* Einkommen
to **incorporate sth (in/into)** *11* etw einbeziehen (in)
increasingly *14* zunehmend, in zunehmendem Maße
indecision *66* Unentschlossenheit
indeed *8* tatsächlich, in der Tat
indelible *92* unlöschbar, nicht entfernbar, unauslöschlich
independent study *22* Selbststudium
to **indicate** *39* (an)zeigen, darauf hindeuten, hinweisen auf
indifferent *105* gleichgültig
indispensable *8* unentbehrlich, unverzichtbar
indistinguishable *154* nicht unterscheidbar
individual *10* einzeln, individuell
indoor *50* im Haus, Innen-
to **indulge in sth** *8* sich etw gönnen, genehmigen

inequality *153* Ungleichheit
inevitably *132* zwangsläufig
inexorable *170* unaufhaltsam
infancy *87F* (frühe) Kindheit
to **inflate sth** *20* etw aufpumpen, etw aufblasen
influx *106* Zustrom
information: ~ sharing *151* Informationsaustausch; to **feed sb (with) ~** *99* jdn mit Informationen versorgen
to **inhabit (a region)** *74T* (eine Region) bewohnen
inhabitant *78* Einwohner/in, Bewohner/in
to **inherit sth** *115* etw erben
initial *68* anfänglich, erste(r,s)
initially *53* anfangs, anfänglich
to **initiate sth** *171* etw einleiten, etw initiieren
to **inject sth** *57* etw injizieren, etw (ein)spritzen
to **injure sb** *133* jdn verletzen
injury *20* Verletzung
innocence *53* Unschuld, Arglosigkeit
innocent *136* unschuldig
to **innovate (sth)** *163* Neuerungen einführen, (etw neu) einführen
innovator *151* Neuerer, Neuerin
insane *26* irrsinnig, verrückt
to **insert sth (in)** *71* etw einführen (in), etw (hin)einstecken (in)
insight (into) *141* Einblick (in), Verständnis (von)
to **insist** *98* darauf bestehen, beteuern
inspector *58* Kontrolleur/in
installation *81* Anlage
instance: for ~ *78* zum Beispiel
instantly *100* sofort, unmittelbar
instructional *11* Lehr-, Schulungs-
to **insulate sth** *90* etw isolieren
to **insult sb** *172* jdn beleidigen
insults: to **hurl ~ (at sb)** *126* (jdn) beschimpfen, (jdn) beleidigen
insurance: medical ~ *33* Krankenversicherung
intake *36* Zufuhr, Aufnahme
to **intend sth** *82* etw beabsichtigen
intended *10* gedacht, vorgesehen
intense *32T* intensiv
intensity *15* Intensität
intent on doing sth *87* entschlossen sein, etw zu tun
to **interact** *22* interagieren, aufeinander eingehen
to **interlock sth (with sth)** *32T* etw (mit etw) verbinden
intern *80* Praktikant/in
internship *32* Praktikum
interrogation *138* Befragung, Verhör
interviewer *32* Person, die ein Vorstellungsgespräch führt
intimate *32T* intim, eng, persönlich
to **introduce** *(a law)* *106* *(ein Gesetz)* einbringen
to **introduce sb to sb/sth** *10* jdm jdn/etw vorstellen
intrusion *15* Eindringen, Störung
invasive *74T* eindringend, invasiv
to **invent sth** *92* etw erfinden, sich etw ausdenken
to **invest sth** *51* etw investieren
to **investigate sth** *99* etw ermitteln, etw untersuchen
investigation *101F* Untersuchung, Nachforschung
investment *74* Investition
to **invigorate** *53* stärken, beleben, anregen
invincible *60T* unbesiegbar
to **involve sb** *88T* jdn (mit) einbeziehen
to **involve sth** *33* etw mit sich bringen, etw umfassen
involvement (in) *53* Engagement (bei), Beteiligung (an), Einbindung (in)
iron *60F* Eisen
issue *8* Streitpunkt, Frage, Problem, Thema
italics *(pl)* *90* Kursivschrift
item *12* Artikel, Gegenstand, Punkt *(auf einer Liste)*
itinerary *64* Reiseroute, Reiseplan

J

jail *137* Gefängnis
to **jam sth somewhere** *154* etw an einen Ort klemmen, (fest) drücken
jar *78* Glas, Gefäß
to **join sb/sth** *39* sich jdm/einer Sache anschließen
to **jostle** *154* (sich) drängeln
joyous *46T* froh, freudig
judge *134* Richter/in; to **~** *172T* (be)urteilen, ermessen
judging by … *20* … nach zu urteilen, … nach zu schließen
judgment *95* Urteilsvermögen, Urteil, Einschätzung
to **juggle sth** *154* etw miteinander vereinbaren, (mit) etw jonglieren
juicy *35* saftig
to **jumble sth up** *102F* etw (kunterbunt) durcheinanderwerfen
to **jump on the bandwagon** *92* auf den fahrenden Zug aufspringen
junior *(AE)* *123* *Schüler/in im vorletzten Schuljahr*
jury *137* die Geschworenen
just about *(infml)* *132* nahezu, so ziemlich
justice *138* Gerechtigkeit
to **justify sth** *7* etw begründen, etw rechtfertigen
juvenile *134* Jugend-, jugendlich

K

keen: to **be ~ on sth** *8* auf etw versessen/scharf sein, etw gerne haben/tun
to **keep to sth** *13* sich an etw halten, etw einhalten, bei etw bleiben
kennels *(pl)* *18F* (Hunde-)Zuchtbetrieb
key: ~ card *71* Schlüsselkarte; **~ stage 2** *46T* *(GB:) die Grundschuljahrgänge 3 – 6 für Schüler/innen zwischen 7 und 11 Jahren*
keyword *68* Schlagwort, Schlüsselwort
kick: to **~ against sth** *(infml)* *71* gegen etw aufmucken, sich gegen etw wehren; to **~ back** *18* abschalten, relaxen; **alive and ~ing** *51* gesund und munter
kidney *56* Niere
killer: serial ~ *32T* Serienmörder/in
to **knock off** *(infml)* *155* Feierabend machen
knowledge *22* Wissen, Kenntnis(se)
knowledgeable *144T* bewandert, kenntnisreich
known: it is ~ to be/do … *9* man weiß, dass es … ist/tut

L

labor: Bureau of Labor Statistics *32T* *(USA)* Agentur für Arbeitsstatistiken
laboratory *164* Labor
labour exchange *109* Arbeitsvermittlung
to **lack sth** *134* etw nicht haben
lack (of) *95* Mangel (an)
landfill site *78* Mülldeponie
lap *32T* Schoß; *46T* Runde *(Sport)*
large-scale *43* groß, groß angelegt
to **last** *60T* dauern, andauern, so bleiben
Latino *32* US-Amerikaner/in lateinamerikanischer Abstammung
laughable *99* lächerlich
to **launch sth** *46T* etw ins Leben rufen, etw starten
laureate *102* Preisträger/in
law enforcement *98* Gesetzesvollzug, Polizeigewalt
lawyer *137* (Rechts-)Anwalt/Anwältin
to **lay sth out** *43* etw ausführen, etw niederlegen *(aufschreiben)*
layer *39* Schicht, Ebene
laziness *15* Faulheit, Trägheit
lead: to **~ (to)** *14* führen (zu), leiten; to **~ sb astray** *144T* jdn vom rechten Weg abbringen
lead researcher *39* Forschungsleiter/in
leadership *46T* Führung
leakage *165* Leck, Austreten
lean *36* schlank, hager, mager *(Fleisch)*
leap *162* Sprung
lease *70* Mietvertrag, Pachtvertrag; *88T* Miete, Pacht
to **leave a lot to be desired** *149* sehr/viel zu wünschen übrig lassen
to **lecture sb** *141* jdm einen Vortrag halten
legal proceedings *(pl)* *139* Gerichtsverfahren, gerichtliche Schritte
legislator *39* Mitglied der Legislative, Abgeordnete/r
leisure *7* Freizeit, Muße
lenient *134* milde, nachsichtig

Lent *35* (die) Fastenzeit
lentil *42* Linse *(Lebensmittel)*
to **lessen sth** *18T* etw mindern, etw verringern
letter to the editor *52* Leserbrief
level: at (the) grass-roots ~ *50* an der Basis; **sea ~** *78* Meeresspiegel
to **liaise** *144T* zusammenarbeiten, Bindeglied sein
to **liberate sb** *67* jdn befreien
liberation *120* Befreiung
liberty *105T* Freiheit
life expectancy *43* Lebenserwartung
lifespan *162* Lebensdauer
lifetime *62* lebenslang, (ganzes) Leben
light-hearted *172* heiter, unbekümmert
like: ... and the ~ *71* ... und dergleichen
likely: to **be ~ to do sth** *15* etw wahrscheinlich tun (werden)
to **limit sth** *8* etw begrenzen, etw einschränken
limitation *165* Einschränkung
literal *34* wörtlich, buchstäblich
liveable *84* lebenswert, bewohnbar
lively *172* lebendig, lebhaft, munter
livestock *81* Vieh
living: to **make a ~** *50* seinen Lebensunterhalt verdienen
load: a ~ of sth *(infml)* *28* eine Menge (von etw)
local *64* Einheimische/r; **(~) authority** *46T* (Kommunal-)Behörde
located in/on *33* in/an (... gelegen)
long: in the ~ run *18* auf lange Sicht, langfristig; to **go a ~ way toward(s) doing sth** *11* zu einer Sache viel beitragen
longer: no ~ *15* nicht mehr
long-term *10* langfristig, Langzeit-
loo *(infml)* *112* Klo
loose: all hell would break ~ *109* hier wäre der Teufel / die Hölle los
lose: to **~ graciously** *54T* mit Anstand verlieren; to **~ heart** *158T* den Mut verlieren; to **~ out on sth** *164* bei etw schlecht wegkommen; to **~ out to sb/sth** *(infml)* *157* von jdm/etw verdrängt werden; to **~ weight** *35* abnehmen *(Körpergewicht reduzieren)*; to **~ your touch** *39* nachlassen
loss *42* Verlust
loudspeaker *13* Lautsprecher
to **lower sth** *18* etw senken, etw herabsetzen
luggage *18F* Gepäck
lung *40* Lunge

M

mad on: to **be/go ~ sth** *43* nach etw verrückt sein/werden
magistrate *137* (US) Untersuchungsrichter/in, (GB) Laienrichter/in; **~s' court** *138* Amtsgericht
to **maintain sth** *32T* etw aufrecht erhalten
maize *42* Mais
major *37* Haupt-, wesentlich, größer
majority: vast ~ *53* (bei weitem) größter Teil, Löwenanteil
make: to **~ a contribution** *20* einen Beitrag leisten; to **~ a living** *50* seinen Lebensunterhalt verdienen; to **~ a payment** *150* eine Zahlung vornehmen, leisten; to **~ sense** *43* Sinn ergeben, sinnvoll sein; to **~ sense of sth** *127* etw verstehen, aus etw schlau werden; to **~ sth up** *36* etw erfinden, sich etw ausdenken; to **~ sth your own** *12* sich etw aneignen, sich etw zu eigen machen; to **~ sure** *22* sicherstellen; to **~ the most of sth** *7* das Beste aus etw machen
maker *112* Hersteller/in
makings: to **have the ~ of sth** *130* das Zeug zu etw haben
malfunction *164* Fehlfunktion
mammal *85* Säugetier
to **man sth** *148* etw *(mit Personal)* besetzen, etw bemannen
mandatory *73* verpflichtend, vorgeschrieben, obligatorisch
man-made *89* künstlich, menschlichen Ursprungs
manner *32T* Art, Wesen
manslaughter *133* Totschlag
manual *148* handbetrieben, Hand-, manuell
to **manufacture sth** *174* etw fertigen, etw herstellen
manufacturing *149* Fertigung, Herstellung
manure *80* Dung, Mist
marine *85* Meeres-
marriage *120* Ehe, Heirat
to **marshal sth** *(fml)* *154* etw (an) ordnen, etw arrangieren, etw kontrollieren
to **mask sth** *95* etw verdecken, etw verbergen
to **master sth** *67* etw meistern, etw bewältigen
to **match sth** *172* zu etw passen, mit etwübereinstimmen
match-fixing *50* Spielmanipulation
mate *28* Kumpel, Freund/in
material: ~s science *150* Werkstoffkunde, -wissenschaft; **raw ~** *86* Rohstoff
maternal leave *158* Mutterschaftsurlaub
matter: ... is a ~ of choice *99* ... hat man selbst in der Hand, ... liegt im eigenen Ermessen; **no ~ what/how/who** *11* (ganz) egal, was/wie/wer
mattress *20* Matratze
maturity *67* Reife
meaningless *40* unbedeutend, sinnlos
means, *pl* **means** *64* Möglichkeit, Mittel; **by no ~** *120* keineswegs
measure *40* Maßnahme; to **~** *18T* messen
measurement *130T* Abmessung, Maß
median *113* mittlere/r/s, durchschnittlich
medical insurance *33* Krankenversicherung
medical condition *37* Leiden, Erkrankung
medium, *pl* **media** *14* Medium, Medien; **a happy ~** *16* ein goldener Mittelweg
meet: to **~ sth** *15* *(Bedarf, Norm etc.)* erfüllen, etw befriedigen, einer Sache entsprechen; to **make ends ~** *134* über die Runden kommen
to **melt** *78* schmelzen, abschmelzen
memorandum, *pl* **memoranda** *165* Absichtserklärung
memory (of) *115* Erinnerung (an)
menial *106* niedere(r,s), untergeordnet *(Arbeit)*
mental *10* geistig, psychisch, seelisch; **~ health** *127* psychische/seelische Gesundheit
to **mention sth** *9* etw erwähnen, etw nennen
mere: a ~ ... *95* bloß ..., lediglich ...
merely *14* bloß, nur
to **merge sth** *106* etw verschmelzen, etw mischen
merit *47* Vorzug, Verdienst
message: to **get the ~ across** *16* die Botschaft rüberbringen
meticulous *108* sorgfältig, gewissenhaft, gründlich
mill *60T* Fabrik *(insbesondere Textilfabrik)*
millennials *(pl)* *92* Generation Y *(Generation der zwischen 1980 und 1999 Geborenen)*
mind *28* Geist, Verstand, Gedanken, Denkweise; to **change people's ~s** *38* die Menschen zum Umdenken bewegen; to **change your ~** *138* seine Meinung ändern; to **come to ~** *21* einem einfallen
mind you *109* allerdings
mine *60T* Bergwerk, Mine
mineral *36* Mineral(stoff)
to **mingle (with)** *95* (sich) (ver)mischen (mit), Umgang haben (mit)
mining *149* Bergbau
minor *120* weniger bedeutend, gering(er)
miracle *150* Wunder
miserable *155* erbärmlich, trostlos
misleading *118* irreführend
misplaced *52* fehl am Platz
to **misrepresent sb/sth** *128* jdn/etw falsch darstellen, etw verfälschen
mist *88T* Nebel, Dunst
misunderstanding *137* Missverständnis
to **mitigate sth** *71* etw (ab)mildern
mitigation: in ~ *144T* zur Entlastung
mixture *22* Mischung, Gemisch
to **mock sb** *25* sich über jdn lustig machen
model: role ~ *12* Vorbild
to **model sth** *130* etw vorführen *(z. B. als Fotomodell)*

moderate *15* gemäßigt, maßvoll
modify: to ~ **sth** *14* etw (ver)ändern, etw modifizieren; **GM (genetically modified)** *162* genmanipuliert
to **monitor** *118* überwachen
monotonous *18* eintönig, monoton
mood *36* Stimmung, Laune
moon *168* Mond
moors *(pl)* *18F* Heide(landschaft)
morality *140* Moral *(Wertesystem)*
moreover *40* überdies, zudem
most: to **make the ~ of sth** *7* das Beste aus etw machen
mostly *32* meistens, hauptsächlich
to **motion (to sb)** *32T* (jdm) ein Zeichen geben
mountain range *20* Gebirge, Gebirgszug
mouthguard *(AE)* *49* Mundschutz, Zahnschutz
MP (Member of Parliament) *146* Parlamentsabgeordnete/r
to **murder sb** *26* jdn ermorden
mutual *102* gegenseitig
mythical *74T* mythisch, legendär

N

nail: You ~ed it! *32T* Du hast es geschafft
narcissistic *52* narzisstisch
narrator *24* Erzähler/in
nasty *11* gemein, hässlich, böse
naturopath *43* Naturheilkundige/r
nauseam: ad ~ *95* bis zum Überdruss, bis zum Abwinken
neat *32T* ordentlich, sauber
necessarily: not ~ *64* nicht unbedingt
neck: to **breathe down sb's ~** *54T* jdm im Nacken sitzen
to **neglect sb/sth** *11* jdn/etw vernachlässigen
negligent (about) *104* nachlässig (bei), fahrlässig
to **negotiate sth** *126* über etw verhandeln, etw aushandeln
neither … nor … *16* weder … noch …
nervous breakdown *76* Nervenzusammenbruch
net *151* netto, Netto-
nevertheless *67* trotzdem, dennoch
news: to **break the ~ (to sb)** *92* (jdm) die Nachricht(en) überbringen
newsroom *102T* Nachrichtenredaktion
niche *50* Nische(n-)
nightmare *146* Albtraum
to **nip** *(infml)* *155* schnell irgendwo hingehen, huschen, flitzen
nitrogen *84* Stickstoff
no: ~ longer *15* nicht mehr; **there is ~ doing sth** *13* man kann etw nicht tun, es ist unmöglich etw zu tun
non: ~-fiction *10* Sachliteratur, Sachbücher; **~-profit** *74F* gemeinnützig, nicht auf Gewinn ausgerichtet
nor: neither … ~ … *16* weder … noch …
notable *126* bedeutend, bemerkenswert
notably *141* insbesondere
to **note sth** *14* etw zur Kenntnis nehmen, etw feststellen, etw beachten
noticeable *95* erkennbar, auffällig
notion *70* Vorstellung, Auffassung
novel *24* Roman
novelty *166* Neuheit
nuclear: ~ family *120* Kernfamilie, Kleinfamilie; **~ power station** *90* Kernkraftwerk
nursery school *46* Kindergarten
nutrient *85* Nährstoff
nutrition *36* Nahrung, Ernährung
nutritionist *36* Ernährungswissenschaftler/in, Ernährungsberater/in

O

obedience *120* Gehorsam
obese *36* fettleibig
obesity *19* Fettleibigkeit
to **obey sth** *143* etw beachten, etw befolgen
observation *94* Beobachtung
to **observe sth** *141* etw beobachten
obsessed with *127* besessen von
to **obtain sth** *164* etw erhalten, an etw gelangen
obvious *29* offensichtlich, klar
occasion *94* Anlass, Gelegenheit
occasional *9F* gelegentlich
to **occupy sth** *148* etw einnehmen, etw besetzen, etw innehaben
to **occur** *71* stattfinden, passieren, geschehen
odd *109* gelegentlich
odds: to **be at ~ with sb** *108* mit jdm uneinig sein, sich mit jdm streiten
off *25* seltsam, eigentümlich, befremdlich; **on and ~** *16* mit Unterbrechungen, hin und wieder; to **play people ~ against each other** *129* Menschen gegeneinander ausspielen; to **step ~ the beaten track** *70* ausgetretene Pfade verlassen
offence *134* Straftat, Vergehen
offender *126* Straftäter/in, Übeltäter/in
offensive *95* beleidigend, anstößig
office-holder *51* Amtsinhaber/in
official *50* Beamte/r, Funktionär/in
offspring, *pl* **offspring** *107* Sprössling, Nachwuchs
often: more ~ than not *125* meistens
oftentimes *(AE)* *158T* oftmals
oily *36* ölig, fett
to **omit sth** *127* etw auslassen, etw weglassen
on and off *16* mit Unterbrechungen, hin und wieder
once *67* sobald, wenn (erst); **for ~** *128* ausnahmsweise, dieses eine Mal
one: ~ another *150* einander, sich (gegenseitig); **~ way or another** *11* so oder so, auf die eine oder andere Art
ongoing *120* laufend
on-site *33* vor Ort, im Betrieb
onus *106* Pflicht, Verpflichtung
to **operate sth** *80* etw unterhalten, etw bedienen
opponent *54T* Gegner/in
opportunity *11* Gelegenheit, Möglichkeit, Chance
to **oppose sth** *97* gegen etw opponieren, sich gegen etw widersetzen
opposed: to **be ~ to sth** *43* gegen etw sein
opposite *81* gegenüber (von), gegenüberliegend
opposition *109* Widerstand
oppression *102T* Unterdrückung
opt: to **~ for sth** *118* sich für etw entscheiden; to **~ out of sth** *43* sich gegen etw entscheiden, bei etw nicht mitmachen
ordeal *134* Qual, Tortur
order *25* Reihenfolge, Rangordnung; **in ~ to** *25* um … zu
orienteering *50* Orientierungslauf
to **originate from** *115* kommen aus
ostensibly *155* angeblich, scheinbar
otherwise *20* ansonsten, andernfalls
ought to: it ~ make … *39* es sollte … machen
outcome *13* Ergebnis, Resultat
outdated *107* veraltet, nicht mehr aktuell
to **outdo sb** *118* jdn übertreffen
outdoor (play/sport) *14* (Spiel/Sport) im Freien, draußen
to **outline sth** *55* etw skizzieren, etw grob beschreiben
outlook *8* (Zukunfts-)Aussicht(en)
to **outnumber sth** *112* etw *(zahlenmäßig)* übertreffen
to **outplay sb** *170* besser als jd spielen, jdn an die Wand spielen
outright *95* total, völlig, offen, direkt
outsider *27* Außenseiter/in
outspoken *126* freimütig, direkt, unverblümt
outstanding *129* hervorragend, überragend, außergewöhnlich
outward *120* äußere/r/s, äußerlich
to **outweigh sth** *71* schwerer als etw wiegen
over time *14* im Laufe der Zeit
overall *71* allgemein, insgesamt, im Großen und Ganzen
to **overcome sth** *56* etw überwinden
to **overcook sth** *44* etw verkochen *(zu lange kochen)*, etw verbraten
overcrowded *70* überfüllt, übervölkert
to **overdo (sth)** *15* (es) übertreiben (mit etw)
overdrive: to **go into ~** *84* hochaktiv werden
overhaul *118* Überholung, Revision
to **overlook sth** *74T* etw überblicken
overly *14* allzu
to **override sth** *71* sich über etw hinwegsetzen, etw außer Kraft setzen
to **overstate sth** *71* etw übertreiben

to **overuse sth** *64* etw überstrapazieren, etw übermäßig beanspruchen
overweight *19* Übergewicht, übergewichtig
to **overwhelm sb** *97* jdn überwältigen, jdn überschütten
to **owe sb sth** *98* jdm etw schulden
own: in your ~ right *50* eigenständig; to **make sth your ~** *12* sich etw aneignen, sich etw zu eigen machen
oxygen *57* Sauerstoff
oxymoron *64* Oxymoron, Widerspruch in sich

P

pace *18F* Tempo, Schritt, Geschwindigkeit; to **gather ~** *160* Fahrt aufnehmen
pack *39* Packung
package *(AE)* *18F* Schachtel, Verpackung, Paket; **~ tour** *64* Pauschalreise
to **package sth** *39* etw (ver)packen
packet soup *37* Tütensuppe
pad *108* Notizblock
pain: to **be a ~ (in the arse)** *(infml)* *43* jdm auf die Nerven gehen
painful *108* schmerzhaft, schmerzlich
palm *32T* Hand(fläche)
to **pamper sb** *154* jdn verwöhnen
panacea *155* Allheilmittel, Patentlösung
panel *74T* Platte, Tafel, Kollektor; *145* Gremium, Jury
panel discussion *73* Podiumsdiskussion
paradoxically *8* paradoxerweise
paraphrase *13* Umschreibung
parental *15* Eltern-, elterlich
parole *134* Bewährung; to **be eligible for early ~** *134* für eine vorzeitige, bedingte Haftentlassung infrage kommen
part: to **take ~ (in sth)** *8* (an etw) teilnehmen
participant *42* Teilnehmer/in
to **participate (in sth)** *8* (an etw) teilnehmen, sich (an etw) beteiligen
participation (in) *9* Teilnahme, Beteiligung (an)
particular *22* bestimmt, speziell
particularly *11* besonders, insbesondere
partner *157* Gesellschafter/in, Teilhaber/in
partnership: registered ~ *120* eingetragene Partnerschaft
part-time *29* Teilzeit-
passer-by *95* Passant/in
passion *8* Leidenschaft
passionate *9* leidenschaftlich
pastry *36* Teig, Gebäck(stück)
pathetic *25* erbärmlich, jämmerlich
patrol *146* Streife, Rundgang
patron *71* Gast *(z. B. Hotel)*, Besucher/in *(z. B. Konzert)*, Kunde/Kundin
paycheck *(AE)* *147* Gehalt(sscheck)
payment: to **make a ~** *150* eine Zahlung vornehmen, leisten
peace *102* Frieden
pedalo *74F* Tretboot
to **pen sb in** *105* jdn einpferchen, jdn einsperren
penalty *144* Strafe
penchant *126* Vorliebe, Schwäche
pension *104* Rente, Pension
pensioner *106* Rentner/in
to **perceive sth** *100* etw wahrnehmen, etw erkennen
percentage *116* Prozentsatz, Anteil
perception *98* Wahrnehmung
performance *24* Vorstellung, Aufführung
period *22* (Unterrichts-)Stunde; *25* Zeit(raum), Periode
permission *174* Erlaubnis, Genehmigung
to **permit sth** *166* etw erlauben
persecution *106* Verfolgung
personal statement *22* Selbstbeschreibung
perspective: to **put sth in ~** *11* etw relativieren, etw ins rechte Licht rücken
to **persuade sb** *38* jdn überreden, jdn überzeugen
pervasive *151* um sich greifend, durchdringend
pervasiveness *151* Verbreitung
petroleum *87F* Erdöl
petty crime *134* Kleinkriminalität, Bagatelldelikt
physical *8* körperlich, physisch
pick: to **~ at sth** *32* an etw herumzupfen; to **~ sth up** *68* etw aufschnappen, sich etw aneignen
to **pile sth on** *28* etw aufstapeln
to **pin sth (to a place)** *103* etw (an einem Ort) befestigen, etw (an einen Ort) heften, stecken
to **pinch sb** *109* jdn kneifen
to **pinpoint sth** *84* etw genau lokalisieren, etw feststellen
pint *76* Glas Bier (ca. ein halber Liter), Halbe
to **pioneer sth** *74T* etw zum ersten Mal anwenden, etw entwickeln
pipe *88T* Rohr(leitung), Röhre
pitch *49* Platz, Spielfeld
place: in the first ~ *134* überhaupt (erst mal), am Anfang (schon), an erster Stelle
placement: work ~ *22* Praktikum
plain *32T* einfach, schlicht
plant *81* Fabrik, Werk, Anlage, Kraftwerk
play: to **~ people off against each other** *129* Menschen gegeneinander ausspielen; **All work and no ~ makes Jack a dull boy.** *8* Arbeit alleine macht (auch) nicht glücklich. *(Sprichwort)*
to **plead guilty** *144T* sich schuldig bekennen
pleasure *9* Vergnügen, Freude
to **pledge** *57* sich verpflichten
plentiful *25* reichlich, im Überfluss (vorhanden)
plenty (of) *165* reichlich, viel
ploughshare *114* Pflugschar
plumbing *114* Klempnerei, Sanitär
point: to **~ sth out** *15* auf etw hinweisen; **tipping ~** *85* Kipppunkt, kritischer Punkt, Wendepunkt; to **have a valid ~** *172T* ganz Recht haben, einen berechtigtes Argument vorbringen
pointless *53* zwecklos, sinnlos
poison *133* Gift
poisonous *79* giftig
to **police sth** *140* etw überwachen, etw kontrollieren
to **polish sth** *31* etw (auf)polieren
poll *8* Umfrage
pollutant *87F* Schadstoff
to **pollute sth** *74T* etw verschmutzen
pollution *18F* (Umwelt-)Verschmutzung
poor *19* schlecht, mangelhaft
pope *93* Papst
populous *123* bevölkerungsreich
portable *71* tragbar
to **pose sth** *56* etw darstellen
to **position sb/sth** *127* jdn/etw platzieren, jdn/etw (auf)stellen
to **possess sth** *135* etw besitzen
possession *30* Besitz, Besitztum
post *148* (Arbeits-)Stelle, Posten
poverty *63* Armut
power: ~ station *78* Kraftwerk; **geothermal ~** *89* Erdwärme; **nuclear ~ station** *90* Kernkraftwerk; to **cut ~** *164* den Strom abstellen
powerful *12* stark, mächtig, kräftig
powerhouse *88T* treibende Kraft
practice: common ~ *120* gängige/übliche Praxis; to **put sth into ~** *38* etw in die Praxis umsetzen
practitioner *53* Fachmann/frau, Praktizierende/r
prankster *95* Witzbold
to **pray** *109* beten
prayer *18T* Gebet
to **preach sth** *141* etw predigen
to **precede sth** *150* einer Sache vorausgehen, einer Sache vorangehen
precedent *150* Präzedenzfall, Beispiel, Tradition
precious *7* wertvoll, kostbar
preconception *130T* vorgefasste Meinung, Vorstellung
predator *85* Raubtier
predecessor *100* Vorgänger/in, Vorläufer/in
predictable *126* voraussagbar, vorhersehbar
predominantly *113* überwiegend
preferable to sth *156* besser als etw
preference *32T* Präferenz, Vorliebe
pregnant *140* schwanger
prehistoric *42* vorgeschichtlich, prähistorisch
premier *33* führend; erstklassig

premise *25* Prämisse, Voraussetzung
premises *(pl) 47* Betrieb(sräume), Geschäft(sräume), (Betriebs-)Gelände
prepared: to **be ~ to do sth** *7* bereit sein, etw zu tun
to **present sth** *12* etw vorstellen, etw präsentieren
preservation *79* Erhaltung, Bewahrung
to **preserve sth** *70* etw bewahren, etw erhalten
presidency *118* Präsidentschaft
to **presume sth** *67* etw annehmen, etw vermuten, etw voraussetzen
pretty much *16* (so) ziemlich, fast
to **prevail** *120* (vor)herrschen; *168* siegen, sich durchsetzen
to **prevent sb from doing sth** *11* jdn davon abhalten, etw zu tun
to **prevent sth** *36* etw (ver)hindern, einer Sache vorbeugen
preventable *39* vermeidbar
prevention *40* Prävention, Prophylaxe
previous *33* vorherig, früher
priced: reasonably ~ *163* zu einem vernünftigen Preis
priceless *50* unbezahlbar, von unschätzbarem Wert
pricey *88T* kostspielig, teuer
pride *52* Stolz
primal *42* ursprünglich, Ur-, urweltlich
primarily *53* vorrangig, hauptsächlich
primary *84* Haupt-, hauptsächlich; **~ education** *22* Primarstufe, Grundschulausbildung; **~ school** *46* Grundschule
principle *32T* Grundsatz, Prinzip
prior to *33* vor *(zeitlich)*
to **prioritize sth** *11* etw der Wichtigkeit nach ordnen, etw priorisieren
priority *74T* Priorität, Vorrang
prisoner *138* Strafgefangene/r
privacy *91* Privatsphäre
probation *134* Bewährung
process *22* Ablauf, Vorgang, Prozess
process: ~ed food *36* industriell verarbeitete Lebensmittel; to **process sth** *37* etw (weiter)verarbeiten
production line *148* Fließband, Fertigungsband
profession *22* Beruf
proficiency *92* Können, Kenntnisse, Fähigkeiten
profit: non-~ *74F* gemeinnützig, nicht auf Gewinn ausgerichtet
profound *87F* tief greifend, tief gehend, fundiert
to **programme sth** *42* etw programmieren
to **progress** *22* vorankommen, weiterkommen
to **project sth** *134* etw vermitteln
prolongation *150* Verlängerung
prominent *114F* bekannt, bedeutend
to **promote sth** *64* etw fördern, etw unterstützen
prompt *130* Stichwort, Vorgabe
to **pronounce sth** *83* etw aussprechen
to **propagate sth** *(fml) 151* etw propagieren, etw verbreiten
proper *23* ordentlich, angemessen
property *70* Grundstück, Eigentum an Grund und Boden
prophecy: self-fulfilling ~ *169* selbsterfüllende Prophezeiung
proposal *18* Vorschlag
to **propose sth** *39* etw vorschlagen, etw unterbreiten, etw darlegen
prosecutor *134* Staatsanwalt/-anwältin, Ankläger/in
prospect *68* Aussicht, Perspektive
prospective *164* (zu)künftig, potenziell
to **prosper** *113* florieren, gedeihen
prosperity *115* Wohlstand
protection *79* Schutz
protein *36* Eiweiß, Protein
to **prove** *53* sich erweisen (als)
provide: to **~ for sb/sth** *147* für jdn/etw sorgen; to **~ sb with sth** *18F* jdn mit etw versorgen, ausstatten; to **~ sth** *36* etw (an)bieten, etw zur Verfügung stellen
provision *64* Bereitstellung, Versorgung
psychiatric *15* psychiatrisch
psychiatrist *7* Psychiater/in
psychologist *18* Psychologe/-in
public health *39* öffentliches Gesundheitswesen
to **publicise sth** *126* auf etw aufmerksam machen
to **publish sth** *39* etw veröffentlichen
pulp *78 (Papier-, Holz-)* Brei
to **punch sb** *140* jdn schlagen
to **punish sb** *60* jdn bestrafen
punishment *57* Strafe, Bestrafung
to **purchase sth** *(fml) 130T* etw kaufen
purpose *23* Absicht, Zweck; **~-built** *18F* eigens dafür gebaut, speziell entwickelt; to **serve a ~** *99* einem Zweck dienen
to **pursue sth** *8* einer Sache nachgehen, etw verfolgen
pursuit *8* Betätigung, Beschäftigung; **in ~ of sth** *64* beim Streben nach etw, auf der Suche nach etw
pushy *32T* penetrant, Druck ausübend
pussy bow *130T* Schleifenkragen (an Blusen)
put: to **~ it** *154* es formulieren, es ausdrücken; to **~ on weight** *36* zunehmen *(Körpergewicht erhöhen)*; to **~ sth forward** *103* (Argument/Vorschlag) vorbringen, etw zur Diskussion stellen; to **~ sth into practice** *38* etw in die Praxis umsetzen; to **~ up with sth** *71* sich mit etw abfinden, etw ertragen
puzzle *18T* Rätsel, Puzzle

Q

to **quadruple** *84* (sich) vervierfachen
to **question sth** *47* etw infrage stellen
queue *33* Warteschlange
quota *106* Kontingent, Quote
quote *7* Zitat
quoted: to **be ~ on the stock exchange** *50* an der Börse notiert werden

R

race *127* Abstammung, Rasse
racial *106* rassisch, Rassen-
racket *49* Schläger *(Tennis, Squash)*
RAF (= Royal Air Force) *109 britische Luftwaffe*
to **raid a place** *94* einen Ort überfallen, durchsuchen
railway *133* Eisenbahn
raise: to **~ (children)** *120* (Kinder) erziehen, aufziehen; to **~ sth** *15* etw erhöhen, etw (an)heben, etw steigern; to **~ your eyebrows (at sth)** *81* (über etw) die Stirn runzeln
rampage *141* Randale
random *46T* zufällig, beliebig
range *22* Bereich, Bandbreite, Palette; **mountain ~** *20* Gebirge, Gebirgszug
to **rank sb/sth** *133* jdn/etw einstufen, jdn/etw (ein-)ordnen
ranking *51* Rangfolge; **~ (list)** *12* Rangliste
rant, rape *133* Vergewaltigung
to **rant (about sth)** *95* (über etw) schimpfen
rate *19* Rate, Quote, Anteil; **at a ~ of …** *98* mit einer Geschwindigkeit von …
rather than *23* anstatt
to **rave** *95* toben, phantasieren, wirres Zeug reden
ravenous *87* ausgehungert
raw material *86* Rohstoff
to **reach an agreement** *31* übereinkommen
to **react (to)** *27* reagieren (auf)
readership *96* Leserschaft
realm *164* Bereich
reasonable *97* vernünftig; **reasonably priced** *163* zu einem vernünftigen Preis
reasoning *99* Argumentation, Logik
to **recall sth** *95* sich an etw erinnern
to **receive sth** *34* etw erhalten, etw empfangen
recent *50* jüngst, aktuell
recently *52* kürzlich, in letzter Zeit
receptive (to sth) *165* (etw gegenüber) aufgeschlossen
recipient *126* Empfänger/in
recognition *126* (An-)Erkennung, (Wieder-)Erkennen; to **modify sth beyond ~** *14* etw so verändern, dass es nicht wiederzuerkennen ist
recognizable (by) *74T* (wieder)erkennbar (an)

to **reconcile sth (with sth)** 155 etw (mit etw) vereinbaren
record: to **put the ~ straight** 28 etw gerade rücken, etw klarstellen
to **record sth** 18T etw dokumentieren, etw verzeichnen, etw aufzeichnen
to **recover** 8 sich erholen
recreation 60T Freizeit, Erholung
recreational 157 Freizeit-, Erholungs-
to **recruit sb** 33 jdn anwerben, jdn neu einstellen
reduction 141 Verringerung, Senkung
redundant: to **be made ~** 159 entlassen werden, den Arbeitsplatz verlieren
refer: to **~ sb to sb/sth** 32T jdm jdn überweisen, jdn an etw verweisen; to **~ to sth** 15 sich auf etw beziehen
reflect: to **~ sth** 92 etw reflektieren, etw widerspiegeln; to **~ upon sth** 28 etw reflektieren, über etw nachdenken
reflection 78 Spiegelbild
reformed 42 geläutert, ehemalig
refrigerator 103 Kühlschrank
refusal 30 Ablehnung, Verweigerung
to **refuse to do sth** 104 sich weigern etw zu tun
to **refute** 69 widerlegen, zurückweisen, bestreiten
to **regard sth (as)** 74 etw ansehen, etw betrachten (als)
regardless of sth 120 ungeachtet einer Sache
register: ~ed partnership 120 eingetragene Partnerschaft; to **not ~** 137 nicht wahrgenommen werden
to **reintroduce sth** 74T etw wieder einführen, etw wieder heimisch machen
to **reinvent sth** 154 etw wieder/neu erfinden
rejection 28 Ablehnung
to **rejuvenate sth** 81 etw verjüngen
to **relate to sb/sth** 150 einen Bezug zu jdm/etw haben, mit jdm/etw in Zusammenhang stehen
related: to **be ~ to sth** 23 mit etw in Zusammenhang stehen
relation 165 Beziehung, Verhältnis
release 10 Befreiung; to **~ sb/sth** 78 etw freisetzen, jdn entlassen
relevance: to **be of ~** 172T von Bedeutung sein
to **relieve sth** 11 etw erleichtern, *(Druck)* verringern, etw lindern
to **relocate** 148 umziehen, umsiedeln
to **rely on sb/sth** 67 sich auf jdn/etw verlassen
to **remain** 10 bleiben
remainder 81 Rest(bestand)
remains *(pl)* 42 (Über-)Reste, Relikte
remarkably 42 erstaunlicherweise
remedial class 116 Förderklasse
reminder 74 Erinnerung, Mahnung
remotely 150 aus der Ferne
to **remove sth** 15 etw entfernen, etw beseitigen
to **rename sb/sth** 113 jdn/etw umbenennen, jdn/etw umtaufen
rendition 32T Vortrag
renewable 71 erneuerbar
rental 64 Verleih, Vermietung
reparation 144 Entschädigung, Wiedergutmachung
repetitive 32T sich ständig wiederholend, *(z.B. Arbeit)* monoton
to **replace sth** 12 etw ersetzen, etw austauschen
replacement 108 Ersatz, Ersetzung, Austausch
to **represent sth** 7 etw ausmachen, etw darstellen
representative 144T Vertreter/in, Beauftragte/r
to **request sth** *(fml)* 154 etw (an)fordern, etw erbitten, um etw bitten
to **require sth** 8 etw erfordern, etw benötigen
requirement 33 Voraussetzung, Bedingung, Anforderung
research: body of ~ 39 Forschungsmaterial, Forschungsarbeiten
to **research sth** 24 etw recherchieren, Nachforschungen über etw anstellen
researcher 39 Forscher/in, Wissenschaftler/in
to **resemble sth** 43 einer Sache ähneln, einer Sache gleichen, etw widerspiegeln
to **resent sth** 124 sich über etw ärgern
resentment 106 Unmut, Groll, Ressentiment
reserved 67 reserviert, zurückhaltend
reservoir 87F Stausee, Staubecken
residential area 142 Wohngebiet
residue 90 Rückstand
resilience 84 Widerstandsfähigkeit
to **resist sth** 104 einer Sache widerstehen
resistant to sth 163 resistent gegen etw
to **resolve sth** 70 etw (auf)lösen
respective 128 jeweilig
respondent 159 Befragte/r
responsibility 28 Aufgabe, Zuständigkeit
to **restock sth** 74F etw wieder auffüllen
to **restore sth** 81 etw restaurieren, etw wieder aufbauen
to **restrict (to)** 11 einschränken, beschränken (auf)
restriction 47 Beschränkung, Einschränkung
to **result in sth** 59 zu etw führen
résumé *(AE)* 11 Lebenslauf
retail 32T Einzelhandel(s-)
retailer 64 Einzelhändler/in
retailing 149 Einzelhandel
to **retain sb/sth** 100 jdn/etw behalten, etw beibehalten, etw bewahren
retired 56 pensioniert, im Ruhestand
retirement 147 Ruhestand, Rente
retiring 32T zurückhaltend
return 151 Ertrag, Rendite; **~ flight** 33 (Hin- und) Rückflug; **in ~** 55 im Gegenzug, als Ausgleich
returnable bottle 78 Mehrwegflasche
reusable 78 wiederverwendbar
to **reuse** 70 wiederverwenden
revenue 72 Einkünfte, Einnahmen
to **reverse sth** 85 etw umkehren
to **review sth** 28 etw bewerten, etw prüfen
to **revise sth** 22 *(Lernstoff)* wiederholen
to **revitalize sb/sth** 10 jdn/etw wieder beleben
to **revive sth** 74T etw wieder beleben, etw wieder aufleben lassen
reward: financial ~ 50 (finanzielle) Entlohnung, Entgelt
rewarding 9 lohnend, erfüllend
to **rid sth of sth** 57 etw von etw befreien
to **ridicule sb** 127 jdn lächerlich machen
ridiculous 125 lächerlich, unglaublich
rig: (oil) ~ 122 (Öl-)Bohrinsel, Förderturm
right: ~ away 48 sofort; **~-wing** 106 rechtsgerichtet; **in your own ~** 50 eigenständig
rink 49 Eisbahn, Rollschuhbahn
riot 111 Aufstand, Aufruhr
rise 98 Aufschwung, Aufstieg
to **rob sb** 67 jdn be-/ausrauben
robbery 133 Raub, Überfall
robotics 150 Robotertechnik
rock pooling 74F *bei Ebbe Gezeitentümpel untersuchen/nach Tieren absuchen*
rocket stove 71 Raketenofen/-herd (der Brennstoff besonders effizient verbrennt)
role model 12 Vorbild
root 74T Wurzel
rosy-cheeked 46T mit (rosigen/roten) Wangen
rough: to **sleep ~** 145 im Freien übernachten, auf der Straße leben
roughly 92 ungefähr, etwa
routinely 127 routinemäßig, regelmäßig
row 128 Streit, Krach
rules: to **bend the ~** 51 über die Regeln hinwegsehen, die Vorschriften beugen
to **ruminate (on/over/about)** 18 grübeln, nachsinnen (über)
rumour 60 Gerücht
run: in the long ~ 18 auf lange Sicht, langfristig
rung 158T Sprosse *(einer Leiter)*
runoff 74T Abfluss, abfließendes Wasser
rusty 140 rostig
ruthless 107 rücksichtslos, skrupellos

S

to **sacrifice sth** 74 etw opfern
to **safeguard sth** 73 etw schützen
said: it is ~ that ... 74T man sagt, dass ...

sales *(pl)* *47* Verkauf, Vertrieb, Verkaufs-
salmon, *pl* **salmon** *36* Lachs
satisfaction *8* Zufriedenheit
to **satisfy sb** *9* jdn zufriedenstellen, jdn befriedigen
saturate: to ~ **sth** *37* etw sättigen *(chemisch)*; **(un)~d fat** *36* (un) gesättigte Fettsäure
scale *84* Ausmaß, Umfang
scapegoat *115* Sündenbock
scarf, *pl* **scarves** *50* Schal, Halstuch
scheme *46* Programm, Projekt
school: ~ **run** *155* „Elterntaxi" zur/von der Schule; **vocational** ~ *22* Berufsschule, berufsbildende Schule
scientific *44* wissenschaftlich
scope *150* Rahmen, Umfang
scores (of ...) *46T* eine Menge (...), viel/e (...)
to **scramble** *74F* klettern, krabbeln; ~ **(for sth)** *32T* Gerangel (um etw)
to **scrap sth** *29* etw aufgeben, etw wegwerfen
to **scratch sth** *32T* etw (zer)kratzen
scrutiny: under ~ *127* auf dem/den Prüfstand
sea level *78* Meeresspiegel
seafood *42* Meeresfrüchte
seamless *154* nahtlos
seaside *132* (Meeres-)Küste, Strand
second: to **have** ~ **thoughts** *40* es sich anders überlegen
secondary education *22* Sekundarstufe 1 und 2
secure *13* sicher; to ~ **sth** *165* (sich) etw sichern, etw sicherstellen
sedentary *8* sitzend
seed *42* Samen, Saat(gut), *(AE)* Kern
to **seek sth** *15* (nach) etw suchen, etw anstreben
to **select sb/sth** *12* jdn/etw (aus) wählen
self-esteem *8* Selbstachtung, Selbstwertgefühl
selfish *87* egoistisch, selbstsüchtig
self-sufficient *80* autark
senior *(AE)* *25* Schüler/in der Abschlussklasse *(US High School)*
sense *32T* Sinn; ~ **of agency** *127* Handlungsbewusstsein, Handlungskompetenz; **common** ~ *46T* gesunder Menschenverstand; to **make** ~ *43* Sinn ergeben, sinnvoll sein; to **make** ~ **of sth** *127* etw verstehen, aus etw schlau werden
sensible *13* vernünftig, sinnvoll
sensitive *32T* heikel
sensitivity *67* Sensibilität, Einfühlungsvermögen
sentence *134* Haftstrafe; to ~ **sb (to sth)** *134* jdn (zu etw) verurteilen; **youth custodial** ~ *144T* Jugendstrafe
sequin *123* Paillette
serial killer *32T* Serienmörder/in
serve: to ~ **(as)** *12* dienen (als); to ~ **a purpose** *99* einem Zweck dienen
serviceman *109* Militärangehöriger
session *66* Sitzung, Termin, Treffen, (Unterrichts-)Stunde
set: to ~ **about sth** *108* sich über etw hermachen, sich auf etw stürzen; to ~ **off an alarm** *165* Alarm auslösen; to ~ **sb back sth** *67* jdn etw kosten; to ~ **sb up** *11* jdm eine Falle stellen; to ~ **sth up** *158T* etw eröffnen, etw einrichten
to **settle in(to sth)** *46T* sich (in etw) eingewöhnen, (bei/in etw) ankommen
settlement *87* Siedlung, Kolonie
severe *165* ernst, schwer
to **sew** *18* nähen
sewage *74* Abwasser
shape *32T* Form; to ~ **sth** *162* etw formen
shareholder *60T* Aktionär/in, Teilhaber/in, Gesellschafter/in
sharing: information ~ *151* Informationsaustausch
sharp *135* stark
shed: tool ~ *32T* Geräteschuppen, „Kuhstall"
sheer: the ~ **enormity** *137* das ungeheure Ausmaß
shelter *106* Unterkunft
shift *33* Schicht; *92* Verschiebung, Verlagerung, Wandel
to **shift** *84* (sich) verlagern, (sich) verändern
shin pad *49* Schienbeinschoner
shiny *105T* glänzend
to **shiver** *137* zittern
shock *39* Schock
to **shock sb** *40* jdn schockieren
to **shoot for sth** *(AE, infml)* *158T* auf etw aus sein
shoplifting *133* Ladendiebstahl
short: ~**-sighted** *95* kurzsichtig; ~**-term** *18* kurzfristig, Kurzzeit-; to **be** ~ **on sth** *155* etw nicht haben, von etw zu wenig haben
shortage (of) *94* Mangel, Knappheit (an)
shrewd *109* klug, scharfsinnig, geschickt
to **shrink** *106* schrumpfen
siblings *(pl)* *129* Geschwister
sick: to **get** ~ **of sth** *97* von etw zuviel bekommen
sighted: short-~ *95* kurzsichtig
to **sign up for sth** *123* sich für/bei etw anmelden
to **signify sth** *32T* etw bedeuten, etw bezeichnen
similarly *10* in ähnlicher Weise, ebenso
simulated *168* simuliert
simultaneous *80* gleichzeitig
since *39* weil, da, seit
single *20* einzelne/r/s
site: landfill ~ *78* Mülldeponie; **on-**~ *33* vor Ort, im Betrieb
skilled *114* qualifiziert, Fach-
skillful *53* geschickt, gut
to **skim (a text)** *10* (einen Text) überfliegen
sled *18F* Schlitten
sleep: to ~ **rough** *145* im Freien übernachten, auf der Straße leben; to **not** ~ **a wink** *138* kein Auge zutun
to **slice bread** *157* Brot in Scheiben schneiden
slick *18F* glatt, raffiniert (gebaut)
slightly *28* leicht, geringfügig
slope *35* (Ab-)Hang, Piste
slot *60T* Platz, Zeitfenster; *71* Schlitz, (Karten-)Einzug
to **slouch** *32T* sich lümmeln
slow: to ~ **down** *7* (sich) verlangsamen; to ~ **sth** *168* etw verlangsamen, etw eindämmen
slowdown *170* Verlangsamung
small-scale *74T* Klein-, klein angelegt
smart *25* intelligent, pfiffig, geschickt
to **smuggle sth** *136* etw schmuggeln
snub *108* Abfuhr, Brüskierung
to **soar** *84* steigen
sobering *8* ernüchternd
to **socialize (with)** *14* sich treffen (mit), unter Leute gehen
societal *130T* gesellschaftlich, sozial
soft drink *38* alkoholfreies Getränk
soil *78* Erde, Boden
solid *90* fest, solide; ~ **waste** *74T* Feststoffabfall, Hausmüll
solitary *15* einsam, solitär, Einzel-
sombre *130* traurig, düster, betrübt
somewhat *76* etwas, ziemlich
soot *84* Ruß
sophisticated *78* raffiniert, anspruchsvoll
sorrow *35* Kummer, Leid
to **sort sth out** *137* etw klären, etw lösen
sought after *148* begehrt, gefragt
sound *97* solide, vernünftig
source *11* Quelle
spa *74F* Wellnessbereich
spare time *104* Freizeit
to **speak volumes** *97* Bände sprechen
species, *pl* **species** *74T* Art *(Biologie)*
specific *13* bestimmt, speziell, spezifisch
speck *32T* Fleck
to **spectate** *51* zuschauen
spectator *50* Zuschauer/in
to **speculate about sth** *138* sich über etw Gedanken machen
to **speed sth up** *155* etw beschleunigen
speedy *98* schnell, zügig
sperm count *56* Spermienzahl
spirit *10* Geist, Seele
to **spit sth out** *123* etw ausspucken
to **split (into)** *103* (sich) aufteilen (in)
spokesman *28* Sprecher
spokesperson *46* Sprecher/in
spokeswoman *43* Sprecherin
sponsorship *33* Förderung
to **sport sth** *132* etw (stolz) tragen *(z. B. Kleidungsstück)*
sportswear *50* Sportkleidung
to **spot sb/sth** *20* jdn/etw entdecken
square *35* (Spiel-)Feld

stable *84* stabil, konstant
to **stack sth** *109* etw stapeln
staff: waiting ~ *33* Servicepersonal, Bedienung
to **staff sth** *158* etw *(mit Personal)* besetzen
stag party *64* Junggesellenabschied (des Bräutigams)
stage: key ~ 2 *46T (GB:) die Grundschuljahrgänge 3 – 6 für Schüler/innen zwischen 7 und 11 Jahren*
to **stage sth** *126* etw inszenieren, etw veranstalten, etw aufführen
to **stain sth** *120* etw beschmutzen, *(Ruf)* (be)schädigen
stand: to ~ **out** *22* auffallen, herausstechen; **I can't/couldn't ~ ...** *45* ich kann/konnte ... nicht ausstehen; to **not ~ for sth** *109* sich etw nicht gefallen lassen
starch *37* Stärke *(in Lebensmitteln)*
starchy *36* stärkehaltig
start: head ~ *99* Vorsprung
starter *144T* Eingangs-
startling *158T* alarmierend, erschreckend, erstaunlich
starvation *42* Hunger
starved: to **be ~ of sth** *76* unter (...-) Mangel leiden, nicht genug von etw bekommen/haben
to **state sth** *22* etw darlegen, etw festlegen
statement: personal ~ *22* Selbstbeschreibung
station: nuclear power ~ *90* Kernkraftwerk; **power** ~ *78* Kraftwerk
stationary *18* ruhend, bewegungslos
statutory *46T* gesetzlich (vorgeschrieben)
staying power *131* Ausdauer, Durchhaltevermögen
steady *32T* kontinuierlich, stabil
steam *148* (Wasser-)Dampf
steel *60F* Stahl
to **step off the beaten track** *70* ausgetretene Pfade verlassen
steps: to **take** ~ *99* Schritte unternehmen
stick *49* Schläger *(Hockey)*
stick: to ~ **sth** *41* etw (an)kleben, etw (an)hängen; to **stick to sth** *16* bei etw bleiben, sich an etw halten
to **stimulate sth** *165* etw anregen, etw stimulieren
stir: to ~ **sth up** *107* etw schüren; to ~ **the pot** *95* Bewegung in die Sache bringen
stock: to **be quoted on the ~ exchange** *50* an der Börse notiert werden
stone-baked oven *18F* Steinbackofen
to **stop sth** *36* etw verhindern
storage *90* Speicherung, Speicher-
to **store** *78* speichern; **grocery** ~ *(AE)* *39* Lebensmittelgeschäft
storeman *109* Lagerist
straight: ~ **away** *48* sofort; to **put the record** ~ *28* etw gerade rücken, etw klarstellen
stranded: to **be** ~ *164* festsitzen, gestrandet sein
strategic body *46T* Organisation, strategisches Organ/Gremium
to **strengthen** *170* kräftigen, stärken
to **stress sb out** *11* jdn stressen
strike: to **go on** ~ *99* streiken
striker *54T* Stürmer/in
string *30* Kette, Reihe
to **strip sb of sth** *56* jdm etw aberkennen
to **strive** *53* streben, bemüht sein
stroke *36* Schlaganfall
to **stroll** *18F* spazieren, bummeln
stuck: to **be** ~ *158T* stecken bleiben, festsitzen, nicht weiterkommen; to **be ~ with sth** *95* etw am Hals haben, etw nicht wieder loswerden
stuff *29* Zeug, Sache(n)
stuffy *71* stickig
to **stumble over your words** *123* stottern
stunned *94* fassungslos
stunning *74T* phantastisch, umwerfend
subconscious *32T* unterbewusst
subgroup *66* Untergruppe
subject: elective ~ *22* Wahlfach
to **submerge** *155* untertauchen
to **subscribe to sth** *8* einer Sache beipflichten, sich *(einer Meinung, Aussage etc.)* anschließen
subscriber *92* Abonnent/in
to **subsidize sb/sth** *74T* jdn finanziell unterstützen, etw subventionieren
to **substitute for sb/sth** *151* jdn/etw ersetzen
subtitles *(pl)* *74* Untertitel
such as *15* wie (zum Beispiel)
to **suck sb into sth** *155* jdn in etw hineinziehen
to **suffer (from sth)** *15* (an etw) leiden
sufficient *88T* ausreichend, hinreichend
sugary *36* zuckerhaltig, süß(lich)
suicide *102F* Selbstmord
suit: to **follow** ~ *46T* gleichziehen
to **suit sb/sth** *46T* zu jdm/etw passen
suitability *28* Eignung
suitable *18* geeignet, passend
suited: (well-)~ to/for sb/sth *155* für jdn/etw (gut) geeignet
summer camp *33* (Sommer-)Ferienlager
summit *113* Gipfel(treffen)
to **supervise sb** *33* jdn beaufsichtigen
to **supply sth** *81* etw liefern, etw bieten, etw bereitstellen
supply-side *150* angebotsorientiert, was das Angebot betrifft
to **support sb/sth** *40* jdn/etw unterstützen
supporter *42* Anhänger/in
supportive *46T* (unter)stützend
supposedly *53* vermeintlich, angeblich
suppression *120* Unterdrückung
sure: to **make** ~ *22* sicherstellen
surgeon *155* Chirurg/in
surgery: open-heart ~ *123* Operation am offenen Herzen
to **surround sth** *88T* etw umgeben
surrounding area *71* Umgebung
surroundings *(pl)* *74T* Umgebung
surveillance *91* Überwachung
survey *15* (Meinungs-)Umfrage
to **survey sb** *14* jdn befragen
to **suspect sth** *59* etw vermuten
to **suspend sth** *134* etw zeitweilig aufheben, etw aussetzen
suspicion *51* Verdacht
to **sustain sth** *46T* etw (aufrecht) erhalten, etw (unter)stützen
sustainability *74* Nachhaltigkeit
to **swear sb in** *118* jdn vereidigen
sweeping *127* pauschal, umfassend, weit reichend
swell *74F* Woge, Seegang
swift *158T* schnell, rasch
syndicate *50* Syndikat, Interessensgemeinschaft
syringe *59* (Injektions-)Spritze

T

table water *74T* Grundwasser
tabloid *92* Boulevardzeitung
to **tackle sth** *56* etw *(z. B. ein Problem)* angehen, etw bewältigen
tag: electronic ~ *144T* elektronische Fessel
tailored *113* maßgeschneidert
tailor-made *162* maßgeschneidert
take: to ~ **advantage of sth** *64* sich etw zunutze machen, etw ausnutzen; to ~ **care** *92* vorsichtig sein, aufpassen; to ~ **care to do sth** *120* (sorgfältig) darauf achten, etw zu tun; to ~ **effect** *16* wirken, Wirkung zeigen; to ~ **it in turns** *35* sich abwechseln; to ~ **part (in sth)** *8* (an etw) teilnehmen; to ~ **sth into account** *98* etw (mit) berücksichtigen
tan *28* Sonnenbräune
to **tap (into) sth** *154* etw erschließen, sich etw zunutze machen
tax *46* Steuer; ~ **evasion** *134* Steuerhinterziehung
taxpayer *104* Steuerzahler/in
to **team up with sb** *74F* mit jdm zusammenarbeiten, sich mit jdm zusammentun
to **tear sth down** *156* etw abreißen, etw einreißen
technical college *22* Technische Universität
tee *49* Tee *(Abschlag beim Golf)*
temporary *70* vorübergehend, befristet
to **tempt sb** *51* jdn in Versuchung führen, jdn verleiten
temptation *50* Versuchung
to **tend to do sth** *10* dazu neigen, etw zu tun
tension *106* Spannung
term *9* Begriff

terms: a contradiction in ~ *52* ein Widerspruch in sich; **in ~ of …** *121* was … betrifft/angeht
terrifying *138* Furcht erregend
tertiary *22* tertiär
thankful *124* dankbar
thanks to *64* dank
the … the … *68* je … desto …
thee *105T* dich, dir *(veraltet oder auf Gott bezogen)*
theft *92* Diebstahl
there is no doing sth *13* man kann etw nicht tun, es ist unmöglich etw zu tun
thereby *71* dabei, dadurch
therefore *10* daher, deshalb, demzufolge
thermal *90* thermisch, Wärme-
thesis, *pl* **theses** *42* These
thief, *pl* **thieves** *133* Dieb/in
thoroughly *109* gründlich, aufmerksam
thought *40* Gedanke; to **have second ~s** *40* es sich anders überlegen
threat *56* Bedrohung
thrill *18F* Nervenkitzel, (aufregendes) Gefühl
to **thrive on sth** *22* bei etw (richtig) aufblühen
throughout *57* überall, in der ganzen Zeit … hindurch
to **throw in the towel** *(infml)* *155* das Handtuch werfen
thus *14* daher, deshalb, somit
tight *168* eng; to **hang ~** *32T* ruhig abwarten
to **tilt** *32T* kippen, sich neigen
time: big ~ *28* so richtig; *134* ganz groß; to **fall on hard ~s** *148* schwere Zeiten durchleben
timely *154* zeitgerecht, zur rechten Zeit
tipping point *85* Kipppunkt, kritischer Punkt, Wendepunkt
tiredness *42* Müdigkeit
to **be to do sth** *123* etw tun sollen
tobacco *40* Tabak
toe-touch meeting *71* kurzer Vor-Ort-Termin, geschäftliche „Stippvisite"
tool *15* Werkzeug, Instrument; **~ shed** *32T* Geräteschuppen, „Kuhstall"
tooth decay *36* Karies, Zahnfäule
to **top sth up** *28* etw vollständig machen, etw ergänzen
topical *96* thematisch
top-notch *130T* erstklassig
tops *(slang)* *28* super, toll
torn: to **be ~ between A and B** *106* zwischen A und B hin und her gerissen sein
torture *43* Folter
touch: to **lose your ~** *39* nachlassen
tournament *52* Turnier
towel: to **throw in the ~** *(infml)* *155* das Handtuch werfen
toxic *78* giftig, Gift-
to **trace sth** *112* etw (zurück)verfolgen
track *46* Rennstrecke, Laufbahn
trade *113* Branche, Gewerbe
trafficker: human ~ *106* Schleuser/in, Menschenhändler/in
trafficking: drug ~ *134* Drogenhandel
trainee *23* Auszubildende/r
trait *53* Wesenszug, Eigenschaft
to **transform** *15* umwandeln, (sich) verwandeln
transgenic *162* transgen, genmanipuliert
transition *81* Übergang, Umstellung
to **translate** *48* übersetzen, (sich) übertragen (lassen)
translation *129* Übersetzung
to **transmit sth** *162* etw übertragen
travel agent *76* Reisebüro(angestellte/r)
treadmill *42* Tretmühle
to **treat sth** *74T* etw behandeln, *(Abwasser)* klären
treatment *174* Behandlung
trial *42* Versuch, Test, Probe; *137* Verfahren, Prozess
triangle *32T* Dreieck
tribute (to) *112* Würdigung, Anerkennung
to **trick sb into doing sth** *136* jdn mit List / mit einem Trick dazu bringen, etw zu tun
to **trickle** *88T* tropfen, tröpfeln
to **trigger sth** *87* etw auslösen
trinket *18F* Modeschmuck, *(kleines, billiges)* Schmuckstück
trolley *18F* (Hand-)Wagen
trout, *pl* **trout** *36* Forelle
truancy *134* Schwänzen, unentschuldigtes Fernbleiben
to **truant** *144T* Schule schwänzen
truly *95* wahrhaftig, wirklich, tatsächlich
trunks *(pl)* *49* Badehose
tub *35* Becher, Packung *(z. B. Eiscreme)*
tuition *31* Unterricht, Anleitung
tuna *36* Thunfisch
turn: ~ of events *97* Wende der Ereignisse/des Schicksals; **~ of the century** *96* Jahrhundertwende; **in ~** *151* wiederum, seiner-/ihrerseits; **it's the ~ of sth** *52* etw ist an der Reihe; to **take it in ~s** *35* sich abwechseln
turn: to **~ into sth** *29* zu etw werden (lassen); to **turn out** *18T* sich herausstellen; to **turn out to be …** *68* sich erweisen/herausstellen als …
tutor *28* Lehrer/in, Dozent/in, Kursleiter/in
to **tweak sth** *32T* etw optimieren
twinkle: … was still a ~ in sb's eyes *154* … war für jdn noch Zukunftsmusik
twist *130T* *(überraschende)* Wendung, *(überraschende)* (Geschmacks-)Note
to **typify sth** *151* etw verkörpern, für etw typisch sein

U

ubiquitousness *40* Allgegenwart
unbearable *101F* unerträglich, *(Mensch)* unausstehlich
unbelievable *42* unglaublich
uncertainty *106* Ungewissheit, Unsicherheit
unchallenged *53* unwidersprochen
to **uncover sth** *50* etw aufdecken
underage *142* minderjährig
to **underestimate sb/sth** *9* jdn/etw unterschätzen
to **undergo sth** *23* sich einer Sache unterziehen
underlying *77* zugrunde liegend
to **underpin sth** *84* etw (ab)stützen, etw untermauern
to **undertake sth** *164* etw unternehmen, etw in Angriff nehmen
underwear *130T* Unterwäsche
uneasiness *152* Unbehagen, Unwohlsein
uneasy *153* besorgt, unbehaglich, mulmig
unemployment *32T* Arbeitslosigkeit
unequivocal *18* eindeutig, unzweideutig
unexpected *60* unerwartet
unfortunately *23* leider
to **unfurl sth** *105T* etw entfalten, etw auseinanderrollen
unique *57* einzigartig
universal *25* universell, allgemein, weltweit
unless *41* es sei denn, außer wenn
unnoticed: to **go ~** *40* unbemerkt bleiben
unpleasant *111* unangenehm, unschön
unprecedented *84* beispiellos, einmalig
unreliable *100* unzuverlässig
unrest *15* Unruhe(n)
unsightly *94* unschön, hässlich
unskilled *148* ungelernt
unspoilt *70* unverdorben, unberührt *(Landschaft)*
unsweetened *36* ungesüßt
to **unveil sb/sth** *130T* jdn vorstellen, etw enthüllen
to **unwind** *8* sich entspannen
up: ~ to date *34* aktuell, auf dem/den neuesten Stand; **~s and downs** *95* Höhen und Tiefen; **it is ~ to sb (to do sth)** *15* es ist jds Sache / es liegt an jdm (etw zu tun)
to **update sb** *123* jdn auf den neusten Stand bringen
uprising *94* Aufstand
upset *109* verstimmt, verärgert
urbanization *87* Verstädterung, Urbanisierung
to **urge sb** *28* jdn drängen
urgent *77* dringend
to **usher sb** *108* jdn führen, jdn geleiten

to **utilize sth** *90* etw einsetzen, etw (be)nutzen

utter *123* völlig, vollkommen

V

vacation *(AE)* *8* Urlaub

valid: to **have a ~ point** *172T* ganz Recht haben, einen berechtigtes Argument vorbringen

valley *20* Tal

valuable *10* wertvoll

value *11* Wert

to **value sth** *67* etw (wert)schätzen

to **vanish** *70* verschwinden, aussterben

vanity *52* Eitelkeit

variability *84* Schwankung, Unbeständigkeit

variety *36* Sorte, Art, Variante; **a ~ of** *14* eine Vielzahl (von)

various *16* verschieden, mehrere, allerlei

to **vary** *28* variieren, schwanken

vast *84* riesig, sehr groß; **~ majority** *53* (bei weitem) größter Teil, Löwenanteil

vein: in this ~ *127* dieser Art

velocity *150* Geschwindigkeit

vending machine *38* (Verkaufs-)Automat

to **vent on sb/sth** *95* sich über jdn/etw auslassen

to **ventilate sth** *75* etw belüften

venue *119* Veranstaltungsort, Veranstaltungsstätte

verdict *138* Urteil

versus *151* gegen

viability: financial ~ *74T* finanzielle Realisierbarkeit, Durchführbarkeit

vibes *(pl)* *32T* Ausstrahlung, Atmosphäre

vicinity: in the ~ (of …) *64* in der Nähe (von …), in der näheren Umgebung (von …)

vicious circle *72* Teufelskreis

victim *22* Opfer

to **victimise sb** *144T* jdn schikanieren

vigilance *57* Wachsamkeit

vigorous *36* kräftig, energisch

vine *74T* Weinrebe

vineyard *74T* Weinberg

to **violate sth** *56* gegen etw verstoßen, etw verletzen

violation *172* Verstoß, Verletzung *(von Gesetzen, Rechten)*

viral: to **go ~** *92* sich *(im Internet)* rasend schnell verbreiten

virtually *40* praktisch, nahezu

visa *33* Visum

visible *36* sichtbar

to **visualize sth** *13* etw bildlich darstellen, etw visualisieren

vital *36* lebensnotwendig, unerlässlich

vocational school *22* Berufsschule, berufsbildende Schule

voltage *88T* Spannung

volumes: to **speak ~** *97* Bände sprechen

voluntary *8* freiwillig, ehrenamtlich

volunteer *22* freiwillig, ehrenamtlich; to **~** *8* freiwillig/ehrenamtlich arbeiten *(unbezahlt)*

to **vote on sth** *27* über etw abstimmen

vulnerable *74* verletzlich, verwundbar

W

waiting staff *33* Servicepersonal, Bedienung

waking hours *(pl)* *14* die Stunden, in denen man wach ist

wall bars *(pl)* *15* Sprossenwand

wallet *140* Brieftasche, (Herren-)Portemonnaie

war bonds *(pl)* *113* Kriegsanleihen

warfare *172T* Krieg(führung)

waste *78* Müll; **domestic ~** *78* Hausmüll; **hazardous ~** *78* Sondermüll; **solid ~** *74T* Feststoffabfall, Hausmüll

to **waste sth** *104* etw verschwenden, etw vergeuden

wasteful *9* verschwenderisch

wastewater *74T* Abwasser

to **watch out (for sth)** *20* (auf etw) aufpassen, (auf etw) achten

waterfront *33* Ufer

way: in harm's ~ *172T* in Gefahr; **one ~ or another** *11* so oder so, auf die eine oder andere Art; to **find your ~ around** *69* sich zurechtfinden (in); to **go a long ~ toward(s) doing sth** *11* zu einer Sache viel beitragen; to **go ~ back** *(infml)* *120* schon lange bestehen

wayward *(fml)* *127* ungehörig

to **weaken** *40* (sich) (ab)schwächen, nachlassen

wealth *151* Wohlstand, Reichtum

wealthy *106* wohlhabend, reich

weapon *39* Waffe

to **weave** *74T* weben

to **weigh sth up** *16* etw abwägen, etw einschätzen, etw beurteilen

weight: to **lose ~** *35* abnehmen *(Körpergewicht reduzieren)*; to **put on ~** *36* zunehmen *(Körpergewicht erhöhen)*

weirdness *169* Verrücktheit

welfare *147* Wohl, Wohlergehen

well: ~-being *8* Wohl(befinden); **as ~** *15* auch (noch), ebenfalls; **as ~ as** *9* sowohl … als auch …, ebenso wie, sowie

wetsuit *74F* Tauchanzug, Surfanzug

whatever *22* was auch immer

wheat *37* Weizen

whereas *86* während, wohingegen

wherever *114* wo (auch) immer

which: … ~ is why … *17* …, weswegen …

whichever *120* wer/was (auch immer), egal welche/r/s

whilst *144T* während

to **whip** *108* flitzen

white-collar crime *134* Wirtschaftskriminalität

wholegrain *36* Vollkorn-

why: … which is ~ … *17* …, weswegen …

widespread *22* (weit) verbreitet, allgemein, groß

wilderness *20* Wildnis

will *25* Wille

willing: to **be ~ to do sth** *18* bereit sein, etw zu tun

willingly *120* bereitwillig, gern

window dressing *75* Schönfärberei, Augenwischerei

wing: right-~ *106* rechtsgerichtet

wink: to **not sleep a ~** *138* kein Auge zutun

wisdom *69* Weisheit, Klugheit

to **wobble** *113* schwanken, wackeln

to **wonder** *30* sich fragen

word power *12* Wortverständnis, Wortschatz, Wortgewandtheit

words: to **stumble over your ~** *123* stottern

work: ~ experience *22* Praktikum; **~ placement** *22* Praktikum; **All ~ and no play makes Jack a dull boy.** *8* Arbeit alleine macht (auch) nicht glücklich. *(Sprichwort)*

workforce *106* Erwerbstätige, Erwerbsbevölkerung

working life *22* Arbeitsleben

workload *131* Arbeitsbelastung

worldly *67* welterfahren, weltlich

worries *(pl)* *33* Sorgen, Bedenken

worse: to **change for the ~** *14* (sich) zum Schlechteren wandeln, (sich) verschlechtern

to **worsen sth** *173* verschlechtern

worth (millions) *40* (Millionen) wert

worthwhile *7* lohnend

X

xenophobia *106* Fremdenfeindlichkeit, Ausländerhass

Y

to **yell** *108* schreien, brüllen

yet *39* (und) doch, dennoch

to **yield sth** *151* etw erzielen, etw hervorbringen, etw einbringen

youngster *16* Jugendliche/r

youth custodial sentence *144T* Jugendstrafe

Quellenverzeichnis

S. 7/ob.li.: Shutterstock / goir; **S. 7/ob.re.:** Shutterstock / Rawpixel.com; **S. 7/mi.li.:** Shutterstock / Lightspring; **S. 7/mi.re.:** Shutterstock / wavebreakmedia; **S. 7/un.li.:** Shutterstock / Kritchanut; **S. 7/un.re.:** Shutterstock / Aila Images; **S. 8:** Shutterstock / Africa Studio; **S. 11:** Fotolia / Pixsooz; **S. 12:** Shutterstock / Sergey Nivens; **S. 13:** Fotolia / Jacob Lund; **S. 14:** Image Source / Rick Becker-Leckrone; **S. 17:** Fotolia / Syda Productions; **S. 19:** Cartoonstock/Jerry King; **S. 21/ob./1:** Shutterstock / dotshock; **S. 21/ob./2:** Fotolia / BillionPhotos.com; **S. 21/ob./3:** Shutterstock / Volt Collection; **S. 21/mi./1:** Fotolia / Photographee.eu; **S. 21/mi./2:** Fotolia / Christian Schwier; **S. 21/mi./3:** Fotolia / grimaldello; **S. 21/un./1:** Fotolia / Feel good studio; **S. 21/un./2:** Shutterstock / Monkey Business Images; **S. 21/un./3:** Shutterstock / Lucky Business; **S. 22:** Shutterstock / RMIKKA; **S. 25:** vario images / blend; **S. 27/ob./1:** Fotolia / Andrey Kiselev; **S. 27/ob./2:** Fotolia / JJAVA; **S. 29:** Shutterstock / J. Henning Buchholz; **S. 30:** Shutterstock/mangostock; **S. 33:** Cartoonstock / James Whitworth; **S. 36:** Fotolia / goir; **S. 39/oben:** vario images / eyecandy pro; **S. 39/unten:** vario images / Tetra Images; **S. 41/oben:** Your Photo Today / phanie; **S. 41/un./1:** Fotolia / ErikSvoboda; **S. 41/un./2:** Fotolia / chrisdorney; **S. 41/un./3:** Fotolia / Afanasiev Oleksii; **S. 41/un./4:** Fotolia / valentint; **S. 41/un./5:** Fotolia / bobnevv; **S. 41/un./6:** Fotolia / chrisdorney; **S. 41/un./7:** Fotolia / creative soul; **S. 42:** Shutterstock / Mountain Brothers; **S. 45:** Shutterstock / ifong; **S. 46:** Murdo MacLeod; **S. 49/ob./1:** Fotolia / Shariff Che'Lah; **S. 49/ob./2:** Fotolia / justasc; **S. 49/ob./3:** Fotolia / Igor Mojzes; **S. 49/ob./4:** Fotolia / massimhokuto; **S. 49/ob./5:** Fotolia / Dasha Petrenko; **S. 49/ob./6:** Fotolia / razihusin; **S. 49/ob./7:** Fotolia / SolisImages; **S. 49/ob./8:** Fotolia / SolisImages; **S. 50:** Fotolia / Dusan Kostic; **S. 52:** Fotolia / BillionPhotos.com; **S. 54/un.li.:** Fotolia / berc; **S. 54/un.mi.:** vario images / Image Source; **S. 54/un.re.:** vario images / Image Source; **S. 55:** Shutterstock / Igor Vkv; **S. 56:** Fotolia / Valeriy Velikov; **S. 58:** Fotolia / Fisher Photostudio; **S. 59:** Fotolia / Fisher Photostudio; **S. 60:** Picture-Alliance / empics; **S. 61:** ddp images / ZUMA; **S. 63/1:** Fotolia / giorgios245; **S. 63/2:** Fotolia / giorgios245; **S. 64:** Shutterstock / Sirikunkrittaphuk; **S. 66/ob./1:** Shutterstock / Julia Karo; **S. 66/ob./2:** Shutterstock / Rawpixel.com; **S. 66/ob./3:** Shutterstock / Syda Productions; **S. 66/mi./1:** Shutterstock / p.studio66; **S. 66/mi./2:** Shutterstock / Irina Ovchinnikova; **S. 66/mi./3:** Shutterstock / ChameleonsEye; **S. 66/un./1:** Shutterstock / gpointstudio; **S. 66/un./2:** Fotolia / panomacc; **S. 66/un./3:** Shutterstock / Alvov; **S. 68:** Fotolia / .shock; **S. 70:** mauritius images / Alamy Stock Photo / Eagle Visions Photography / Craig Lovell; **S. 71:** Fotolia / DutchScenery; **S. 72:** Fotolia/olly; **S. 74:** Shutterstock / travel mania; **S. 75/Nadel:** Shutterstock / schab; **S. 75/Photo:** Fotolia/seaphotoart; **S. 77/Hintergr./1:** Shutterstock / Yulia Glam; **S. 77/Hintergr./2:** Shutterstock / Panacea Doll; **S. 77/ob./1:** Shutterstock / Lisa S.; **S. 77/ob./2:** Shutterstock / Panacea Doll; **S. 77/ob./3.:** Shutterstock / orxy; **S. 77/mitte:** Shutterstock / Dmytro Balkhovitin; **S. 77/un./1.:** Shutterstock / sdecoret; **S. 77/un./2.:** Shutterstock / Dudarev Mikhail; **S. 78:** Fotolia / Yuriy Mazur; **S. 80:** laif / Zenit / Paul Langrock; **S. 81/ob.re.:** Reuters / Tobias Schwarz; **S. 81/mi.li.:** laif / Zenit / Paul Langrock; **S. 81/un.re.:** F1online / Holger Peter; **S. 82:** Picture-Alliance / dpa; **S. 83:** laif / Malte Jaeger; **S. 85:** Reuters / Pawan Kumar; **S. 86:** Shutterstock / Amethista777; **S. 87:** Shutterstock / Vadim Sadovski; **S. 89:** Seppo Leinonen; **S. 92:** Shutterstock / Oleksiy Mark; **S. 95:** PHOTOMORPHIC PTE. LTD.; **S. 96:** Fotolia / tom_nulens; **S. 97:** Fotolia / aey; **S. 98:** action press / Sipa Pressaction press; **S. 100:** Fotolia / Dmitry Vereshchagin; **S. 101:** Fotolia / stockphoto mania; **S. 103/ob.mi.:** Shutterstock/Iconic Bestiary; **S. 103/ob.re.:** Fotolia / highwaystarz; **S. 105/Hintergr.:** Fotolia / william87; **S. 105/ob.re.:** Shutterstock / Janossy Gergely; **S. 105/mi.li.:** Fotolia / Prazis; **S. 106:** Shutterstock / doom.Ko; **S. 108:** ddp images / CAMERA PRESS / Richard Stonehouse; **S. 109/ob.re.:** ddp images / interTOPICS; **S. 109/un.re.:** Picture-Alliance / Photoshot; **S. 110:** Shutterstock / Blend Images; **S. 112:** Shutterstock / Denise Lett; **S. 115/un.re.:** Fotolia / sldesign; **S. 115/ob.re.:** Shutterstock / francesco de marco; **S. 117:** Cartoonstock/Alexei Talimonov; **S. 119/Hintergr.:** Shutterstock / strizh; **S. 119/ob./1:** Fotolia / javiindy; **S. 119/ob./2:** Fotolia / Duncan Andison; **S. 119/ob./3:** Fotolia / sebra; **S. 119/ob./4:** Shutterstock / saschanti17; **S. 119/ob./5:** Fotolia / Astarot; **S. 119/ob./6:** Fotolia / Aytunc Oylum; **S. 119/ob./7:** Fotolia / alphaspiri; **S. 119/ob./8:** Fotolia / mikhail_kayl; **S. 119/ob./9:** Fotolia / razoomanetu; **S. 119/ob./4:** Shutterstock / saschanti17; **S. 120:** Image Source / Laura Doss.; **S. 122/un./1:** Fotolia / delkoo; **S. 122/un./2:** Shutterstock / RGtimeline; **S. 122/un./3:** Shutterstock / Christine Langer-Pueschel; **S. 122/un./4:** Fotolia / tunedin; **S. 122/un./5:** Shutterstock / Mindscape studio; **S. 122/un./6:** Fotolia / elivagar; **S. 122/un./7:** Fotolia / Svyatoslav Lypynskyy; **S. 122/un./8:** Shutterstock / Valery Sidelnykov; **S. 122/un./9:** Fotolia / briagin; **S. 124:** Fotolia / Michael Schindler; **S. 125:** Fotolia / thinglass; **S. 126:** action press / Picturegroupaction press / Frank Micelotta; **S. 128:** Shutterstock / Thinglass; **S. 129:** Fotolia / Konstantin Yuganov; **S. 130:** Reuters / Lucas Jackson; **S. 131:** Fotolia / Faithie Photography; **S. 133/Hintergr.:** Shutterstock / Mario Savoia; **S. 133/ob.li./1:** Fotolia / highwaystarz; **S. 133/ob.li./2:** Shutterstock / vicvic13; **S. 133/ob.li./3:** Shutterstock / Ppictures; **S. 133/ob.re./1:** Shutterstock / VeronikaChe; **S. 133/ob.re./2:** Fotolia / highwaystarz; **S. 134:** Image Source / Craig Robinson; **S. 137:** Shutterstock / Photographee.eu; **S. 139:** Shutterstock / Jakkrit Orrasri; **S. 140:** Shutterstock / Deviant; **S. 141:** Fotolia / ifh85; **S. 143/ob.re.:** Shutterstock / argus; **S. 143/un.li.:** Shutterstock / hafakot; **S. 145/un.re.:** Cartoonstock / FRAN; **S. 145/un.li.:** Cartoonstock / FRAN; **S. 147/ob.li.:** Shutterstock / Yuriy Rudyy; **S. 147/ob.re.:** Shutterstock / Halfpoint; **S. 147/mitte:** Fotolia / jaymast; **S. 147/un.li.:** Fotolia / Scott Griessel; **S. 147/un.re.:** Fotolia / michaeljung; **S. 148:** Nataliya Hora; **S. 150:** Fotolia / alphaspirit; **S. 152:** Shutterstock / Montri Nipitvittaya; **S. 155:** Shutterstock / Suchota; **S. 156:** Shutterstock / one photo; **S. 161/Hintergr.:** Shutterstock / vs148; **S. 161/ob.li.:** Shutterstock / Georgejmclittle; **S. 161/ob.re.:** Shutterstock / NH; **S. 161/mitte:** Shutterstock / kirill_makarov; **S. 161/un.li.:** Shutterstock / Thorsten Schmitt; **S. 161/un.re.:** Fotolia / ktsdesign; **S. 162:** Fotolia / Sergey Nivens; **S. 164/un.li.:** ddp images / robertharding / Michael; **S. 164/un.mi.:** ddp images / robertharding / Frank F; **S. 164/un.re./1:** ddp images / robertharding / Robert; **S. 164/un.re./2:** mauritius images / Alamy / Wiskerke; **S. 166:** Image Source / PAUL VENNING; **S. 167:** Fotolia/ GKSD; **S. 169:** Picture-Alliance / AP Photo; **S. 171:** Fotolia / stevecuk; **S. 172:** ddp images / United Archives; **S. 173:** CartoonStock / Universal Uclick; **S. 188/ob.li.:** Fotolia / Petair; **S. 188/mi.re.:** Shutterstock / COO7; **S. 188/mi.li.:** Shutterstock / Dioniya; **S. 188/un.re.:** Alamy / ATStockFot; **S. 189/Nadeln:** Shutterstock / schab; **S. 189/ob.li.:** Shutterstock / POSSOHH; **S. 189/mi.re.:** Shutterstock / Gail Johnson; **S. 189/un.li.:** Fotolia / TTstudio; **S. 190/ob.re./1:** Fotolia / arm2528; **S. 190/ob.re./2:** Fotolia / arm2528; **S. 190/mi.re./1:** Fotolia / arm2528; **S. 190/mi.re./2:** Fotolia / arm2528; **S. 190/un.re./1:** Fotolia / petovarga; **S. 190/un.re./2:** Fotolia / robsonphoto; **S. 190/links:** Shutterstock / pingebat; **S. 191/ob.li.:** Cartoonstock / Larry Lambert; **S. 191/ob.re.:** Cartoonstock / Aaron Bacall; **S. 191/mi.li.:** Cartoonstock / Chris Wildt; **S. 191/mi.re.:** Cartoonstock / Alan Rose; **S. 191/un.re.:** Cartoonstock / Harley Schwadron; **S. 196:** Shutterstock / Voronin76; **S. 197/mi.re./Hintergr.:** Shutterstock / 89studio; **S. 197/mi.re./Vordergr.:** Shutterstock / KULI; **S. 287:** Cornelsen / Carlos Borrell Eiköter; **S. 288:** Cornelsen / Carlos Borrell Eiköter

Canada & United States of America

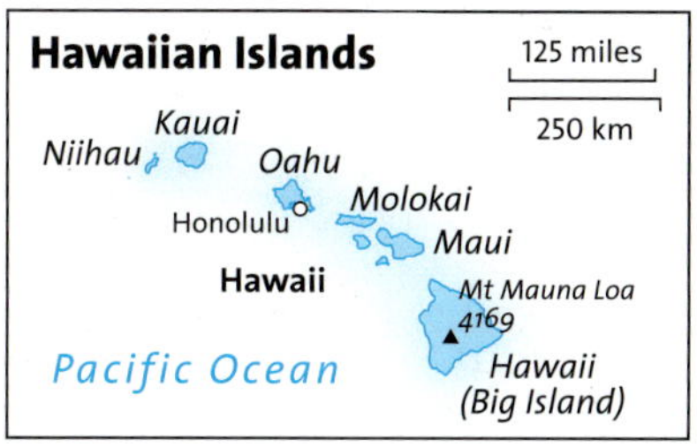

Abbreviations CANADA:
NB = New Brunswick
P.E.I. = Prince Edward Island

Abbreviations UNITED STATES:
CT = Connecticut
DE = Delaware
NH = New Hampshire
NJ = New Jersey
MA = Massachusetts
MD = Maryland
PA = Pennsylvania
RI = Rhode Island
VT = Vermont

The World

Greenland
Canada
United States of America
Mexico
Montreal
New York
San Francisco
Las Vegas
Mexico City
Atlantic
Ocean
Pacific
Ocean
Bahamas
Cuba
Dominican Rep.
Jamaica
Haiti
Puerto Rico
Guatemala
Honduras
El Salvador
Nicaragua
Costa Rica
Panama
Venezuela
Guyana
Surinam
Fr. Guyana
Columbia
Ecuador
Peru
Brasil
Bolivia
Paraguay
Rio de Janeiro
Chile
Uruguay
Buenos Aires
Argentina
Iceland
Norway
Finland
Sweden
United Kingdom
Leeds
London
Ireland
Germany
Paris
France
Portugal
Spain
Italy
Greece
Ukraine
Moscow
Russia
Kazakhstan
Mongolia
Georgia
Uzbekistan
Turkmenistan
Kyrgystan
Tajikistan
Turkey
Tunisia
Morocco
Algeria
Libya
Egypt
Western Sahara
Mauretania
Mali
Niger
Chad
Sudan
Eritrea
Senegal
Burkina Faso
Guinea
Sierra Leone
Liberia
Côte d'Ivoire
Ghana
Nigeria
Cameroon
Central African Rep.
South Sudan
Ethiopia
Somalia
Gabun
Congo
Dem. Rep. of Congo
Uganda
Kenya
Tanzania
Angola
Zambia
Malawi
Zim-babwe
Mo-zam-bique
Namibia
Bots-wana
South Africa
Swaziland
Lesotho
Madagascar
Iraq
Iran
Afghanistan
Kuwait
Saudi Arabia
UAE
Dubai
Oman
Yemen
Pakistan
Nepal
India
Mumbai
Bangla-desh
Sri Lanka
Indian
Ocean
China
Beijing
North Korea
South Korea
Japan
Tokyo
Yokohama
Shanghai
Taiwan
Hong Kong
Myan-mar
Laos
Vietnam
Thai-land
Cam-bodia
Philippines
Kuala Lumpur
Malaysia
Indonesia
Jakarta
Papua New Guinea
Pacific
Ocean
Australia
Sydney
New Zealand